# Courts, Politics, and the Judicial Process

*Second Edition*

## Christopher E. Smith

*Michigan State University*

**Wadsworth**
Thomson Learning™

Australia • Canada • Denmark • Japan • Mexico • New Zealand • Philippines
Puerto Rico • Singapore • South Africa • Spain • United Kingdom • United States

**Wadsworth/Thomson Learning**
**10 Davis Drive**
**Belmont CA 94002-3098**
**USA**

For information about our products, contact us:
**Thomson Learning Academic Resource Center**
**1-800-423-0563**
http://www.wadsworth.com

For permission to use material from this text, contact us by
Web:http://www.thomsonrights.com
Fax: 1-800-730-2215
Phone: 1-800-730-2214


Project Editor: Laura Weber
Compositor: Precision Typographers
Manufacturer: Capital City Press
Cover Painting: "What A Piece of Work Is Man," by Robert Gadomski

**Library of Congress Cataloging-in-Publication Data**

Smith, Christopher
    Courts, politics, and the judicial process / Christopher Smith.
    — 2nd ed.
        p.    cm.
    Includes bibliographical references and index.
    ISBN 0–8304–1481–9
        1. Courts—United States.    2. Judicial process—United States.
    3. Political questions and judicial power—United States.
    I. Title.    II. Series.
    KF8700.S586    1997
    347.73'16DC21                                    96–53218
                                                     CIP

Manufactured in the United States of America

10  9  8  7  6  5  4

For A.V.H., W.M.C., D.R.V., C.S.A., and J.D.P.

# Contents

# Preface

Several years ago, I had the unique opportunity to attend the first week of classes at a law school to take notes for a family member who was hospitalized for surgery. As a lawyer and a political scientist, I found it fascinating to analyze the scene of my legal education through the lens of my subsequent professional training in political science. Although the discussions and interactions in first-year classes on contracts, torts, and civil procedure were very similar to those I remembered from my own experience as a law student, I was struck by the complete omission of many fundamental topics: the structure and functions of courts; the nature of law; the connections between the judiciary and the political system. In the first five minutes of their very first law school classes, brand-new law students jumped immediately into appellate legal opinions on narrow aspects of tort law, contract law, and civil procedure without any knowledge of what the court system looks like, what functions it serves for society, or how it produces the legal opinions that are the focus of law school study. Equally troubling was the fact that these future lawyers began to study the specifics of case law without any general discussion about what law is, how it is developed, or how it affects society. I know from my own experience that law students may never address these issues as they study specific legal subjects in preparation for their eventual bar examination and careers in the legal profession. Without examining the court system and its operations critically, these future lawyers will continue to perpetuate the naive expectations shared by most sectors of the American public about neutral law and equal justice.

This second glimpse of legal education remains with me as I teach and write. The experience contributed to my motivations for writing this book. There is a continuing need for greater dissemination and reinforcement of knowledge about courts and the judicial process that has been generated by contemporary research. No book or set of books can counteract the legal imagery perpetuated in American society by politicians, television, eighth-grade civics classes, law schools, and other sources of information. However, if college students have the opportunity to examine the court system critically, those who later attend law school may gain clearer insights into law and justice, and those who move to other careers may better understand the behavior of lawyers and the processes of the judicial branch of government. As citizens and voters, we can use accurate assessments of the judicial system in choosing our state judges who make decisions, our legislators who reform and fund the courts, and our presidents who select future federal judges.

Because events involving courts and law have such prominence in the public consciousness, the need for accurate understanding of the roles of courts, judges, and lawyers is stronger than ever. Since the first edition of this text was written, Los Angeles experienced significant loss of life during civil disturbances after the acquittals of police officers who were videotaped beating Rodney King. O. J. Simpson's murder trial divided public opinion and spurred debates on race relations, unequal justice, cameras in the courtroom, and a variety of other subjects. President Clinton became the first Democratic president in more than a quarter of a century to appoint a new justice to the Republican-dominated Supreme Court. Unfortunately, actual information about these events and other aspects of the judicial process sometimes produces disillusionment because reality falls so far short of people's idealized expectations. It is my hope that readers of this book can avoid disillusionment by accepting the inevitability of human, political influences on courts and law. Readers should be able to focus their energy and attention toward considering how these influences may be reorganized and reshaped to move our inherently imperfect system closer to the unattainable ideals we learned in eighth-grade civics classes.

The purpose of this book is to provide a broad, critical examination of the role of political influences on the judicial process. Most assuredly, these are modest intentions rather than grand pretensions, because the imagery of law and justice will certainly continue to cast its spell over most of the American public. The structure and content of this book, however, are fashioned in the hope that insights into the true nature of the judicial process will ''stick'' in the minds of readers and not become subsequently overwhelmed by ingrained reverence for conceptions of ''law.'' I hope that this underlying objective will be facilitated by the book's continual emphasis on political aspects of the court system and by the numerous examples from scholarly literature.

Although a comprehensive book of this nature necessarily contains a descriptive component, several chapters raise provocative issues confronting the courts that receive much less attention in other books (e.g., judicial salaries, appointment of lay judges to appellate courts, bureaucratic decision making, coercive consequences of alternative dispute resolution, etc.). In addition, the chapter comparing the American courts with aspects of judicial systems in other countries provides readers with a broader perspective on the widespread and inevitable influence of politics on the judicial process. Thus, this book provides both a broad, research-based examination of the structures, processes, and consequences of the American legal system and a vehicle for analyzing the underlying issues and problems that continue to face the judicial branch.

I am indebted to many people for their contributions to my continuing development as a student of and writer about courts and law. My experiences as a writer have been much richer during the past few years because of my collaborations with co-authors on various projects. I am especially grateful for my working relationships and friendships with George F. Cole of the University of Connecticut, Thomas R. Hensley of Kent State University, Joyce A. Baugh of Central Michigan University, and David A. Schultz of the University of Wisconsin at River Falls. I am deeply indebted to Elliot Slotnick of The Ohio State University and to anonymous reviewers for saving me from several errors and omissions in both editions. The Law and Society Association generously granted permission to use the data in figure 5.1 drawn from Richard E. Miller and Austin Sarat. "Grievances, Claims, and Disputes: Assessing the Adversary Culture," *Law and Society Review* 15 (1980–81): 544.

My colleagues in the School of Criminal Justice at Michigan State University deserve my thanks for welcoming me into a new professional environment that has enhanced the quality of my life and career in many ways. Beverley Bockes deserves special thanks for her efforts to provide the resources I needed to complete this and other projects. In addition, Stephen Ferrara and Richard Meade at Nelson-Hall have earned my eternal gratitude for providing me with opportunities (and encouragement) that have shaped my life and career in profound ways.

As always, my wife Charlotte and my children Alica and Eric remain incomparable sources of encouragement, patience, and support.

This book is dedicated to my closest friends from whom I learned the most about human behavior and other important subjects.

# Chapter 1

# Courts, Politics, and the Judicial Process

W hat images come to mind when Americans hear the words "government" and "politics"? Politicians making campaign speeches. . . . Legislators debating controversial public policies. . . . The president being followed by reporters, microphones, and television cameras. It is unlikely, however, that many people immediately visualize black-robed judges presiding over solemn, ornate courtrooms. Yet, the judicial system constitutes one of the three branches of government. In the United States Constitution, after Article I describes the structure and powers of the legislative branch and Article II describes the president's authority, Article III establishes the Supreme Court and describes the jurisdiction of the judicial branch. Although the courts are a component of government, generally accepted beliefs about the proper role and behavior of judicial actors differ from expectations about the actions and motivations of officials in the other branches of government. For example, when legal commentators speak about "the independence of the judiciary from the political branches [of government],"[1] they are clearly identifying the courts as different from the other branches. Unlike the judicial branch, the legislative and executive branches are recognized as "political" in nature.[2] Justice Felix Frankfurter echoed this theme when he warned that the judicial system should be kept separate from political issues and institutions: "It is hostile to a democratic system to involve the judiciary in the politics of the people."[3] When Americans discuss the court system, they convey the image of a governmental branch which, by its very nature, is distinctively different from other components of government. Courts are unique among government institutions because of their association in the public mind with *law* rather than *politics*.

The public is periodically confronted with clear evidence of the influence of politics on courts, especially when a president nominates a new justice for

1

the United States Supreme Court. When President George Bush nominated Judge Clarence Thomas to replace retiring Justice Thurgood Marshall in 1991, the news media embarked on weeks of speculation about the potential effect that a future Justice Thomas might have on controversial policy issues such as affirmative action, abortion, and school prayer.[4] This discussion of the highest court's impact on public policy accurately indicates that political parties attempt to shape the judiciary's composition as a means of influencing and changing important social policies.

The "political" nature of Supreme Court appointments becomes all the more obvious when the media examine a president's motives in selecting particular judicial nominees. Despite the obvious evidence to the contrary, politicians try to persuade the public that political considerations do not affect decisions about the judiciary. For example, Judge Thomas demonstrated his politically conservative viewpoints through his speeches criticizing liberal judicial decisions on various civil liberties issues and through his work as a loyal bureaucrat in the conservative Reagan administration. Despite the nominee's reputation for conservative views, President Bush attempted to convey the impression that the nomination was not based on Thomas's well-known political viewpoints. According to Bush, "I don't know whether he'll agree with positions that our administration takes or overthrow decisions. . . . [b]ut that doesn't matter. What matters is that he faithfully interpret the Constitution."[5] By asserting that he was only concerned that Thomas would "faithfully interpret the Constitution," Bush was employing the language of neutrality to mask his underlying expectation that Thomas's interpretations would support the president's partisan policy preferences.

In another example, when President Ronald Reagan's nominee for the Supreme Court, Judge Robert Bork, was rejected by the United States Senate in 1987, Bork's supporters claimed that the judge had been rejected as the result of a "rancorous *political* campaign" [emphasis in original].[6] Bork's opponents countered that President Reagan selected the nominee for the purely political purpose of seeking reversal of specific judicial decisions affecting social policies, such as abortion and affirmative action. Thus, according to Senator Joseph Biden, chairman of the Senate Judiciary Committee, senators were justified in examining Bork's political views before voting on his confirmation.[7] As this example illustrates, clashing partisans seek to stake out the "high ground" in debates about the judiciary by accusing the opposing side of injecting "politics" into the judicial selection process. The accusations exchanged between opponents imply that there is something improper about the appearance of "politics" in judicial affairs.

The selection of federal judicial appointees is not always based exclusively on presidential predictions on how the appointee may affect court decisions and public policy. Other kinds of political considerations may also influence the choice of appointees. When President Clinton nominated Judge Ruth Bader Ginsburg to fill a Supreme Court vacancy in 1993, he sought two specific political benefits. First, because Ginsburg had been a noted civil rights lawyer whose ideas shaped constitutional law concerning gender discrimination, her nomination appealed to Clinton's liberal constituency in the Democratic party. Second, Ginsburg's record as a moderate federal appellate judge increased the likelihood that Democratic *and* Republican senators would support her nomination, thereby avoiding any embarrassing or divisive confirmation battles.[8] Thus, various kinds of political considerations affect the decisions of presidents, both Republicans and Democrats, concerning whom to appoint to the Supreme Court and other federal judgeships.

Politics also affects the selection of judges for state courts. As chapter 6 will describe in greater detail, many states use elections to permit the voters to select trial and appellate judges. Those elections may involve the same kinds of political elements as elections for other governmental offices: political parties, campaign fund-raising, political advertisements criticizing opponents, and judgeship candidates selected for their political connections rather than for their legal experience. Even when political parties are less active in states that use nonpartisan elections or judicial selection committees, interest groups, such as the Chamber of Commerce, labor unions, and lawyers' associations, may attempt to influence the selection of judges through endorsements, lobbying, or political advertisements.

Although the public can see that political maneuvering affects the judiciary's composition and thereby shapes judicial decisions about controversial public policy issues, the judicial branch retains its distinctive image as the nonpolitical branch of government. After judges don their black robes, many members of the public lose sight of the connections between the courts and the highly publicized political battles that sometimes surround the judicial nomination process. Americans revert to traditional myths concerning the neutrality of courts and law. In a study of college students' attitudes toward the Supreme Court, Dean Jaros and Robert Roper found that students "exhibit a high degree of mythical belief about the Supreme Court."[9] Although college students possess higher levels of education than most Americans and, therefore, "can hardly be numbered among the naive and credulous masses," Jaros and Roper found that "less than a third admitted that the [Supreme] Court would respond to political demands."[10] A national survey of American adults found that more than 40 percent acknowledged that justices' political beliefs influence the Court's decisions. Yet in comparison with views about Congress, twice as many respondents rated the Supreme Court's performance as "good" or "excellent."[11] Thus, courts maintain an image of being less influenced by the political forces that affect other institutions within the American governing system.

The underlying theme of this book is that court organization and the outcomes produced by the judicial process are actually the products of politics. Although political scientists who study the judicial branch recognize the influence of political forces on courts, the public's understanding of the judicial process is distorted by an idealized image of apolitical judges dispensing justice through the application of neutral laws. "Politics" has been defined as "activity which expresses the will and interests of individuals in the ordering of public affairs."[12] The goal of politics is the creation and advancement of policies which set societal goals and determine the allocation of resources and benefits in a society.[13] Many lawyers and judges object to the idea that the outcomes produced by the judicial process are the product of "the wills and interests of individuals." Such a characterization of the judicial branch clashes directly with the idea that neutral principles of law govern the courts. As the chapters of this book will discuss in detail, the image of neutral law is far removed from the reality of the judicial process.

Like other institutions of government, court operations and judicial outcomes are determined by politics, specifically by the advancement of policy preferences through the assertion of human beings' interests and values. Many of the same "political" actors and influences that shape decisions and outcomes in the legislative and executive branches also affect judicial processes. For example, interest groups seek to attain their policy goals by lobbying in favor of sympathetic judicial nominees and by sponsoring litigation. Just as interest groups influence the issue agendas of legislatures through lobbying and campaign contributions, political interests can determine which issues receive attention from the judicial branch through the cases that they initiate. Inequalities in wealth and resources affect both the effectiveness of interest groups in the legislative process and the success of litigants in the judicial process. The judicial branch's image, organization, and processes may differ from those of the other governmental branches, but political forces still shape the decisions and outcomes produced by the courts.

## THE IMAGE OF LAW AND JUSTICE

When citizens view the president of the United States or the governor of a state, they see an official who is connected to a political party, who makes promises to the public in order to win elections, and who cooperates with legislators, interest groups, and the news media. A politician employs these tactics in order to achieve policy goals, to maintain public popularity, and to win reelection. Similarly, state legislators and members of Congress campaign for office by making promises to the public, raising money from interest groups, and currying favor with voters and wealthy contributors by proposing and selectively supporting legislation. It is well recognized that the behavior of elected officials (and their assistants) in the executive and legislative branches of government is motivated by politics. These government officials and other politicians are engaged in perpetual competition to gain and maintain power. Their tactics and public statements are designed to generate public support for their efforts to control the policy-making mechanisms of government. Because elected government officials and other officeholders whom they appoint are intimately connected to political parties, campaigns, and elections, the public knows that a politician's viewpoints and actions will be guided by political interests rather than by firm philosophical principles. For example, when Republican and Democratic political strategists consider the pronouncements their respective candidates will make about controversial issues during elections, their primary goal is usually to attract votes rather than to articulate a coherent policy position.[14] In the early stages of the 1996 presidential campaign, Senator Robert Dole and President Clinton were accused of changing their public pronouncements to please whichever constituent group they happened to be wooing at the time.[15] The political maneuvering that underlies the development of governmental policies breeds public cynicism about the elected branches of government. Unfulfilled campaign promises, interest group politics, negative campaigning, and periodic government scandals reinforce the perception that politicians in the legislative and executive branches are unduly influenced by partisanship and the desire for reelection. Elected officials appear to lack the courage to move beyond special interest politics and safe, symbolic opposition to taxes.

Public perceptions about the judiciary are quite different. Citizens presume that courts are not guided by the overt partisanship so pervasive in the other branches of government. Unlike the elected branches in which it is widely recognized by the American public that political considerations influence decisions, the judicial branch is presumed to be governed by law. With their specialized training in law and their professional experience as lawyers, judges are expected to make decisions according to the principles of law which are designed to achieve justice. Thus, even if a poor person cannot make political contributions to gain the attention and support of elected officials, that citizen can nevertheless receive the benefit of neutral, objective decision making by initiating a case in court. In reality, however, as subsequent chapters will show, poor people may have a difficult time gaining access to and fair treatment from the judicial branch.

The attributes of the judicial branch serve to reinforce its image as the lone governmental forum devoted to neutral, principled decision making. Although the judicial branch's entire range of symbolic attributes may not be visible during the routine plea bargaining and civil lawsuit settlements that absorb the time of local trial courts, the imagery of law is especially apparent during jury trials and appellate court proceedings. The arguments and opinions produced by judicial actors, namely judges and lawyers, are infused with the language of neutral justice—''equal protection,'' ''due process,'' and ''rights of the accused.'' The legal language of the judicial process conveys the impression that judges and lawyers, unlike legislative and executive branch officials, draw from their specialized knowledge to identify established, principled rules for settling controversies. Presumably, judges do not rely on partisanship or on their personal attitudes in decision making, yet the language of law can hide politics' influence on judges' decisions.

Judges also wear black robes and sit at high benches elevated above other people in the courtroom. Everyone must stand when a judge enters or leaves a courtroom and they must address the judge as "your honor." These traditional, formal procedures give judicial officers at all levels of state and federal court systems a unique measure of symbolic deference and respect that is unmatched within the American governing system except for the formal treatment accorded the president as the national head of state. In addition, judges work in buildings that project a sense of majesty which instills reverence and awe in the citizens who enter the impressive, wood-paneled courtrooms. The architectural use of marble columns, high ceilings, velvet curtains, and inscribed mottoes, such as the "Equal Justice Under Law" chiseled in stone at the top of the U.S. Supreme Court, are reminiscent of the design of religious temples rather than that of functional government buildings. In sum, the physical environment of the courthouse and the use of traditional, formal procedures convey the image of a governmental branch which upholds the esteemed principles of justice. The courts appear to be removed from and, indeed, sit above the swirling turmoil of imperfect human society. In fact, however, courts are populated with human beings whose decisions are shaped by their own attitudes, values, and policy preferences.

Judges and lawyers work to maintain the judicial system's image as the branch of government guided by legal principles rather than by politics. United States Supreme Court justices have noted that the judiciary's effectiveness depends on its success in maintaining public faith in the neutral application of law by judges. As Justice Felix Frankfurter once wrote, "[T]he Court's authority—possessed of neither the purse nor the sword—ultimately rests on sustained public confidence in its moral sanction."[16] Justice Harry Blackmun reiterated this idea that "[t]he legitimacy of the Judicial Branch ultimately depends on its reputation for impartiality and nonpartisanship."[17] Scholars claim that, to protect judicial credibility and power, judges and lawyers must behave as if their actions are guided by legal principles:

> [T]he legitimacy of courts rests in their fidelity to the law and its enforcement.
> . . . If courts do not preserve their distinctiveness from other political bodies,
> if they cease being "courts," then their claim to legitimacy—and their power—
> will erode.[18]

In order to maintain the courts' image, judges cloak their judicial opinions in the language of law. They cite previous cases and develop elaborate justifications that appear to make their current decisions consistent with previously established principles, even when they decide something entirely new or abruptly move legal interpretations in a new direction. Judges and lawyers can go to great lengths to preserve the courts' image as a legal institution. In fact, the obsession with maintaining the judicial image can lead to very revealing actions. In 1990, for example, the Ohio Supreme Court barred a lawyer from ever practicing law again because he had violated the judicial system's dignified legal image by accusing judges of lying. The justices of the Ohio Supreme Court declared that

"[W]e find the flagrant disrespect that [the attorney] demonstrated toward the entire judicial system deserving of the legal profession's most severe sanction."[19] As a newspaper report on the case noted, "[L]awyers found to have committed seemingly more serious offenses—like stealing money from their clients—regularly receive less severe punishment."[20] Thus, it appears that tarnishing the judicial system's dignified image may be a more serious offense for attorneys than committing an actual crime. Judicial actors' determination to protect the court system's image stems from strongly held and deeply ingrained beliefs about the reverence that ought to be accorded to the law. Although judges and lawyers may genuinely believe that the judicial system deserves special deference and respect, a pragmatic observer cannot help but note that such beliefs also protect the elevated status, power, and incomes of the professionals who work in the courts.

Despite being clothed in the symbols of detachment and neutrality, the judicial branch remains a component of the American government system and, as such, it is inevitably influenced by politics. The purpose of this book is to illuminate the myriad ways in which courts and the judicial outcomes produced by courts are guided by the same kinds of political factors which influence actors and outcomes elsewhere in the political governing system.

On first encountering academic literature that cuts through the legal imagery shrouding the judicial system, some people feel a keen sense of disappointment because their beliefs in the neutrality of law have been shattered. The illumination of the political factors underlying the judicial system should not, however, breed cynicism about courts and law. A fundamental premise throughout this book is that "politics" is not a dirty word. Instead, politics is an inevitable component of the human institutions and interactions that regulate behavior, distribute benefits and burdens, and produce social policies. Despite judicial officers' good faith efforts to render fair decisions according to their own definitions of fairness, political influences affect the structure and composition of the judicial branch and subsequently determine the case decisions, policies, and outcomes produced by courts. The judicial process, like other political and governing processes, involves human beings in establishing goals and values for society. By recognizing how much the judicial branch has in common with other components of the political system, people can move beyond their preconceived beliefs about the unique neutrality of courts and law and question and analyze how judicial processes actually operate.

## JUDICIAL FUNCTIONS

Courts perform several important functions for society. As *dispute-processing forums*, courts provide the environment and procedures for processing conflicts between different entities within society. Trial courts are more important than appellate courts in fulfilling this function. As chapter 2 will describe in greater detail, cases enter the judicial system at the trial-court level and most do not proceed to higher levels in the court system. Disputes may involve individuals, government agencies, corporations, and other organizations. During a dispute, one or both of the parties to the controversy may seek the assistance of an authoritative outsider, namely the judiciary, with the hope that the government's coercive power will be exercised to settle the dispute. Frequently, courts simply provide an environment in which the disputants must negotiate with their opponents during structured interactions as part of the litigation process. For example, prior to trial, civil litigation forces disputants to shape their assertions into the form of legal arguments and then meet together over the course of several months to exchange relevant information and evidence about the dispute. As they interact together in the forced, structured encounters required by the judicial process, the disputants usually negotiate a compromise resolution. Because of the ever-present threat that one side might win a total victory if the case were to go to trial, most cases end with negotiated settlements as each party seeks to avoid the risk of complete defeat. In the few cases that are not settled, judges and juries must determine outcomes by utilizing court procedures and legal justifications that cloak their decisions in the image and legitimacy of law.

Because of the judicial branch's image as a legal rather than a political institution, the dispute-processing function contributes to stability in society. The disputants are often willing to accept decisions that emanate from the esteemed, robed elders who reside in the marble temples of justice. People might be less willing to accept the decisions of governmental actors whom they view as self-interested politicians.[21]

In processing disputes, whether by creating a structured environment for negotiation or by deciding which disputant will prevail, courts *allocate benefits and burdens for society*. The judicial process determines whether people will receive compensation for injuries, enjoy their rights to free speech and other protected liberties, and maintain their ownership of disputed property. In settlements and court decisions, resources such as money and property are transferred between disputants within the structured environment of the judicial system. For example, in the case of *Hickey v. Zezulka*, a college student committed suicide by hanging himself while in custody of the campus police after being arrested for drunk driving. Courts faced questions concerning who bore the responsibility for the student's death. Was the student solely responsible for his own death, since his life was taken by his own hand, thereby imposing the complete burden for his death on his grieving family? Or were the campus police and university responsible for the death by placing him in a holding cell without confiscating his belt, thereby placing a financial burden on the officer and university while transferring a financial benefit to the student's family? In this case, a jury ordered the officer on duty to pay the student's family $1 million and ordered the university to pay an additional $650,000. In allocating benefits and burdens in this fashion, courts have a broad impact on society.[22] In this example, the jury's verdict affected society by forcing the campus police to develop new procedures for monitoring holding cells, by reducing the university's financial resources available for education, and by increasing the cost of the university's insurance.

Courts also allocate less tangible benefits and burdens, such as when judicial orders require someone to take a particular action (e.g., a factory must install pollution control equipment, a neighbor must keep a dog on a leash, etc.). There are also judicial orders that forbid actions, such as injunctions that prevent political protesters and labor union picketers from blocking access to streets and buildings.

Courts also *enforce society's norms for behavior.* In the criminal justice context, courts exercise society's power to punish citizens who exhibit harmful or undesirable behavior that has been forbidden by legislative enactments. Such statutes prescribe the application of governmental coercive power and societal stigma in the form of criminal punishments for individuals' harmful conduct. Prosecutions for robbery, murder, fraud, and other crimes provide examples of this function.

In civil litigation, courts enforce other social norms, such as ordering people to fulfill their contractual obligations and to provide compensation in situations of undesirable behavior—such as negligent damage to property—for which legislators have chosen not to apply criminal punishments. The existence of the judicial process as a forum for dispute processing reinforces the expectation that people's irreconcilable differences can be settled through legal proceedings rather than through socially undesirable behavior, including violence or other forms of self-help justice. If there were no courts to prosecute robbers, for example, people within a neighborhood might attack suspected robbers in a form of vigilante justice—a practice that causes grave risks for increasing the level of violence in society and for erroneously imposing punishment on innocent people. The courts' reputation for neutrality and justice contributes to public acceptance of the behavioral expectations enunciated and enforced by the judicial system.

Courts *mediate between citizens and government* by providing a mechanism to ensure that governmental actors follow the guidelines of constitutions and statutes. If Congress or the President attempts to exceed constitutional powers, citizens can challenge legislative or executive actions in court. Similarly, if an executive branch agency does not obey its legislative mandate, the courts offer a forum for citizens seeking to alter the government bureaucracy's actions. A judicial decision in such cases may change the government's behavior by, for example, ordering a welfare agency to pay benefits that were improperly withheld from a claimant or by invalidating a congressional statute. Alternatively, a judicial decision favoring the government may confer the legitimacy of ''law'' on innovative actions undertaken by legislative or executive actors and thereby enhance public acceptance of controversial government programs and policies.

The greatest impact of courts on society may be felt when judicial outcomes allocate benefits and enforce norms on a broad scale, with consequences that reach beyond the specific conflict between individual disputants. In its *policy-making function*, the judicial branch allocates values for society through structured settlements and judges' decisions that determine governmental policies in education, housing, employment, and other important areas of public policy. Although judges frequently claim that they merely follow the law and do not create public policy, the consequences of judicial actions can unquestionably shape large-scale governmental actions. Because courts influence the power, resources, priorities, and actions of other branches of government, judicial policy making frequently elicits reactions from other political actors, and those reactions can affect subsequent court decisions. As the policy-making function of courts leads to continuing interaction between the judicial system and other actors in the political system, public policies may be repeatedly reshaped in light of the shifting preferences, strategic tactics, and relative political strength of interested actors, including lawyers and judges. Chapter 10 will present a more complete discussion of this important judicial function.

## LAW AS POLITICS

In fulfilling its functions for society, the judicial branch enhances the acceptance and effectiveness of its decisions by clothing them in the language of law. Contrary to the image conveyed by the judiciary, law does not consist of clear, coherent principles to guide judicial outcomes. Law is the malleable product of politics and its malleability is one vehicle for the infusion of political interests into the functions of the judicial branch.

American law is not based on neutral, enduring principles of justice. As the authoritative rules for society, which are backed by the coercive power of government, laws are produced by the interactions of political interests. Laws change as different political values are expressed by the actors and institutions of the governing system. In the legislative context, statutory law shifts in conjunction with the changing balance of power between political parties, interest groups, and other political actors. Indeed, the public expects changes in statutory law when one political party loses control of the presidency, Congress, a governorship, or a state legislature. The political party assuming power will inevitably seek to write new laws intended to advance its policy preferences.

Case law generated by judicial decisions is similarly affected by changing political forces. Like legislators, judges make decisions that reflect the values of their historical era. For example, the relevant words in the Constitution concerning "equal protection" did not change between 1896 and the 1960s, but the meaning given those words by judges changed dramatically as societal support for official racial discrimination policies diminished. In 1896, racial segregation was accepted by society, endorsed by judges, and enforced by many local governments. In fact, the justices of the Supreme Court endorsed such racial discrimination by an 8 to 1 margin.[23] By contrast, the Supreme Court of the 1960s interpreted the very same words of the Constitution to mean that legal segregation must end immediately.[24] It would be difficult to claim that the justices in 1896 were mistaken in their interpretation of the Constitution and that the justices of the mid-twentieth century had found the "true" meaning. After all, the members of the post-Civil War Congress who actually wrote the words "equal protection" and placed that right in the Constitution's Fourteenth Amendment clearly supported racial segregation in the Washington, D.C., public schools[25] and in the visitors' galleries of Congress itself.[26] The meaning of "equal protection" in constitutional law changed because the ideas of the human beings who don black robes and interpret the law changed with the shifting values of twentieth-century American society.

The judicial development and definition of law rests in the hands of human beings who inevitably apply their experiences, attitudes, and values to the decisions they make. Lawyers' values and preferences influence their arguments in court, which, in turn, serve as the basis for legal decisions by judges. In appellate courts, judges' attitudes and beliefs affect judicial decisions and the justifications for those decisions which comprise the published opinions designed to serve as guiding precedents for subsequent cases. Thus, the precise content of legal interpretations and case law are determined by the particular human beings who happen to be chosen to preside over courtrooms. In trial courts, judges' attitudes and beliefs affect their rulings on the admissibility of evidence and the sentences that they impose on convicted offenders. Because judges are selected through political system processes, no one should be surprised that they can differ significantly from each other in their patterns of decisions. The American judiciary is composed of liberals, conservatives, Republicans, Democrats, and people who have a variety of demographic characteristics (e.g., age, religious affiliation, gender, etc.) that affect their experiences and values. Just as the substance of statutory law is determined by the values and preferences of the political partisans who win elective office, the substance of court decisions is determined by the political partisans who become judges. Judicial decisions do not merely embody the societal values reflected by judges who live in a particular historical era; those decisions also reflect the judges' individual political orientations. Law does not merely change gradually as society changes from era to era. Because the definition of law rests in human hands and not upon fixed, enduring principles, law can also change rapidly as the partisan composition of the judiciary changes.

The rapidity with which law can change in conjunction with changes in the political system is well illustrated by President Ronald Reagan's influence over the decisions by the federal judiciary. President Reagan was critical of the judicial decisions produced by federal courts during the 1960s and 1970s. In the course of defining constitutional law, the U.S. Supreme Court and lower federal courts during those decades gave legal force to such controversial policies as affirmative action, school desegregation, and legal abortion. When Reagan served as president from 1981 to 1989, he appointed to the Supreme Court and other federal courts new justices and judges who agreed with his values and policy preferences and would oppose the case law decisions established in preceding years concerning criminal justice, abortion, and affirmative action. Reagan's conservative Republican appointees in both trial and appellate courts made different decisions than their Democratic colleagues, especially in cases affecting criminal justice and civil rights.[27] The impact of new judicial appointees was most pronounced on the U.S. Supreme Court.

During Reagan's two terms in office, the retirements of three justices permitted him to make three appointments and to elevate his favorite incumbent on the Court, William Rehnquist, to Chief Justice. President Bush, who was Reagan's vice president, subsequently appointed two additional justices during his four years in the White House. As a result of these appointments, the political balance of power on the Supreme Court changed. The newly powerful political conservatives on the Court could reshape constitutional law to fit with their values and preferences. In 1987 and 1989, for example, the Supreme Court decided cases in which the justices forbade states from using "victim impact statements" in determining whether convicted murderers should receive the death penalty.[28] Victim impact statements are testimony about the adverse consequences of the victim's death on the victim's family, friends, and community. The Supreme Court was concerned that such testimony would inject emotional considerations into the death penalty decision and effectively treat some victims' deaths as more important than others. However, when President Bush appointed Justice David Souter in 1990, the Court's composition shifted and the conservative justices gained the majority vote needed for issuing a new decision that endorsed the use of victim impact statements.[29] Thus, the law completely reversed precedents established only a few years earlier. As with other constitutional issues, the law of the land changed simply because of a change in the political composition of the Court.

Sudden, politically influenced shifts in the judicial definition of law need not move in any particular ideological direction. Changes in the composition of the judiciary can lead to either liberal or conservative legal developments, depending on the political values and policy preferences of judicial appointees in a specific historical era. Although the 1980s and 1990s witnessed the rewriting of case law by conservative judicial officers appointed by Presidents Reagan and Bush, President Franklin Roosevelt's liberal judicial appointees in the 1930s and 1940s created comparable liberal shifts in constitutional law. The Roosevelt appointees invalidated four decades of case precedents that had hampered the government's ability to regulate the economy. The Roosevelt appointees also led the Court into a new era with decisions expanding the rights of individuals.

Law should not be conceptualized as a set of fixed principles. Instead, law should be regarded as changeable rules which emerge from the interactions of political actors within legislatures, the courts, and the other institutions of government. This is not to say that case precedents and the enunciation of legal principles are irrelevant to the judicial decisions which shape the law. As subsequent chapters will discuss, judges may draw guidance from or feel bound by principles that they regard as firmly established. However, the development and application of consistent legal principles is not, as judges and lawyers sometimes claim, the essence of judicial decision making. As illustrated by the behavior of the contemporary Supreme Court, existing principles are only one factor to be considered (and possibly discarded) if the legal principles do not fit the values and preferences of the judicial decision makers. Law and judicial decision making are influenced by political human factors which frequently remain unrecognized as the judicial actors hand down case decisions under the symbolic imagery of neutral law and justice.

## THE POWER OF AMERICAN JUDGES

It is especially important to recognize the political influences which actually affect judicial outcomes because American judges, unlike judges in most other countries, are exceptionally powerful in the governing system. In the federal court system, judges' power is enhanced by the term in office granted to them by the Constitution. Federal judges "hold their Offices during good Behaviour,"[30] which effectively means life tenure as long as they do not commit any crimes or gross ethical improprieties. In some state court systems, judges may be removed in periodic elections, but incumbent judges normally win reelection repeatedly without much difficulty. Job security alone, however, does not create strong judicial power, as evidenced by the life-tenured British judges whose authority is narrower than that of their American counterparts.

Broad American judicial power derives from the nature of the United States Constitution. Because state constitutions are frequently based on the U.S. Constitution, state courts' power has an analogous basis. The limited specificity of the Constitution's language is considered one of its greatest strengths because the governing system can adapt to changing social conditions. According to Archibald Cox:

> [T]he genius of the Framers [of the U.S. Constitution] was partly a talent for saying enough but not too much. . . . [I]mportant questions were left open, questions that the Framers could not foresee and questions on which they could not agree. [The Framers] left those questions to be decided as [the unanswered questions] came to a head in accordance with the dominant needs of each generation.[31]

Judges are the authoritative political actors with responsibility for giving meaning to the ambiguous provisions of the Constitution. The definitions of constitutional provisions enunciated by judges do not remain constant. Judges have shaped and altered the definitions of constitutional law as society and the political composition of the judiciary have changed.

Judges' authority as the ultimate interpreters of the Constitution was not granted by any specific language in the Constitution. Although the judicial branch is vested with the power to decide all cases arising under the Constitution, some early participants in the development of the U.S. government argued that all three branches of government possessed the power to define the meaning of the Constitution.[32] Others who helped to write the Constitution agreed with Alexander Hamilton who wrote: ''A constitution is, in fact, and must be regarded by the judges, as a fundamental law. It therefore belongs to them to ascertain its meaning. . . .''[33]

Historically, judicial supremacy over constitutional interpretation was established by the Supreme Court's famous 1803 decision in *Marbury v. Madison*.[34] A minor judicial appointee nominated in the final hours of John Adams' presidential administration sued the next presidential administration—that of President Thomas Jefferson and Secretary of State James Madison—for failing to deliver the signed commission that would empower Marbury to assume his duties as justice of the peace in the District of Columbia. Chief Justice John Marshall, who ironically had failed to deliver the contested commission in his previous position as Secretary of State under President Adams, wrote a landmark opinion which advanced judicial power and simultaneously avoided a direct clash between President Jefferson and the Supreme Court. Chief Justice Marshall asserted that the Supreme Court possessed the power to order the president to deliver the commission. However, Marshall deftly avoided issuing such an order (which President Jefferson might have refused to obey) by declaring that the lawsuit was invalid because it was based on a congressional statute that violated the Constitution. Without discussing the issue of constitutional interpretation at length, Marshall declared an act of Congress to be unconstitutional. This case created the fundamental precedent for the courts' power of *judicial review*, the power to decide whether actions by the other branches of government violate the Constitution. Although very few legislative enactments were declared unconstitutional during the first century of the country's existence, the *Marbury* decision laid the groundwork for judicial actions that asserted judges' power to act as the ultimate interpreters of the Constitution. The power to determine the validity of actions by other branches of government is an awesome power indeed. As chapter 10 will discuss, American judges' application of judicial review has led critics to charge that the judiciary is too powerful within the American governing system.[35]

An additional factor that enhances the influence of judges in the United States is the American adherence to the *common law system*. The United States inherited the British legal system's practice of permitting judges to develop new law through decisions in court cases. Judges are expected to examine the rulings in prior cases. These judicial decisions are supposed to serve as precedents for subsequent cases presenting similar factual situations and legal issues. Theoretically, American judges are bound by *stare decisis,* which means they are to adhere to prior case decisions. The application of case precedents provides several benefits for society and for the judicial system. By utilizing case precedents, the legal system gains stability because similar cases are decided in a consistent manner. People can guide their own behavior in initiating or avoiding conflicts based on prior court decisions that enable them to predict how similar conflicts are likely to be resolved by the judiciary. Similarly situated people are treated equitably when cases are decided consistently, and the judicial system gains administrative efficiency because judges do not have to "start from scratch" in making a decision in each case.

Despite the theoretical benefits of *stare decisis*, as a practical matter, judges have the option of making new decisions by expanding or contracting prior interpretations of the law or by directly reversing prior precedents. Trial judges are limited in their ability to shape law because their decisions may be overturned by appellate courts above them in the judicial hierarchy. Appellate judges, by contrast, tend to have greater ability to use their decisions to create new law. This is especially true for justices serving on state supreme courts and on the U.S. Supreme Court.

By incorporating references to prior cases in their opinions, judges can cloak their decisions in the image of legal legitimacy even as they mold case outcomes to fit their own values and preferences. The common law system permits case law to be flexible and to change with developments in American society as judges incrementally change the interpretations established in prior cases. Thus, judges can create new rules and policies for society while they purport merely to make adjustments in established legal precedents.

Judges also draw from concepts in prior cases when creating new laws to deal with unanticipated issues. For example, judges had to create new rules when advances in medical technology led to custody disputes between infertile married couples and the women they had hired as "surrogate mothers" to bear children for them.[36] By empowering judges to make new laws, the common law system enables case decisions to remain responsive to new developments in society. American legislatures possess the authority to enact statutes that can change the common law developed by judges. Despite legislative activity that limits judges' power, judges affect the consequences of legislative enactments by shaping the meaning of such laws through their authority to interpret statutes. In addition, various issues inevitably remain under judicial control because legislatures are unable to act on every issue that confronts modern society. The inherent empowerment granted to judges within the common law system makes judges especially important regarding a variety of decisions affecting constitutional law and other legal matters, such as private disputes between individuals or property disputes.

In contrast to the American common law system, which grants significant power to judges, many countries, including France and Germany, employ the *civil law system* in which judges apply detailed legal codes that have been written by legislatures. Although judges influence outcomes in both systems, the common law system grants judges much greater power through its deliberate endorsement of judge-made law.

In addition to the foregoing elements, which in the United States make judges powerful actors in the governing system, judges are also immune from nearly all lawsuits. Although many other government officials can be sued for violating citizens' rights or for acting beyond the scope of their official authority, judges are subject to lawsuits only when they act in a "clear absence of all jurisdiction."[37] It is difficult to imagine the circumstances that would constitute a "clear absence of all jurisdiction," because the Supreme Court has said that judges are immune from suit even when they act maliciously or exceed their judicial authority.[38] Moreover, it is other judges, rather than officials outside the judicial system, who ultimately decide whether a judge may be sued for harmful conduct. The basis for this nearly absolute immunity for judges, for prosecutors,[39] and for the President of the United States, stems from the need to protect these decision makers from being influenced by the threat of lawsuits from people who disagree with their decisions. The effect, however, is to make judges even more powerful by removing one constraint in effect on many other governmental officials, namely lawsuits.

If judges merely followed established legal principles and actually fulfilled the judicial system's image for providing neutral decision making, the special powers possessed by American judges would be less interesting and less important. However, these powers and protections are possessed by inherently biased and fallible human beings who gain office through the workings of the political system. Thus, a concrete understanding of courts and of the judicial process requires analysis of the underlying influences which affect the actions of these powerful decision makers.

## COURTS AND THE POLITICAL SYSTEM

The connections between the courts and the political system include more than the political selection of judges and the judges' political values which influence judicial decisions. Although one must recognize the influence of politics on judicial decision making in order to escape from the pervasive and commonly accepted imagery of neutral law and justice, many other connections between courts and politics affect the content and consequences of judicial decisions.

The most well-known and useful illustration of the connections and interactions between courts and the political system was developed by Sheldon Goldman and Thomas Jahnige in their model of the federal courts as a political system.[40] Drawing from David Easton's work on political systems,[41] Goldman and Jahnige developed a model in which the court system is recognized as operating within the larger environment of American society. As in other American social institutions, decision makers in the judiciary are affected by the same historical, political, economic, and social forces which influence the experiences, viewpoints, preferences, and beliefs of actors in government, in business, and throughout society. The most obvious examples of larger historical forces affecting judicial decisions involve court cases that have arisen during wartime. Despite glaring issues concerning whether the American government properly exercised its power, the Supreme Court during World War II ignored all "due process" rights and endorsed the mass incarceration of Japanese-Americans in concentration camps.[42] The justices apparently feared, as did other Americans, the possibility of military attacks from Japan in the aftermath of Pearl Harbor and, blinded by this fear, a majority of justices ignored the Constitution and deferred to the wishes of American military leaders despite the devastating personal, financial, and legal consequences for innocent Japanese-American families.

Although defenders of the judicial system's legal image might claim that the court system is insulated from the influence of social forces, the courts are one component of American society and government. If economic problems affect the country, the courts, like other government agencies, may find their budgets reduced. When courts do not have enough personnel, space, and other resources for processing cases, judicial outcomes are affected, and cases are either prevented from entering the system, processed very slowly (causing some parties to surrender their claims in inequitable settlements), or processed too quickly to give adequate attention to each party's claims. Other examples can illustrate the swirl of social forces around the judicial system. Even so simple an example as the recognition that judges live in society, read newspapers, send their children to schools, and shop at grocery stores reveals that judicial decision makers cannot avoid having their experiences and viewpoints affected by the same social, economic, and political factors that affect the lives of other Americans. These experiences affect judicial decision making, in part, by shaping judges' predictions about how particular kinds of case decisions might affect society.

Conflicts—between individuals, government agencies, corporations, or other organized entities—that are not solved informally by the disputants arrive in the court system as legal cases. These cases are, in effect, demands on the court system's resources by disputants seeking judicial assistance to gain or protect some benefit, resource, or right. Cases move through the processing mechanisms at the trial, appellate, and Supreme Court levels of the court system. Most cases will leave the system at the trial court level through dismissal or negotiated settlement, but a small number of cases move on to the appellate courts, and a still smaller number are subsequently decided in the Supreme Court. When the Supreme Court and other courts make judicial decisions, the decisions have an impact on society. Sometimes the impact is limited to a redistribution of resources between two disputing individuals. In other cases, however, judicial decisions affect millions of people by, for example, restructuring public school systems, creating new policy choices for individuals (e.g., abortion), or transferring millions of dollars between corporations involved in a substantial lawsuit. Although the image of authoritative, powerful courts implies that judges make decisions that resolve pressing conflicts and then move on to new issues, in fact, societal reactions to judicial decisions frequently force courts to decide the same issues over and over again. Actions by other actors in the political system create pressures on judicial decision makers to produce different outcomes in subsequent cases. In other words, the courts do not merely affect society; the judicial process has an interactive relationship with society in which the political system also influences the decisions of the courts.

The interaction between the courts and the political system can be illustrated by the example of Supreme Court decisions on abortion. After 1973 the Supreme Court established a constitutional right for women to make choices about abortion in *Roe v. Wade*,[43] but the abortion issue was not settled. Interest groups mobilized to generate political activity supporting or opposing the Supreme Court's initial abortion decision. State legislatures reacted to the Supreme Court's decision by passing new laws to confront or evade the case precedent in the hope of forcing the Supreme Court to reconsider the abortion issue. Each new state statute was challenged in a legal case in the federal court system. Around and around the judicial process goes, as each new decision produces reactions from political actors, subsequently leading to the introduction of new cases into the court system. As long as there is powerful opposition to court decisions in the political system, case law on a particular issue may not necessarily be settled—the case precedents can be challenged again and again. Goldman and Jahnige characterize political reactions and the new cases they generate as one form of "feedback" that informs and influences the judges' perceptions about how to formulate decisions that can be successfully implemented.

Ronald Reagan's opposition to the Supreme Court's initial abortion decision led to a presidential reaction during the 1980s: the systematic appointment of new federal judges and Supreme Court justices who shared Reagan's opposition to abortion.[44] Because political actors outside the judicial system, namely the president and the Senate, control the appointment of federal judges, these actors can react against decisions with which they disagree by gradually installing new decision makers who will render different judicial outcomes. The appointment of new judges is another form of "feedback" stemming from political reactions to judicial decisions and affecting subsequent judicial decisions by changing the decision makers. Reagan's strategy eventually advanced his goals when his appointment of Justice Anthony Kennedy in 1987 provided the necessary vote to move the judiciary away from its consistent fifteen-year pattern of guarding against state regulations that might impinge on women's right of choice regarding abortions.[45] Although the Supreme Court ultimately preserved the availability of abortions, it created new opportunities for states to regulate abortions so long as those regulations do not place an undue burden on the right of choice.[46]

Members of Congress reacted to the Supreme Court's initial abortion decision in *Roe v. Wade* by proposing constitutional amendments that would eliminate the Court's ability to determine law on that issue. Although the proposed constitutional amendments were not successful, Congress passed several statutes limiting the right of choice for some women (i.e., poor women) by banning the use of federal funds for abortions. There were also proposed statutes to limit the courts' ability to decide abortion cases. Adverse political reactions from legislatures and the public may lead some judges to soften or change their views. As subsequent chapters will explain in greater detail, there are indications that the Supreme Court has sometimes modified its decisions when congressional reactions to those decisions led to proposals for limiting the jurisdiction of the federal courts.

The public, government officials, and others affected by judicial decisions may react by refusing to implement or obey those decisions. Because the courts have limited ability to enforce their decisions without assistance from the other branches of government, negative public reactions may lead judicial decision makers to modify and reshape their subsequent decisions in order to seek public cooperation or to avoid the turmoil caused by widespread noncompliance.

Connections between the courts and the political system can also be identified on numerous other issues. For example, judicial decisions on school desegregation, criminal defendants' rights, prayer in the public schools, and burning the American flag as a form of political expression have led to clashes between the judiciary and other political actors and these conflicts have generated additional court cases. Sometimes the reactions of other actors in the political system do not lead to changes in the judicial development of law. Other issues, such as school desegregation[47] and criminal defendants' rights,[48] are similar to the abortion issue because "feedback" from the political system led to new judicial decisions that moved the prevailing case law away from the policies established in the original court cases.

## CONCLUSION

Courts fulfill important functions for American society. Americans have grown to accept and rely on judicial actions that shape public policies, enforce societal norms, and allocate benefits and burdens throughout society. Americans also look to courts to protect them from excessive or improper actions by other branches of government. Courts are not the sole source of protection for the American citizenry because the democratic electoral system permits voters to oust and replace legislators, governors, and presidents whose actions are opposed by large segments of the public. However, courts play an especially important role in providing a forum in which citizens can air their grievances and seek protection and redress.

In the course of fulfilling the courts' functions, judges attempt to perpetuate the judicial branch's image as the neutral, nonpolitical component of government.

This image is important in preserving the courts' legitimacy in the public's eyes and thereby encourages people to respect and obey judicial decisions. Despite the efforts to maintain this image, however, courts can never fulfill the ideal of apolitical neutrality. The effects of politics are evident throughout the judicial branch from the selection of judges to constitutional interpretation. Subsequent chapters will discuss in much greater detail the connections between the courts and the political system. The discussion and examples in this chapter merely illustrate the underlying themes of this book: first, courts are political institutions, and the judicial process is guided by many of the same political influences that affect other governmental institutions. Second, the structure, processes, and functions of the judicial branch differ from those of other branches of government, but all branches are intimately connected as components of the political system.

## NOTES

1. Owen M. Fiss, "The Bureaucratization of the Judiciary," *Yale Law Journal* 92 (1983): 1443.
2. Warren E. Burger, "The Bill of Rights: What It Means to Us," *Parade Magazine*, 27 January 1991, p. 6.
3. *Colegrove v. Green*, 328 U.S. 549, 553–54 (1946).
4. Richard L. Berke, "Judge Thomas Faces Bruising Battle with Liberals Over Stand on Rights," *New York Times*, 4 July 1991, p. A12; Evan Thomas, "Where Does He Stand?" *Newsweek,* 15 July 1991, p. 16.
5. Maureen Dowd, "Conservative Black Judge Clarence Thomas Is Named to Marshall's Court Seat," *New York Times*, 2 July 1991, p. A3.
6. William Bradford Reynolds, "Adjudication as Politics by Other Means: The Corruption of the Senate's Advice and Consent Function in Judicial Confirmations," in *Judicial Selection: Merit, Ideology, and Politics* (Washington, D.C.: National Legal Center for the Public Interest, 1990), p. 15.
7. Jean Jackman, "Advice and Consent: Biden Discusses Senate's Role in Judicial Selection Process," *Law Quadrangle Notes* 34 (1990): 22–23.
8. Joyce Ann Baugh, Christopher E. Smith, Thomas R. Hensley, and Scott Patrick Johnson, "Justice Ruth Bader Ginsburg: A Preliminary Assessment," *University of Toledo Law Review* 26 (1994): 1–10.
9. Dean Jaros and Robert Roper, "The U.S. Supreme Court: Myth, Diffuse Support, Specific Support, and Legitimacy," *American Politics Quarterly* 8 (1980): 95.
10. Ibid.
11. John M. Scheb II and William Lyons, "Public Holds U.S. Supreme Court in High Regard," *Judicature* 77 (1994): 273–74.

12. *Dictionary of Political Science*, ed. Joseph Dunner (New York: Philosophical Library, 1964), p. 418.
13. Ibid.
14. Thomas B. Edsall, "A Political Powder Keg: The Parties Can't Ignore the Quota Issue," *Washington Post National Weekly Edition*, 14–21 January 1990, p. 6.
15. Michael Kramer, "Will the Real Bob Dole Please Stand Up?," *Time*, 20 November 1995, pp. 58–65; James Carney, "Correcting His Posture," *Time*, 20 November 1995, p. 77.
16. *Baker v. Carr*, 369 U.S. 186, 267 (1962) (Frankfurter, J., dissenting).
17. *Mistretta v. United States*, 488 U.S. 361, 407 (1989).
18. Joel Grossman and Richard Wells, *Constitutional Law and Judicial Policy Making*, 3rd ed. (New York: Longman, 1988), p. 11.
19. David Adams, "Top Court Disbars Outspoken Akron Attorney Spittal," *Akron Beacon Journal*, 31 May 1990, p. A5.
20. Ibid.
21. Christopher E. Smith, "The Supreme Court in Transition: Assessing the Legitimacy of the Leading Legal Institution," *Kentucky Law Journal* 79 (1990-91): 322–26.
22. Hickey v. Zezulka, 443 N.W. 2d 180 (Michigan Court of Appeals, 1989).
23. See *Plessy v. Ferguson*, 163 U.S. 537 (1896).
24. See *Griffin v. School Board*, 377 U.S. 218 (1964); *Alexander v. Board of Education*, 396 U.S. 1218 (1969).
25. Richard Kluger, *Simple Justice* (New York: Random House, 1975), p. 635.
26. Raoul Berger, *Government by Judiciary: The Transformation of the Fourteenth Amendment* (Cambridge, MA: Harvard University Press, 1977), p. 125.
27. C.K. Rowland, Donald Songer, and Robert Carp, "Presidential Effects on Criminal Justice Policy in the Lower Federal Courts: Reagan Judges," *Law and Society Review* 22 (1988): 191–200; Christopher E. Smith, "Polarization and Change in the Federal Courts: *En Banc* Decisions in the U.S. Courts of Appeals," *Judicature* 74 (1990): 133–37.
28. *Booth v. Maryland*, 482 U.S. 496 (1987); *South Carolina v. Gathers*, 109 S. Ct. 2207 (1989).
29. *Payne v. Tennessee*, 111 S. Ct. 2597 (1991).
30. U.S. Constitution, Article III, sec. 1.
31. Archibald Cox, *The Court and the Constitution* (Boston: Houghton Mifflin, 1987), pp. 377–78.
32. Louis Fisher, *American Constitutional Law* (New York: McGraw-Hill, 1990), pp. 49–50.
33. Alexander Hamilton, "The Federalist, No. 78," in *The Federalist*, ed. Jacob E. Cooke (Cleveland: World Publishing Co., 1961), p. 525.
34. *Marbury v. Madison*, 5 U.S. (1 Cr.) 137 (1803).

35. See, e.g., Christopher Wolfe, *Judicial Activism* (Pacific Grove, CA: Brooks/
    Cole, 1991); Jeremy Rabkin, *Judicial Compulsions: How Public Law Dis-
    torts Public Policy* (New York: Basic Books, 1989); Richard E. Morgan,
    *Disabling America* (New York: Basic Books, 1984).
36. See, e.g., In the Matter of Baby M, 109 NJ 396 (NJ 1988).
37. *Stump v. Sparkman*, 435 U.S. 349, 357 (1978).
38. Ibid.
39. Prosecutors receive only limited immunity for their actions in giving legal
    advice to the police. *Burns v. Reed*, 111 S. Ct. 1934 (1991).
40. The discussion in this section draws heavily from Sheldon Goldman and
    Thomas Jahnige, *The Federal Courts as a Political System*, 3rd ed. (New
    York: Harper & Row, 1985).
41. See David Easton, *The Political System*, 2nd ed. (New York: Knopf, 1971).
42. *Korematsu v. United States*, 323 U.S. 214 (1944).
43. *Roe v. Wade*, 410 U.S. 113 (1973).
44. See Herman Schwartz, *Packing the Courts: The Conservative Campaign to
    Rewrite the Constitution* (New York: Charles Scribners' Sons, 1988).
45. *Webster v. Reproductive Health Services*, 492 U.S. 490 (1989).
46. *Planned Parenthood v. Casey*, 505 U.S. _____, 112 S.Ct. 2791 (1992).
47. See, e.g., *Oklahoma City Board of Education v. Dowell*, 488 U.S. 237
    (1991) (judicial desegregation orders may be removed even if schools are
    racially segregated due to housing patterns), described in Linda Greenhouse,
    "Justices Rule Mandatory Busing May Go, Even If Races Stay Apart," *New
    York Times*, 16 January 1991, pp. A1, B6.
48. See, e.g., *Duckworth v. Eagan*, 492 U.S. 195 (1989) (police may alter the
    substance of traditional *Miranda* warnings even if new wording may confuse
    defendant's understanding of rights). See also, Christopher E. Smith, "Police
    Professionalism and the Rights of Criminal Defendants," *Criminal Law
    Bulletin* 26 (1990): 155–66.

# Chapter 2

# Court Organization

The design of governmental institutions, including courts, affects citizens' access to those institutions and the outcomes produced by each branch of government. The committee system which divides the workload in Congress, for example, permits the legislative branch to address many more issues than the entire body of elected representatives could consider as one group. On the other hand, because issues must work their way through committee hearing processes before consideration by Congress, the committee system also gives members of particular committees extra power to facilitate or obstruct proposed legislation within their committees' spheres of authority. Just as the organization of Congress affects its decision-making processes, the organization of courts affects the way cases are processed.

## THE "DUAL COURT SYSTEM"

The United States has a dual court system in which separate state and federal courts coexist in the same geographic areas. While the court systems of each state possess authority only over legal conflicts within their own state's boundaries or involving their state's residents, the federal court system reaches across the entire country. Some countries have a single, unified court system. By contrast, the system of federalism in the United States permits states to run their own governmental affairs—including their own court systems—to address issues which are not placed under the exclusive authority of the federal government by the U.S. Constitution.

Courts can only handle cases that fall within their designated jurisdiction which encompasses the people, places, and legal issues that are placed under their legal authority by constitutions (state or federal) and statutes. A local small claims court, for example, will usually be able to accept only cases arising from disputes within a particular city and in which the amount of money at issue is less than $1,000 (or some other modest, set amount). Because of the specific provisions in its authorizing state statute or city ordinance, the small claims court's jurisdiction is limited to cases which meet these criteria. Similarly, although the U.S. Supreme Court is the highest court in the land, its jurisdiction has boundaries, too. For example, if a case concerns a contested interpretation of a state constitution and raises no issue concerning the U.S. Constitution or any federal statutes, then the relevant state supreme court rather than the U.S. Supreme Court is the final decision maker. It is state courts rather than federal courts which have jurisdiction over such an issue. The U.S. Supreme Court's jurisdiction is primarily limited to cases concerning issues arising from the U.S. Constitution or federal laws. State supreme courts control the interpretation of their own state's laws and thereby serve as the final authorities for many cases. Thus, no court in the United States has jurisdiction over all possible legal conflicts.

When a dispute develops and one party, wishing to utilize the dispute-processing benefits of the judicial process, initiates a court case, that party's lawyer must determine which court has jurisdiction. In some instances, more than one court may possess jurisdiction, especially if the conflict involves disputants who are residents of different states. In such circumstances, the attorney will make a strategic choice about which court is most likely to produce favorable results for the claimant. This choice may be based on a number of factors. The claimant may choose to file the case in the courthouse closest to his or her home, thereby forcing a distant opponent to endure the hassle and expense of traveling to contest the case. A geographic location may create pressure on the distant party to settle the case so as to avoid substantial travel expenses for repeat court appearances. Alternatively, the political backgrounds of judges in different courts may lead a claimant to believe that one judge will be more sympathetic than another. Suppose a corporation initiates a lawsuit, and one potential judge is a former corporate attorney while the other is a former environmental lawyer who litigated cases against corporations. The corporation will probably file the case in the court of the judge whom it believes will best understand and identify with a business's legal arguments. Thus, the corporation's assessment of the judges' experiences and values may cause it to initiate the lawsuit in the former corporate attorney's court. Lawyers' decisions may also be affected by the judges' political party affiliations. For example, a litigant may assume that the Republican party's traditional identification with business will make a Republican judge more receptive to a corporation's arguments. Conversely, a litigant may believe that a Democratic judge will be more sympathetic toward labor unions or racial minorities, traditional constituencies of the Democratic party.

As they pursue their public policy objectives through litigation, interest groups use "court shopping" strategies to enhance their likelihood of success. When an interest group seeks a judicial decision that will advance its policy preferences, it attempts to file the case in a court made up of judges whose political characteristics might incline them to sympathize with the group's arguments. For example, according to Richard Kluger, when prominent civil rights lawyer and future Supreme Court Justice Thurgood Marshall filed cases challenging racial discrimination in South Carolina in the late 1940s and early 1950s, he sought to have the cases heard in federal district court by Judge J. Waties Waring, because "Marshall knew he had a friend on the bench and [he] shaped his pleadings with that friendliness in mind."[1]

Lawyers may initiate a case in a particular court when that court's governing law, either state or federal, is most favorable. For example, a coal mining company was sued over the deaths of 125 people after one of the company's dams burst, causing a major flood. The claimants' attorney sought to file the suit in federal rather than state court, because West Virginia law limited recoveries in wrongful death actions to ten thousand dollars. In federal court, however, the claimants could sue for millions of dollars.[2] Thus, the overlapping jurisdictions of U.S. courts can allow attorneys to exploit political considerations, such as the prevailing law within particular jurisdictions or the political backgrounds of judges, when developing litigation strategies.

Although lawyers make strategic choices about which judge will be most receptive to their arguments, they frequently cannot make certain that their cases will be handled by a particular judge. If the case concerns an issue of state or federal law and involves local litigants, the lawyer may be required to file the case in the state or federal court that has jurisdiction. In addition, even if lawyers can choose the court in which to file a claim, many courthouses have more than one judge. In such instances, lawyers cannot be certain which judge in a courthouse will be assigned to the case.

Most cases are handled by state courts since most criminal cases and lawsuits concerning contracts, personal injuries, real estate, and other matters are governed by state law. A case may enter the federal courts, including a case that has already been heard in a state court, if it fits in one of the categories of federal court jurisdiction. For example, in 1991 several Los Angeles police officers were videotaped by a bystander as they beat motorist Rodney King after chasing and apprehending him for speeding. The officers were charged with various criminal offenses under California state law. When a jury in state court acquitted the officers,[3] Los Angeles exploded in a deadly riot in which more than fifty people died.[4] Amid public outcry against the acquittals, the U.S. government filed federal charges against some of the officers for violating King's civil rights. After a trial in federal court, two of the officers were convicted and sentenced to prison.[5] When the case concerned state criminal charges, it was tried in state court. When the same defendants were subsequently charged with federal civil rights offenses, the case was tried in federal court.

In general, federal courts accept only cases that fall within one of three specific categories. First, federal courts hear *federal question cases*—disputes concerning issues of federal law or the U.S. Constitution. Although thousands of such cases arise each year, the overwhelming majority of legal cases in the United States are filed in state courts. Most cases concern property damage, personal injury, breach of contract, and other issues governed by state law. Second, federal courts handle cases in which *the United States government is a party*. If the federal government initiates a legal action or is sued by an individual or corporation, the case is heard in federal court. Third, federal courts may hear *diversity of citizenship cases* in which the dispute is between residents of different states *and* the amount being claimed is at least fifty thousand dollars. Thus, personal injury cases, contract disputes, and many other legal issues may be heard in federal courts if they concern a sufficiently large sum of money and if the dispute is between residents of different states. These diversity cases can also be filed in state courts, but the existence of concurrent federal court jurisdiction permits attorneys to make strategic choices about where to file a lawsuit.

The definition of federal court jurisdiction embodied in these three categories of cases developed from political considerations about the characteristics of state and federal courts. Federal courts possess authority over federal law and the U.S. Constitution for several reasons: the desire for uniformity in the interpretation of federal law and the significant likelihood of contradictory and self-serving interpretations if state judges had equal authority to define federal law. Throughout American history, there have been numerous disputes between states and the federal government over the limits of the federal governmental authority. Indeed, the Civil War is the most graphic example of the divisive consequences of such disputes. Because state judges are drawn from a state's political system, there is legitimate concern that these judges' interpretations of federal law would favor the interests of their home states, particularly because judges in many states must run in periodic elections in order to stay on the bench. Thus, state judges are under political pressure to make decisions that will be popular with the local electorate. Similar reasons dictate that the U.S. government should not be subject to decisions by state judges. Local political pressures might influence state judges to make judgments against the federal government. Although federal judges are also drawn from state political systems, they are presumably better able to make independent and potentially unpopular decisions because they have protected life tenure in office.

The attempt to insulate federal judges from political pressure does not mean that judges are actually unaffected by local politics. As Jack Peltason found in his study of school desegregation in the South, "Federal judges do not live in a vacuum. Whatever formal [legal] doctrine may be, community attitudes have been a crucial if unmentionable factor. . . . The judges' awareness of the . . . important factor of public opinion . . . in areas of maximum [public] resistance" affected judges' willingness to implement desegregation orders.[6] During school desegregation controversies, judges, who came to the bench after growing up in and being prominent members of their local communities, were ostracized, threatened, and even subjected to violence (in some cases, the judges' homes were bombed) when their decisions went against prevailing local opinion.[7] Thus, according to Peltason, local pressures contributed to judges' reluctance to enforce Supreme Court mandates regarding racial discrimination.[8]

The federal courts' diversity jurisdiction also stems from fears that state judges will show favoritism when cases arise between local residents and out-of-state residents. If a case involved a multi-million dollar lawsuit between a local corporation and an out-of-state corporation, it has been questioned whether state judges will be inclined to favor local interests rather than transferring significant economic resources to a distant locale. Because most state judges are now more professional—through formal education and legal experience—than in previous eras, many federal judges and members of Congress believe that diversity jurisdiction should be eliminated and federal courts relieved of the burden of run-of-the-mill contract, personal injury, and property suits, and other cases involving issues normally heard in state courts.[9] Earlier in American history, many lawyers and judges had little or no formal education. Prior to the twentieth century, an aspiring lawyer studied with an attorney and subsequently received that attorney's endorsement, certifying the new lawyer's competence. These lawyers might eventually become judges with no formal education. By contrast, most contemporary judges, both state and federal, are college graduates with law degrees. Because state judges today are generally educated legal professionals, many people believe that these educated professionals are less likely to show favoritism in deciding diversity cases. Congress modified the federal courts' diversity jurisdiction in 1988 by changing the required amount in controversy from ten thousand to fifty thousand dollars, thus reducing the number of diversity cases subject to the federal courts. Practicing attorneys, however, continue to exert political pressure on Congress to retain diversity jurisdiction. Attorneys want to ensure that they will retain the opportunity to make strategic choices among courts.

## THE HIERARCHY OF STATE COURTS

Court systems in every state are hierarchical, offering opportunities for litigants to appeal to higher courts if they have received unsatisfactory decisions in lower courts. As illustrated by the examples in figure 2.1, state court systems vary widely. Most states have a top appellate court, an intermediate appellate court, and a general trial court. Some states have more than one court at each level. Others have no intermediate appellate court or have additional low level courts with limited jurisdiction. As the discussion of court reform will present in greater detail, states' differing organizational structures are the products of their individual histories and political environments. Although states would enjoy administrative and financial benefits from South Dakota's streamlined, centralized organization, many states maintain fragmented systems, especially at the trial court level. A fragmented structure, which is often inefficient and confusing, benefits certain

**Figure 2.1: Examples of State Court Organization, 1993.**

|  | South Dakota | Maryland | Indiana |
|---|---|---|---|
| Court of Last Resort | Supreme Court | Court of Appeals | Supreme Court |
| Intermediate Appellate Courts |  | Court of Special Appeals | Court of Appeals<br>Tax Court:<br>(admin. agency appeals) |
| Courts of General Jurisdiction | Circuit Court | Circuit Court | Circuit Court<br>Superior Court |
| Courts of Limited Jurisdiction |  | District Court<br>Orphan's Court:<br>(estate cases) | County Court<br>Probate Court<br>Municipal Court<br>City Court<br>Town Court<br>Small Claims Court |

*Source:* David B. Rottman, Carol R. Flango, and R. Shedine Lockley, *State Court Organization, 1993* (Washington, D.C.: U.S. Government Printing Office, 1995), pp. 362, 368, 390.

interests, such as political parties that use local courthouses as a source of patronage jobs for party loyalists. Figure 2.2 provides a complete comparison of the differences in court organization among state judicial systems.

At the bottom of the hierarchy within state court systems are *courts of limited jurisdiction*. These courts generally have jurisdiction over minor cases, including traffic offenses, parking tickets, and misdemeanors (i.e., crimes punishable by less than one year in jail). Civil lawsuits in such courts are normally limited to those in which the contested amount is relatively small (often under $10,000). In California, for example, there are municipal courts in districts whose population exceeds 40,000 and justice courts in smaller areas. These courts handle civil cases involving $25,000 or less as well as traffic and criminal misdemeanor cases.[10] States apply a variety of names to their lowest level courts. Police court (Arkansas), justice of the peace court (Louisiana), and county court (Indiana), for example, designate courts of limited jurisdiction. Some states have many different limited jurisdiction courts, each responsible for a specific category of cases (such as traffic, misdemeanor, or small claims). Other states have only one court of limited jurisdiction, and a few have no limited jurisdiction courts.

Typically, large numbers of cases are quickly and informally processed in limited jurisdiction courts. Most cases conclude with negotiated settlements (civil) or plea bargaining (criminal). For trials, these courts frequently do not use juries. Cases are heard before a judicial officer who may be called a judge, a magistrate, a referee, or a justice of the peace. For small claims, traffic, and other minor cases, citizens may simply tell the judge their version of events after the case against them has been presented by a police officer or opposing disputant. The presiding judicial officer renders a quick decision at the close of testimony and then moves on to the next case. Lawyers are likely to represent claimants in civil cases exceeding the $500 to $1,000 limit.

Lay judges preside over the lowest level courts in several states.[11] For example, Mayors' Courts in Ohio enable small town mayors, whether or not they are lawyers, to preside over cases concerning traffic offenses and other misdemeanors. The use of nonlawyers as judges for minor legal matters has produced horror stories about improper procedures and openly prejudiced decisions of these untrained judicial officers.[12] However, judges with law degrees may also violate procedures and make biased decisions. Fallible human beings exercise judicial authority from beneath the black robes, and formal education for judges does not ensure consistent or proper decisions. A study of lay judges concluded that "the ultimate irony in the debate over lay judges is that lay and lawyer judges in comparable courts are not so very different [in the decisions that they make]."[13]

All states have *courts of general jurisdiction*, which are the basic trial courts empowered to provide initial processing for a complete range of legal issues. These courts often have exclusive jurisdiction over felony cases—criminal offenses punishable by one or more years in prison. Also, general jurisdiction courts do not limit the monetary amount in question in civil cases. Litigants suing for large sums of money initiate their cases in the general jurisdiction court. Some courts have minimum jurisdictional amounts (often $1,000), but others set no minimum amount. In the latter category, disputants in minor civil cases may initiate their suits in the courts of either general or of limited jurisdiction. General jurisdiction courts bear different names in different states, but they are usually called superior courts (Alaska), district courts (Nebraska), circuit courts (Maryland), or courts of common pleas (Ohio).

Most cases in general jurisdiction courts are resolved through dismissals or negotiated settlements. In the criminal context, these negotiated settlements are plea bargains in which defendants receive reduced charges or less severe punishment in exchange for a guilty plea. Thus, judges often loosely supervise the negotiations between opposing attorneys and subsequently approve the pleas or settlements. In the minority of cases not resolved through plea bargaining (criminal) or negotiated settlements (civil), general jurisdiction courts are the forums for courtroom dramas like those portrayed in television shows and Hollywood films. These basic trial courts provide the opportunity for jury trials, presentation of evidence, and cross-examination of witnesses. In most states, a single judge presides over the trial court and stays out of the fray except when necessary—for example, to keep the attorneys from making improper statements or from presenting inadmissable evidence—not unlike the referee of a sporting event. The judge also rules on lawyers' motions concerning the admissibility of evidence and other objections. The trial court judge instructs the jury on the relevant law to consider and determines the appropriate sentence for convicted criminal offenders.

**Figure 2.2: State Court Organization.**

| State | Last Resort (# of justices) | Intermediate Appellate | General Jurisdiction | Limited Jurisdiction (not exhaustive) |
|---|---|---|---|---|
| AL | Supreme Ct.(9) | Ct. of Civil App.<br>Ct. of Crim. App. | Circuit | Municipal, Probate, Dist. |
| AK | Supreme Ct.(5) | Ct. of App. | Superior | District |
| AZ | Supreme Ct.(5) | Ct. of App. | Superior | Justice of Peace, Municipal |
| AR | Supreme Ct.(7) | Ct. of App. | Circuit Chancery | County, Police, City, Municipal |
| CA | Supreme Ct.(7) | Ct. of App. | Superior | Municipal, Justice |
| CO | Supreme Ct.(7) | Ct. of App. | District | Water, County, Municipal |
| CT | Supreme Ct.(7) | Appellate Ct. | Superior | Probate |
| DE | Supreme Ct.(5) | — | Superior Chancery | Common Pleas, Municipal, Justice of Peace |
| FL | Supreme Ct.(7) | Dist. Ct. of App. | Circuit | County |
| GA | Supreme Ct.(7) | Ct. of App. | Superior | Civil, Probate, Magistrate |
| HA | Supreme Ct.(5) | Intermed. Ct. of App. | Circuit | District |
| ID | Supreme Ct.(5) | Ct. of App. | District | — |
| IL | Supreme Ct.(7) | App. Ct. | Circuit | — |
| IN | Supreme Ct.(5) | Ct. of App.<br>Tax Ct. | Superior Circuit | County, Probate, Municipal, City |
| IA | Supreme Ct.(9) | Ct. of App. | District | — |
| KS | Supreme Ct.(7) | Ct. of App. | District | Municipal |
| KY | Supreme Ct.(7) | Ct. of App. | Circuit | District |
| LA | Supreme Ct.(8) | Ct. of App. | District | Justice of Peace, City, Parish |
| ME | Supreme Judicial Ct.(7) | — | Superior | District, Probate |
| MD | Ct. of App.(7) | Ct. of Special App. | Circuit | District, Orphan |
| MA | Supreme Judicial Ct.(7) | App. Ct. | District Superior Municipal | Juvenile, Housing, Probate |
| MI | Supreme Ct.(7) | Ct. of App. | Circuit Recorder's | District, Probate, Municipal |
| MN | Supreme Ct.(7) | Ct. of App. | District | — |
| MS | Supreme Ct.(9) | — | Circuit Chancery | County, Family, Municipal |
| MO | Supreme Ct.(7) | Ct. of App. | Circuit | Municipal |
| MT | Supreme Ct.(7) | — | District | Water, City, Justice of Peace |
| NE | Supreme Ct.(7) | Ct. of App. | District | Juvenile, County |
| NV | Supreme Ct.(5) | — | District | Municipal, Justice of Peace |

**Figure 2.2: Continued.**

| State | Last Resort (# of justices) | Intermediate Appellate | General Jurisdiction | Limited Jurisdiction (not exhaustive) |
|---|---|---|---|---|
| NH | Supreme Ct.(5) | — | Superior | Probate, District, Municipal |
| NJ | Supreme Ct.(7) | App. Div. | Superior | Municipal, Tax |
| NM | Supreme Ct.(5) | Ct. of App. | District | Magistrate, County, Probate |
| NY | Ct. of App.(7) | App. Div. | County Supreme | Claims, Family, District, City, Surrogate, Town |
| NC | Supreme Ct.(7) | Ct. of App. | Superior | District |
| ND | Supreme Ct.(5) | Ct. of App. (temp. 1987-96) | District | County, Municipal |
| OH | Supreme Ct.(7) | Ct. of App. | Common Pleas | County, Mayor, Municipal |
| OK | Supreme Ct.(9) Ct. of Crim. App.(5) | Ct. of App. | District | Tax, Municipal |
| OR | Supreme Ct.(7) | Ct. of App. | Circuit | Tax, County, District, Municipal |
| PA | Supreme Ct.(7) | Commonwealth Superior | Common Pleas | District, Traffic, Municipal |
| RI | Supreme Ct.(5) | — | Superior | District, Family, Municipal |
| SC | Supreme Ct.(5) | Ct. of App. | Circuit | Family, Probate, Municipal, Magistrate |
| SD | Supreme Ct.(5) | — | Circuit | — |
| TN | Supreme Ct.(5) | Ct. of App. Ct. of Crim. App. | Circuit Chancery Criminal | Probate, Municipal, Gen'l Sessions |
| TX | Supreme Ct.(9) Ct. of Crim. App.(9) | Ct. of App. | District | County, Probate, Municipal, Justice of Peace |
| UT | Supreme Ct.(5) | Ct. of App. | District | Circuit, Juvenile, Justice of Peace |
| VT | Supreme Ct.(5) | — | Superior District | Probate |
| VA | Supreme Ct.(7) | Ct. of App. | Circuit | District |
| WA | Supreme Ct.(9) | Ct. of App. | Superior | Municipal, District |
| WV | Supreme Ct. of App.(5) | — | Circuit | Magistrate, Municipal |
| WI | Supreme Ct.(7) | Ct. of App. | Circuit | Municipal |
| WY | Supreme Ct.(5) | — | District | Justice of Peace, Municipal, County |

*Source:* David B. Rottman, Carol R. Flango, and R. Shedine Lockley, *State Court Organization, 1993* (Washington, D.C.: U.S. Bureau of Justice Statistics, 1995), pp. 347–399.

Initial appeals from trial court decisions go to *intermediate courts of appeals*—in the thirty-nine states that have such courts. In some states, there is one intermediate court of appeals but in other states, there are several, with jurisdiction over cases presented from specific geographic districts within the state. Ohio, for example, is divided into twelve appellate districts. In some states, there is one court of appeals with many judges, who may sit in panels of three to hear cases, so that the court can process many cases simultaneously. The number of intermediate appellate judges may vary dramatically from state to state. For example, although the states of Michigan and Ohio are similar in size and appellate caseload, the Ohio intermediate appellate courts have fifty-nine judges while Michigan's courts have only twenty-eight.[14]

Appellate courts do not conduct new trials or hear testimony. They do not decide a defendant's guilt or innocence. Such courts merely consider specific questions concerning alleged mistakes in the trial court, such as the admission of invalid evidence or the improper application of state law. The appellate judges consider detailed written arguments called appellate briefs that the lawyers for each side submit to argue the narrow question or questions at issue. In many cases, the lawyers will be permitted to present limited oral arguments, normally about thirty minutes in duration. The judges then discuss the case with one another and vote to determine the outcome. One judge in the majority will write an opinion explaining the court's decision, and other judges may write opinions explaining why they applied different reasoning (in concurring opinions) or arrived at different outcomes (in dissenting opinions). Obviously, the judges' responsibilities and methods for processing cases in appellate court are quite different from those employed in trial courts where a single judge typically supervises negotiated outcomes or courtroom trials.

All states have a *court of last resort*, usually called the state supreme court. Oklahoma and Texas are unique in having separate courts of last resort for criminal and civil cases. The court of last resort is an appellate court which receives cases from the intermediate appellate court (if there is one) or from the general jurisdiction court. The responsibilities and methods of the court of last resort are very similar to those of the intermediate appellate courts, except that the highest courts usually consist of a larger number of judges, who are called "justices." These justices receive appellate briefs, hear oral arguments, discuss the cases, and issue written opinions to explain decisions. Courts of last resort range in size from three justices (Oklahoma Court of Criminal Appeals) to nine (Texas Supreme Court) members, with most state supreme courts consisting of five or seven members. Although most state supreme court justices hear cases as a group, a few states divide their highest courts into panels for some cases. As chapter 8 will discuss in greater detail, courts of last resort frequently have discretionary jurisdiction permitting them to select the cases they wish to hear and to decline to review others.

# THE POLITICS OF COURT REFORM

The proliferation of lower level courts within a state can create problems. Many state courts have overlapping jurisdictional authority. While some states have clear divisions defining separate jurisdictions, (e.g., in Kentucky civil cases involving less than twenty-five hundred dollars go to the limited jurisdiction district court and suits for larger amounts are heard in circuit court,[15]) other states lack clear boundaries. In North Dakota, for example, civil cases for less than ten thousand dollars can be filed in the limited jurisdiction county court or in the general jurisdiction district court.[16] Overlapping jurisdictions can create confusion and invite "forum shopping" by lawyers—deciding which judge they want to hear a particular case and then filing the lawsuit in that judge's court.

In addition, administrative difficulties increase when there are many different courts. Because lower level courts in many states are linked to local political units (e.g., county, city, or village governments), the funding and administrative efficiency of these courts vary greatly. Some governmental units have well-organized court systems with secure funding, while others suffer from organizational and financial problems. The internal administration of a court is usually overseen by a chief judge. The chief judge in a given district, circuit, or county has significant authority over the distribution of cases, the introduction of new court procedures, and the allocation of resources. When a different decision maker oversees the administration of each court, courts may define and implement their individual procedural rules, creating confusion for lawyers and litigants unfamiliar with local idiosyncracies. Litigants risk having their cases dismissed if they inadvertently fail to follow some local court rule unique to a particular courthouse. The priorities and effectiveness of key administrative decision makers vary from court to court. Such diversity among courts can lead to administrative difficulties which, in turn, can affect the courts' ability to process cases efficiently and effectively. The importance of court structure and administration for case processing is demonstrated by research which indicates that trial judges' ability to control cases and encourage settlements depends on the timing and manner of case assignments.[17]

Reformers have sought to change the structure and administration of state courts for most of the twentieth century.[18] According to advocates of reform, a streamlined, unified state court system increases the courts' effectiveness by implementing uniform procedural rules, distributing cases efficiently, and allocating resources equitably. A state-wide administrative system can tackle the pressing management issues that face courts: case-flow management, adequate funding, distribution of personnel, and record keeping.[19] A centralized administrative office for all of a state's courts can monitor the effectiveness of case processing and subsequently adjust the allocation of resources or implement new procedures. If one courthouse has a backlog of cases, a centralized court system may be able to assign an additional judge to that court or increase other resources. By contrast, under a system of independent, locally administered courts, the courthouse with the greatest need for resources may be located in the county or city that can least afford to provide them.

The arguments for court reform sound strong, but there are barriers to their adoption and implementation. In many states, political parties compete to control the local courthouses. Because judges in decentralized court systems frequently appoint the court clerks, bailiffs, clerical staff, and other judicial support personnel, political parties use courthouses to dispense traditional political patronage. In the limited jurisdiction municipal court in Akron, Ohio, for example, the clerk of court is an elected official. The clerk's office is prized by the political parties because it controls fifty-three patronage jobs.[20] If a centralized administration controlled the hiring of court personnel and turned court jobs into civil service positions, political parties would lose a primary benefit of winning local elections. By keeping courthouses under local control, successful politicians can reward loyal partisans with jobs and can motivate their loyalists to work in subsequent elections. Thus, there are strong political interests opposing the consolidation and professionalization of court administration.

In his studies of state court systems, Henry Glick has identified the political interests that typically clash over the issue of court reform.[21] State and national legal organizations support court reform to dispel any public perception that the legal system is connected to local politics. The federal government and its constituent agencies that come into contact with state courts favor unified court systems as a step toward innovation and efficiency in judicial administration. High-status corporate lawyers frequently lead campaigns for court reform for two reasons. First, they "are usually the most financially successful and prestigious attorneys who have the time and financial independence to become involved in bar association and other political activities."[22] Second, "[T]heir social, economic, and legal status usually means also that these lawyers are Republicans who work and live in large cities that are dominated by the Democratic party."[23] Thus, their efforts to weaken the linkages between courts and local politics are also intended to reduce Democratic control of judgeships and court administration. In addition, middle-class, civic-oriented reform organizations "are likely to endorse the ideals of court reform and the vision of separating justice from politics."[24]

General practice and trial lawyers often oppose court reforms because their success depends on intimate knowledge of the personnel and procedures of local courts. Any structural change in court administration may reduce the usefulness of the expertise and personal connections that they have developed. Judges and other court employees sometimes oppose court reform because restructuring could reduce their power and autonomy and might eliminate some jobs. Obviously, the dominant political party and its interest group allies oppose court reform because it is aimed directly at reducing their influence over the judicial branch and their ability to reward party loyalists with patronage positions.[25]

There are other reasons reform is resisted. The Mayors' Courts in Ohio, for example, place local politicians in a position to generate revenues for their own local governments by levying fines against traffic offenders. While this system is advantageous for local authorities, it can raise serious questions about the neutrality of the "judges" (i.e., mayors) who determine guilt and impose fines upon defendants.[26]

According to Glick, the political interactions of these opposing groups frequently produce compromise reforms:

> Most compromises follow a familiar political pattern. Reformers propose a far reaching package of judicial changes, but various legislators, lawyers, and judges criticize and lobby against them. Finally, the reformers agree to withdraw some reforms, publicly stating regret, but they also are pleased at what they could get.[27]

There are serious questions about whether court reform initiatives actually produce the intended result—increased efficiency of the judicial system. State court systems that appear streamlined and unified on paper may still include a variety of divisions in their general and limited jurisdiction courts. Although these various divisions may technically be components of a single circuit or district court, they often continue to operate relatively independently as separate probate, juvenile, small claims, and other specialized courts. In unified court systems, judges may wield considerable power over administrative matters through their willingness or reluctance to accept and implement uniform court procedures created by the state's administrative office for courts. Because no one can directly control what judges do in their own courtrooms, individual judges may ignore or alter new procedures. Centralized administration may also deter innovative experimentation by individual judges with creative ideas for processing cases more effectively.

## THE ORGANIZATION OF THE FEDERAL COURTS

Although the Supreme Court is the only court established by the U.S. Constitution, that document also vests judicial power "in such inferior Courts as the Congress may from time to time ordain and establish."[28]

### Historical Background

There was considerable sentiment at the nation's founding to permit state courts to handle trial-level adjudication and thereby leave federal courts to focus on appeals. However, Congress enacted the Judiciary Act of 1789 to establish a dual court system with federal trial and appellate courts operating side by side with state courts.[29]

Because the initial federal judicial districts coincided with state boundaries, "the federal courts that the [Judiciary Act of 1789] created were not designed to be completely free of the influence of their states' politics and legal culture."[30] The district court boundaries could have been drawn to cover portions of several states in order to avoid close relationships with specific states. Instead, the use of state borders as federal judicial district boundaries ensured close contact between local federal courts and state political systems. For example, federal district judges have always been appointed from the states in which their courts are located. As chapter 6 will discuss in greater detail, lawyers who become federal judges are usually politically active and well-connected in their states' electoral politics in order to receive judicial appointments.

## The Contemporary Federal Courts

### District Courts

As illustrated in figure 2.3, the federal judicial system consists of 94 district courts which are divided into 12 geographic circuits. The 94 districts contain more than 600 district judges plus numerous semi-retired senior judges whose work ranges from continued full-time handling of cases to occasional stints as visiting judges. As the federal judicial system's primary trial courts, the district courts are courts of general jurisdiction that process disputes through the various stages of litigation under the supervision of a single judge. District courts also handle federal criminal cases. The district court provides the forum for trials heard by either a judge and a jury or a judge alone. Although some states are divided into multiple districts, the connections between the federal courts and political systems remain intact because district boundaries lie within individual states. Within each district there may be more than one courthouse and more than one judge in each courthouse. The Western District of Michigan, for example, has judges in Grand Rapids, Kalamazoo, and Lansing. By contrast, all judges in a small district may be located in a single courthouse. In the district of New Hampshire, for example, both judges sit in Concord.

A small number of cases may be heard by special three-judge district courts, which must include at least one district judge and one circuit judge. These specially constituted courts can hear cases in which an individual challenges the constitutionality of a state or federal statute by seeking a judicial order (injunction) preventing enforcement of the statute. Such cases may be appealed directly from the special district court to the U.S. Supreme Court.[31]

Bankruptcy judges are considered "adjuncts" of the district courts. These judges do not have the protected life tenure granted to judges of the U.S. District, Circuit, and Supreme Courts. Instead, they are appointed to fourteen-year terms by the circuit courts of appeals. The regular federal judiciary controls the

**Figure 2.3: Federal Circuit Courts and Their Constituent District Courts**
(excluding District of Columbia Circuit and Federal Circuit).

| 1st Circuit | 2nd Circuit | 3rd Circuit |
|---|---|---|
| Maine | Connecticut | Delaware |
| Massachusetts | Eastern New York | New Jersey |
| New Hampshire | Northern New York | Eastern Pennsylvania |
| Puerto Rico | Southern New York | Middle Pennsylvania |
| Rhode Island | Western New York | Western Pennsylvania |
| | Vermont | Virgin Islands |

| 4th Circuit | 5th Circuit | 6th Circuit |
|---|---|---|
| Maryland | Eastern Louisiana | Eastern Kentucky |
| Eastern North Carolina | Middle Louisiana | Western Kentucky |
| Middle North Carolina | Western Louisiana | Eastern Michigan |
| Western North Carolina | Northern Mississippi | Western Michigan |
| South Carolina | Southern Mississippi | Northern Ohio |
| Eastern Virginia | Eastern Texas | Southern Ohio |
| Western Virginia | Northern Texas | Eastern Tennessee |
| Northern West Virginia | Southern Texas | Middle Tennessee |
| Southern West Virginia | Western Texas | Western Tennessee |

| 7th Circuit | 8th Circuit | 9th Circuit |
|---|---|---|
| Central Illinois | Eastern Arkansas | Alaska |
| Northern Illinois | Western Arkansas | Arizona |
| Southern Illinois | Northern Iowa | Central California |
| Northern Indiana | Southern Iowa | Eastern California |
| Southern Indiana | Minnesota | Southern California |
| Eastern Wisconsin | Eastern Missouri | Western California |
| Western Wisconsin | Western Missouri | Guam |
| | Nebraska | Hawaii |
| | South Dakota | Idaho |
| | North Dakota | Montana |
| | | Nevada |
| | | Northern Mariana Islands |
| | | Oregon |
| | | Eastern Washington |
| | | Western Washington |

| 10th Circuit | 11th Circuit |
|---|---|
| Colorado | Middle Alabama |
| Kansas | Northern Alabama |
| New Mexico | Southern Alabama |
| Eastern Oklahoma | Central Florida |
| Northern Oklahoma | Northern Florida |
| Western Oklahoma | Southern Florida |
| Utah | Middle Georgia |
| Wyoming | Northern Georgia |
| | Southern Georgia |

procedures and resources of bankruptcy courts, and decisions by bankruptcy judges can be reviewed in district and circuit courts. Bankruptcy judges handle cases in which individuals and businesses seek to restructure or discharge their debts when financial circumstances make it impossible for them to fulfill contractual obligations to their creditors. Regional and national economic conditions significantly affect the caseloads of bankruptcy judges.

Congress attempted to give bankruptcy judges broad powers to handle all legal matters related to bankruptcy proceedings. This congressional effort elicited political opposition from federal judges unwilling to see the power and prestige of bankruptcy judges enhanced. The battles surrounding the congressional reform of the bankruptcy system illustrated the roles of various judicial system actors, including judges and lawyers, as components of political interest groups seeking to shape the judicial branch to suit their own interests and preferences.[32] The Supreme Court ultimately invalidated the legislation by declaring that Congress had granted to bankruptcy judges power that could be exercised only by judges with constitutionally protected tenure and other attributes of the federal judiciary.[33]

### Circuit Courts of Appeals

Appeals from district court decisions go to the specific circuit court of appeals which has jurisdiction over the geographic area that includes the district court. There are twelve geographic circuits plus the U.S. Court of Appeals for the Federal Circuit. The Federal Circuit handles nationwide appeals for cases concerning trademarks, patents, copyrights, and claims against the government. While the Court of Appeals for the District of Columbia Circuit has geographic responsibility for federal appellate cases in the nation's capital, it has special importance because it can also hear appeals from other parts of the country in cases involving federal agencies.

The circuit courts divide into three-judge panels to hear cases. Each panel considers cases for two weeks or some other specified time period, then the judges in the circuit are reconstituted into different three-judge panels. If two different panels in a circuit reach contradictory conclusions in similar cases, or if a majority of judges in the circuit believe that a particular panel's decision deserves further consideration, a case may be reconsidered *en banc*, with all judges in the circuit deciding the case. For example, a three-judge panel in the Sixth Circuit invalidated an Ohio state statute that limited claimants' ability to file civil rights actions in federal courts. Subsequently, the Sixth Circuit judges voted to have the case reargued in front of all of the circuit's judges. When the case was scheduled for reargument, one judge *recused* himself. In other words, he voluntarily removed himself from participation in the case because of his involvement in developing the statute during his service in the Ohio state legislature. After the second round of arguments, the circuit's remaining judges voted eight to six to reverse the panel's decision and uphold the constitutionality of

the Ohio statute.[34] *En banc* hearings involve all of a court's judges in every circuit except the Ninth. The number of judges in each circuit ranges from fewer than ten to more than twenty-five. Because there are so many judges in the huge Ninth Circuit, *en banc* cases are heard by panels formed by randomly drawing the names of eleven judges.

### U.S. Supreme Court

At the top of the judicial system is the U.S. Supreme Court. As chapter 9 will describe in greater detail, the Supreme Court is composed of nine justices who have discretion to decide which of the thousands of cases submitted each year that they will hear. In its 1994 term from October 1994 to July 1995, for example, the Supreme Court received 6,996 petitions. Ultimately, the justices heard oral arguments and provided complete written opinions in only 82 cases.[35] They handle cases—some of which flow from the federal system, others from state court systems—that raise issues concerning federal law or the U.S. Constitution. Because the Supreme Court is at the top of the judicial hierarchy, it can guide and shape decisions in lower courts through its power to reverse state, district, or circuit court decisions. Supreme Court justices can define the meaning of the Constitution and of federal statutes, but their power is not absolute. Subsequent chapters of this book will discuss the Court's interactions with other governmental institutions and political actors, as well as other limitations on its power and effectiveness.

### Specialized Courts

In addition to general jurisdiction and appellate courts in the federal system, there are courts with special functions and narrow jurisdictions. The previously mentioned Court of Appeals for the Federal Circuit handles trademark, patent, and related cases. The Court of International Trade, formerly the U.S. Customs Court, handles cases concerning duties levied on products and other issues concerning imports. Appeals from this court go to the Federal Circuit Court of Appeals. These special courts have their own judges, appointed by the president through the normal constitutional process and confirmed by the U.S. Senate. Other special courts borrow federal judges on a temporary basis to hear cases. These courts include the Temporary Emergency Court of Appeals, which handles cases concerning energy regulation, the Rail Reorganization Court, and both the trial and appellate divisions of a Foreign Intelligence Surveillance Court, which considers government requests for warrants to conduct surveillance.[36]

The judges on the Federal Circuit, the Court of International Trade, and the temporarily constituted special courts are *Article III judges*, which means that, like judges of the U.S. District Courts, Circuit Courts of Appeals, and Supreme Court, they are appointed by the president, and confirmed by the senate to lifetime terms ("during good Behaviour") in accordance with the Constitution's provisions concerning the judicial branch. By contrast, *Article I judges* preside over different judicial proceedings. Article I of the Constitution establishes the powers of the legislative branch (Congress), and Article I judges and courts were created and empowered by Congress to handle limited tasks without protected tenure or the presidential appointment process mandated by Article III. The U.S. Court of Military Appeals, which provides civilian judicial review of military courts-martial, is an Article I court.[37] Among district judges, the judges for territorial district courts (e.g., Guam, the Virgin Islands, the Northern Mariana Islands) have limited terms in office despite presiding over general jurisdiction courts. Although Article I judges are not constitutional judicial officers, they perform adjudicative functions, and their decisions are reviewable by Article III courts.

The *Court of Claims* is a trial court that considers monetary claims against the federal government. Appeals from this court are heard in the Federal Circuit Court of Appeals.[38] The Tax Court considers tax disputes at the trial level. Judges of the Court of Claims and Tax Court are appointed by the president to fifteen-year terms instead of to life tenure. In 1988 Congress created the Court of Veterans Appeals to hear cases concerning benefits claims brought by veterans against the government. The court was created to reduce the burden of veterans' claims cases on the regular federal judicial system.

One motivation for congressional creation of Article III and Article I special-ized courts was pressure from political interests hoping to win advantages for themselves by restructuring the judicial forums in which their cases would be heard. According to one study, the primary political interest was the federal government.[39] It is no accident that the specialized courts focus on disputes be-tween individuals and the federal government:

> In several situations where government decisions were already subject to judicial review . . . federal policymakers have preferred that this review be undertaken by specialized courts . . . [because of] the belief that a specialized court was less likely than generalists to rule against the validity of government decisions and to intervene in government programs.[40]

Although not part of the federal judicial system, one other category of govern-ment adjudicative agencies deserves mention. The executive branch of govern-ment includes more than one thousand Administrative Law Judges (ALJs) who preside over quasi-judicial proceedings concerning government regulations and benefits. The ALJs are selected through a civil service process and serve for a fixed number of years. The Social Security Administration's eight hundred ALJs make up over 60 percent of the total ALJs in thirty administrative agencies.[41] Social Security ALJs hear appeals from claimants who have been denied Social Security disability benefits. The ALJs consider the medical evidence and the legal criteria for eligibility to decide whether to approve the disbursement of benefits. They hold informal hearings not governed by the rules of procedure and evidence that apply in regular judicial processes. The Social Security ALJs and their colleagues in other agencies are not entirely separated from the federal judiciary, however, because their decisions can subsequently be appealed in federal courts. Thus, the adjudicative decisions of federal agencies may become the basis for cases entering the federal judicial process and may thereby consume a portion of the federal courts' limited resources.

## Court Administration

Several administrative and policy-making organizations affect the development of procedures and the allocation of resources in the federal judicial system. The Judicial Conference of the United States is the primary policy-making body for the judicial branch. The Chief Justice presides over the Judicial Conference, which is composed of chief judges representing each of the circuit courts plus one district judge from each circuit. The work of the Judicial Conference is assisted by committees composed of federal judicial officers appointed by the Chief Justice to study specific kinds of issues. The Judicial Conference represents the federal judiciary in making recommendations to Congress about policies, procedures, and resource needs of the judicial branch.

The Judiciary and Appropriations Committees in Congress play important roles in considering and recommending legislation to restructure the judiciary, change court procedures, and provide resources for the judicial branch. Federal judges lobby Congress and try to maintain reputations for sound financial management to convince the legislature to allocate requested resources. While federal statutes forbid judges from spending the judiciary's funds on lobbying activities, judges communicate their views to Congress through testimony before congressional committees, official communications emanating from the Judicial Conference, and informal communications with congressional staff members.[42] In sum, the judges employ political strategies in seeking the support of the legislative branch. For example, the Budget Committee of the Judicial Conference of the United States is usually comprised of judges ''having ability, legislative experience, and congressional associations,''[43] who can effectively influence Congress.

The Administrative Office of the U.S. Courts was created in 1939 to serve as the administrative agency for the judicial branch. The Administrative Office gathers statistics to track what kinds of cases enter the federal courts and how long it takes various courts to process them. The Administrative Office's statistics serve as the basis for the Judicial Conference's requests for personnel, computer equipment, and other resources. Officials in the Administrative Office assist the Judicial Conference in developing legislative proposals for submission to Congress. The Administrative Office also serves as the central management office for individual judges' requests for additional secretaries, law clerks, computers, photocopiers, and other resources.[44]

The Federal Judicial Center was established in 1967 to conduct research on the federal courts. The Center conducts studies on case processing, on consequences of particular procedural rules, on innovations developed and implemented by specific judges, and on other aspects of the federal judicial process.[45] The Center publishes booklets for distribution to judges and law libraries throughout the country. In addition, the Center organizes annual seminars to teach new judicial appointees—including judges, court clerks, and other court personnel—to perform their jobs effectively. The Center also offers continuing education programs to keep judges and other court personnel abreast of changes and innovations affecting the judiciary.[46]

In addition to these system-wide administrative entities, each circuit has its own annual conference with guest speakers who address various legal topics. These conferences are opportunities for judicial officers in a given circuit to exchange ideas. Each circuit has a judicial council composed of circuit and district judges that monitors the case-processing effectiveness of district courts within the circuit.[47] Judges in individual districts can institute their own procedures and innovations, provided that those procedures supplement and do not conflict with rules established by Congress, the Judicial Conference, and the circuit councils.[48] Full-time court administrators in each circuit and in several districts are called circuit executives and district executives, respectively. These administrators prepare and manage annual budgets, plan for court space and facilities needs, collect data on case management, and undertake other administrative tasks that might otherwise fall on the judges.[49]

In addition to the administrative staff, other personnel affect the efficiency of the judiciary. For example, in each district, a U.S. attorney acts as the federal prosecutor for criminal cases and represents the federal government in civil cases. When these political appointees develop good relationships with judges, there is likely to be greater cooperation in scheduling conferences, arriving at acceptable guilty pleas, and performing other aspects of civil and criminal litigation affecting judicial efficiency. Other officials can also affect the smooth processing of cases in the federal courts. The court clerk, for example, is responsible for organizing and monitoring the multitude of papers filed with the court during the course of litigation. United States marshals guard prisoners and provide security for judges. Although these tasks may not appear significant in the administration of justice, consider how judges' time can be wasted if the marshals are not well-organized in escorting incarcerated defendants and prisoners to court for scheduled hearings.

## ISSUES FACING COURTS

### Bureaucratization

Federal and state courts experience significant caseload pressure. As legislatures enact more statutes, new opportunities are created for lawsuits to clarify the meaning of or to assert entitlements created by these statutes. In addition, some observers theorize that Americans are litigious people prone to suing each other without seeking alternative means to resolve disputes. Others wonder whether the large and ever-increasing number of lawyers in the United States solicit clients and initiate more litigation simply to make a living. Whatever the cause, the large number of cases initiated in both state and federal court systems cause judges to complain about insufficient time and resources to properly complete their responsibilities. One consequence of increasing caseloads has been a growth in the number and kinds of personnel who assist judges in processing cases.

In federal courts, judges receive assistance from several unseen and little-known actors within the court system. In undertaking case processing and other responsibilities, judges delegate tasks to assistants who conduct research and make recommendations affecting outcomes produced by the courts. The introduction and proliferation of judicial subordinates in the federal courts has elicited warnings from judges and scholars that the federal judiciary has become "bureaucratized."[50] Cases may be improperly screened and terminated by subordinates without receiving appropriate consideration by judges. Judith Resnik warns that judges' traditional responsibility for decision making has become submerged in managerial responsibilities for supervising subordinates, scheduling the litigation process, meeting with disputants to encourage negotiated settlements, and other aspects of modern litigation management and court administration.[51] In addition, Resnik argues that the proliferation of judicial subordinates who are not Article III judges improperly places actual decision-making power in the hands of subordinate officials rather than under the control of duly appointed judges who supervise these officials.[52] In effect, bureaucratization can lead to routine, administrative decision making rather than the careful, considered judgments that the public expects from the judicial branch.

Similar concerns have been expressed regarding the use of judicial subordinates in state courts. For example, the seven justices on the Illinois Supreme Court each have three law clerks as well as shared oversight responsibilities for twenty-four legal staff members who work for the entire court. On the Washington State Court of Appeals forty-three legal staff members serve the seventeen judges as well as two law clerks per judge.[53] Can judges adequately supervise and control staff members while simultaneously handling their judging responsibilities, including presiding over oral arguments and drafting judicial opinions? A study of the Michigan Court of Appeals raised serious questions about the risk of staff members actually handling substantive decision-making responsibilities in legal cases.[54]

Political factors can influence the creation and proliferation of judicial subordinates. For example, even when the federal courts are experiencing burdensome caseloads, many members of Congress may not be willing to create new judgeships if an opposing political party controls the White House and will fill the positions with its own members. In the 1960s, despite mounting caseloads in the federal courts, reluctance to create new judgeships led Congress to create an entirely new judicial officer—the U.S. magistrate judge who would not be appointed by the president.

U.S. magistrate judges are the most authoritative subordinates assisting the federal district judges. Magistrate judges are appointed by district judges to serve for renewable eight-year terms (or four-year terms for part-time magistrate judges). Because they were originally called U.S. magistrates when their office was created by Congress in 1968, lawyers sometimes confused these federal judicial officers with state magistrates, who are often lay justices of the peace in rural areas.[55] In an effort to enhance magistrates' status, Congress changed the title to "magistrate judge" in 1990.[56] These subordinate judicial officers are empowered to undertake any judicial tasks performed by district judges except for certain tasks related to felony criminal cases (e.g., jury selection, trials, sentencing, etc.). When a magistrate judge undertakes certain tasks that may directly dispose of a case—such as considering a motion by a disputant to have his or her opponent's case dismissed—the magistrate judge makes a recommendation to the district judge. For other tasks, such as ruling on a motion about the admissibility of evidence, magistrate judges make binding decisions. Magistrate judges may even preside over full civil trials with the consent of both litigants.[57]

Magistrate judges are considered adjuncts of the federal district court, appointed, assigned, and supervised by district judges. Because of the breadth of their authority, however, there is a risk that a magistrate judge's role and decision-making power in federal court might prevent a disputant's claim from receiving the attention of a regular district judge. One study of magistrate judges found that when district judges prefer not to hear certain cases, they sometimes pressure litigants to accept a magistrate judge. Such pressure directly violates the federal statute requiring all such consents to be completely voluntary and uncoerced.[58] In addition, the caseload of district judges may lead them to "rubber stamp" magistrate judges' recommendations without reviewing the analysis and conclusions.[59] The most significant risk of bureaucratization stems from the wholesale delegation of prisoners' cases and Social Security disability appeals to magistrate judges. Because such cases are routine, repetitive, and filed by despised (e.g., prisoners) or less affluent (e.g., disability claimants) people, some magistrate judges do not give them adequate attention and district judges often fail to monitor decision making in these categories of cases that some judicial officers regard as boring or unimportant.[60] Such outcomes reflect the organization of politics and distribution of power in American society. People with enough money to hire their own attorneys and pay for sustained litigation expenses are best able to make use of the judicial branch's resources and processes. Less affluent people may not be able to enter the judicial process at all or, if they manage to enter, their cases may receive less than careful attention.

Law clerks assist judicial officers at all levels in the federal court system, from magistrate judges through Supreme Court justices. Law clerks also assist state appellate judges and even state trial judges in some places. Law clerks are

generally recent law school graduates with outstanding academic credentials. They spend one or two years working closely with judicial officers before moving into careers in law firms, government, and teaching. Clerkships with federal judges and state supreme courts are highly prized as prestigious work experiences, so the competition for such positions is keen. The most desirable clerkships are those with judicial officers on the U.S. Courts of Appeals and the U.S. Supreme Court.[61]

Law clerks perform a variety of tasks. They conduct research on cases, review petitions from claimants, write memoranda on the case law underlying particular issues, and even draft preliminary judicial opinions. Since Supreme Court justices began to employ law clerks at the end of the nineteenth century, there has been a proliferation of such assistants. Today, most magistrate judges have one law clerk, many district judges have two, circuit judges may have three, and Supreme Court justices have three or four law clerks apiece.[62] State supreme court justices in thirty-four states have two or more law clerks, and justices on California's Supreme Court each have five law clerks.[63] The increase in staff requires judges to spend more time monitoring and supervising assistants and creates a risk that judges will not be able to devote themselves to traditional adjudicative functions.

Because law clerks play important roles in researching issues and in making recommendations for the substance of judicial opinions, it is possible that a judge may be subtly influenced by a law clerk's values and preferences.[64] For example, because appellate judges frequently rely on the law clerks to provide them with memoranda summarizing pending cases prior to oral argument, the law clerks' perceptions of the facts or value preferences concerning the issues in the case may intentionally or unwittingly slant the information provided to the judge. After serving as law clerk to Justice Robert Jackson in the early 1950s, future chief justice William Rehnquist wrote a national magazine article in which he asserted that Supreme Court law clerks' ''left of center . . . political views could to some extent influence the action of the Court in deciding whether to grant a hearing in a particular case.''[65]

Law clerks are usually very inexperienced but are given the important task of reviewing petitions to determine which cases deserve judicial attention. These reviews by law clerks are undertaken at all levels of the federal courts, including the U.S. Supreme Court. The inexperienced law school graduate's recommendations may influence the determination of which cases will be heard and which will be dismissed, or at the appellate level, which will be terminated through summary decisions without oral arguments and complete written opinions. Clerks are potentially influential because judges frequently read only the summaries and recommendations and may never see the actual petitions.

Some judges recognize that an inexperienced clerk's evaluation may suffer from a constant burden of petitions, so they attempt to vary the quantity and content of the clerk's assigned tasks.[66] Other judges delegate a constant flow of petitions and other tasks to law clerks because the judges are so burdened by their own case-processing responsibilities.

In addition to the law clerks who work directly for federal judicial officers, some courthouses have independent law clerks working for all judges. These law clerks are generally responsible for reviewing *pro se* petitions filed by people representing themselves without the assistance of an attorney.[67] Such cases are usually filed by prisoners, civil rights claimants, and other less affluent people. These untrained claimants often file confusing documents that reveal a lack of understanding of legal procedures, as well as deficiencies in basic spelling and grammar. Law clerks are responsible for determining whether these *pro se* petitions contain any claims that merit the court's attention. The repetitive nature of such claims can incline law clerks to dismiss them without adequate consideration.[68] Yet no judge directly monitors all the work undertaken by *pro se* law clerks.

The risk that judicial decisions may be affected by this proliferation of invisible decision makers is illustrated by the manner in which Social Security disability appeals are handled in some federal courthouses. When claimants' appeals arrive at the district court, the district judge frequently refers the review of the ALJ decision to a magistrate judge. The magistrate judge then, in turn, assigns the review to his or her law clerk. In some courts, the law clerk may delegate the review to a law student working part-time as an intern. The review of the petition usually produces a memorandum recommending that the court uphold the ALJ's decision denying benefits, and the claim is dismissed. The intern's memo is sent to the magistrate judge's law clerk, who sends it to the magistrate judge, who sends it to the district judge's law clerk, who sends it to the district judge, who usually signs an order implementing the recommendation. Because the initial decision maker—often an inexperienced law student or law clerk—is usually the only person who has actually read the claim and the medical evidence file, some judicial decisions become administrative, with each layer of the judicial hierarchy merely "rubber stamping" the decisions passed up from below.

Different variations on bureaucratization exist in different courts. In the circuit court of appeals, for example, additional decision makers, known as staff attorneys, make recommendations about which appeals ought to be accepted for full hearing and which ought to be dismissed. As with *pro se* law clerks at the district level, staff attorneys often do not work under the direct supervision of any particular circuit judge.

## The Caseload "Crisis"

Over the past several decades, the number of cases filed in American courts has increased significantly. Although the numbers have not increased every year, the overall trend of the late twentieth century has made judges feel exceptionally burdened by caseload pressures. Table 2.4 illustrates the increased burden on

**Table 2.4: Federal District Court Caseload, 1969–1995.**

| Year | District Judges | Criminal Cases | Civil Cases | Total Cases | Cases per Judge |
|------|-----------------|----------------|-------------|-------------|-----------------|
| 1969 | 327 | 33,585 | 77,193 | 110,778 | 339 |
| 1973 | 384 | 40,367 | 98,560 | 138,927 | 362 |
| 1977 | 373 | 39,786 | 130,567 | 170,353 | 457 |
| 1981 | 472 | 30,413 | 180,576 | 210,989 | 447 |
| 1985 | 496 | 38,546 | 273,670 | 312,216 | 629 |
| 1988 | 544 | 43,503 | 239,634 | 283,137 | 520 |
| 1995 | 649 | 45,800 | 248,300 | 294,099 | 453 |

*Source:* Committee on the Judicial Branch of the Judicial Conference of the United States, *Simple Fairness: The Case for Equitable Compensation of the Nation's Federal Judges* (1988), p. 17; *Federal Judicial Workload Statistics* (Washington, D.C.: Administrative Office of the U.S. Courts, 1993), pp. 2–4; "Chief Justice Recaps 1995 Year-end Report," *The Third Branch* 28 (January 1996): 4–5.

federal district judges. In 1969, 33,585 criminal cases and 77,193 civil cases were initiated in the district courts. By 1995, those numbers had jumped to 45,800 and 248,300, respectively.[69] Although the number of district judges increased from 327 to 649 during that period, caseloads continued to mount: the number of cases per judge increased from 339 to 453 in the district courts.[70] These are average caseload figures, so the burden actually varies by district judge. Some districts may face special burdens, such as courts in Florida and Texas that handle an extraordinary number of prosecutions for narcotics smuggling by virtue of being located along key border and entry points. In a 1990 report, a committee of judges and lawyers concluded that the pressure on the federal courts had reached a "crisis" stage:

> [T]he expanded federal effort to reduce drug trafficking has led to a recent surge in federal criminal trials that is preventing federal judges in major metropolitan areas from scheduling civil trials, especially civil jury trials, of which there is now a rapidly growing backlog. It appears that the long-expected crisis of the federal courts, caused by unabated growth in case filings, is at last upon us.[71]

This "crisis" affecting the federal judiciary is exacerbated by the slow process of filling judicial vacancies through presidential appointment and senatorial confirmation. Many courts are left with long-standing personnel shortages. As of January 1, 1996, there were thirteen vacant circuit judgeships with only seven nominees awaiting Senate confirmation and thirty-seven district court vacancies with only twenty-two nominees awaiting Senate confirmation. Fourteen judgeships, vacant for eighteen months or more, were therefore publicized as "judicial emergencies" in the federal judiciary's monthly newsletter.[72]

Recommendations for improving the federal courts' effectiveness were formulated in 1989 and 1990 by specially formed committees of the Brookings

Institution and the federal judiciary.[73] The recommendations suggested a variety of reforms intended to improve the case-processing efficiency of the federal courts. For example, some reformers suggested decreasing the number of cases permitted to enter the federal courts by eliminating diversity jurisdiction and forcing regular civil suits into the state courts—even if the disputants were from different states. The consequence of such an action in the American dual court system, however, would increase the burdens on state court systems, many of which have fewer resources than does the federal judiciary. Other suggested reforms included the creation of additional specialized courts, such as a special Article I court of appeals for Social Security cases, and the implementation of more alternative dispute resolution procedures to encourage disputants to negotiate settlements. Such suggestions would alter the nature of the judicial process by reducing the opportunities for disputants to be heard by federal judges. In addition, the diversion of certain categories of litigants and issues from the judicial process would affect the development of federal case law. Certain kinds of cases may cease to reach judges for the consideration and decision-making that normally shape and change legal precedents.

Any reform of the judicial process, even one with the best of intentions, will have both obvious and subtle consequences for disputants, for the nature of judicial attention to cases, for the distribution of the caseload among courts, and for the outcomes of litigation. Because reforms inevitably affect the interests of specific individuals and groups, various interest groups, bar associations, judges, and lawyers urged Congress to act (or to refrain from acting) on the reforms that could affect their political and financial interests. Ultimately, Congress took the modest step of requiring district courts to evaluate themselves and develop plans for reducing case-processing delays. In addition, ten districts were selected for a three-year pilot project to implement ideas for managing litigation.[74]

To improve the situation, federal judges must continually push Congress to increase the judicial budget, create new judgeships, limit the kinds of cases permitted to enter the judicial process, and increase judges' salaries. Although judges, unlike some other political interest groups, are not entirely self-interested, their well-intentioned efforts to improve judicial efficiency by reforming court organization and jurisdiction are mixed with self-interested desires to increase their own salaries[75] and prestige.[76]

## Judicial Malapportionment

The adequacy of resources for addressing rising caseloads affects individual courts as well as the judicial system as a whole. To provide citizens with access to the judicial process and to fulfill its dispute-processing functions, the federal judicial system's resources must be equitably distributed among the various districts or other jurisdictional subunits. For example, in 1988 there was one federal district judge for every 237,666 people in South Dakota, a sharp contrast to the one judge for every 801,000 people in Nebraska.[77] Such disparities are likely to cause long delays in court proceedings for people in resource-poor judicial districts, even though they may be in dire need of monetary damages to remedy a personal injury or of protection of constitutional rights.

In federal courts, the allocation and distribution of judicial resources are determined by political interactions with Congress and by the internal politics of the federal judiciary. Members of Congress and federal judges seek resources, such as additional judgeships, for their districts and circuits. Thus, they seek to influence recommendations to Congress from the Judicial Conference and the Administrative Office of the U.S. Courts, as well as the ultimate decisions by Congress itself. Because the district and circuit courts are responsible for specific geographic areas, any maldistribution of resources affects the court access and judicial outcomes of specific constituencies—the people who live in a specific state or region. As Richard Richardson and Kenneth Vines have observed, judicial malapportionment is similar to legislative malapportionment in depriving specific constituencies of equitable access to governmental resources and power:

> Certainly the adequacy of judicial staff helps determine both the accessibility to and effectiveness of courts, and inequalities in judicial staff may affect the expectations of litigants as well as create unfavorable environments for the presentation of policy demands. For these reasons, figures on case litigation are not an entirely satisfactory measure of institutional adequacy. The number of judges available for actions, it can be argued, might well create conditions favorable for litigation and increase it substantially. A constituency deprived of institutional representation in the judiciary may suffer some of the same ills as similarly situated constituencies in legislative malapportionment.[78]

## CONCLUSION

Because of their diversity, American court systems provide abundant examples of the impact of politics on the organization, administration, and reform of judicial institutions. The structure and operations of state court systems are based on local political traditions and the interactions of partisan interests in a given political environment. Many fragmented state court systems—with their traditional dispersals of power and patronage to local political interests—provide stark contrasts to unified state court systems and the federal judicial system, which contain components consciously created in response to specific problems. Although some court systems have initiated changes to cope with caseload growth or to improve administrative efficiency, specific reforms were developed and implemented through strategic interactions of political interests. Because the organization of courts, the distribution of authority among judicial officers, and systemic responses to emerging judicial problems are influenced by the interactions of political parties, interest groups, and elected officials, politics effectively determines claimants' access to courts, procedures employed to process claims, and outcomes produced by the judicial process.

## NOTES

1. Richard Kluger, *Simple Justice: The History of* Brown v. Board of Education *and Black America's Struggle for Equality* (New York: Random House, 1975), p. 301.
2. Gerald Stern, *The Buffalo Creek Disaster* (New York: Vintage, 1976), pp. 20–21, 52–64.
3. Seth Mydans, "The Police Verdict: Los Angeles Policemen Acquitted in Taped Beating," *New York Times*, 30 April 1992, p. A1.
4. David Ellis, "L.A. Lawless: The Violence Sparked by the King Verdict Reveals Racial Divisions That Have Plagued the City for Years," *Time*, 11 May 1992, pp. 26–28.
5. Seth Mydans, "The 81 Seconds That Shaped 2 Years Return to Center Stage in Los Angeles," *New York Times*, 22 February 1993, p. A12.
6. Jack Peltason, *Fifty-Eight Lonely Men* (New York: Harcourt Brace, 1961), p. 132.
7. Kluger, *Simple Justice*, 300–301.
8. Peltason, *Fifty-Eight Lonely Men*, pp. 133–34.
9. See *Report of the Federal Courts Study Committee*, 2 April 1990, pp. 39–42.
10. *Almanac of California Government and Politics* (Sacramento, CA: California Journal, 1987), pp. 98–99.
11. See D. Marie Provine, *Judging Credentials: Nonlawyer Judges and the Politics of Professionalism* (Chicago: University of Chicago Press, 1986).
12. Harry P. Stumpf, *American Judicial Politics* (New York: Harcourt Brace Jovanovich, 1988), pp. 81–85.
13. Provine, *Judging Credentials*, p. 190.
14. Greg J. Borowski, "Case backlog cut in half," *Lansing State Journal*, 29 December 1995, p. B1.
15. *BNA's Directory of State Courts, Judges, and Clerks*, 2nd ed. (Washington, D.C.: Bureau of National Affairs, 1988), p. 123.
16. Ibid., p. 236.
17. See John Paul Ryan, Allan Ashman, Bruce D. Sales, and Sandra Shane-DuBow, *American Trial Judges* (New York: Free Press, 1980), pp. 71–75.
18. See James A. Gazell, *The Future of State Court Management* (Port Washington, NY: Kennikat Press, 1978), pp. 5–27.
19. See David J. Saari, *American Court Management* (Westport, CT: Quorum Books, 1982), pp. 68–93.

20. Steve Hoffman, "Clerk Hits Political Roadblock," *Akron Beacon Journal*, 13 February 1991, p. D1.

21. Henry R. Glick, "The Politics of State-Court Reform," in *The Politics of Judicial Reform*, ed. Philip L. DuBois (Lexington, MA: Lexington Books, 1982), pp. 17–33.

22. Ibid., p. 22.

23. Ibid.

24. Ibid., p. 23.

25. Ibid., pp. 23–25.

26. Sheryl Harris, "Lawsuit Challenges Peninsula Mayor's Court," *Akron Beacon Journal*, 5 January 1993, p. C1.

27. Glick, "The Politics of State-Court Reform," p. 25.

28. U.S. Constitution, Article III, sec. 1.

29. Russell R. Wheeler and Cynthia Harrison, *Creating the Federal Judicial System* (Washington, D.C.: Federal Judicial Center, 1989), pp. 4–6.

30. Ibid., p. 8.

31. Robert A. Carp and Ronald Stidham, *The Federal Courts*, 2nd ed. (Washington, D.C.: Congressional Quarterly Press, 1991), p. 28.

32. See Carroll Seron, "Court Reorganization and the Politics of Reform: The Case of Bankruptcy Court," in *The Politics of Judicial Reform*, ed. Philip L. DuBois (Lexington, MA: Lexington Books, 1982), pp. 87–98.

33. See Comment, "Is the Federal Magistrate Act Constitutional After *Northern Pipeline*?" *Arizona State Law Journal* (1985): 189–212.

34. Ann Woolner, "Tug of War Gets Intense," in *Reagan Justice: A Conservative Legacy on the Appellate Courts* (special supplement to *The American Lawyer*) [May/June 1988]: 36). Discusses *Leaman v. Ohio Department of Mental Retardation*, 825 F.2d 946 (6th Cir. 1987).

35. "Chief Justice Recaps 1995 in Year-end Report," *The Third Branch* 28 (January 1996): 4–6.

36. Lawrence Baum, *American Courts: Process and Policy*, 2nd ed. (Boston: Houghton Mifflin, 1990), pp. 36–38.

37. Carp and Stidham, *The Federal Courts*, p. 29; Stumpf, *American Judicial Politics*, p. 140.

38. Stumpf, *American Judicial Politics*, pp. 138–39.

39. See Lawrence Baum, "Specializing the Federal Courts: Neutral Reforms or Efforts to Shape Judicial Policy?" *Judicature* 74 (1991): 217–24.

40. Ibid., p. 224.

41. Donna P. Cofer, *Judges, Bureaucrats, and the Question of Independence* (Westport, CT: Greenwood Press, 1985), p. 14.

42. Christopher E. Smith, *Judicial Self-Interest: Federal Judges and Court Administration* (Westport, CT: Praeger Publishers, 1995), pp. 15–43.

43. Thomas G. Walker and Deborah J. Barrow, "Funding the Federal Judiciary: The Congressional Connection," *Judicature* 69 (1985): 50.

44. Carp and Stidham, *The Federal Courts*, pp. 65–67.
45. See, e.g., *Recommended Procedures for Handling Prisoner Civil Rights Cases in the Federal Courts* (Washington, D.C.: Federal Judicial Center, 1980); Carroll Seron, *The Roles of Magistrates in the Federal District Courts* (Washington, D.C.: Federal Judicial Center, 1983).
46. Carp and Stidham, *The Federal Courts*, pp. 67–70.
47. Ibid., pp. 70–72.
48. See, e.g., *Rules of the United States District Court, Northern District of Ohio*, 4 April 1984.
49. Steven Flanders, "Court Executives and Decentralization of the Federal Judiciary," *Judicature* 70 (1987): 273–79.
50. See, e.g., Owen Fiss, "The Bureaucratization of the Judiciary," *Yale Law Journal* 92 (1983): 1442–1468; Wade McCree, Jr., "Bureaucratic Justice: An Early Warning," *University of Pennsylvania Law Review* 129 (1981): 777–97.
51. Judith Resnik, "Managerial Judges," *Harvard Law Review* 96 (1982): 374–448.
52. Judith Resnik, "The Mythic Meaning of Article III Courts," *University of Colorado Law Review* 56 (1985): 581–617.
53. David B. Rottman, Carol R. Flango, R. Shedine Lockley, *State Court Organization 1993* (Washington, D.C.: Bureau of Justice Statistics, 1995), pp. 187–89.
54. Mary Lou Stow and Harold Spaeth, "Centralized Research Staff: Is There a Monster in the Judicial Closet?," *Judicature* (1992): 216–221.
55. See Christopher E. Smith, "The Development of a Judicial Office: United States Magistrates and the Struggle for Status," *The Journal of the Legal Profession* 14 (1989): 175–97.
56. See "Judiciary Fares Well in Legislation Passed by 101st Congress," *The Third Branch* 11 (November 1990): 5.
57. Christopher E. Smith, *United States Magistrates in the Federal Courts: Subordinate Judges* (New York: Praeger Publishers, 1990), pp. 15–28.
58. Smith, *United States Magistrates in the Federal Courts*, pp. 165–66.
59. Ibid., p. 131.
60. Ibid., pp. 174–78.
61. See, generally, John Bilyeu Oakley and Robert S. Thompson, *Law Clerks and the Judicial Process* (Berkeley, CA: University of California Press, 1980).
62. Ibid., pp. 19–21.
63. Rottman, Flango, and Lockley, pp. 187–90.
64. Carp and Stidham, *The Federal Courts*, pp. 75–79.
65. William H. Rehnquist, "Another View: Clerks Might 'Influence' Some Actions," *U.S. News & World Report*, 21 February 1958, p. 116.

66. Christopher E. Smith, "United States Magistrates and the Processing of Prisoner Litigation," *Federal Probation* 52 (December 1988): 15.

67. See Donald H. Zeigler and Michele G. Hermann, "The Invisible Litigant: An Inside View of Pro Se Actions in the Federal Courts," *New York University Law Review* 47 (1972): 159–257.

68. Smith, *United States Magistrates in the Federal Courts* pp. 176–77.

69. Committee on the Judicial Branch of the Judicial Conference of the United States, *Simple Fairness: The Case for Equitable Compensation of the Nation's Federal Judges* (1988), p. 17; "Chief Justice Recaps 1995 in Year-end Report," *The Third Branch* 28 (January 1996): 4–5.

70. Committee on the Judicial Branch, *Simple Fairness*, p. 17.

71. *Report of the Federal Courts Study Committee*, p. 6.

72. "Judicial Boxscore," *The Third Branch* 28 (January 1996): 11.

73. See *Justice for All: Reducing Costs and Delay in Civil Litigation* (Washington, D.C.: Brookings Institution, 1989); *Report of the Federal Courts Study Committee* (2 April 1990).

74. William H. Rehnquist, "1990 Year-End Report of the Federal Judiciary," *The Third Branch* 23 (January 1991): 5.

75. See Christopher E. Smith, "Federal Judicial Salaries: A Critical Appraisal," *Temple Law Review* 62 (1989): 849–73.

76. For example, Justice Scalia said the federal judiciary should be a "natural aristocracy . . . of ability rather than wealth." Stuart Taylor, "Scalia Proposes Major Overhaul of U.S. Courts," *New York Times*, 16 February 1987, p. 1.

77. Christopher E. Smith, *Courts, Politics, and the Judicial Process* (Chicago: Nelson-Hall, 1993), p. 51.

78. Richard J. Richardson and Kenneth N. Vines, *The Politics of Federal Courts* (Boston: Little, Brown, 1970), pp. 44–45.

# Chapter 3

# The Legal Profession

A lthough the courts constitute a branch of government, citizens do not enjoy free access to the dispute-processing resources of the judicial branch. One potential barrier to judicial access is the inability to obtain representation by an attorney. It is extremely difficult for lay people to utilize the judicial process effectively to settle disputes or to protect their constitutional rights without the assistance of an attorney. Court procedures are technical and intricate, and such procedures are not designed to encourage people to present their own claims to the judiciary. Because it is so difficult for lay people to represent themselves effectively in court, they must rely on lawyers, the professionals trained in the procedures and tactics of the judicial process.

Lawyers are more readily available for certain kinds of cases. In criminal cases, the Sixth Amendment constitutional guarantee of a ''right to counsel'' has been interpreted to require governments to provide free representation for indigent defendants who face charges that might lead to incarceration.[1] For civil litigation, several mechanisms have reduced the absence of privately retained counsel as a barrier to access to the courts. The federal Legal Services Corporation and local legal aid societies provide representation for claimants whose incomes are sufficiently low. Interest groups sponsor cases by litigants whose legal claims might lead to judicial decisions that will advance the groups' public policy goals. Federal legislation provides for the awarding of attorneys' fees to victorious claimants in certain civil rights and other cases. Despite the existence of these mechanisms, many people still have difficulty obtaining the services of lawyers.

The foregoing mechanisms for increasing access to legal counsel and the courts are available to relatively few litigants. Very few claimants will receive sponsorship from interest groups. Only society's poorest citizens are entitled to free representation in civil and criminal cases. Only a limited number of claims are eligible for attorney fee awards. Thus, most people must use their own resources to hire a lawyer when they confront legal problems. Nearly 70 percent of American lawyers are in private practice.[2] These are the lawyers available to pursue—or decline to pursue—most legal claims through the judicial process. As a result, private, profit-seeking lawyers are key figures in determining whether citizens will gain access to and enjoy the benefits of the judicial branch of government.

The recognition that private actors exert significant control over citizens' access to a branch of government raises significant questions about the interests and behavior of these legal professionals. How does lawyers' self-interest influence litigants' access to and outcomes from the judicial process? Which political interests in American society benefit from private attorneys' influence over the judicial process?

Although this chapter devotes significant attention to the majority of lawyers who are in private practice, it should be noted at the outset that the American legal profession is not monolithic. Government agencies employ thousands of attorneys whose jobs entail pursuing legal cases on behalf of the public in order to protect consumers, prevent pollution, redress discrimination, and fulfill a variety of other public-service governmental functions. Hundreds of interest groups are represented by attorneys whose sustained attention to specific public policy issues differentiates them from the private attorneys who are available to represent the narrow interests of specific individual clients. Despite these differences in goals and clients that distinguish attorneys from each other, unifying elements of education, socialization, and professional norms bind lawyers together and determine the distribution of prestige and political influence among members of the legal profession.

# THE ROLE OF LAWYERS IN AMERICAN SOCIETY

Lawyers serve several important functions for the judicial process and for society. Although lawyers and their organizations (''bar associations'') attempt to cultivate and project the image of a public-service profession, lawyers' decisions and behavior are not necessarily guided by their assessments of what is ''best for society.'' Attorneys in private practice are in business to make money. Some lawyers object to the characterization of a law practice as a ''business,''[3] but private practitioners seek to secure paying clients, charge fees to ensure healthy profits, build an increasingly large volume of clients and profits, and otherwise behave like any businessperson seeking to make money by providing goods or services. Lawyers' self-interest affects the performance of the legal profession's functions. In a political world in which people's decisions and behavior are influenced by their values, attitudes, and interests, it should be neither surprising nor disappointing that lawyers' actions are influenced by these same human, political factors. The problematic aspect of lawyers' self-interest and its effect on their actions stems from the significant control that these private actors exert over the structure and processes of a governmental branch that affects the lives of all citizens.

A primary function performed by lawyers is that of *gatekeepers* for the judicial system. When people wish to pursue claims through the judicial process, they generally must seek the advice and assistance of attorneys. Attorneys may encourage these claimants and assist them in presenting their cases in court. Alternatively, lawyers may discourage the claimants from pursuing the cases. The advice of an attorney can be very influential in determining whether cases are brought to court. If an attorney tells someone that a case is not worth pursuing, the person is likely to abandon the claim. Lawyers' calculations about whether a claim should be filed in court are not based merely on their assessments of the case's merits. Lawyers also take into consideration the costs and potential economic profitability of legal action. If a case is not worth enough money to generate revenues for the attorney, he or she may not wish to waste time on it, no matter how meritorious the claim may be. For example, a poor person who wishes to sue a landlord for $150 wrongly withheld from a security deposit will have trouble finding an attorney to pursue the case. Many attorneys charge more than $150 per hour of work, so they know that it is not financially feasible to pursue the claim even if the tenant *was* wronged. Lawyers take cases on a contingency-fee basis for personal injury claims. Under this arrangement the lawyer receives a set percentage, usually 30 percent, of whatever the plaintiff wins from the settlement or court victory. If the injury is slight (e.g., a sprained wrist), a lawyer may decline to pursue the case because there is not enough money at issue to justify the expenditure of effort and attention. Thus, the judicial process is not freely available to all disputants. The judicial process is normally activated only when a lawyer believes that the potential recovery will be sufficiently large to make the legal efforts profitable or when the client is sufficiently wealthy to pay the lawyer's hourly fees. A study of lawyers' advice to clients in consumer cases found that lawyers were more inclined to encourage cases initiated by businesses or by wealthy persons than those pursued by ordinary consumers.[4]

Lawyers who work for government agencies or who are salaried staff members for corporations and other organizations do not make the same financial calculations in deciding to pursue a case. As salaried employees, their incomes do not depend on the number of clients they represent. They may, however, apply their self-interest in other forms by discouraging their employers from pursuing cases that they regard as overly difficult, too time consuming, or especially uninteresting.

In addition to screening cases for entry into the judicial process, lawyers are also *transformers* who must translate people's grievances into the language of recognizable legal claims. If a woman complains to a lawyer that she was unfairly fired from her job, the lawyer must determine whether this allegation may be pursued within the legal system. Was she fired for poor job performance? Or was she fired because of gender discrimination, racial discrimination, age discrimination, or some other legally improper reason? The lawyer must fit the client's factual situation into existing statutes and case precedents and present the grievance in a form that courts may recognize and can remedy. This process of transforming a human grievance into a legal claim is one of the most difficult tasks for lay people to undertake. For example, prisoners in correctional institutions frequently file cases, without the assistance of attorneys, alleging violations of their constitutional rights. Prisoners tend to include every aspect of prison life that bothers them, from a lack of padding on furniture to physical abuse by corrections officers, with no idea which claims qualify as proper constitutional issues that may be examined by a court.[5] These cases force judicial officers and their law clerks to spend extra time and energy determining whether a legal claim is hidden among the amateurs' petitions.[6] Lawyers may damage claimants' interests by declining to accept and transform legitimate claims that do not advance the lawyers' personal and financial self-interest; but, as the prisoner example illustrates, in other cases lawyers help conserve the resources of the court system by ensuring that claims are presented in an understandable, processable form.

In transforming grievances into legal cases, lawyers may utilize their creativity to *present new arguments and legal theories* to the courts. These new theories may provide judges with the tools to move law and social policy in new directions through the common law process of establishing new judicial precedents. In tort law cases concerning injuries to people and property, the concept of holding people who commit negligent acts responsible for the consequences of their behavior was developed and refined through arguments presented to judges by lawyers. Judges in the American judicial system are relatively passive. The procedures governing courts' institutional processes limit judges' ability to pursue issues of interest to them. Judges must wait until cases and arguments are brought to them before they make decisions. Thus, lawyers play a significant role in shaping law and judicial policy by formulating and presenting creative arguments and evidence in court. Ground-breaking cases concerning racial discrimination, for example, were not based entirely on judges' desires to alter the U.S. policy of racial segregation. The decisions made by the Supreme Court culminating in the landmark case of *Brown v. Board of Education*[7] resulted from arguments presented over several decades by Thurgood Marshall and other lawyers from the National Association for the Advancement of Colored People (NAACP), arguments that led the justices to question the propriety of the fifty-year-old doctrine of ''separate but equal'' segregation.[8]

Lawyers also function as *prominent decision makers* whose actions and judgments determine the outcomes of cases in the judicial process. Over 90 percent of criminal cases that are not dismissed result in plea bargains rather than in trials. A similar percentage of civil cases end in negotiated settlements rather than in adversarial courtroom battles. Lawyers are the key negotiators between the opposing parties, guiding the processing of both criminal and civil cases. Although the clients possess the ultimate authority to approve or disapprove negotiated guilty pleas or civil case settlements, clients usually follow lawyers' recommendations. Thus, the lawyers' decisions in the negotiation process concerning the necessity and acceptability of a plea or settlement are the primary determinants of case outcomes. Because negotiation affects the overwhelming majority of cases in the judicial process, lawyers have more influence than judges over most case outcomes. As chapters 4 and 5 will show in regard to criminal and civil cases, respectively, lawyers' self-interest in financial considerations and in maintenance of relationships with other judicial actors sometimes overrides the clients' best interests.

Lawyers are also prominent decision makers in commercial transactions that shape the American economy. When companies and corporate assets are bought and sold, lawyers serve as essential advisors, helping to shape and facilitate such deals. In any potential transaction, lawyers analyze the interested parties' potential tax consequences, a process that may either encourage or inhibit completion of transactions. Lawyers also help to design the structure of transactions. How will a contract for the sale of corporate assets be designed? What kind of financing will be available for the deal? These decisions ultimately affect whether companies stay in business, move to new locations, or develop new products—results that inevitably affect the jobs and livelihoods of many workers as well as the economic vitality of communities.

Lawyers also wield enormous *influence over public policy decisions* through their overrepresentation in legislatures. Out of 535 members of the ninety-ninth Congress, for example, there were 251 lawyers.[9] Although researchers studying legislative behavior question whether lawyer-legislators vote differently than do other legislators,[10] other studies indicate that "lawyer-legislators . . . are in a position to define the meaning of legislation before it becomes law" because of deference by nonlawyers.[11] Senator Robert Byrd of West Virginia demonstrated his belief that lawyers are especially powerful in Congress by spending ten years attending evening law school in order to earn a law degree and thereby "join the club," though he was already a member of Congress. According to Byrd, "I saw that the lawyers were in the main, the movers and shakers. . . . They were the elected leadership. They chaired most of the committees. On the floor of the House and Senate, they seemed to be the most effective legislators."[12] Whether or not attorneys have a special influence in legislatures, lawyers have succeeded in controlling the rules and procedures that have direct bearing on the size and financial health of the legal profession, including legal education, credentials for the practice of law, and attorney discipline for misbehavior. All of these subjects could be regulated by governmental commissions of lay members or by other mechanisms, but legislatures, with their disproportionate representations of lawyers, grant the legal community the privilege of self-regulation. This may stem, in part, from the fact that lawyer-legislators typically have positive feelings toward the legal system and are less likely to acknowledge the role of politics as an influence on judicial decisions.[13] As Richard Abel has described in great detail in his book *American Lawyers*, lawyers have controlled entry into the legal profession and have undertaken other actions to preserve their elite status and lucrative monopoly over dispute-processing activities within the judicial branch.[14]

Lawyers' influence on public policy also stems from their status as members of the pool of potential candidates from which judges are selected. Controlled entry into the legal profession shapes the eventual composition of the judiciary. The common socialization process and development of profession-centered interests that lawyers experience as law students and later as beginning attorneys shape the legal professionals who will later determine law and public policy as judicial officers. Lawyers' control over their profession's standards and their influential role in society are consequences of the legal profession's development during the past century.

## HISTORICAL DEVELOPMENT OF THE AMERICAN LEGAL PROFESSION

The historical development of the American legal profession has shaped the structure of lawyers' organizations, including law firms and bar associations, the client interests that receive judicial resources, and the legal profession's influence over the availability (or lack thereof) of legal resources for certain segments of American society. Judge Arlin Adams has observed that the growth of large law firms, lawyers' increasing emphasis on profit maximization, and the trend toward specialization in the legal profession have diminished lawyers' historical roles as civic-minded professionals who provide leadership in the American democracy.[15] As the legal profession developed, lawyers and their organizations tended to apply their specialized skills and political influence to the preservation of their own professional stature and to the advancement of the interests of politically powerful corporate clients.

When the earliest American colonies were composed of small, tightly knit communities controlled by religious sects, there was little need for lawyers. Social behavior and relationships were governed according to the local churches' proscriptions. The growth of a commercial economy in colonial towns and cities, however, created new relationships and new conflicts that demanded the services of legal professionals. Contractual disputes between merchants in different cities could not be resolved through the same consensual, religion-based rules and interactions that governed interpersonal disputes in small, homogeneous agrarian communities. As lawyers pursued disputes in growing colonies through litigation, legal professionals' prominence and power expanded. Lawyers tended to be generalists who practiced law on their own or with a few partners. In the era of the American revolt against Great Britain, more than half of the signers of the Declaration of

Independence were lawyers as were a similar proportion of representatives at the Constitutional Convention.[16] When Alexis de Tocqueville toured the United States in the early nineteenth century and produced his classic observations in *Democracy in America*, he identified lawyers as the "American aristocracy" who possessed disproportionate power and who pursued their own interests.[17]

Although Tocqueville's characterization of lawyers appears aimed at elite attorneys in the larger cities, country lawyers in early American society enjoyed the same prestige and influence—though not the same wealth—as their urban brethren. Small-town attorneys were usually self-taught professionals who served as community leaders. They were generalists who cultivated the respect of the townsfolk and who established their reputations through eloquence in the courtroom:

> Practicing alone in a small town, [the nineteenth century lawyer] prepared for his profession by reading Blackstone and Kent and by apprenticing himself to an established practitioner for whom he opened and cleaned the office, copied documents, and delivered papers. . . . Whether he rode circuit or lounged around the local courthouse, he absorbed the camaraderie of his profession and cherished the respect of his neighbors. As an independent generalist, he served all comers, with no large fees to turn his head toward a favored few.[18]

Abraham Lincoln is remembered as the quintessential self-educated, country lawyer. Like other lawyers who practiced alone or with a few partners, Lincoln became a respected leader by serving the general legal needs of people in his local community.

Although lawyers from affluent families may have received some formal education, they were not likely to have studied law. The few students who gained entry into institutions of higher education normally studied only Latin, Greek, moral philosophy, and mathematics.[19] No specific educational requirements were mandated for entry to the legal profession. White males were eligible for the bar after studying law with attorneys and receiving recommendations from lawyers stating that they were sufficiently qualified and capable to practice law. Because of the lack of opportunities for formal education in frontier and rural areas, some lawyers could enter practice without any formal education whatsoever.

In the aftermath of the Civil War, as the predominantly rural, agricultural United States was transformed by accelerating industrialization, immigration, and urbanization, the legal profession began to change. Coinciding with the rise of powerful manufacturing businesses, railroads, and other corporate structures, corporate law firms arose to serve the needs and interests of industrialists. As described by Harry Stumpf:

> Differences between the pre- and postbellum practice of law amounted to differences originating not in the legal profession itself but rather in the economic and social character of American society. With the great concentrations of wealth

required for and produced by corporate industrialization came the need for legal devices and doctrines to aid in the creation and use of that wealth. Lawyers were thus called upon to play a new role, to attach themselves to the great corporate machines of America as quasi-independent entities.[20]

This era and the continued development of the legal profession thereafter made clear that lawyers could make no special claim to professional public service motivated by the pursuit of justice. Instead, the practice of law became another kind of business in which lawyers' dispute-processing services, financial planning advice, challenges to governmental regulation, and creation of new arguments for the development of law and social policy advance attorneys' incomes at the behest of those clients best able to pay for legal services. In the American context, businesses and affluent individuals can best afford to hire attorneys and are, therefore, able to enjoy disproportionate benefits from lawyers' expertise. The same profit-seeking motivations that caused lawyers to link with businesses in the late nineteenth century have served ever after to skew the distribution of legal resources in favor of the affluent.

## The Development of Professional Stratification

Jerold Auerbach has identified ethnicity and social class as two primary factors that have influenced the development of the legal profession through the twentieth century. The expanding urbanization and industrialization of the United States built on swelling immigration from Europe in the late nineteenth and early twentieth centuries. The new social relationships and conflicts produced by urbanization inevitably created new opportunities for lawyers to direct their services toward individual clients. Many immigrants sought legal careers in order to gain social status and income. Although some immigrants and lower-class Americans gained social mobility through legal careers, according to Auerbach, the established Anglo-Saxon elites worked to protect their own privileged positions as elite professionals:

> The proportion of Anglo-Saxon Protestants within the legal profession and American society was diminishing as changing immigration and demographic patterns swelled cities and the profession with the foreign-born and their children. Native[-born] American lawyers were determined to repel a dual challenge: to their ascendancy in professional life and to the economic institutions of industrial capitalism which they served. First they consolidated their position within corporate law firms and professional associations. Once these enclaves were secure, they wielded their power to forge an identity between professional interest and their own political self-interest.[21]

The result of lawyers' historic efforts to exclude various groups from membership in the legal profession was not merely to limit social mobility for those aspiring attorneys who came from emerging demographic groups (i.e., immigrants, women, and racial minorities). The monopolization of the legal profession also served to prevent the entry of attorneys who might provide legal services to a broader range of clients. Controlled entry into the profession helped to reserve the benefits of legal resources for the affluent interests that possessed preexisting connections to the established legal profession.

After the Civil War, most states had no formal preparation requirements for entry to the practice of law—provided that the aspiring lawyer was a white male. Those states with entry requirements usually specified a period of apprenticeship with an attorney, the training that had historically been the basis for lawyers' legal knowledge. Law schools began to proliferate during the late nineteenth century. These were nothing like contemporary law schools. The first law schools generally required no previous formal training for admission, and their programs could be completed in as little as one year.[22] The flood of aspiring lawyers helped legal education replace apprenticeships as the means of entry into the legal profession. According to Abel:

> Many lawyers did not accept apprentices. Outside larger cities, [apprentice] positions may have become scarce. . . . Immigrants and their sons—a large and expanding proportion of those aspiring to become lawyers around the turn of the century—were not likely to be welcomed as apprentices by lawyers of different class, ethnicity, religion, and culture, whose families had been in America longer. Furthermore, the rate of increase was simply too great to be absorbed through apprenticeship: the profession nearly doubled between 1860 and 1880 and then doubled again by 1900.[23]

Various states introduced bar examinations as the means of entry into the profession. Students flocked to law schools, so the existence of law schools and bar examinations did not prevent a continued proliferation of new lawyers. Many law schools secured a "diploma privilege" for their graduates who thereby automatically become lawyers—without taking the bar examination—simply by completing law school courses. Because law schools did not have entrance requirements or standardized curricula, many immigrants and others seeking social mobility could become lawyers by taking advantage of the growing number of night law schools that permitted students to study while maintaining full-time employment.[24]

The rapid growth of the legal profession led to the formation of professional associations, including the American Bar Association in 1878, by established attorneys concerned about the future of their profession. These organizations worked to control entry into the profession in order to preserve lawyers' elite status, protect against economic competition, and prevent immigrant ethnic group members from joining the profession. Their efforts were directed at legal education and, in Abel's words, "[T]he history of legal education in the first half of the twentieth century, therefore, is largely a story of the struggle by the ABA to persuade state licensing authorities . . . to adopt entry standards.''[25] The ABA sought to require that lawyers have a minimum number of years of college prior to entry into law school. This requirement had especially significant ramifications for the less affluent, including immigrants, because college scholarships were less plentiful in the early twentieth century. Affluent people, then, enjoyed a great advantage in securing the formal education required to become an attorney. The ABA also sought to standardize legal education by raising accreditation standards for law schools. By persuading states that aspiring attorneys must study for three years in ABA-approved law schools, lawyers managed to eliminate many night law schools, which had served as the vehicles for many immigrants and other less affluent people to enter the legal profession.[26] The effort to standardize legal education succeeded to such a degree that by the 1980s only four states permitted people to bypass law school by studying with an attorney.[27]

The ABA also sought to ensure that state bar examinations would be centrally administered written tests required of all applicants for licenses to practice law. As a result of the ABA's success in influencing entry requirements for the profession, most states have eliminated any "diploma privileges" for graduates from law schools in their states. Bar examination passage rates have fluctuated in a manner that suggests that fewer people pass the bar examination at times when there is a desire to restrict the number of lawyers:

> Stronger trends emerged in the 1930s, as the profession responded to what it saw as the unhappy conjunction of rapid expansion, the entry of increasing numbers of lawyers from immigrant backgrounds, and the contraction of the economy caused by the Depression. In the year following the Crash of 1929, pass rates fell in fourteen of the thirty-six states for which figures are available and rose in only six.[28]

Bar associations have also sought to enforce citizenship and residence requirements for aspiring lawyers, but both of these stipulations were invalidated by the Supreme Court in recent decades.[29] Bar associations also introduced character tests, which "were deliberately introduced in order to exclude immigrants and their sons.''[30] Although established lawyers traditionally applied subjective evaluations of aspiring lawyers' "character and fitness for the practice of law" to prevent members of certain ethnic groups (e.g., Jewish people) and political dissidents from becoming lawyers, contemporary character requirements focus on people with criminal records.[31] All barriers to entry into the legal profession had especially powerful effects on the aspirations of immigrants and less affluent people:

> The profession reinforced the exclusion of immigrants and their sons with every new barrier it erected: increases in the length of prelegal and legal education (especially when many universities discriminated against religious and ethnic

minorities), more stringent standards for ABA accreditation, which curtailed part-time education, character tests, and the requirement of a preceptor or sponsor.[32]

In addition to the entry barriers sought by bar associations and elite attorneys, the bar associations themselves practiced explicit discrimination. Women were not accepted in the ABA until 1918, and African-Americans not until 1943. Small, alternative lawyers' associations developed to provide organizational support for attorneys who were excluded from or otherwise felt unrepresented by the American Bar Association and state bar associations. For example, the National Bar Association became and continues to be an organization of African-American attorneys. The National Lawyers' Guild developed as the organization for lawyers interested in liberal and leftist political action. Because the Guild provided representation for labor organizers and civil rights activists, it was attacked by members of Congress and the Federal Bureau of Investigation as a "subversive" organization.

Stratification within the legal profession was developed and maintained not only through the creation of new entry barriers for aspiring lawyers, but also through the hiring practices of elite corporate law firms. These large law firms gained wealth and influence not only through their legal service to major corporations, but also through connections to the corporate world by placement of their attorneys on corporate boards of directors. These elite law firms were historically composed of white, Anglo-Saxon, Protestant (WASP) men from affluent backgrounds. While many of these lawyers led the efforts to restrict entry to the legal profession, they also utilized discriminatory hiring practices to maintain the homogeneity of their own firms. These firms would consider hiring only graduates of the nation's elite law schools, such as Harvard, Yale, and Columbia. Disadvantaged students could not afford to attend such prestigious and expensive schools. In addition, these schools frequently discriminated against Jewish people and other immigrants in the admissions process. Less affluent students might be brilliant lawyers, but if they attended affordable state universities or night law schools, they would have little hope of consideration for the most important, lucrative, and influential jobs in the legal profession. A few immigrants, such as Supreme Court Justice Felix Frankfurter, a Jewish immigrant from Austria, were outstanding students at elite law schools and worked for major corporate law firms. But most non-WASP lawyers—even if they had attended elite law schools—found barriers to acceptance by exclusive firms. As Auerbach has observed about the early twentieth century, "[P]rofessional discrimination and job retrenchment during the depression virtually eliminated the prospects of Jewish, Catholic, and black lawyers for remunerative employment in the more lucrative sectors of the profession—regardless of their qualifications."[33] Many of these lawyers found their best employment opportunities in government careers with fewer opportunities for wealth and status.

The legal profession's exclusionary practices were accompanied by efforts to protect lawyers' monopoly over dispute-processing activities and to maintain lawyers' incomes at the expense of clients.[34] For example, the legal profession prohibited advertising by lawyers. This prohibition reduced direct competition between lawyers and hindered citizens' ability to "shop around" for less expensive representation. State bar associations maintained minimum fee schedules and punished lawyers who charged less money for legal services. Thus, attorneys' incomes could be maintained at the expense of the public. The legal profession successfully thwarted prepaid legal services plans, which might have benefitted the public but might also have dimished the incomes of lawyers who did not participate.[35] Until they were eliminated in the mid-1970s, these restrictions helped to elevate lawyers' incomes by insulating the practice of law from competitive market forces that might have reduced the price of legal services for consumers.

## THE CONTEMPORARY LEGAL PROFESSION

The second half of the twentieth century introduced changes in American society that reduced many barriers to equal opportunity. Laws against employment discrimination were established and implemented. Women and minority groups were accepted by law schools previously reserved for white, male students. The number of lawyers in the United States increased dramatically after the mid-1960s as the "baby boom" generation reached adulthood, barriers to college education fell, and legal careers increased in popularity.[36] In 1951, there were 221,605 lawyers in the United States. By 1960, that number had grown only to 285,933. Steady growth continued through the 1960s so that there were 355,242 lawyers in 1970. The number mushroomed to 542,205 in 1980 and zoomed to 650,000 by the mid-1980s.[37] By the mid-1990s, the size of the legal profession was estimated to approach, if not exceed, 800,000.[38] Given the continued creation of new law schools in the 1990s (e.g., Texas Wesleyan University and Roger Williams College, Rhode Island) and the rate at which law schools produce new graduates, there could be one million lawyers early in the twenty-first century. In 1950 fewer than 3 percent of attorneys were women, but by the mid-1980s, nearly 13 percent were women.[39] Because women comprise 40 percent of current law school graduates, the percentage of women lawyers will continue to grow each year.[40] The percentage of attorneys from racial minority groups has grown more slowly. For example, in 1900, when legal discrimination and violent intimidation of racial minorities were pervasive in American society, 0.5 percent of attorneys were African-Americans. By 1950, this percentage had grown to 0.8 percent and, even though discriminatory barriers had been reduced and the size of the legal profession had increased rapidly during the 1960s, African-Americans still comprised only 1.3 percent of attorneys in 1970. This percentage should continue to increase, especially because racial minorities now constitute nearly 10 percent of law students.[41] Both women and minorities, however, remain underrepresented among lawyers and, despite a tremendous increase in numbers since 1970, among law students.

Despite societal changes that permitted freer entry into the profession, stratification and discrimination in the legal profession continue to prevent equal access to social mobility, wealth, and status through a legal career. The authors of a major study of lawyers in Chicago confirmed several results of earlier studies that demonstrated continued stratification:

> First, for all the talk about the law being a major avenue of upward mobility for the socially disadvantaged, a very substantial majority of lawyers come from families of at least middle-class, if not higher, socioeconomic standing. Second, those who are from socially disadvantaged backgrounds are much more likely to end up in solo or small firm practices, with individuals [instead of corporations] as their clients and with relatively modest and uncertain incomes. Third, the conversion of the social advantages or disadvantages of one's birth into legal career achievement is accomplished by the channeling of persons into different types of law schools, which are themselves loosely organized into a hierarchical structure of top-flight law schools associated with major universities and local law schools of less certain standing.[42]

The authors of the Chicago study found the legal profession divided into a hierarchy of two distinct groups: lawyers who represent corporations and lawyers who represent individuals. The corporate attorneys constitute the profession's elite in wealth, status, and power: "Because an ever increasing amount of social power has come to be concentrated in corporations, the lawyers who are in a position to influence the affairs of corporations are now likely to have the most impact on the transactions that are of the greatest consequence for our society."[43] Lawyers regard corporate practice specializations as "most prestigious," and the Chicago study found a continuing association between lawyers' backgrounds and their status as corporate attorneys: "Lawyers from less prestigious social origins were overrepresented among those practicing in the less prestigious fields [of legal specialization, such as criminal, divorce, and probate]."[44] The authors also concluded that opportunities for gaining wealth and status as a prestigious corporate lawyer are not based on attorneys' relevant skills: "[T]he professional's proficiency in the lawyerly skills should determine professional success if [an] ideal-type model of the profession prevails. . . . [but] [t]he Chicago bar does not appear to conform closely to the [ideal-type] model."[45] Opportunities for success with prestigious law firms are, as Auerbach described for the early twentieth century, still influenced by "ethnicity and [social] class."[46]

The homogeneity of corporate law firms is less absolute. They still recruit exclusively from the expensive, elite law schools, but those schools now graduate women attorneys and lawyers from ethnic groups that were previously excluded.[47]

The Chicago study found ''most striking . . . the role that elite law schools play in stocking the largest law firms and that local law schools play in producing solo practitioners.''[48] Although members of previously excluded demographic groups may gain toeholds in the prestigious law firms if they have the correct elite credentials, they are much less likely to be promoted to partnerships in these firms. In 1985 women comprised 25 percent of law firm associates (i.e., lawyers employed by law firms) but only 6 percent of law firm partners (i.e., the attorneys who set the firm's policies and share in the substantial profits).[49] By 1989 women constituted 33 percent of the associates in the country's 250 largest law firms, but they were only 9 percent of the partners within those firms.[50] Opportunities for previously excluded groups have expanded, but equal treatment has yet to be achieved.

Women were not permitted to become lawyers until late in the nineteenth century, and some states did not admit women attorneys until 1911.[51] According to Abel, ''Even when women were admitted [to the legal profession], hidden quotas and social and cultural barriers kept their numbers small.''[52] As recently as the 1950s, when future Supreme Court Justice Sandra Day O'Connor graduated third in her class from the prestigious Stanford University Law School, major law firms offered her positions as a legal secretary, but not as a lawyer.[53] After establishing an outstanding record at both Harvard and Columbia, including stints as editor for both the *Harvard Law Review* and the *Columbia Law Review*, future Supreme Court Justice Ruth Bader Ginsburg could not find employment with any New York City law firm.[54] In addition to continuing disparities in promotion opportunities in elite law firms, women attorneys generally have lower average incomes than their male law school classmates with equivalent training and experience.[55]

Racial minorities are also seriously underrepresented in elite law firms. In 1989, for example, African-Americans comprised only 2.2 percent of the associates and only 0.9 percent of the partners in the country's 250 largest law firms, although this racial group constituted over 12 percent of the national population.[56] Lawyers from minority groups are more often found in less prestigious and less lucrative solo practices, small law firms, and government agencies.

While women attorneys and lawyers from racial minority groups still find fewer opportunities for status and wealth in the legal profession, the historical efforts of bar associations and elite lawyers to hinder the entry of male lawyers from immigrant ethnic groups have largely failed or been abandoned. Although Jewish and Catholic lawyers from working-class backgrounds have been overrepresented among solo practitioners and local government attorneys, members of such groups who are recent graduates of elite law schools find fewer barriers to acceptance into prestigious firms.[57]

The diversification of the legal profession on the basis of ethnicity and gender has, according to Abel, exacerbated the profession's exclusion of people with lower socioeconomic status. There is a strong correlation between family income and the high grades and test scores necessary for admission to law school. Thus, the opening of law school admissions to women and members of previously excluded ethnic groups has permitted the affluent members of those groups to fill seats that might previously have gone to less affluent white men. Studies of the social backgrounds of law students confirm that the children of white-collar, professional, and high-income parents are significantly over-represented.[58]

## The Working Lives of Lawyers within the Stratified Profession

In 1980 over 68 percent of lawyers were in private practice. Nearly two-thirds of them were in small firms of five or fewer attorneys, and 48 percent of those in private practice were solo practitioners.[59] Private industry and government each employed 10 percent of attorneys. The remaining 12 percent were fairly evenly divided between other employers, the judiciary, and retirement or other inactive status.[60]

The highest status lawyers in the profession practice with large law firms. This 5 percent of attorneys practice with firms containing more than 50 lawyers.[61] New graduates of elite law schools who work for large, prestigious corporate firms frequently receive starting salaries in excess of $70,000.[62] If, after seven to ten years of diligent and profitable work on behalf of the firm, they are invited to become partners, their annual incomes may exceed $200,000 when they begin to share in the firm's profits.[63] The peak earnings for the top 10 percent of law partners with 25 years' experience (in cities with populations over one million) are reported at approximately $340,000 annually.[64] In order to garner such lucrative compensation, corporate attorneys must attract major corporations and other clients with substantial resources who can pass their significant legal expenses on to consumers in the form of increased prices for their products. Corporations are also better able than individuals to afford expensive legal work because attorneys' fees can be deducted from corporations' taxable income as a "business expense." Corporate lawyers must generate "billable hours"—hours of legal work billed to clients at $150 per hour or more. A firm's lawyers do not actually receive the high legal fees charged for their services. Instead, they are paid a set salary, and the money generated by their billable hours is distributed to the partners who control the firm. Corporate law firms can maintain their ornate, impressive offices and high incomes only by generating a steady flow of billable hours for clients who can afford to pay.

Unlike people who purchase other goods and services, consumers of legal services frequently do not know what they are paying for. When an attorney's client receives a bill for one hundred hours of legal work, she or he cannot see a tangible product, does not know if the lawyers' work is really worth the amount charged, and, indeed, often does not know for certain that the lawyers actually did the research and other tasks listed on the billing statement. Although in recent years many corporations have begun using their own attorneys to monitor the charges submitted by law firms, corporations have traditionally simply paid their substantial legal bills, convinced that their lawyers are producing positive results. The connections between corporate business leaders and corporate lawyers as graduates of the same elite colleges, members of the same exclusive clubs, and leaders in the same community organizations facilitate trust and cooperation between the two sets of actors. Corporate law firms usually foster these networks with business leaders by encouraging their attorneys to join country clubs and elite community groups and seeking to place law partners on the boards of directors of large corporations.

Although they enjoy affluence, prestige, and influence, the working lives of corporate lawyers are not necessarily easy. In order to maintain their positions (and profits), corporate law firms must constantly cultivate and retain wealthy corporate clients. Because the practice of law is very competitive, upstart law firms are continually hiring prominent attorneys and former members of Congress as "rainmakers" to woo desirable clients away from other firms.[65] If there is a downturn in the economy, corporations may cut back on the money they spend for legal services, and corporate law firms may lay off the highly paid young associates to maintain their profitability. Corporations have made large law firms more insecure by choosing a different firm to handle each specific legal matter rather than maintaining a continuing relationship with a single law firm.[66] Corporate law firms have attempted to protect incomes of partners by hiring staff attorneys—salaried employees who will never be considered for partnerships—rather than by hiring all new attorneys as firm associates eligible to work their way toward eventual partnership and shares in the firm's profits.[67] As a *New York Times* analysis of legal developments observed, "[t]he economics of large firms push inexorably toward finding a way to limit the number of [partner] equity-holders who get a share in the profit pool, while expanding the number of people whose billings add to that pool."[68]

Lawyers in corporate law firms are under tremendous pressure to produce billable hours, and lawyers are increasingly abandoning the practice of law because of the stress produced by the expectation that they will keep generating profits for the firm:

A major increase in working hours, coupled with a corresponding rise in stress, has led to an erosion in the quality of life for many lawyers. Law firms often require that each year attorneys do 2,000 to 2,500 hours of work that can be billed to clients, almost a third more than a decade ago. That frequently translates into twelve-hour-plus workdays plus busy weekends as well.[69]

In addition to facing competition and pressure to maintain profits, corporate lawyers must constantly direct their actions toward pleasing the corporate interests. As the authors of the Chicago study observed, "[A] principal reason large firms have given for their reluctance to represent the poor, downtrodden, friendless, and despised, or to take on various public interest causes, is that this sort of thing would give offense to their regular [corporate] clientele."[70] Corporate lawyers may have less ability to select cases of interest and importance or to effectively direct their clients toward recommended courses of action because these lawyers—in their efforts to maintain their high incomes and profits—are especially preoccupied with catering to the desires of corporate clients.

The lower tier of the legal profession, composed of solo practitioners (33.2 percent of all lawyers) and small law firms (21.5 percent of all lawyers in firms with 2–10 attorneys),[71] represents individual clients. Such lawyers may not enjoy the prestige and affluence of their corporate counterparts, but they have more control over their professional lives. These lawyers are likely to handle less prestigious legal matters such as divorces, wills, personal injuries, adoptions, automobile accidents, and other matters that draw ordinary citizens into the judicial process. Despite the image of law as a lucrative profession, solo practitioners who attempt to build a practice by writing wills, handling divorces, and developing a clientele of ordinary citizens may have to struggle to earn even the $26,292 in income earned annually by the average American worker.[72] Some private practitioners earn huge incomes on behalf of individual clients by winning significant personal injury lawsuits in cases of medical malpractice, automobile accidents, or other situations in which severe injuries are caused by an insured business or individual. Other lawyers earn more modest compensation working for middle-class individuals, because the attorneys can charge only as much as their clients can afford to pay. A survey of attorneys in 1984 revealed that 19 percent earned less than $25,000, 44 percent earned between $25,000 and $55,000, and 23 percent earned between $55,000 and $100,000. Only 14 percent earned more than $100,000,[73] yet many of these attorneys earned much more than merely $100,000. Experienced partners in big city law firms can earn in excess of $350,000, and some firms reportedly pay senior partners more than $1 million annually.[74]

Nearly one-third of lawyers pursue careers that are not focused on the business of making money. These lawyers work in many positions in government, from assistant prosecutors in local county courts to senior attorneys in federal government agencies. Such attorneys' salaries may range from $25,000 for an employee of a small unit of local government to $100,000 for supervising attorneys at the top grades of federal government service. These attorneys become specialists in the particular areas of law in which they must advise and represent the government. Other attorneys receive relatively modest salaries to work for public interest groups. For these attorneys, the desire to use their legal skills in order to influence public policy may provide greater motivation and professional satisfaction than the pursuit of a high income.

Attorneys earning mid-range salaries as employees of government agencies or businesses rather than of law firms can frequently avoid having their professional responsibilities swallow their personal lives. They represent a single client (i.e., their employer), and their income is not dependent on the number of cases they handle. They may even begin to keep regular 9-to-5 hours, except when they are preparing or presenting arguments in court. Attorneys in private practice, however, must continually attract new clients and retain old ones. It is not unusual for attorneys at large law firms to spend sixty to seventy hours per week at the office. Unlike the pressured attorneys at large law firms, lower-tier private practitioners can control their own working hours according to their own aspirations for profit and growth. Attorneys who represent individual clients are also better able to control their caseloads, because their clients are more likely to defer to the lawyers' professional expertise and advice.

Lawyers in small towns and rural areas tend to be general practitioners who handle the variety of legal matters that arise in small communities.[75] Although these country lawyers are similar to their lower-tier urban counterparts in their need to attract and retain individual clients, they may be under greater pressure to demonstrate success and to maintain the image of a respectable professional. In the urban context, individual clients come and go as divorces, accidents, and other events produce a continuing flow of individuals needing legal representation. An individual client's dissatisfaction with a lawyer's performance is not likely to have much effect on the lawyer's practice in a large city. In the rural setting, however, there is a relatively small pool of potential clients. As a member of the community, the lawyer encounters that limited number of clients in a variety of settings: at church, at the grocery store, at the Parent-Teacher Association meeting, etc. Country lawyers' multifaceted, continuing relationships with a small pool of clients make these attorneys "very visible and very accountable to their community" so they must "carefully craft . . . reputation[s] for being competent, concerned, helpful, and loyal."[76] Country lawyers may have less ability to control their clients than do their urban counterparts because they must remain highly sensitive to the clients' opinions, feelings, and desires.

## LEGAL EDUCATION AND ENTRY INTO THE PROFESSION

As illustrated by the foregoing discussion, the law school hierarchy is based on prestige of reputation. Students who gain admission to the most esteemed law schools—generally, the Ivy League law schools in addition to Stanford, Chicago, Michigan, and California/Berkeley—will have the broadest range of job opportunities upon graduation. These schools and a few other "national" law schools attract recruiters from all over the country. The recruiters seek to hire new graduates for the most elite corporate firms as well as for government agencies, interest groups, and lesser law firms. A middle tier of law schools, composed of major state universities and prominent private universities, may attract recruiters from several neighboring states, but only the very top students have any hope of getting an interview with the most elite firms. At the bottom of the hierarchy are the lesser known public and private institutions, most of whose graduates have access only to the less lucrative and less elite jobs in government, as solo practitioners, or as associates in small local firms. The impact of law schools' reputations on the hiring practices of the hierarchical legal profession is so great that an outstanding college student, admitted to Harvard or Yale, who decided for personal or financial reasons to attend a lesser institution would have limited job opportunities despite his or her academic abilities.

The irony of the law school hierarchy's effect on employment opportunities for new lawyers is that virtually all law schools teach the same subjects, use the same course materials and methods, and have faculty members trained at elite law schools. Elite schools and schools with larger faculties can offer their students a greater variety of elective courses, but even at these schools students tend to structure their selections around the business-related courses that are the focus of state bar exams.[77] Although students admitted to elite law schools generally have outstanding undergraduate college grades and Law School Aptitude Test (LSAT) scores, it would be difficult to argue that they necessarily receive a superior education by virtue of attending a highly regarded law school.

Law schools utilize the "case method" of instruction, in which students study judges' appellate opinions and, in response to persistent questioning in the classroom by law professors, attempt to discern the legal principles and reasoning contained in the opinion. Dean Christopher Columbus Langdell of Harvard Law School is often erroneously credited with creating the case approach to the study of law in the late nineteenth century.[78] Although Langdell did not create this teaching method, he was responsible for popularizing it during his tenure as dean of the Harvard Law School and for influencing its adoption by American law schools following Harvard's example. Langdell also helped to make legal education a three-year course of study requiring a four-year college degree prior to admittance,[79] and thus his efforts contributed to the goal of eliminating unaccredited and evening law schools.

The case method of instruction, which one scholar has noted "rather pretentiously came to be known as the Socratic method,"[80] is a narrow approach to the study of law. By studying opinions in appellate cases, law students learn relatively little about the skills necessary for practicing law. The case method does not teach law students how to counsel clients, prepare cases for court, negotiate settlements, or fulfill the myriad responsibilities that absorb the daily lives of working lawyers. In addition, former Chief Justice Warren Burger and other judges have criticized the poor advocacy skills evidenced by lawyers during appellate oral arguments, and American law schools have been criticized for not providing better training in this important area. To redress these weaknesses, many law schools have, since the 1970s, added skills courses (e.g., client counseling, negotiation, etc.) and clinical programs to help students to master these skills. In clinical courses, law students represent low-income people in court under the supervision of professors. Because these courses are electives, however, many students do not choose to enroll in them. Like most new lawyers, they will learn how to act as attorneys through on-the-job training in their first positions. In a large law firm, this initially means doing limited tasks under the supervision of an experienced attorney. By contrast, a solo practitioner or a lawyer in a small law firm learns to be a lawyer by "trial and error" at the expense of individual clients.

The case method also instills in law students the belief that legal principles guide the resolution of legal cases. The continual focus on appellate opinions—without discussion of the political factors affecting the selection of judges, judicial decision making, and the implementation of judicial decisions—reinforces lawyers' acceptance and defense of "the law" as a neutral instrument for achieving justice. Thus, the case method hinders lawyers' ability to recognize connections between the judicial process and the political system. In particular, lawyers may be blind to the social context in which legal cases arise and to the human consequences of judicial decisions. Law schools have attempted to redress this weakness by offering upper-level seminars and "perspectives" courses that integrate law with other academic disciplines such as history and sociology. As with the clinical programs, law students enroll in few such courses because these subjects are not useful for passing the bar exam.

Law school curricula and students' selection of courses are shaped by continuing connections between the legal profession and the business world. The legal profession became intertwined with corporate interests during the industrialization period of the late nineteenth century, and the leading lawyers and law firms continue to work for such clients. The device that orients law students toward business is the bar examination. After four years of college and three years of law school, a law school graduate must pass a state bar exam in order to become a lawyer. For most students, this requires paying an additional one thousand dollars or more to private businesses that conduct bar review courses, concentrated instruction on legal subjects in the eight weeks prior to the bar exam. The bar exam tests law graduates' knowledge of a variety of legal subjects and requires significant memorization skills. In all but a few states, the exam does not test legal skills; it merely gauges whether the applicant can apply memorized legal principles to hypothetical cases. If you give any group of lawyers, including law professors, a bar exam as an unannounced "pop quiz," virtually all would fail. If law school graduates can store sufficient knowledge in their short-term memories to survive a two- or three-day test, they can practice law for the rest of their lives without retaining the information memorized for that one exam. Passing a bar exam does not mean that an attorney possesses lawyering skills or knows anything about various areas of law. The bar exam is essentially an entry barrier designed to control the number of people who can practice law. The arbitrary number established as the minimum passing score bears no relation to any level of necessary knowledge or skill. Moreover, the inherently subjective nature of essay exams gives the lawyers on the examination committee plenty of flexibility for passing or failing students according to their own personal judgments.

Because law students must pass the bar exam to become lawyers, they expect law schools to give them the information they will need to pass the exam. This is why clinical programs and perspectives courses do not attract many students. Those courses may help one become a better lawyer, but they do not contribute to success in the bar exam. As a reflection of the legal profession's association with business, bar exams emphasize business subjects. Thus, law schools offer a preponderance of business subjects, and students normally use their electives to take the courses that will prepare them for the exam.

In Ohio, for example, one day of the bar exam is devoted to the Multi-state Exam, a difficult, six-hour multiple-choice test of six basic legal subjects required at most law schools: contracts, torts, property, constitutional, criminal, and evidence. This exam is also given as part of the bar exams in most other states. The other day (two days in Ohio and some other states) is devoted to essay questions on a particular state's law. Ohio's two additional exam days consist of twenty-four half-hour essay questions, twelve questions during each six-hour day. The business focus of the Ohio bar exam is evident in the distribution of questions. Out of the twenty-four questions, business associations and corporations are usually the focus of four; commercial transactions, three questions; and taxation, two questions. Other subjects concerning accumulation and protection of wealth, property, and trusts and wills, for example, receive two questions each. By contrast, subjects concerned with individual rights and relationships, such as constitutional, criminal, domestic relations, and torts, receive only one essay question each. The remaining subjects on the exam that—except for civil procedure, which is covered in two essay questions—receive only one question each are evidence, legal ethics, and contracts. Most revealing is the list of subjects *not* included on the Ohio bar exam, nor on most others: labor law, environmental law, employment discrimination law, and consumer protection law, to name a few. Thus, a student must pass a business-oriented exam to become a specialist in environmental, labor, or consumer law. Because 15 percent to 40 percent of graduates fail the bar exam (depending on grading criteria), there is significant pressure on law students to take bar-related courses (i.e., business law courses) and not waste time or risk their success on the bar exam by taking such nonbar subjects as environmental or labor law. Even idealistic students who enter law school intending to protect the environment or civil rights find themselves drawn into courses that emphasize the accumulation and protection of wealth and corporate interests. In the words of one critic, legal education leads to ''the immediate destruction of the entering law students' belief that law exists to serve the public good, and the constant fostering of the diametrically opposed idea that law is a business.''[81]

The forces that push law students toward specialization in business are exacerbated by the student loan debts that many students incur while working their way through four years of college and three years of law school. Because the total cost of one year at a private law school exceeded twenty-five thousand dollars in 1995, many students borrow tens of thousands of dollars to earn their law degrees. Such financial pressures can force students to forego an interest in public service and to accept high-paying positions with large law firms. A few law schools have attempted to redress this problem by creating loan waiver programs for graduates who accept low-paying positions in public service organizations. However, few schools possess the resources to fund such programs at anything more than a token level.

## THE DISTRIBUTION OF LEGAL SERVICES

Affluent people and businesses receive a disproportionate share of legal services because most lawyers are private practitioners (68.3 percent in 1985)[82] whose incomes depend on attracting and retaining clients who can afford to pay. Most other attorneys are salaried employees of businesses and government agencies whose services benefit one client: the employer. A substantial portion of the American population cannot afford to pay attorneys' fees, court costs, and other expenses associated with hiring a lawyer and seeking the benefits of the judicial process.[83] In addition to the 13 percent of Americans with incomes below the poverty level,[84] millions more are ineligible for government financial assistance yet find their incomes completely absorbed by food, rent, medical bills, and other living expenses. Despite the fact that a substantial proportion of the U.S. population is too poor to pay for an attorney's services, only 1.5 percent of attorneys work for legal aid and public defender programs that provide legal services to clients who cannot afford legal fees.[85]

As chapter 4 will discuss in detail, poor people receive free legal representation when they are arrested and face the prospect of incarceration. In many places, private practitioners receive modest fees from the government to represent indigent criminal defendants. The quality of this representation is frequently suspect, but the availability of compensation paid by the government ensures that indigent defendants have access to attorneys. In other places, full-time public defenders, salaried employees of a city or state, devote all their time to the representation of indigent defendants. Thus, in criminal cases in which the U.S. Supreme Court requires the government to provide attorneys for the indigent,[86] mechanisms are in place to distribute legal services for the less affluent at government expense.

For civil legal matters, which constitute the bulk of issues that require an attorney's services, poor people have no constitutional right to free representation by a lawyer. In general, if you cannot afford to pay for an attorney, you have no access to the judicial process, and you cannot seek authoritative assistance for the protection of your rights. Because lawyers in private practice are in business to make money, the distribution of legal services favors affluent interests, and poor people generally cannot seek the benefits and protection of the judicial branch of government.

## Redressing the Inequitable Distribution of Legal Services

Historically, American lawyers have resisted efforts to provide legal services for people whose limited financial resources hampered their ability to seek the benefits of the civil judicial process. Until the 1960s, bar associations prevented the introduction of low-cost legal services by maintaining minimum fee schedules and by prohibiting prepaid legal services plans.[87] In addition, American lawyers opposed government programs designed to provide legal services for the poor:

> Bar associations maintained that legal services to the poor should be provided only through the charitable efforts of philanthropies and volunteer lawyers; when Britain established a state-supported legal aid scheme in 1949, American lawyers recoiled in horror at the threat to professional independence posed by this specter of creeping socialism.[88]

Since the 1960s, with prodding from Supreme Court decisions outlawing minimum fee schedules[89] and eliminating prohibitions on advertising,[90] the legal profession has become more receptive to clients of modest financial means. In 1994, for example, the Supreme Court overruled a Florida decision that prohibited attorneys from advertising their other professional qualifications, such as being a Certified Public Accountant (CPA).[91] The introduction of advertising, low-cost clinics, and prepaid plans have made legal services more accessible. These changes are not based on lawyers' benevolence. Instead, these innovations reflect greater competition within the legal profession as the numbers of new lawyers have mushroomed since the 1960s, leading private practitioners to seek new sources of revenue.[92] Thus, some attorneys have sought to attract middle-class and working-class clients who can afford modest fees for simple legal services such as wills, divorces, and adoptions.

The legal profession also now supports government-provided legal services for the poor. The American Bar Association and state bar associations recognize that legal services have not been sufficiently accessible to financially limited people, and they have worked to maintain funding for government programs that provide representation for such individuals.

Some lawyers' support for government legal services programs has not been based entirely on a recognition of the flawed distribution of legal resources. As with reforms in advertising and prepaid legal plans, there is an element of self-interest in some support for government programs—which were opposed in the 1950s and 1960s—in the 1980s:

[T]he profession has pushed steadily (although with limited success) for the diversion of funds from staffed [government] offices employing full-time salaried lawyers to judicare programs that would reimburse any private attorney who represents poor clients. The fear that state intervention would curtail professional autonomy seems to have evaporated in the face of potential economic benefits.[93]

Despite the changes since the 1960s, the distribution of legal services remains strongly skewed in favor of affluent interests. Innovations designed to attract clients with modest incomes, such as legal clinics and advertising, tend to focus on limited legal needs (i.e., wills and divorces) or narrow categories of cases that will be profitable to lawyers on a contingency fee basis (i.e., personal injuries and workers' compensation). Representation in other kinds of cases remains beyond the reach of many Americans because lawyers' services are so expensive. Government programs lack resources and reach relatively few people.

The ABA's Model Rules of Professional Conduct declare that lawyers should ensure that poor people have access to adequate legal representation. There is an expectation that lawyers will accept certain cases without charging a fee because of the ethical obligation to do legal work *pro bono publico*, for the public good. The ABA's Model Rule 6.1 states:

> A lawyer should render public interest legal service. A lawyer may discharge this responsibility by providing professional services at no fee or a reduced fee to persons of limited means or to public service or charitable groups or organizations, by service in activities for improving law, the legal system or the legal profession, by financial support for organizations that provide services to persons of limited means.

The rule is not binding on lawyers unless it is adopted by their state's legislature or supreme court. Many states adopted the provisions of the ABA's earlier Model Code of Professional Responsibility, but that code did not contain a rule concerning public service. The earlier code merely encouraged lawyers to assist in providing legal services for the poor. There are efforts now underway to require lawyers to provide free legal services for underprivileged citizens. For example, an advisory committee urged that New York lawyers be required to devote at least twenty hours each year to public service.[94]

Many lawyers object to the notion that they should be forced to render professional services without compensation. Other professionals, such as medical doctors, teachers, nurses, and accountants, are not required or even formally pressured to donate their time for the benefit of the public. Moreover, because the growth of the legal profession has made law practice increasingly competitive, lawyers may find it more difficult than other professionals to donate their time and services since many of them are struggling to develop a dependable income base for their own firms.

Lawyers and their organizations are deeply divided over the requirment to serve the poor, and the Supreme Court is also divided on the issue. In a split decision in 1989, mixing unusual coalitions of liberal and conservative justices on both sides of the issue, the Supreme Court ruled that a statute passed by Congress cannot be utilized by judges to require attorneys to undertake uncompensated representation of poor clients.[95] In an attempt to orient new lawyers toward public service, a few law schools now require law students to spend a specified number of hours assisting poor people with legal problems. Despite the positive intentions behind the modest initiatives to encourage lawyers to perform *pro bono* work, these efforts have done little to alter the skewed distribution of legal services. According to Paul Wice, lawyers' actions do not fulfill their purported support for service to the poor:

> Although many state and local bar associations do give lip service to their professional obligation to provide legal representation to the economically disadvantaged, the reality of available *pro bono* assistance is almost nonexistent. Individual firms and individual attorneys . . . may dedicate a small percentage of their time to *pro bono* work, but even this small subset of the profession would likely join their professional colleagues in opposition to making such charitable activities mandatory. Even if a program of mandatory *pro bono* work was implemented, it could be expected to have only a limited impact on improving the availability of legal services needed by our nation's indigent.[96]

## *Pro Bono* Cases

The expectation that lawyers will provide uncompensated service to the public clashes with the reality that private attorneys and their firms are profit-making enterprises. Any portion of their time that lawyers donate to the needy cannot be used to gain revenue from paying clients. One study indicates that this clash between lawyers' business goals requiring profit maximization and bar associations' professional ethics statements encouraging voluntary *pro bono* work leads lawyers to apply highly inconsistent criteria when considering acceptance of a *pro bono* case.[97]

Studies of lawyers' *pro bono* work indicate the limited extent to which attorneys donate time to the poor and the differential treatment that less affluent clients receive. One study found that lawyers provide only a modest level of service to the needy. About 60 percent of lawyers responding to a survey indicated that they spend less than 5 percent of their billable hours doing *pro bono* work, and almost half of them spend no time at all. In addition, many of these cases that lawyers consider *pro bono* are actually situations in which clients fail to pay after services have been performed, not instances of attorneys voluntarily donating time to public service. In *pro bono* work outside normal working hours, most lawyers donated time to church or community groups or to family or friends. In sum, there is relatively little *pro bono* work provided for poor individuals who cannot afford to hire attorneys.[98]

Another study found that lawyers work harder for their paying clients. Lawyers quickly negotiate settlements in the cases for *pro bono* clients in order to devote time and energy to the cases of paying clients. In addition, a primary motivation for doing *pro bono* work is not to provide services for the needy, but to cultivate clients who might subsequently hire a lawyer. Lawyers hope that the clients' financial circumstances will change in the future, that the case might generate favorable publicity, or that the client might steer friends and relatives to the attorney. Although this evident self-interest might be perceived as a positive factor encouraging lawyers to provide greater assistance, in fact most *pro bono* work is actually supplied to middle-class people whose immediate circumstances prevent them from paying. The study indicated that *pro bono* work is not provided to the neediest sectors of society because the truly poor lack necessary connections with the intermediaries, such as doctors, ministers, and co-workers, who frequently persuade lawyer-acquaintances to accept cases for middle-class people.[99]

During the 1970s and 1980s, some law firms began to reduce their *pro bono* legal work. Rising overhead costs and increased competition among law firms led to greater limitations on attorneys who wished to donate time to nonpaying clients. Furthermore, law firms moved to limit their attorneys' contributions to complex cases because they preferred their lawyers to volunteer for *pro bono* cases likely to be quickly completed. Despite diminished services for the needy, individual attorneys and bar associations have attempted to increase contributions to *pro bono* work.[100]

# LEGAL SERVICES AGENCIES

The creation of organizations to serve the poor's legal needs in civil matters began with the German Legal Aid Society in New York City in the 1870s. Through the first half of the twentieth century, although agencies were created in several cities to provide legal services for the needy, most cities had no civil legal aid organizations. Existing agencies tended to struggle with tiny budgets supported primarily by private donations.

In the 1960s, as part of President Lyndon Johnson's "War on Poverty," the federal government created neighborhood legal offices throughout the country, offering civil legal aid to indigent people. The agency, which began as a unit of the Office of Economic Opportunity, eventually became a completely separate government agency called the Legal Services Corporation. People who meet the agency's requirements for a very low income and few assets are eligible to receive legal help from Legal Services offices.

## Legal Services and Social Reform Litigation

Attorneys from the Legal Services Program initiated a variety of legal actions to protect the civil rights and governmental benefits granted to less affluent citizens. One measure of the attorneys' success as primary legal advocates for the poor is the fact that the U.S. Supreme Court accepted 119 Legal Services-sponsored cases for review between 1965 and 1974.[101] Legal Services came under attack from local politicians when agency attorneys began to file broad legal actions challenging governmental policies that adversely affected poor people.[102] The strongest attack on Legal Services came from then-Governor Ronald Reagan of California, who was upset when lawsuits by Legal Services lawyers prevented him from dropping 160,000 poor people from a medical assistance program, forced farm owners to pay a minimum hourly wage to agricultural workers, and invalidated an English language literacy requirement for voting. President Richard Nixon's administration assisted the attack on the Legal Services Program (later restructured and renamed as the Legal Services Corporation) by moving the administrative authority from the national director to regional program directors more susceptible to local political pressures.[103] According to one study, this decentralization effectively limited litigation aimed at reforming societal institutions.[104]

Political pressures to limit Legal Services lawyers' efforts on behalf of the poor reached a peak during Ronald Reagan's presidency. President Reagan initially proposed abolishing the Legal Services Corporation. He said that poor people's legal needs could be handled through the voluntary efforts of private attorneys. Because Congress resisted Reagan's efforts to abolish the agency, the Reagan administration adopted the alternative strategy of cutting the agency's budget every year and appointing as directors of the Corporation people opposed to its existence. In the 1990s, Legal Services continues to suffer significant budget cuts, which produce new restrictions on the types of cases that can be accepted.

As Jerome Corsi has noted, the efforts of the Reagan administration to transfer legal aid responsibilities to the private sector reflected either ignorance or apathy concerning the history of legal services for the poor. According to Corsi, "[T]he neglect of the poor by the private bar has been a primary impetus behind legal aid movements throughout [the twentieth] century."[105] One researcher who studied legal services programs concluded that private attorneys cannot adequately serve the needs of the poor because they lack specialized knowledge of issues affecting low-income people. They have no financial or political incentive to pursue cases vigorously, especially cases that might threaten established political or economic interests. In fact, because of frequent connections between lawyers and business interests within communities, attorneys may be reluctant to pursue tenant complaints against landlords or consumer claims against businesses and banks. In such cases, a successful effort on behalf of a needy client may alienate potential paying clients. In addition, similar community pressures can deter lawyers from representing the poor in controversial cases, such as medical malpractice and civil rights.[106]

## CONCLUSION

Lawyers and bar associations devote significant energy to portraying themselves as professionals who work for the public good. Many individual lawyers have made positive contributions to society, but the history and structure of the legal profession reflect the pursuit of self-interested political and economic goals. Historic links between lawyers and businesses, perpetuated through the structures of legal education and bar examinations, provide corporate interests with greater access to the judicial process. By contrast, less affluent people who lack political and economic power have fewer opportunities to seek benefits and protections from the judiciary because they cannot afford to secure the services of lawyers, the ''gatekeepers'' of the court system. The skewed distribution of legal resources in American society prevents equal access to the judicial branch of government, which purports to guarantee ''equal justice under law'' for all citizens.

The lack of equal access not only inhibits a portion of the citizenry from seeking and enjoying the resources and protections of one branch of government, the unequal distribution of legal resources also shapes the development of law and public policy. The interests of affluent entities receive disproportionate attention from judicial decision makers. Those with the greatest legal resources at their disposal (i.e., businesses, interest groups, wealthy individuals) can use litigation selectively to present the judiciary with issues that may produce favorable case decisions. These judicial decisions shape the development of case law and determine public policy outcomes through judges' consideration of the issues and arguments most readily available and most comprehensively presented—that is, the issues and arguments that favor affluent and organized interests. When impoverished people finally gained access to representation through the Legal Services Program, they lost several significant cases before the Supreme Court. However, the Legal Services attorneys became the ''mechanism by which a new class of litigants was able to place its civil claims before the Supreme Court and influence the policy decisions emanating from that institution.''[107] Legal Services' litigation and other such cases have led to judicial consideration of issues beyond those presented by the wealthy, organized, and powerful. Those with ready access to the skills of legal professionals enjoy disproportionate opportunities to present their arguments and interests in the judicial process. Thus, the substantive content of case law and judicial policy making still reflects a skewed distribution of legal resources.

## NOTES

1. *Argersinger v. Hamlin*, 407 U.S. 25 (1972).
2. Barbara A. Curran, ''American Lawyers in the 1980s: A Profession in Transition,'' *Law and Society Review* 20 (1986): 27–28.

3. See, e.g., Leonard S. Janofsky, "Is the 'S' in 'Esquire' Becoming a $ Sign?" *Wisconsin Bar Bulletin* 59 (August 1986): 13–14.

4. Stewart Macaulay, "Lawyers and Consumer Protection Laws," *Law and Society Review* 14 (1979): 130.

5. See Donald H. Zeigler and Michele G. Hermann, "The Invisible Litigant: An Inside View of *Pro Se* Actions in the Federal Courts," *New York University Law Review* 47 (1972): 159–257.

6. Christopher E. Smith, "United States Magistrates and the Processing of Prisoner Litigation," *Federal Probation* 52 (December 1988): 15.

7. *Brown v. Board of Education*, 347 U.S. 483 (1954) (racial segregation in public schools declared an unconstitutional violation of equal protection rights).

8. Richard Kluger, *Simple Justice: The History of* Brown v. Board of Education *and Black America's Struggle for Equality* (New York: Random House, 1975), pp. 214–38.

9. Roger H. Davidson and Walter J. Oleszek, *Congress and Its Members*, 2nd ed. (Washington, D.C.: Congressional Quarterly Press, 1985), p. 110.

10. See, e.g., Justin J. Green, John R. Schmidhauser, Larry L. Berg, and David Brady, "Lawyers in Congress: A New Look at Some Old Assumptions," *Western Political Quarterly* 26 (1973): 440–52.

11. Albert P. Melone, "Rejection of the Lawyer-Dominance Proposition: The Need for Additional Research," *Western Political Quarterly* 33 (1980): 232.

12. Peter Carlson, "Tales Out of Law School," *The Washington Post Magazine*, 2 July 1989, p. 17.

13. Mark C. Miller, "Lawyers in Congress: What Difference Does It Make?" *Congress and the Presidency* 20 (1993): 1–23.

14. See Richard Abel, *American Lawyers* (New York: Oxford University Press, 1989).

15. Arlin M. Adams, "The Legal Profession: A Critical Evaluation," *Judicature* 74 (1990): 77–83.

16. Lawrence Friedman, *A History of American Law*, 2nd ed. (New York: Simon & Schuster, 1985), pp. 94–101.

17. Alexis de Tocqueville, *Democracy in America* (New York: Edward Walker, 1847), pp. 297–306.

18. Jerold S. Auerbach, *Unequal Justice: Lawyers and Social Change in Modern America* (New York: Oxford University Press, 1976), p. 15.

19. Robert Stevens, *Law School: Legal Education in America from the 1850s to the 1980s* (Chapel Hill, NC: University of North Carolina Press, 1983), p. 35.

20. Harry P. Stumpf, *American Judicial Politics* (New York: Harcourt Brace Jovanovich, 1988), p. 246.

21. Auerbach, *Unequal Justice*, p. 5.

22. Abel, *American Lawyers*, pp. 41–44.
23. Ibid., p. 43.
24. Ibid., p. 44.
25. Ibid., p. 47.
26. Ibid., pp. 48–62.
27. Lawrence Baum, *American Courts: Process and Policy*, 2d ed. (Boston: Houghton Mifflin, 1990), p. 60.
28. Abel, *American Lawyers*, p. 64.
29. Ibid., pp. 68–69.
30. Ibid., p. 69.
31. Ibid., p. 69–71.
32. Ibid., p. 85.
33. Auerbach, *Unequal Justice*, p. 185.
34. Richard L. Abel, "The Transformation of the American Legal Profession," *Law and Society Review* 20 (1986): 9.
35. Ibid.
36. Curran, "American Lawyers in the 1980s," pp. 19–25.
37. Ibid., p. 20.
38. James B. Clark, "The New Economics of a Healthy Legal System," *New Jersey Law Journal*, 13 March 1995, p. 11.
39. Curran, "American Lawyers in the 1980s," p. 25.
40. Abel, *American Lawyers*, p. 96.
41. Ibid., pp. 99–100.
42. John P. Heinz and Edward O. Laumann, *Chicago Lawyers: The Social Structure of the Bar* (New York: Russell Sage Foundation, 1982), pp. 172–73.
43. Ibid., p. 321.
44. Ibid., p. 331.
45. Ibid., p. 332.
46. See Auerbach, *Unequal Justice*, p. 5.
47. Marc Galanter and Thomas Palay, *Tournament of Lawyers: The Transformation of the Big Law Firm* (Chicago: University of Chicago Press, 1991), p. 57.
48. Heinz and Laumann, *Chicago Lawyers*, p. 192.
49. "Women Still Facing Bias in Law Profession, Schools," *Cleveland Plain Dealer*, 21 August 1988, p. 6A.
50. Galanter and Palay, *Tournament of Lawyers*, p. 57.
51. Abel, *American Lawyers*, p. 90.
52. Ibid.
53. Baum, *American Courts: Process and Policy*, p. 141.
54. David Von Drehle, "The Quiet Revolutionary," *Washington Post National Weekly Edition* 26 July–1 August 1993, pp. 6–7.
55. Abel, *American Lawyers*, pp. 92–95.

56. Galanter and Palay, *Tournament of Lawyers*, p. 57.

57. Abel, *American Lawyers*, pp. 86–87.

58. Ibid., pp. 88–90.

59. Curran, "American Lawyers in the 1980s," pp. 27–28.

60. Ibid.

61. Ibid.

62. Francisco Badillo, "Law Schools Hot, but Few Grads Getting Rich," *Akron Beacon Journal*, 12 September 1988, p. C1.

63. See Committee on the Judicial Branch of the Judicial Conference of the United States, *Simple Fairness: The Case for Equitable Compensation of the Nation's Federal Judges* (Washington, D.C.: Administrative Office of the United States Courts, 1988), p. 72.

64. Ibid., pp. 71–72.

65. See David Margolick, "The Problems of the A.B.A. President's Firm Mirror Ills in the Legal Profession," *New York Times*, 3 November 1989, p. B7.

66. Heinz and Laumann, *Chicago Lawyers*, p. 368.

67. Tamar Lewin, "Law Firm's Add Second Tier," *New York Times*, 11 March 1987, p. D1.

68. Ibid., p. D3.

69. Andrea Sachs, "Have Law Degree, Will Travel," *Time*, 11 December 1989, p. 106.

70. Heinz and Laumann, *Chicago Lawyers*, p. 371.

71. Curran, "American Lawyers in the 1980s," p. 28.

72. In 1992, $26,292 was the median income for families with one wage earner. U.S. Census Bureau, *Money Income of Households, Families and Persons in the United States: 1992*, (Washington, D.C.: U.S. Government Printing Office, 1993), p. 40.

73. Abel, *American Lawyers*, p. 161.

74. Committee on the Judicial Branch, *Simple Fairness*, pp. 71–72.

75. See Donald D. Landon, *Country Lawyers: The Impact of Context on Professional Practice* (New York: Praeger, 1990).

76. Ibid., p. 151.

77. See Stumpf, *American Judicial Politics*, p. 252.

78. Stevens, *Law School*, p. 52.

79. Ibid., pp. 36–37.

80. Ibid., p. 53.

81. Chris Goodrich, "A Problematic Profession," *The Nation*, 12 February 1990, p. 206.

82. Curran, "American Lawyers in the 1980s," p. 26.

83. See Christopher E. Smith, *Courts and the Poor*, (Chicago: Nelson-Hall, 1991) pp. 3–5.

84. Bureau of the Census, *Poverty in the United States: 1987*, Series P-60, No. 163 (February 1989): p. 1.
85. Curran, "American Lawyers in the 1980s," p. 26.
86. See *Gideon v. Wainwright*, 372 U.S. 335 (1963).
87. Abel, "The Transformation of the American Legal Profession," p. 9.
88. Ibid.
89. *Goldfarb v. Virginia State Bar*, 421 U.S. 773 (1975).
90. *Bates v. State Bar of Arizona*, 433 U.S. 350 (1977).
91. *Ibanez v. Florida*, 512 U.S. _____, 114 S.Ct. 2084 (1994).
92. Abel, "The Transformation of the Legal Profession," pp. 11–14.
93. Ibid.
94. David Margolick, "Required Work for Poor Urged for Lawyers," *New York Times*, 11 July 1989, p. A1.
95. *Mallard v. U.S. District Court*, 490 U.S. 296 (1989). See also Linda Greenhouse, "Law on Free Legal Service Narrowed," *New York Times*, 2 May 1989, p. 8.
96. Paul Wice, *Judges and Lawyers* (New York: HarperCollins, 1991), p. 126.
97. See Dorothy L. Maddi and Frederic R. Merrill, *The Private Practicing Bar and Legal Services for Low-Income People* (Chicago: American Bar Association, 1971).
98. Joel F. Handler, Ellen J. Hollingsworth, and Howard Erlanger, *Lawyers and the Pursuit of Legal Rights* (New York: Academic Press, 1978), pp. 91–110.
99. Philip R. Lochner, Jr., "The No Fee and Low Fee Legal Practice of Private Attorneys," *Law and Society Review* 9 (1975): 448–49.
100. Nan Aron, *Liberty and Justice for All* (Boulder, CO: Westview Press, 1989), pp. 80–82.
101. Susan E. Lawrence, "Legal Services Before the Supreme Court," *Judicature* 72 (1989): 267.
102. See Harry P. Stumpf, *Community Politics and Legal Services* (Beverly Hills, CA: Sage, 1975).
103. Jerome R. Corsi, *Judicial Politics: An Introduction* (Englewood Cliffs, NJ: Prentice-Hall, 1984), p. 236.
104. Mark Kessler, *Legal Services for the Poor: A Comparative and Contemporary Analysis of Interorganizational Politics* (Westport, CT: Greenwood Press, 1987), p. 143.
105. Corsi, *Judicial Politics*, p. 243.
106. Kessler, *Legal Services for the Poor*, pp. 148–49.
107. Lawrence, "Legal Services Before the Supreme Court," p. 272.

# Chapter 4

# Criminal Justice Processes

During 1995, the American public was captivated by the murder trial in which Hall of Fame football star O. J. Simpson was accused of stabbing his ex-wife and an acquaintance of hers to death. Because the court proceedings were televised, people were able to follow the daily progress of the case from arrest to preliminary hearing to trial to jury decision. While the Simpson case drew public attention to the criminal justice process, it did relatively little to educate the public about how the justice process affects most criminal cases. Instead, the Simpson case reinforced the image of criminal cases as portrayed in television, motion pictures, novels, and news reports, which all focus on violent crimes and subsequent courtroom battles concerning the guilt or innocence of criminal defendants. If someone's only knowledge of judicial processes comes through news and entertainment media images, he or she may easily assume that criminal cases consume most of the judicial system's time, attention, and resources. In fact, criminal matters constitute only a portion of the cases that enter state and federal courts. For example, in the federal courts in 1995 criminal cases comprised less than 16 percent of the cases filed in U.S. district courts.[1] While criminal cases constitute a larger percentage of the caseload in many states, with a national average typically closer to 25 percent, such cases represent only a minority of the cases presented to U.S. courts. In state courts, there were 19.7 million civil cases filed in 1992, compared to only 13.2 million criminal cases.[2]

Criminal cases dominate the public's awareness of the judicial system because the fear of crime touches people's daily lives. Whether or not they are personally threatened by serious crime, many Americans think about the risk of crime every day as they lock their doors and cast suspicious glances at passersby on the streets. Moreover, politicians emphasize their opposition to crime as a safe, but essentially symbolic, issue that exploits voters' fears and will not offend any segment of the voting public.[3] The news and entertainment media both draw from and feed into the public interest in crime to capture television ratings or sell newspapers.

As Lawrence Friedman has noted, "Cop shows aim for entertainment, excitement; they are not documentaries. They exaggerate ludicrously, for dramatic effect. Crime shows, for example, overrepresent violent crimes; shoplifting is not great audience holder, but murder is."[4] By contrast, civil disputes, despite their abundance and their predominant position in the court system, catch public and media attention less frequently.

Although criminal cases constitute only a small portion of state and federal court caseloads, such cases are important because the outcomes produced by the criminal justice system have tremendous impact on the lives of individuals who are drawn into the system. Through criminal justice processes, the government exercises its distinctive power to punish those who violate the societal rules embodied in the criminal laws. As a result of decisions made by actors in the criminal justice system, some people will spend decades of their lives locked behind iron bars and barbed wire. Other people's lives will end when state governments employ electrical shocks, poison gas, lethal injections, the hangman's noose, and the firing squad to execute defendants convicted of capital offenses. The human beings in black robes who exercise judicial authority frequently face difficult and troubling decisions in criminal cases. Sometimes it is evident that judges agonize over the appropriate punishment for a criminal offender. In most cases, however, the political characteristics of the criminal justice system lead to outcomes that are the cumulative result of decisions by numerous actors in the judicial process. Thus, in most criminal justice cases, no individual decision maker is forced to bear the sole burden of difficult decisions.

For example, O.J. Simpson's acquittal can be seen as the product of cumulative decisions rather than simply as a controversial jury verdict. The evidence presented was defined through a series of decisions by various actors. The Los Angeles Police Department's detectives' questionable decision to enter and search Simpson's property without a warrant may have tainted some of the evidence. This decision and the subsequent attempts to justify it apparently made some jurors doubt the detectives' motives when they claimed they entered the property to check on the inhabitants' safety rather than to search for incriminating evidence. The prosecution's decision to demonstrate that Simpson was the owner of the murderer's bloody glove backfired when, in front of the jury and television cameras, Simpson struggled to fit the glove over his hand. The defense's decision to emphasize the Los Angeles Police Department's reputation of treating African-American suspects unfairly may have succeeded in casting doubt on the evidence and testimony presented. In addition, Judge Lance Ito made several decisions about evidence admissibility and the propriety of arguments advanced. The cumulative impact of these individual decisions shaped the jury's decision.

Although the Simpson case, like all cases, illustrates the point that case outcomes are the products of cumulative decisions, the Simpson case is clearly not representative of the majority of cases processed in criminal court proceedings. Most cases do not involve violent crimes, and very few cases involve notable celebrity defendants. More importantly, very few case outcomes are determined through jury trials, and even fewer cases involve defendants able to pay for defense attorneys, investigators, and expert witnesses, matching the expertise and resources available to prosecutors.

## CRIMINAL LAW AND POLITICS

Many criminal laws, such as those defining murder, are drawn from traditional English common law. The definitions of other crimes, however, are explicitly linked to decisions of officials in the American political system. Criminal laws are defined by elected officials in Congress, state legislatures, and city councils. These politicians are elected by and represent the majority of active voters, who possess middle-class values—and fears—about the protection of private property, the preservation of public morality, and the maintenance of personal security in American society. Criminal laws are not based on natural morality, but on political decisions by elected officials who wish to please their middle-class constituents. Because of underlying political influences on the selective definition and enforcement of criminal laws, such laws may favor dominant political interests. According to a comprehensive study of narcotics regulation, for example, "[C]lass consciousness was a recurrent element in mari[j]uana prohibition even in its infancy."[5] The poor, minority group members who used marijuana lacked the political power to protect their intoxicant of choice, but those in power protected their own addictive, physically harmful intoxicant—alcohol—because it was deemed socially acceptable to the political majority. Eventually, when middle- and upper-class youths began to use marijuana, formal decriminalization efforts developed in several states. Law enforcement officers in other states reduced the attention given to investigating and prosecuting cases involving the possession and use (as opposed to the sale) of marijuana.[6]

Because political influences in an evolving society determine the selective definition and enforcement of crimes, criminal laws can change over time. Such laws are not necessarily tied to any enduring natural morality. For example, in inner-city neighborhoods, many poor people traditionally placed bets in local, privately run lotteries called "numbers games." If you placed your bet on the day's winning number, you won a cash prize drawn from a portion of the day's bets. Police officers frequently harassed and arrested people participating in such lotteries because their betting constituted illegal gambling.[7] In the 1970s, however, state governments began to change their views on gambling. Gradually, certain lotteries were no longer regarded as violating criminal laws; in fact, these lotteries were operated and advertised by the state governments themselves, which exploited this form of gambling as a means to raise government revenue. Presumably, gambling remained just as "immoral" as it was before state-sponsored lotteries, but the status of these gambling games changed for a political reason:

State governments wanted and needed the financial benefits that had once gone to "criminal" entrepreneurs in poor neighborhoods.

There is a consensus in society that certain acts should be outlawed. Homicide, armed robbery, kidnapping, and other offenses are universally acknowledged as sufficiently harmful to society to deserve application of the government's authority to provide punishment. Other offenses, such as public drunkenness, gambling, and prostitution, involve value choices by the political interests that dominate legislative institutions. Although criminal laws are similar in many cities and states, there are notable differences across the United States in the criminalization of pornography, gun ownership, and other behaviors. For example, Nevada has legalized prostitution. Some states permit people to carry concealed handguns. These examples demonstrate that politics, not merely morality, underlies the development of criminal laws. The representation of different values within specific state legislatures and city councils produces these differences in definition.

## The Politics of Law Enforcement

The political power and values possessed by dominant interests also influence enforcement of criminal laws. In observing police behavior in San Francisco, criminologist John Irwin described a scene in which he was part of a well-dressed audience standing outside a theater during intermission. The affluent crowd spilled out into the street and drank champagne while they waited for the show's second act to begin. Two police officers came toward the crowd. Instead of arresting people for violating the city's law against drinking alcoholic beverages from open containers in public or asking them to stop interfering with traffic by standing in the street, the police officers walked around the elite citizens without saying a word. Why should these officers risk creating problems for themselves by confronting people who probably have political influence? Irwin observed that, by contrast, when police officers encounter poorly dressed young men drinking beer on a public sidewalk or even in an alley hidden from public view, the officers act to stop the criminal activity.[8] Irwin concluded that police officers selectively exercise their authority to "control the rabble" in society as a means to hide behavior offensive to mainstream society, even when that behavior is not illegal.[9] The criminalization and selective enforcement of vague laws against "public drunkenness" and "loitering" provide police with discretionary power to remove offensive social problems, such as alcoholism and homelessness, from public view. The discretionary enforcement of such laws may be used to control people who are disturbing public order, but they may also be used against quiet people who are merely unsightly or otherwise offensive to the officers' perceptions of mainstream values. Such arrests will not necessarily produce criminal convictions and punishment. They may simply be a discretionary means to temporarily move selected people off the public streets.

Another aspect of the political nature of law enforcement involves the emphasis by police and prosecutors on so-called street crimes—personal and property offenses such as robbery that occur in public and are commonly committed by less affluent citizens. This is not an irrational choice in light of the fact that the public is most fearful of violent crimes. However, criminal acts committed by more affluent and politically powerful white-collar workers and corporations receive less law enforcement attention and less severe penalties despite the fact that corporate and white-collar crimes, such as fraud and embezzlement, create the greatest annual economic losses for society.[10] The selectivity of law enforcement determines which people are affected by criminal sanctions. As described by one scholar:

> The prisons are disproportionately black not primarily because of racial discrimination in sentencing for particular crimes but because of a bias against crimes committed by lower-class persons. . . . Public policy does not give anything like the same emphasis to white-collar crimes, even though in dollar terms, they cost us about ten times as much as all robberies and burglaries combined. . . . If all of our criminal statutes were enforced, . . . [p]risons would be filled with vast numbers of additional white offenders. The differential treatment given perpetrators of different types of crimes represents a form of discrimination based on social class. This is undoubtedly the most consistent pattern of bias within the criminal justice system.[11]

# THE CRIMINAL JUSTICE SYSTEM

When the actors and institutions in the criminal justice process are characterized as a "system," this does not imply that they work together efficiently in a planned and coordinated manner. In fact, there is significant fragmentation among criminal justice institutions as they guard their authority over separate responsibilities and compete with each other for political attention and financial resources. There are thousands of different police departments and prosecutors' offices throughout the country that operate independently without oversight or coordination from any central authority. These actors and institutions form a "system" because, despite fragmentation, they are interdependent components of the criminal justice process, which must interact in order to enforce criminal laws and move defendants through the various processing stages from investigation to punishment.

## Characteristics of the Criminal Justice System

The criminal justice system has been characterized as an open system with the introduction of new cases, new personnel, and shifting political conditions affecting the environment in which criminal laws are implemented. A state of scarcity exists in regard to time, money, information, and personnel, thereby preventing the system's actors and institutions from processing every case according to formally prescribed criteria.[12] Hypothetically, all defendants are presumed innocent and will have the opportunity to force the prosecution to prove guilt ''beyond a reasonable doubt'' in front of a jury of citizens during an adversarial trial before any punishment is imposed. In reality, however, the forces affecting the criminal justice system lead to discretionary dismissals and plea bargaining in the overwhelming majority of cases, and fewer than 10 percent of all cases result in a jury trial. In a famous discussion of the criminal justice system, Herbert Packer presented two competing models that describe how cases are processed.[13]

The *Due Process Model* represents the idealized conception of criminal justice in which defendants are presumed innocent, suspects' rights are protected, and the process strives to ensure that no innocent person is convicted. In this model, the outcomes of cases are determined in the courtroom after an adversarial battle before the judge and jury during a trial. Although this model comports with popular notions, reinforced by television and books, about how the criminal justice system works, the model actually applies to fewer than 10 percent of cases—usually those involving either very serious offenses (e.g., first-degree murder) or defendants who can afford to hire attorneys to pursue cases to the very end.

While O.J. Simpson's murder case provided an example of the Due Process Model in action, most criminal cases are processed through the discretionary decisions of police officers, prosecutors, defense attorneys, and judges who may decide to decline to arrest, to dismiss charges, to bargain for guilty pleas, and to otherwise conserve system resources by filtering out cases prior to trial. For example, a study of felony cases found that, although murder cases had the lowest rate of guilty pleas, negotiated pleas accounted for more than half of the convictions (58 percent) even on this serious charge.[14] In larceny cases, by contrast, guilty pleas accounted for 92 percent of convictions.[15] These actual operations of the criminal justice system, which apply to most cases, were characterized by Packer as the *Crime Control Model*. Suspects are presumed guilty and are processed administratively by the discretionary decisions of actors within the system. If there are serious doubts about a suspect's guilt, the prosecutor may drop the case or lower charges to facilitate a negotiated guilty plea. The plea process helps to move cases out of the system without absorbing too much of its limited time and resources. The actual operations of the criminal justice system and its hidden, informal processes reflect the most important characteristics of the system.[16]

First, actors in the system have a high degree of *discretion*. Individuals vested with authority in the system make decisions in specific cases about how the criminal laws will or will not be applied. After political institutions have defined the laws, police make decisions—based on a complex mix of factors that may be applied differently in each situation—about whether to arrest people.

Police officers' decisions in situations in which the criminal laws may have been violated depend on departmental policies, situational pressures, and the officers' personal biases.

When spouses are fighting, for example, police officers can use their discretion to ignore criminal behavior (i.e., assault and battery), cool the combatants' tempers, or make an arrest. Because male police officers have historically been unresponsive to women's complaints about abusive husbands, many cities have adopted formal regulations to prevent police from characterizing a physical assault as merely a "domestic disturbance." In the absence of a formal policy requiring an officer to make an arrest whenever there is a complaint about a physical assault by a spouse, the officer's decision about whether to make an arrest will be affected by several factors: how the officer was treated by each spouse; the officer's views of how husbands should treat their wives (and vice versa); the officer's perceptions of the impact of the arrest on the couple's family; and even the amount of paperwork generated by a formal arrest. Obviously, individual officers react differently in similar situations, thus ensuring that criminal laws are not applied equally to all citizens.

Other actors in the criminal justice system also exercise significant discretion. Each application of a discretionary decision affects people's lives by determining whether they will move forward to the next stage in the system and possibly face loss of liberty, execution, or some other punishment. Prosecutors decide whether to pursue criminal charges and then decide *which* charges to pursue. Bail bondspersons decide whether to assist an incarcerated defendant in securing release before trial. Judges use discretion in determining sentences. Corrections officials determine whether to punish prisoners for breaking institutional rules, and these decisions affect parole boards' discretionary decisions about whether an offender deserves an early release.

A second important characteristic of the criminal justice system is the *sequential nature* of tasks and decisions. Actors have authority to make discretionary decisions at separate stages of the process, and those decisions affect the decisions by actors who control the later stages. For example, if police officers and prosecutors vigorously pursue all cases, corrections officials and parole boards may be forced to use their discretion to release offenders and alleviate prison overcrowding.

A third characteristic of the system is produced by the sequential nature of discretionary decisions. In order for the actors to achieve their respective objectives, they must be dependent on other actors. Police officers cannot succeed in imprisoning offenders unless prosecutors and judges follow through with convictions and sentencing. Thus, *exchange relationships* develop as actors cooperate to enforce the criminal laws.

A final characteristic of the system is *resource dependence*. Police officers, prosecutors, judges, and corrections officials must be sensitive to the demands of legislators and the public in order to maintain resource support for themselves and for the system. Although the public has little awareness of what happens in most criminal cases, judges and prosecutors, as elected officials in many states, risk their positions if they make controversial decisions in highly publicized cases. In order to maintain favorable relationships with the politicians who control the purse strings of government, police chiefs frequently publicize crime statistics and focus law enforcement efforts at specific crimes or neighborhoods in response to requests from elected officials. Thus, political pressures and public opinion can affect discretionary decisions about how justice system resources will be deployed.

## The Federal Criminal Justice System

The foregoing key characteristics of the criminal justice system affect both federal and state systems. There are, however, several notable differences between the federal and state systems. Federal law covers a relatively limited range of crimes and encompasses only a few serious "street crimes"—notably kidnapping, bank robbery, and narcotics offenses—that are of grave concern to citizens. Thus, federal officials devote their attention and their decision making to different kinds of crimes, such as smuggling and tax fraud, than those that absorb the attention of state and local law enforcement officials. Other kinds of crimes, such as drug trafficking and firearms violations, may violate both federal and state laws.

Because of their "elite" status, federal law enforcement officials are frequently better paid and better educated than their state and local counterparts. These differences may affect the federal officials' discretionary decisions and exchange relationships. Despite these differences, the federal system also has much in common with state systems. There are federal police officers (i.e., Federal Bureau of Investigation; Bureau of Alcohol, Tobacco, and Firearms; Customs Service; Secret Service; Drug Enforcement Administration) whose discretionary decisions concerning investigations and arrests produce cases for federal prosecutors (i.e., U.S. Attorneys). The federal prosecutors, in turn, engage in plea bargaining and other interactions with defense attorneys, including federal public defenders for indigent defendants. Cases may then proceed to trial before federal district judges. After conviction and sentencing, prisoners enter the federal corrections system governed by the U.S. Bureau of Prisons. All actors in the federal system are dependent on Congress and the president for the provision of adequate resources. Although this chapter focuses on state and local criminal justice officials, who process the bulk of criminal cases in the United States, the concepts presented also apply to the federal system.

## Stages in the Criminal Justice Process

The key characteristics of the criminal justice system affect various sequential steps as criminal defendants are located, apprehended, and processed. Because there are so many decision points in the stages of processing criminal cases, there are numerous opportunities for application of discretionary judgments, which can either filter suspects out of the system or push them on toward punishment.

Before individuals enter the criminal justice system, there must first be an *investigation* to identify people whom police officers seek to arrest. If the investigation is conducted by a prosecutor who subsequently files an ''information'' indicating that there is evidence against a certain individual, police officers will be instructed to make an arrest. Similarly, when a grand jury hears evidence indicating that a particular individual has committed a crime, the ''indictment'' issued by the grand jury leads to a prosecutor's instruction to the police to make an arrest.

Sometimes an investigation is an elaborate, time-consuming process of piecing together bits of evidence from a crime scene and from witnesses. An investigation can also be brief if the police receive a complaint from a victim who can identify the perpetrator at the scene of the crime. Officers' own observations of suspicious behavior constitute a form of ''investigation'' which, although potentially based on personal biases, can lead to arrests. The investigation phase includes important discretionary decisions concerning which cases to pursue, which evidence to examine, which witnesses to believe, and which suspects to question. Each seemingly small decision has enormous consequences for the individuals eventually identified for further processing.

After officers obtain information about a possible crime, whether through a lengthy investigation or a quick observation, they must decide whether to make an *arrest*. Officers bring people into the criminal justice system by formally taking arrestees into custody on suspicion of having committed a crime. The arrest decision presumably means that an officer believes there is sufficient evidence of criminal behavior to support a valid case. Police officers may, however, utilize their power to arrest even if they lack sufficient evidence. An arrest may also provide a brief period of supervised control in which an individual can ''sober up'' or be referred to a social service agency.

Soon after the arrest, there are several processing stages through which discretionary decisions may filter suspects out of the system or increase their likelihood of conviction and punishment. *Bail* may be set by a police officer at the station, if the case involves a minor charge, or by a judge after a hearing if a serious charge is pending. As subsequent sections of this chapter will discuss, the decision concerning whether a criminal defendant will be released prior to trial ultimately affects the defendant's ability to assist in preparing a defense.

In a *preliminary hearing*, the prosecutor and police must present enough evidence to persuade a judge that there is sufficient reason to bring criminal charges against the defendant. Many cases are dismissed by the prosecutor prior to this stage either because there is insufficient evidence to win the case or because the prosecutor believes the person has been adequately punished by being arrested and jailed. Judges dismiss other cases for lack of evidence or for misconduct by the police and prosecutors in obtaining evidence.

Defense attorneys can often use bail hearings and preliminary hearings to see the prosecutor's evidence and begin preparing an appropriate plea bargain offer or trial defense strategy. In order to strengthen their plea-bargaining posture, prosecutors attempt to present enough evidence to justify continued prosecution without revealing all of their evidence. Thus, they hope to bluff the defendants and defense attorneys into believing that there is more incriminating evidence in the possession of the police. If defendants and their attorneys are fearful about the existence of additional damning evidence, they may be more inclined to offer a quick guilty plea in exchange for a reduced charge or sentence.

At the *arraignment*, the defendant is formally told of the charges lodged by the prosecutor. The defendant enters a plea—usually by saying "not guilty"—and the attorneys for each side begin the plea negotiations in earnest. Although most defendants whose cases are not dismissed by the prosecutor or judge prior to arraignment will eventually plead guilty, many do not enter a guilty plea until their lawyers have time to seek a favorable deal from the prosecutor.

As cases are carried forward over weeks or months, both prosecutors and defense attorneys may simultaneously continue their investigations, prepare their arguments and evidence, and negotiate possible plea bargains. Studies indicate that nearly half of all arrestees have their cases dismissed by prosecutors and judges. Of the remaining cases, approximately 90 percent result in *negotiated guilty pleas*, and only 10 percent (or fewer) will lead to a *trial*.[17]

In a trial, the defendant's fate hinges on the actions and decisions of several actors in the courtroom. The attorneys must not only gather favorable evidence and witnesses, they must also make persuasive presentations to the judge and jury. Evidence of guilt or innocence alone may not win a case that is not effectively presented. Thus, a defendant's criminal conviction may be affected by the prosecutor's or defense attorney's skill as well as by the substance of the evidence. The judge's ruling on evidentiary motions and other matters can determine the outcome of the trial, especially if the judge decides to admit or exclude controversial evidence important to one side's case. The biases and memory capabilities of witnesses and jurors also affect the defendant's fate. In sum, as illustrated by the O.J. Simpson case, the outcomes of trials are determined by a complex combination of interactions of human beings with varying capacities for memory, impartial judgment, communication, and persuasion.

After conviction, the court's probation officer frequently plays a significant role in determining punishment. The probation officer will usually prepare a *presentence report* for the judge, describing the defendant's characteristics, skills, and experiences. The probation officer will also frequently make a recommendation to the judge, about a desirable sentence. The quality of the report and the credibility of the probation officer can have significant influence on the *sentence*.

In a growing number of jurisdictions, sentencing decisions are regulated by mandated guidelines that instruct judges on the punishments they must impose for specified crimes. If the judge has discretion in the sentencing process, however, the prosecutor and the defense attorney will attempt to persuade the judge to hand down the sentence they respectively envision. Ultimately, after listening to recommendations from other actors, the judge will apply his or her own philosophy, attitudes, and biases when pronouncing a sentence. Because judges' backgrounds and viewpoints can differ dramatically, the sentences imposed on similarly situated offenders can vary from courthouse to courthouse. Offenders in some states may receive long prison terms for drug, weapons, and other charges that are frequently dismissed or punished with probation in other locales. Variations in sentencing practices may also be influenced by resource scarcity (e.g., burdensome caseloads, overcrowded jails and prisons, etc.). Judges may not be able to punish offenders as they wish if their state's courts and corrections system cannot adequately absorb the number of cases presented.

Criminal offenders may be sentenced to a variety of punishments: restitution, fines, community service, home confinement, probation, incarceration, or execution. In carrying out these sentences, additional criminal justice actors, including probation officers and correctional officials, make judgments about the offenders' cooperative behavior and rehabilitative progress. These discretionary assessments subsequently affect the length of the offenders' correctional supervision. If correctional officials and prison counselors do not provide positive assessments of a prisoner's behavior, it reduces the likelihood that the offender will benefit from parole boards' discretionary decisions for early release. In the *corrections* stage, as in the other steps of the criminal justice process, there are opportunities for authoritative officials to affect the treatment of people being processed through the system.

The discretionary decisions, exchange relationships, and other key characteristics of the system are influential at each stage of the process. As illustrated in figure 4.1, the outcomes produced by the criminal justice process result from a

**Figure 4.1: Sequence of Primary Actors' Potential Discretionary Decisions in the Stages of Criminal Justice System.**

| Police | Prosecutor | Judge | Corrections Officials |
|---|---|---|---|
| Respond to citizen complaints | Recommend bail amount | Set bail | Classify prisoners |
| Investigate crimes | File or dismiss specific charges | Approve plea bargain | Award "good time" credit toward early release |
| Decide to arrest | Plea bargain | Rule on trial motions | Decide to grant parole |
| | Plan trial strategy | Instruct jury | |
| | Recommend sentence | Render verdict | |
| | | Determine sentence | |

variety of discretionary decisions by authoritative officials. The decisions and interactions that affect each individual case can potentially produce myriad outcomes: avoidance of arrest, dismissal of charges, plea-bargained conviction, conviction after trial, or acquittal. Because specific outcomes are determined by the particular sequence of decisions by actors in the system, similarly situated defendants may experience vastly different treatment. For example, the antagonists in one bar fight may receive only a stern warning from busy police officers who are at the end of their shift and eager to go home rather than bother with paperwork needed to process arrests. Similar participants in a fight at another bar may, however, ultimately receive prison sentences if the police officers, prosecutors, and judges that they encounter exercise their discretion to press criminal charges and push the case through the system. Even the average citizen who has little contact with police can see (or experience) the impact of discretion when observing that some motorists who exceed the speed limit are given citations while others are merely given warnings. The roles of discretion, exchange relationships, and the other characteristics of the system in determining case outcomes can be illustrated by examining the authority and behavior of the primary actors at each stage of the criminal justice process.

# POLICE

## Relationships with Political Institutions

Historically, the police were a component of the prevailing political establishment. According to Samuel Walker, they ''enforced the narrow prejudices of their constituencies, harassing 'undesirables' or discouraging any kind of 'unwelcome' behavior.''[18] The twentieth century witnessed a trend toward greater police professionalism. This trend was generated, in part, by the scandalous revelations of investigatory commissions beginning in the 1930s. The trend accelerated in the mid-twentieth century as the U.S. Supreme Court began to enunciate rules for appropriate police treatment of criminal defendants.[19] The imposition of judicial policies coincided with increased training and professionalism among police officers to diminish their roles as partisan political enforcers.

Policies, training, and professionalization can never eliminate the risk that individual police officers will abuse their discretionary power. In 1991, for example, many Americans were shocked by a videotape of Los Angeles police officers beating and kicking motorist Rodney King. In the aftermath of this abusive behavior, Los Angeles experienced a major riot, and two of the officers served terms in prison.[20] While the Rodney King case represents an extreme example of improper police actions, the mere existence of broad discretionary authority always creates the possibility that officers will use their authority in ways that treat people unfairly.

## Arrests

One of the most significant decisions made by law enforcement officers is the decision to make an arrest and enter that person into the criminal justice process. In Michael Lipsky's terminology, police officers are "street-level bureaucrats" who represent the government in direct contacts with the citizenry, particularly in situations eliciting hostile reactions and danger.[21] Most direct contacts between police officers and members of the public occur under stressful circumstances in which someone is angry or upset and a police officer is called on to resolve the situation. In an environment of inadequate resources in which their authority is regularly challenged, police officers use their discretion to avoid confrontations and maintain rapport with citizens. An altercation at a bar, for example, may lead officers to order certain people to leave the premises without making any arrests. On the other hand, officers may assert their authority by making arrests, especially if a criminal harm (e.g., assault-related injury, theft of money, etc.) is too significant to ignore. Research on police officers' decision making indicates that situational factors, such as the seriousness of the alleged offense and the existence of a complaining witness, affect officers' decisions to arrest. Two primary factors encourage officers to make arrests: 1) the officers encounter antagonistic suspects; or 2) there are bystanders observing the officers' interactions with the suspects.[22] Thus, the decision to arrest may also be affected by the officer's desire to maintain his or her image and authority. The officer's decision to arrest is the key triggering event that places people's fates under control of criminal court processes.

# BAIL

When people are arrested and charged with criminal violations, they face the possibility of months in jail prior to any determination of their guilt or innocence. If a defendant is too poor to afford bail or if a judge utilizes his or her discretionary authority to set a high bail, the accused will sit behind bars despite the "presumption of innocence" that supposedly underlies the American criminal justice process. In the bail system, defendants must put up a specified amount of money that will be forfeited if they fail to appear at scheduled court dates. Prosecutors and defense attorneys play crucial roles in influencing the amount of money that the judge will require for pretrial release. Prosecutors make recommendations to judges about bail, and judges frequently adopt the prosecutors' recommendations. This deference by the judges is based on the prosecutor's presumed familiarity with the details of the case and the defendant's background. In practical terms, however, the judge could assert decision-making authority to prevent the public outcry that would follow if the defendant committed another crime or fled while out on bail. The defense attorney is important because solid advocacy on behalf of the accused can often result in a reduction in bail. Poor defendants, who are represented by public defenders or appointed counsel, often do not benefit from well-prepared arguments at the bail hearings because their attorneys, unlike privately retained counsel, have not yet had time to investigate and prepare the case.

Traditionally, bail was intended to insure the appearance of the defendant at trial. In addition, pretrial detention, if bail is not granted or paid, can protect the public by keeping potentially dangerous offenders off the streets. Judges can also utilize bail to punish a defendant by setting bail so high that the accused cannot gain release. Judges and prosecutors may use bail to pressure defendants into pleading guilty. In some cases, the defendant may be given the option of pleading guilty to a lesser charge and going free on probation or, if the defendant wishes to assert his or her innocence, facing incarceration as a result of high bail set for a serious felony charge. In such cases, the guilty go free, and the presumably innocent remain in jail. For people who face the loss of jobs and disruptions in their families' lives from being detained pending trial, it may be easier to offer a guilty plea and receive probation rather than to hold out for an assertion of innocence.

The bail process is also affected by a private, profit-seeking actor—the bail bondsperson. The bail bondsperson receives a fee, often 10 percent of the bail amount, in order to put up bail for a defendant who cannot afford to pay the entire amount. Because the bondsperson forfeits money if the defendant does not appear in court, the bondsperson serves the system by reminding the defendant of trial dates and making certain the defendant appears. The participation of a profit-making actor in the bail process creates risks of corruption as bondspersons pay police officers and jailers to steer clients to their offices. Moreover, bondspersons may work behind the scenes with judges, prosecutors, and police officers to refuse bail to defendants whom officials are intent on punishing prior to trial.[23]

The bail amount is usually based on discretionary decisions by the judge and prosecutor. When these decisions prevent a defendant's pretrial release, the accused suffers serious consequences. As indicated by Malcolm Feeley's well-known study of a city jail, *The Process is the Punishment*, people are punished through their contacts with the criminal justice system whether or not they are eventually found guilty of a crime.[24] While in jail, defendants can lose their jobs, default on their mortgages and car payments, lose any ability to support their families, and have their lives otherwise disintegrate while they wait for the slow-moving wheels of justice to turn. In addition, they forfeit many constitutional rights while they remain behind bars and continually face threatening situations from an ever-changing jail population of substance abusers, violent criminals, former mental patients, and other unstable and unpredictable individuals. Moreover, research indicates that failure to secure release on bail leads to a greater probability of subsequent conviction, regardless of the strength of the prosecutor's evidence.[25]

Although suspects may spend months in jail prior to trial, they should not languish there indefinitely because constitutional and statutory guarantees of a right to a "speedy trial" in criminal cases normally insure that criminal cases move forward within specified time limits. "Speedy trial" laws can contribute to delays of months or years in civil cases by requiring that new criminal cases take precedence over civil cases that have been pending for months.

Efforts to reform the bail system in order to reduce excessive burdens on poor defendants have been initiated in many cities. Frequently such reforms involve programs for interviewing and monitoring defendants so that they can be released on their own recognizance. Although these programs claim to be successful, many of them were never adequately evaluated. Moreover, these reforms were not institutionalized in the criminal justice system because the established actors in the system had little incentive for putting their authority and resources behind the reforms.[26] For example, judges and prosecutors have an interest in keeping some offenders behind bars prior to trial, both to avoid the risk that a suspect will commit an additional crime and to demonstrate to the voting public that the system is "tough on criminals."

## PROSECUTION

Prosecutors are central figures in criminal cases processed in the courts. They can make discretionary decisions to dismiss charges or to bring more serious charges. Prosecutors may also decide whether arrestees should enter substance abuse or psychological treatment programs instead of the criminal justice system. Prosecutors make recommendations for bail and sentencing, and they also control the plea-bargaining process through their willingness, or lack thereof, to negotiate with defense attorneys. Prosecutors are especially powerful because their decisions are not reviewable by any higher authority. If a prosecutor drops charges against a suspect, no one can order him or her to re-initiate the criminal case. As elected officials in every state except Alaska, Connecticut, Delaware, New Jersey, and Rhode Island,[27] prosecutors are presumably held accountable by the voters if they dismiss charges or make other controversial decisions. Prosecutors' decisions are, however, virtually invisible to the electorate. How often does the public hear about prosecutors dropping charges? It happens every day, but most cases receive very little publicity between the initial arrest and the sentencing that concludes the case. The myriad discretionary decisions in the intervening stages of the criminal justice process rarely receive public attention except in cases involving serious crimes, such as homicide, or in cases with well-known defendants. In most criminal cases, the public never really notices whether the arrestee was convicted and sentenced.

Because of their central role in processing criminal cases, prosecutors develop exchange relationships with actors throughout the system. Prosecutors need to cultivate and maintain good relationships with the police in order to ensure that criminal laws are enforced in accordance with the prosecutor's desires. If the prosecutor wants to impress the voting public with a crackdown on drug dealing, the police must follow through with arrests to provide the prosecutor with defendants. Some cities and states are implementing formal police-prosecutor investigation teams to make certain that there is no "cooperation gap" between law enforcement officials.[28] Prosecutors must also maintain good relationships with judges in order to influence bail and sentencing. If judges are unwilling to incarcerate offenders for whom prosecutors recommend imprisonment, the prosecutors will be unable to impress the electorate with their success in sending criminals to prison. Prosecutors rely on elected officials at the city, county, and state levels for funding for criminal justice agencies, so they must be sensitive to the law enforcement priorities set by politicians who control budgetary decisions.

Because the prosecutor's office is the traditional stepping stone to higher political office, prosecutors seek to maintain a positive image in the minds of the voters. Many members of Congress, governors, judges, and other public officials built their careers on the many positive publicity opportunities gained by assuming responsibility for prosecuting highly publicized cases.

Prosecutors' decisions are normally influenced by their desire to maintain cooperative relationships with other actors in the criminal justice system or to preserve a positive image in the eyes of voters and political elites. In order to process cases efficiently and thereby claim that the system is punishing criminals effectively, prosecutors must maintain good working relationships with defense attorneys and judges. If defense attorneys do not encourage defendants to enter guilty pleas or judges refuse to accept such pleas, prosecutors might be forced to dismiss more cases in order to focus their limited resources on trials for the most serious offenses. Usually, however, prosecutors can develop good relationships with other actors because the other actors, like the prosecutors, have self-interested reasons for facilitating guilty pleas under Packer's Crime Control Model. Because of the actors' shared interests in processing cases effectively, James Eisenstein and Herbert Jacob have identified the operation of "courtroom workgroups" in which prosecutors, defense attorneys, and judges work together to achieve quick, efficient case processing through cooperative plea bargaining.[29]

The negotiated guilty pleas developed by the courtroom workgroup serve the interests of all relevant actors. Prosecutors get a sure conviction and avoid the risk of an acquittal by a jury. Defense attorneys process the case quickly and can move on to new cases. Judges need not spend weeks presiding over a trial. Moreover, the plea agreement frequently contains a particular sentence recommendation, so the judge does not have to grapple with the formulation of an appropriate sentence. The defendant generally pleads to a lesser charge and gets a reduced sentence, thus avoiding the risk that a trial might result in a particularly severe punishment.

Although prosecutors willingly participate in plea bargaining because they benefit from the results of the process, they are not simply "selling out" by taking it easy on criminal offenders. Prosecutors normally hold the upper hand in plea negotiations. It is a common practice for prosecutors to charge defendants with more offenses or more serious charges than the available evidence will support. This "overcharging" gives the prosecutors an advantage in plea negotiations because they can relinquish during negotiations charges that they might not have been able to prove during a trial. Thus, the reduced charge that the defendant ultimately obtains through plea bargaining may in fact reflect the actual charge for which the prosecutor could have obtained a conviction.

In many courthouses, plea bargaining does not involve actual negotiations in which there are give-and-take exchanges between the prosecution and defense (e.g., "We will enter a guilty plea if you drop two of the charges"). Instead, guilty pleas are produced through a process of settling the facts. If the two sides can reach a consensus on the provable facts in the case, then both attorneys are well aware of the "going rate" or typical punishment for the provable offense in that particular courthouse. Established sentencing patterns and a shared consensus about the seriousness of the offenses in the local legal community eliminate any doubt about the punishment to be imposed.[30] Such plea discussions may focus on the quality of witness testimony regarding whether a weapon was carried during a robbery rather than whether the defendant is guilty. The defendant's fate will be determined by the attorneys' joint prediction about which offense (e.g., simple robbery vs. armed robbery) would be provable in court. If the defense attorney can persuade the prosecutor that some element of the more serious crime is unlikely to be proven by the existing evidence, both attorneys can agree on a guilty plea accepting the established punishment for the lesser, provable offense. Such attorney interactions are often characterized as plea bargaining by consensus rather than by negotiation.

## DEFENSE ATTORNEYS

Anyone who is charged with a crime must undertake a major financial expense to obtain the services of a defense attorney. Private defense attorneys usually charge thousands of dollars to handle a felony case. If a defendant manages to hire a defense attorney for less than a thousand dollars, he or she may not realize that one of two possibilities could explain the cut-rate price. First, the defendant may have hired an inexperienced or unsuccessful attorney who is trying to build or maintain a struggling law practice. In such a case, the representation provided by the attorney may be inadequate. Second, the attorney may have already decided, without informing the client, that the case will never go to trial because the attorney will seek a quick plea bargain and then persuade the client that this is the best possible outcome. A top-notch defense attorney may require one hundred thousand dollars or more to undertake a major homicide, drug, or other felony case. These fees must usually be paid in advance because defense attorneys know that clients who are convicted will be unwilling to pay the fee. Thus, defense attorneys do not normally charge by the hour and bill the client after work is undertaken. Convicted defendants will not pay after an unsuccessful case.

In many criminal cases, the defendant is very likely to be convicted. Although the attorney may ''win'' by negotiating a lesser charge or a reduced sentence, the client may still refuse to pay because of an expectation on the client's part that a skilled lawyer can always win an acquittal. Private defense attorneys generally calculate their fees by assessing both how much time the case will require and how much money the defendant can afford to pay. Even middle-class defendants without much money in the bank can frequently come up with large sums of money when facing the prospect of a long prison term. Middle-class families will often rally around their relatives, even taking out additional mortgages on their homes in order to come up with the tens of thousands of dollars that a skilled defense attorney is likely to charge.

Very few lawyers earn their living from criminal defense work. It is estimated that fewer than 5 percent of attorneys accept criminal cases on more than an occasional basis.[31] Many criminal defense lawyers are inexperienced or struggling attorneys who accept small fees from their local governments to handle cases for indigent defendants. In any city, it is rare for more than a small number of law firms to specialize profitably in criminal cases. Most criminal defendants cannot afford to pay much money, if anything, for a defense attorney. Affluent and middle-class defendants will be attracted to the attorneys with highly publicized reputations for handling big criminal cases. Thus, criminal defense attorneys comprise only a tiny segment of the legal profession.

Poor criminal defendants are entitled under the U.S. Constitution's Sixth Amendment right to counsel provision to have a defense lawyer provided for them. Although the right to counsel provision in the Constitution was written in the eighteenth century, the Supreme Court did not apply the provision to all indigent criminal defendants until 1963. The case of *Gideon v. Wainwright* established that all defendants, in state as well as federal courts, must have the assistance of a defense attorney when facing incarceration for six months or more for criminal charges.[32] Prior to 1963, criminal trials in many states were one-sided affairs in which professional prosecutors quickly persuaded judges and juries to convict inarticulate defendants who lacked the resources and ability to defend themselves. The *Gideon* decision and others made by the Supreme Court during the 1960s changed the criminal justice system by ensuring that defense attorneys would participate on behalf of defendants in every serious criminal case. Although the intervention of defense attorneys provided greater protection for the rights and interests of criminal defendants, a lawyer's participation does not guarantee that the defendant's constitutional rights will be protected nor that the prosecution will be forced to prove its case beyond a reasonable doubt.

## Indigent Defense Systems

There are three primary methods of providing attorneys for defendants who are too poor to hire their own counsel. The method chosen in a specific county will depend on the personal preferences of local judges and other political factors.[33] In public defender systems, a salaried staff of full- or part-time lawyers represents indigent defendants. The defense attorneys are usually state or local government employees, although sometimes private, nonprofit corporations provide public defenders under contracts with local governments. Public defender systems exist in 37 percent of counties nationwide but cover a majority of the population because they are used in many large cities. Assigned counsels are used in 52 percent of counties. These are private lawyers who are appointed to represent indigent defendants on a case-by-case basis and are then paid by local governments. Alternatively, nearly 11 percent of counties use contract attorneys. In these systems, private attorneys or law firms submit bids to local governments and a contract is awarded to one firm or attorney to provide representation for all poor defendants during an entire year for a set contract fee.[34]

Specific problems beset each defense system, problems that can detract from the quality of representation received by indigent defendants. The timing of appointment of counsel, for example, can affect case outcomes. Although people with the means to hire private attorneys may acquire private representation immediately, some jurisdictions do not provide attorneys for indigent defendants until the formal arraignment—which can be delayed more than thirty days after the arrest. By this time, the defendant may inadvertently make incriminating statements, and witnesses may disappear, placing the defense at a significant disadvantage. While 39 percent of public defender systems provide counsel to indigent arrestees within twenty-four hours, only 33 percent of assigned counsel and 12 percent of contract counsel are appointed as quickly.[35]

In public defender systems, attorneys' salaries are relatively low, frequently lower than those of other government attorneys (including prosecutors). The low salaries can hinder recruitment of outstanding new attorneys, preclude hiring experienced trial attorneys, and encourage frequent turnover of personnel. As a consequence, inexperienced and less skilled public defenders may be overmatched by the prosecutors opposing them. The heavy caseloads assigned to public defenders in some cities may preclude adequate investigation of cases and may restrict opportunities to communicate with clients. In New York City's public defender program, legal aid lawyers are sometimes each simultaneously responsible for as many as one hundred felony cases.[36]

Prosecutors have the police department to investigate cases for them, but public defenders and other attorneys for indigent defendants may not have investigators at their disposal. Thus, the defense attorneys' time may be absorbed by the time-consuming search for witnesses and evidence. In many instances, time and resource constraints simply force defense attorneys to conduct inadequate investigations.

In assigned counsel and contract systems, attorneys representing indigent defendants may have no genuine knowledge about or interest in criminal law. Unlike the public defenders who have made a commitment to criminal defense work as their career, assigned counsel may be aspiring corporate or tax lawyers who simply desire steady income from assigned criminal cases while they attempt to build their law practices in other fields. In addition, only a fraction of counties with assigned or contract counsel provide any specialized training in criminal defense work for the lawyers who represent indigent arrestees.[37] Defense attorneys' lack of commitment to assigned cases is, in part, a reflection of the low fees paid for such work. The fees, which are sometimes as low as $35 per hour, do not compare with the standard fees charged by most lawyers whose clients can afford to pay for legal services.

The consequences of being represented by appointed counsel have been studied by various researchers who have found mixed results. One study of murder charges over two decades found that privately retained attorneys are more successful in securing bail for their clients than are indigents' attorneys, even when controlling for the severity of the charges.[38] Another study found that representation by a court-appointed attorney and failure to win release on bail led to a greater probability of receiving a prison sentence, even when severity of offense and prior record were eliminated as influential factors.[39] More recent studies examining large groups of cases, however, have found few differences in the case outcomes produced by private counsel, public defenders, and assigned counsel.[40]

## Attorney-Client Relationships and Plea Bargaining

The title of one classic study of indigent criminal defendants neatly sums up the attitude of indigent defendants toward their appointed legal representatives: "Did You Have a Lawyer When You Went to Court? No, I Had a Public Defender."[41] Distrust can develop between attorneys and clients because the defendants perceive their lawyers as representatives of the government. Because public defenders, assigned counsel, and contract attorneys are all paid by the same governmental unit that employs the prosecutors and police, defendants frequently believe that their lawyers have no incentive to wage a vigorous defense. Indigent defendants assume that because they cannot afford to pay for a lawyer's services, they will automatically be provided with inferior legal representation. Moreover, because the first contact between a defense attorney and a client is often in the courtroom moments before a hearing, and the defense lawyers' first words are frequently to the effect, "If you plead guilty, I can get you a reduced sentence," the defendant perceives that the lawyer is not concerned about his or her version of the events underlying the alleged criminal violation and is not interested in pursuing an acquittal.

Defendants also observe their attorneys laughing, joking, and conversing in a friendly manner with the prosecutors who are seeking to convict the defendants. This can convey the impression that the defense attorneys are working for the prosecutor rather than for the defendant.[42] The consequences of the difficult relationships between appointed counsel and indigent defendants can lead lawyers to be hostile to their clients and to focus their efforts on controlling the clients' attitudes rather than on pursuing effective defense strategies.[43]

In fairness to the work of defense attorneys, it must be said that most defendants misperceive the nature of criminal defense work. Like the general public, defendants expect to see their attorneys pursue Packer's Due Process Model of adversarial combat in a complete criminal trial before a judge and jury. In fact, however, most criminal lawyers, from public defenders to highly paid elite private practitioners, try to develop and maintain good personal relationships with prosecutors. The apparently friendly interaction that so disturbs the defendant frequently provides the basis for plea-bargain agreements that are beneficial to the defendant. Cooperation between the defense attorney and the prosecutor is not, however, simply a function of the defense lawyers' calculated attempt to obtain reduced sentences for guilty clients. The defense attorneys' own interests in processing cases quickly also encourage cooperative efforts aimed at obtaining guilty pleas.

The incentive for encouraging guilty pleas by indigent defendants may be especially strong for assigned counsel and contract attorneys, who not only lack interest in criminal cases, but also have a strong financial incentive to dispose of cases quickly. Because judges in many jurisdictions determine the precise fees paid to assigned counsel, there is an incentive to avoid antagonizing the judges by requesting time-consuming trials or by otherwise assuming an adversarial role in representing criminal defendants. In addition, because judges sometimes have authority to appoint assigned counsel, the continuation of income from additional future cases may depend on maintaining a cooperative relationship with the courtroom workgroup rather than on zealously defending the client. The maintenance of good relationships can pay dividends for private attorneys. In Cleveland, judges have the option of assigning cases to private attorneys or salaried public defenders, and the most lucrative cases—such as death penalty cases that pay $12,500 per attorney—always go to private attorneys.[44] This occurs despite the fact that public defenders are already paid a salary no matter what kinds of cases they handle and therefore receive no special fee.

In sum, defense attorneys' behavior is influenced by their own interests in maintaining professional relationships within the courthouse and by their interest in having cases processed efficiently. These factors encourage plea bargaining and help to limit the number of full criminal trials that will absorb the time and resources of defense attorneys, prosecutors, judges, and other actors with the system.

# TRIALS

The relatively few cases that reach the trial stage receive extra attention from authoritative actors in the criminal justice system. Prosecutors and defense attorneys frequently spend months preparing their evidence, witnesses, and arguments for presentation during trial. Adversarial trial procedures in the United States are presumed to reveal the truth through a clash of skilled professionals vigorously advocating competing viewpoints. In reality, the adversarial process creates risks, and the more skilled attorney will overwhelm the less experienced or less skilled, whether or not the victor's position is most meritorious. Moreover, because the adversary system creates incentives for each side to hide or distort unfavorable evidence and testimony, trial proceedings may not produce all relevant information for consideration by the judge and jury. Whether or not the judge and jury have access to complete information, as in other stages in the criminal justice process, decisions that determine the outcomes of trials will be influenced by the decision makers' attitudes, values, and interests.

## Juries

The utilization of juries serves several beneficial functions for the judicial system. Citizens are permitted to participate in authoritative decision making. This participation lends legitimacy to trial outcomes by drawing the verdict from the community, not merely from the professionals who control the criminal justice process. Citizen participation also acts as a check on potential abuses of power by police and prosecutors. If law enforcement officials initiate improper prosecutions, citizens on the jury can restrain those officials by acquitting the mistreated defendant. Jury service also helps to educate the citizenry about the efforts of judicial officials to carry out their responsibilities.

Juries are supposed to be composed of a cross-section of the community. A heterogeneous jury should provide representation from various groups in a community and thereby presumably reduce potential biases that might develop if the jury consisted entirely of people from one race, one gender, or one social class. The composition of juries, however, is not usually completely representative of a community. Although some courts use driver's license lists and welfare rolls to call in potential jurors, many jurisdictions rely on voters' lists. Moreover, jury pools in some localities are narrowed to include only those voters who return a juror questionnaire to the clerk of the court. Research on jury composition indicates that the use of voting lists and questionnaires results in underrepresentation of young people, racial minorities, the poor, and transient people.[45] These people are less likely than are affluent, educated, or older people to register to vote and to complete juror questionnaires. Because jury composition is frequently skewed in favor of certain demographic groups, there is a risk of biased outcomes when not all viewpoints are represented. In other words, if jurors are biased—either consciously or unconsciously—against certain racial groups, age groups, or less affluent individuals, there may be no countervailing voices to counteract such biases. For example, when the white Los Angeles police officers who were videotaped beating African-American motorist Rodney King were tried before a nearly all-white jury in Simi Valley, California in 1992, they were acquitted of state criminal charges. During a second trial on federal charges in 1993 before a multiracial jury in Los Angeles, two officers were convicted and sentenced to prison. Although it is difficult to conclude with certainty that the juries' racial biases produced the differing results, it is possible that the verdicts were influenced by representativeness, or lack thereof, on each jury.[46]

As they screen potential jurors to select the few who will actually serve, the attorneys and the judge question these citizens about their attitudes and experiences in a process called *voir dire*. If any potential jurors describe attitudes or experiences that might make them unable to evaluate the cases with an open mind, the attorneys may exclude them with a *challenge for cause*. For example, if a potential juror was previously the victim of a mugging, the attorneys would challenge the person's capacity to remain emotionally detached from a case of robbery or assault. The potential juror's prior experience provides a cause for removal from the jury with the judge's approval. The judge has discretion in such instances to determine whether the juror's attitude or experience constitutes sufficient cause for exclusion.

After potential jurors are excluded because of suspect attitudes or experiences, the attorneys are usually granted the opportunity to exclude a few more potential jurors through *peremptory challenges*. In other words, the prosecutor and defense attorney can each exclude a set number of potential jurors based entirely on their own discretion and without offering any reason. Attorneys use their hunches about jurors they think will be hostile to their cases. The judge then draws the names of the appropriate number of remaining potential jurors to form the actual jury.

The process of applying peremptory challenges can further skew the composition of juries. Studies indicate that prosecutors use these challenges disproportionately to exclude minorities and young people from jury service.[47] The U.S. Supreme Court has declared that peremptory challenges cannot be used to exclude jurors because of their race[48] or gender.[49] However, these declarations are largely symbolic because the Court has permitted the exclusion of African-Americans from juries for such questionable reasons as a prosecutor's claim that their curly hair and mustaches made them look "suspicious."[50] In essence, when they are accused of using race or gender to exclude jurors through peremptory challenges, attorneys' actions can survive judicial review if they manufacture a nonracial or nongender-based justification. The Supreme Court has said trial judges can accept such manufactured reasons even if they are silly, superstitious, or irrational.[51] The late Justice Thurgood Marshall of the U.S. Supreme Court advocated the elimination of peremptory challenges because they increase the risk of bias and discrimination by juries. His colleagues on the Supreme Court, however, were willing to preserve the practice because it is a long-standing custom in the American judicial process.[52]

Because social scientists are not permitted to study decision making in real juries except through the use of post-trial interviews in which jurors frequently alter their descriptions and perceptions of events, jury decision making has frequently been studied in experimental settings. Mock juries, often composed of college students, are confronted with decisions that might face a real jury. Although these experimental situations do not precisely replicate actual jury composition and courtroom situations, they do provide insights into people's biases in the roles of jurors. In determining the guilt or innocence of the defendant, jurors must interpret facts, decide which witnesses they believe, and assess the lawyers' persuasiveness. In criminal cases, the jury must find the evidence to indicate guilt "beyond a reasonable doubt" in order to render a guilty verdict. This is a high standard of proof, but the jury's application of the standard varies according to attitudes and biases about the defendants, attorneys, and witnesses. For example, experimental studies indicate that when simulated juries are confronted with identical factual situations but with different cues about the defendant's socioeconomic status, the jurors find poor defendants guilty more often than affluent defendants.[53]

Jurors' predispositions can also operate to favor some defendants. Many police officials believe that in the aftermath of the Rodney King incident and other highly publicized police corruption scandals, juries in some urban areas are reluctant to believe police officers' testimony. Such skepticism about the police may have contributed to O.J. Simpson's acquittal since the truthfulness of Mark Fuhrman, one of the investigating detectives in the case, was strongly challenged by the defense attorneys, and eventually even the prosecution sought to disassociate itself from his testimony.[54]

# SENTENCING

The federal government and several states have attempted to reduce the discretion of judges in sentencing decisions and simultaneously encourage greater consistency in punishing criminal offenders by developing sentencing guidelines for judges to follow. The technique, pioneered by the state of Minnesota and emulated by the federal government and other jurisdictions, consists of creating a standardized grid indicating a limited sentence range based on the particular offense and the prior record of the defendant. Thus, for example, a twice-convicted offender who commits an aggravated robbery as a third crime would be sentenced to imprisonment for a period ranging from thirty-eight to forty-four months under the Minnesota grid.[55] The judge's discretion would be limited to selecting a particular sentence from within the mandated range. Legislatures tend to permit judges to deviate from the mandated sentence range if the judges are willing to write opinions justifying individualized, discretionary sentences. In the federal system, the United States Sentencing Commission, which includes federal judges among its members, monitors sentencing nationwide and develops sentencing guidelines for federal judges to follow. Although judges complain about the restrictions on their discretionary sentencing authority, the sentencing guidelines are an effective means of encouraging greater equity in the punishments applied to convicted offenders. Some judges, especially those in the federal courts, have voiced strong protests against sentencing guidelines because they believe such mandates deprive them of the necessary power to tailor punishments to fit particular offenders.

In court systems without sentencing guidelines, judges possess tremendous discretion in determining sentences of convicted criminal offenders. In most cases, the exercise of the judge's discretion is constrained because the plea agreement worked out between the prosecutor and defense attorney includes an understanding about what the sentence will be. Although some judges actually participate in plea negotiations to encourage resolutions and to provide reassurance about the expected sentence, other judges stay removed from the process. When judges are not involved in the plea negotiations, many defense attorneys seek private meetings with judges to get assurances about what the sentence will be.

The sentence formulated by a judge will be influenced by his or her desire to seek one or more of the purposes underlying punishment—rehabilitation, retribution, deterrence, and incapacitation. Sentences vary dramatically, depending on which purpose the judge chooses to emphasize. A rehabilitation sentence may include counseling or substance abuse treatment with periodic monitoring so that defendants can be released when they have shown sufficient improvement in their attitudes and behavior. By contrast, an incapacitative sentence locks defendants up for long periods of time in order to prevent future crimes, whether or not the crime committed was particularly heinous. Thus, offenders labeled as "career criminals" have received life sentences for a series of offenses, including nonviolent felonies, which by themselves would not have justified such a long sentence. In the 1990s such sentencing laws, especially those known as "three-strikes-and-you're-out" laws, became very popular with the public. The actual application of such laws is highly dependent on the prosecutors' discretion in deciding what charges to file and on the juries' and judges' decisions on whether to convict for the most serious charges. Although such laws are frequently touted for their ability to remove violent criminals from the streets, they can also operate to incapacitate less threatening repeat offenders. In one case, Texas applied a life sentence to a man who on three occasions stole small amounts of money totaling only $225 over the course of six years.[56]

Studies of judges' sentencing decisions indicate that attitudes, backgrounds, and values influence their treatment of convicted offenders. One study compared sentences of men convicted of violating Selective Service laws during the Vietnam War era. It found that judges with certain background characteristics who came from particular political environments tended to sentence draft evaders to harsher prison terms than did different judges from other political environments (e.g., Republican judges harsher than Democratic judges; older judges harsher than younger judges; etc.).[57] Other studies have found linkages between sentencing decisions and judges' conceptions of their appropriate roles, the threat of electoral defeat, and judges' connections to the local community.[58] While some studies have found that white judges were harsher than African-American judges in sentencing African-American offenders, other studies have found similar patterns of sentencing among both groups of judges.[59] If judges have discretion in determining sentences, punishments are likely to fit the individual judge's conceptions of rehabilitation, deterrence, and incapacitation. These conceptions, based on the judge's attitudes and values, may be associated with certain demographic factors (e.g., political party affiliation) but will not necessarily differ according to the judge's race.

The public has so little awareness of the sentences received by most convicted offenders that judges seldom generate controversy by imposing different punishments on offenders who have committed identical crimes. Judges usually claim that one defendant was more apologetic than another or that one defendant possessed more potential for rehabilitation. There is a risk that disparate sentences will attract public criticism if they are applied in highly publicized cases and appear to be based on the defendant's fame, wealth, race, or other identifiable attribute that should be irrelevant to punishment decisions.

## COURTS AND CORRECTIONS

When offenders are sentenced to imprisonment, they leave the court system and are transferred to the custody of the state department of corrections or, if serving less than one year, to the sheriff responsible for the county jail. Depending on the criminal sanction's administrative organization, some sentenced offenders may remain under the control and supervision of the court if punished through probation, restitution (i.e., paying money to reimburse the victim), community service, or fines. The administration of criminal punishments can provide challenges for judges and court administrators whose training and interests are typically focused on the processing of legal cases.

Probation is one of the most frequently applied punishments. Probationers retain their freedom but must live under specified conditions, such as not using alcohol, staying in education and counseling programs, or meeting with a probation officer every week. Violations of the conditions of probation can lead to incarceration for the remaining term of the sentence. Probation officers are frequently under the administrative supervision of the courts rather than the state corrections department. They affect offenders' lives through the exercise of discretion concerning whether to report infractions.

Conditions in a state or federal correctional system can affect courts in two ways. First, if correctional institutions have insufficient space and resources to handle additional prisoners, judges may feel pressured to emphasize alternatives to incarceration (e.g., probation, fines, etc.) as punishments for non-violent offenses, even if they believe that the offenders should be locked up. As a result, judges may find themselves helpless pawns in political battles between governors, legislators, and interest groups concerning the need, or lack thereof, for devoting additional state expenditures to corrections.[60]

Second, since judges are the primary interpreters and protectors of constitutional rights, convicted offenders file thousands of lawsuits every year alleging the existence of unconstitutional, cruel, and unusual conditions in prisons and jails. These lawsuits, in effect, ask judges to intervene in the administration of correctional institutions in order to change policies and practices. Frequently, these lawsuits are filed by prisoners in state correctional institutions who want federal judges to investigate and reform a state department of corrections. Relatively few prisoner civil rights lawsuits are successful, but occasionally such a lawsuit will lead a judge to issue intrusive, controversial orders to significantly alter the living conditions or practices in prisons and jails.[61]

## CONCLUSION

The American public places significant reliance on courts for addressing crime problems. Courts are responsible for determining suspects' guilt or innocence while simultaneously protecting their constitutional rights. Moreover, courts are the institutional setting in which criminal punishments are formulated, announced, and, in some instances (e.g., probation, fines, restitution) implemented. As court processes determine citizens' fates by deciding which offenders will lose their liberty or lives, decision making is not guided by neutral principles of law. Instead, criminal justice processes are shaped by external political influences and the courts' political attributes.

Criminal laws that provide the basis for courts' authority are enacted through political processes and value choices advanced by elected officials. The resources available for processing criminal cases and punishing offenders are similarly determined by political processes and politicians' partisan policy choices. In the justice system, individuals' fates are determined by cumulative discretionary decisions by the police, prosecutors, jurors, and judges. Legal rules contribute to the framework and environment in which decisions are made, but the attitudes and values of authoritative decision makers are the influences that significantly shape case outcomes. Among these decision makers, prosecutors and judges are frequently elected officials whose decisions may be influenced by their concerns about protecting their own political futures. They may also be concerned about ensuring smooth case processing by maintaining effective exchange relationships with other attorneys and judges who work within a courthouse. Other decision makers may also be influenced by their self-interest. For example, police officers may use their arrest powers in ways that affirm their own authority. Defense attorneys' recommendations to clients concerning the acceptance of guilty pleas may be influenced by a desire to speed case processing and quickly collect available fees.

The recognition of political influences in the criminal justice process does not mean that the criminal courts have failed to fulfill their proper functions. Instead, the illumination of judicial politics demonstrates that the third branch of government, like its two counterparts, is composed of human beings whose authoritative decisions are inevitably influenced by attitudes, values, and policy preferences. As the discussion of civil litigation in chapter 5 will illustrate, the accessibility and impact of courts and the judicial process are the result of complex interacting factors rather than predictable products generated by the rules of law.

# NOTES

1. "Chief Justice Recaps 1995 in Year-end Report," *The Third Branch* 28 (January 1996): 5.
2. Randall Samborn, "Accelerating Caseloads Threaten to Swamp Courts," *National Law Journal*, 9 May 1994, p. A11.
3. Stuart A. Scheingold, *The Politics of Law and Order* (New York: Longman, 1984), pp. 54–57.
4. Lawrence Friedman, "Law, Lawyers, and Popular Culture," *Yale Law Journal* 98 (1989): 1588.
5. Richard J. Bonnie and Charles H. Whitebread II, *The Marihuana Conviction: A History of Marihuana Prohibition in the United States* (Charlottesville, VA: University of Virginia Press, 1974), p. 36.
6. Albert DiChiara and John F. Galliher, "Dissonance and Contradictions in the Origins of Marihuana Decriminalization," *Law and Society Review* 28 (1994): 41–77.
7. See Charles E. Silberman, *Criminal Violence, Criminal Justice* (New York: Vintage Books, 1978), p. 138.
8. John Irwin, *The Jail: Managing the Underclass in American Society* (Berkeley, CA: University of California Press, 1985), p. 23.

9. Ibid., pp. 23–41.

10. See Ronald C. Kramer, "Is Corporate Crime Serious Crime? Criminal Justice and Corporate Crime Control," *Journal of Contemporary Criminal Justice* 2 (June 1984): 2–10.

11. Samuel Walker, *Sense and Nonsense about Crime*, 2nd ed. (Pacific Grove, CA: Brooks/Cole, 1989), pp. 250–51.

12. George F. Cole, *The American System of Criminal Justice*, 4th ed. (Monterey, CA: Brooks/Cole, 1986), pp. 135–40.

13. See Herbert L. Packer, *The Limits of the Criminal Sanction* (Stanford, CA: Stanford University Press, 1968).

14. Carla Gaskins, "Felony Case Processing in State Courts, 1986," *Bureau of Justice Statistics Special Report* (February 1990): 1.

15. Ibid.

16. The discussion of criminal justice system characteristics is drawn from the work of George Cole. *See* Cole, *The American System of Criminal Justice*, pp. 5–33.

17. Ibid., pp. 143–44.

18. Samuel Walker, " 'Broken Windows' and Fractured History: The Use and Misuse of History in Recent Police Patrol Analysis," *Justice Quarterly* 1 (1984): 84.

19. Christopher E. Smith, "Police Professionalism and the Rights of Criminal Defendants," *Criminal Law Bulletin* 26 (1990): 156–58.

20. Seth Mydans, "The 81 Seconds That Shaped 2 Years Return to Center Stage in Los Angeles," *New York Times* 22 (February 1993): p. A12.

21. Michael Lipsky, "Street-Level Bureaucracy and the Analysis of Urban Reform," *Urban Affairs Quarterly* 6 (1971): 391–409.

22. Douglas A. Smith and Christy A. Visher, "Street-Level Justice: Situational Determinants of Police Arrest Decisions," *Social Problems* 29 (1981): 175.

23. See Forest Dill, "Discretion, Exchange, and Social Control: Bail Bondsmen in Criminal Courts, " *Law and Society Review* 11 (1976): 644–74.

24. Malcolm Feeley, *The Process Is the Punishment* (New York: Russell Sage Foundation, 1979), pp. 199–243.

25. See William Landes, "Legality and Reality: Some Evidence in Criminal Procedure," *Journal of Legal Studies* 3 (1974): 287–337; Stevens H. Clarke and Gary G. Koch, "The Influence of Income and Other Factors on Whether Criminal Defendants Go to Prison," *Law and Society Review* 11 (1976): 57–92.

26. See Malcolm Feeley, *Court Reform on Trial* (New York: Basic Books, 1983), pp. 40–79.

27. Cole, *The American System of Criminal Justice*, p. 285.

28. John Buchanan, "Police-Prosecutor Teams: Innovations in Several Jurisdictions," *National Institute of Justice Reports* (May/June 1989): pp. 2–8.

29. James Eisenstein and Herbert Jacob, *Felony Justice: An Organizational Analysis of Criminal Courts* (Boston, MA: Little, Brown, 1977), pp. 19–39.

30. See James Eisenstein, Roy Flemming, and Peter Nardulli, *The Contours of Justice* (Boston: Little, Brown, 1984).

31. Paul Wice, *Criminal Lawyers: An Endangered Species* (Beverly Hills, CA: Sage, 1978), p. 29.

32. *Gideon v. Wainwright*, 372 U.S. 335 (1963).

33. Alissa Pollitz Worden and Robert E. Worden, "Local Politics and the Provision of Indigent Defense Counsel," *Law and Policy* 11 (1989): 401–24.

34. U.S. Department of Justice, "Criminal Defense for the Poor, 1986," *Bureau of Justice Statistics Bulletin*, (September 1988): pp. 3–4.

35. Robert L. Spangeberg, Beverly Lee, Michael Battaglia, Patricia Smith, A. David Davis, *National Criminal Defense Systems Study* (Washington, D.C.: Bureau of Justice Statistics, 1986), p. 35.

36. Robert Hermann, Eric Single, John Boston, *Counsel for the Poor: Criminal Defense in Urban America* (Lexington, MA: Lexington, 1971), p. 67.

37. Spangeberg et al., *National Criminal Defense Systems Study*, p.36.

38. Victoria L. Swigert and Ronald A. Farrell, "Normal Homicides and the Law," *American Sociological Review* 42 (1977): 24–25.

39. Clarke and Koch, "The Influence of Income and Other Factors on Whether Criminal Defendants Go to Prison," p. 83.

40. See Roger Hanson and Joy Chapper, *Indigent Defense Systems* (Williamsburg, VA: National Center for State Courts, 1991).

41. Jonathan D. Casper, "Did You Have a Lawyer When You Went to Court? No, I Had a Public Defender," *Yale Review of Law and Social Action* 1 (1971): 4–9.

42. Ibid.

43. See Roy B. Flemming, "Client Games: Defense Attorney Perspectives on Their Relations with Criminal Clients," *American Bar Foundation Research Journal* (1986): 253–77.

44. Ulysses Torassa, "Public Defenders Do Little Public Defending," *Cleveland Plain Dealer*, 27 June 1993, p. 3B.

45. Valerie P. Hans and Neil Vidmar, *Judging the Jury* (New York: Plenum Press, 1986), p. 54.

46. Christopher E. Smith, "Imagery, Politics, and Jury Reform," *Akron Law Review* 28 (1994): 77–95.

47. Ibid., p. 75.

48. *Batson v. Kentucky*, 476 U.S. 79 (1986); *Georgia v. McCollum*, 505 U.S. ____, 112 S. Ct. 2348 (1992).

49. *J.E.B. v. Alabama* ex rel. T.B., 511 U.S. ____, 114 S. Ct. 1419 (1994).

50. *Purkett v. Elem*, 115 S. Ct. 1769 (1995).

51. Ibid.

52. See *Holland v. Illinois*, 493 U.S. 474 (1990).

53. James M. Gleason and Victor A. Harris, "Race, Socio-Economic Status, and Perceived Similarity as Determinants of Judgments by Simulated Jurors," *Social Behavior and Personality* 3 (1975): 175–80; James M. Gleason and Victor A. Harris, "Group Discussion and Defendant's Socio-Economic Status as Determinants of Judgments by Simulated Jurors," *Journal of Applied Social Psychology* 6 (1976): 181–91. Another study found no significant discrimination: Robert I. Gordon and Paul D. Jacobs, "Forensic Psychology: Perception of Guilt and Income," *Perceptual and Motor Skills* 28 (1969): 143–46.

54. Richard Lacayo, "An Ugly End to It All," *Time*, 9 October 1995, p. 34–35.

55. Todd R. Clear and George F. Cole, *American Corrections* (Monterey, CA: Brooks/Cole, 1986), p. 121.

56. *Rummel v. Estelle*, 445 U.S. 263 (1980).

57. Beverly Blair Cook, "Sentencing Behavior of Federal Judges: Draft Cases—1972," *University of Cincinnati Law Review* 42 (1973): 597–633.

58. James Gibson, "Environmental Constraints on the Behavior of Judges: A Representational Model of Judicial Decision-Making," *Law and Society Review* 14 (1980): 343–70. *See also* Gregory Caldeira, "Courts and Public Opinion," in *American Courts: A Critical Assessment*, eds. John B. Gates and Charles A. Johnson (Washington, D.C.: Congressional Quarterly, 1991), pp. 316–19.

59. Samuel Walker, Cassia Spohn, and Miriam DeLeone, *The Color of Justice: Race, Ethnicity, and Crime in America* (Belmont, CA: Wadsworth, 1996), pp. 168–70.

60. Judy Daubenmier, "Legislators Dispute Prison Overcrowding," *State News* (East Lansing, MI), 29 January 1996, p. 9A.

61. Christopher E. Smith, *Courts and Public Policy* (Chicago: Nelson-Hall, 1993), pp. 93–109.

# Chapter 5

# Civil Justice Processes

C ourts are forums for airing disputes between individuals, groups, and organizations. In civil cases, one party requests a judicial declaration concerning allocation of property, compensation for injury, performance of a contract, or some disputed matter. Although courts function as a branch of government by providing a forum for litigation, this forum is not equally accessible to all citizens and corporations. In order to make effective use of civil litigation, litigants need resources such as time and money. If a litigant has a dire need for immediate compensation after suffering a personal injury or property loss, he or she may not be able to wait for the lengthy litigation process to run its course over many months or even years. Such a litigant may settle the claim quickly for immediate payment, thereby accepting a sum other than that necessary for actual compensation, simply because the litigation process is so time-consuming, burdensome, and in many cases, the source of uncertain outcomes. Effective litigants also need sufficient financial resources to hire attorneys and sustain the many litigation expenses.

## CIVIL CASES

As a formal matter, the initiating party (e.g., individual, interest group, business, or government agency) seeks a favorable decision by a judge or jury. In fact, however, the judicial process does not usually produce such a result. The primary function of courts is to *process* disputes rather than to *resolve* them. Just as most criminal cases result in a negotiated plea bargain, most civil cases leave the judicial process after a negotiated settlement between the parties. For example, when one cadet died and others were seriously injured during training at the Massachusetts State Police Academy in 1988, their families sued the state for compensation. Although the lawsuit ostensibly sought a judicial decision finding the state at fault for the injuries (and death), the injured cadets and their families settled their cases in 1990. The widow of the deceased cadet accepted one million dollars, and the injured cadets accepted individual settlements in excess of thirty thousand dollars.[1] Were these disputes resolved? It seems unlikely that the widow of the cadet who died from kidney problems due to a lack of water during physical training would feel compensated by a monetary sum for the loss of her spouse. Instead, the disputes were processed. The courts created a structured environment with a set of rules and procedures that facilitated the payment of compensation as a formal conclusion to the dispute. Negotiated settlements may or may not personally satisfy all individuals involved, but they do enable each side as well as the judicial system to move ahead with other matters.

The settlement process is sometimes guided directly by the judicial officers, although litigants frequently negotiate settlements on their own. Even without intervention by judges, settlement discussions are inevitably influenced by the threat of continued court action, with its potential for uncertain "winner-take-all" outcomes. Litigants feel pressure to negotiate compromises because they fear losing in a trial. The threat of an adverse judicial decision looms over all litigants. Thus, the processing of civil cases has been characterized as "bargaining in the shadow of the law."[2] As the scheduled trial date approaches, parties in civil litigation increase the pressure on themselves to reach a compromise because of their mutual but unspoken fear that a judge or jury might award everything to the opponent. The civil justice process does not merely provide rules and procedures for processing disputes, it also creates an environment that may induce disputants to settle conflicts that they were originally unwilling or unable to settle.

In criminal cases, the government seeks to enforce specific laws that prescribe formal punishments for unlawful behavior. Despite receiving inordinate attention from television and the news media, the distinctive characteristics of criminal cases (i.e., government action against one or more individuals and laws mandating formal punishment) apply in a minority of cases. In general, all other cases are classified as civil cases in which the courts process disputes between two parties. In 1992, there were 19.7 million civil cases filed in state courts compared to 13.2 million criminal cases.[3] Civil cases comprise an even greater proportion of the federal courts' caseload. In 1995, there were 248,300 civil cases filed in federal courts and only 45,800 criminal cases were filed during the same year.[4]

The government may be one of the parties in a civil case, but unlike the criminal context—in which the government is always the initiator (prosecutor)—in civil cases the government can be either the initiator (plaintiff) or the target (defendant) of the lawsuit. As chapter 10 will discuss in greater detail, interest groups sometimes sue the government to seek favorable judicial decisions that will advance their policy preferences. Usually, civil cases stem from disputes between two private parties, which can be individuals, businesses, and various other kinds of organizations. Plaintiffs are often individuals seeking compensation for injuries while defendants are often insurance companies who have accepted the obligation of defending their individual and business customers. For example, in a study of jury trials concerning tort, contract, and real property cases in the nation's seventy-five largest counties, 88 percent of the plaintiffs were individuals and 50 percent of the defendants were insurance companies or other businesses.[5]

## TYPES OF CASES

Civil cases involve many areas of law. *Tort* suits seek compensation for injuries to persons or property. Such legal actions may pursue compensation for a broad range of alleged injuries, from harm to one's reputation caused by slanderous statements to personal injury and wrongful death resulting from intentional actions or accidents. A single event may give rise to both a criminal case and a tort suit. Because the criminal law is aimed primarily at punishing improper behavior, some crime victims file separate civil tort suits to seek compensation for personal injuries inflicted by the criminal offenders.

In O.J. Simpson's case, after Simpson was acquitted on charges of murdering his wife and Ron Goldman, the families of the victims filed lawsuits against Simpson. Although such lawsuits will nearly always be successful after the offender is convicted because the perpetrator has admitted responsibility or been found guilty by a jury, crime victims frequently do not bother pursuing these actions because many criminal offenders have no money with which to compensate their victims. In Simpson's case, however, the tort lawsuit created the possibility of recovering a substantial monetary award. Moreover, it provided an opportunity to further investigate and potentially punish Simpson for the crimes. It is also easier to prevail in a civil case because the civil judicial process is different than the criminal judicial process. In Simpson's criminal case, the prosecutors, in order to convict Simpson, would have had to gain a unanimous guilty-beyond-a-reasonable-doubt verdict—a very high standard of proof—from twelve jurors. By contrast, the families' success in the civil case would require only nine out of twelve jurors to agree that it was more likely than not that Simpson killed the two people.

*Contract* actions seek either to recover damages for the failure of one party to fulfill obligations under a reciprocal agreement or to require that party to carry out the contractual agreement. Thus, the threat of judicial enforcement of contract law keeps professional athletes, for example, from freely changing teams after they have signed an agreement to play for a particular team for a specified salary.

Other common types of civil cases are also filed primarily in state courts: *probate*, the settlement of wills and distribution of property left by a deceased person; *real estate*, the sale and transfer of land, houses, and other real property; and *domestic relations*, the dissolution of marriages, custody of minor children, child support, and adoption. Domestic relations cases are the fastest growing segment of civil caseloads, comprising one-third of the 19.7 million state court civil cases in 1992.[6]

As with criminal cases, the overwhelming majority of civil cases are filed in state rather than federal courts. There are two primary circumstances under which torts, contracts, and other traditional civil cases can be filed in federal courts. First, such cases can enter federal courts if they meet the requirements for "diversity of citizenship"—in other words, if the case stems from a dispute between residents of two different states, *and* the money or property in question has a value of at least fifty thousand dollars. Second, if the United States government is suing or being sued, the case will be heard in federal court. In addition, a variety of other civil actions can be initiated in federal courts when the underlying claims are based on federal statutes or the U.S. Constitution. For example, federal laws govern certain subjects that may be sources of disputes: labor disputes between unions and companies; employment discrimination based on race, gender, age, or other factors; pollution of the air and water; and false and deceptive advertising of products. Civil cases concerning such subjects may be initiated by private citizens, but other cases are initiated by the federal government agencies responsible for protecting the public against potentially harmful conduct by businesses and private citizens.

## FROM DISPUTES TO LITIGATION: INITIATING THE CIVIL JUDICIAL PROCESS

Although some commentators have characterized Americans as "the most litigious people in the world,"[7] this perceived level of litigation is generated by only a fraction of the conflicts in American society. Most disputes are *not* taken to court. Thus, civil litigation embodies only the minority of disputes in which litigants' motivations, expectations, and resources permit them to seek judicial assistance.

Research on civil litigation has developed the model of the "dispute pyramid" to describe disputes and their relation to the judicial process.[8] At the base of the pyramid are numerous injuries, perceived or unperceived, for which people may potentially seek compensation or other remedies. At the top of the pyramid are the relatively few cases filed in court. The middle of the pyramid consists of the various stages at which grievances stop moving toward the judicial process.

Disputes in American society develop from the myriad interactions among citizens. In Marc Galanter's characterization, "[D]isputes are drawn from a vast sea of events, encounters, collisions, rivalries, disappointments, discomforts, and injuries."[9] As Galanter has noted, disputes are based on individuals' perceptions, expectations, and reactions to the contacts that they have with others: "Disputes are not discrete events like births or deaths; they are more like such constructs as illnesses and friendships, composed in part of the perceptions of those who participate in and observe them."[10] For example, if your neighbor takes your lawnmower from your garage and uses it without asking you, the neighbor's action may or may not generate a dispute. The development of a dispute depends not on the neighbor's action in itself, but on your reaction to the use of the lawnmower. Are you and your neighbor close friends? If so, you may not challenge him or her even if you are annoyed about this casual borrowing. Maintaining a positive relationship with the neighbor may be very important to you. Do you often borrow items from each other without asking? If so, the neighbor's actions— although objectionable when described to an outside observer—fall within the realm of expected behavior. These and other considerations will determine whether the borrowed lawnmower ignites a dispute. Similar considerations determine whether individuals will pursue claims against others in the myriad conflicts that are potential sources of litigation.

At the base of the dispute pyramid—or perhaps more accurately, on the ground beneath the pyramid—are unperceived injuries. The perception of injury requires knowledge and expectations of entitlements. Many people do not recognize that they have suffered an injury that may be remediable. When consumers buy a defective product, for example, those with higher incomes are much more likely to complain. Lower status people often accept such events as their own bad luck, a misfortune that cannot be remedied.[11]

Out of the pool of injuries, only a small portion will be recognized. Perceived injuries for which a person attributes fault to another person or entity are "grievances."[12] A person must believe that someone else is to blame for the perceived injury in order for it to develop into a lawsuit. Some of these grievances will be voiced to the perceived offenders. These grievances become "claims." Other grievances never advance because the injured person believes that the issue is not worth pursuing or does not wish to generate conflict with whomever they blame for the injury—especially if that person is a friend, family member, or co-worker. Although conflicts arise between friends, neighbors, and others with continuing relationships, litigation usually is reserved for conflicts with strangers or between people who are severing their relationship:

> In the American setting, litigation tends to be between parties who are strangers. Either they never had a mutually beneficial continuing relationship, as in the typical automobile injury case, or their relationship—marital, commercial, or organizational—is ruptured. In either case, there is no anticipated future relationship. In the American setting, unlike some others, resort to litigation is viewed as an irreparable breach of the relationship.[13]

Some claims terminate because, confronted with the grievance, the offending party voluntarily apologizes, provides compensation, or otherwise satisfies the injured person. Full-blown disputes arise when the grievance is voiced to the offending party in the form of a claim, and the offender refuses to provide satisfaction.[14] Some disputes proceed no further because claimants are deterred by the costs of litigation. Some claimants do not believe that continuing the dispute will yield worthwhile results. Other claimants experience self-doubt and wonder whether they are actually at fault in the conflict.

Research indicates that there are differences in the types of grievances that are likely to be pursued depending on the feelings of the aggrieved party, the relationship between the perceived victim and the alleged perpetrator, and the environment in which the injury occurred. Interviews with people who have been victimized by discrimination reveal the many psychological barriers to the pursuit of claims. According to Kristin Bumiller's research on discrimination cases, aggrieved individuals often decline to pursue disputes because they do not wish to be cast into the role of "victim."[15] In their minds, pursuing a discrimination complaint would transform "a social conflict into a psychological contest to reconcile a positive self-image with the image of the victim as powerless and defeated."[16] Claimants may resist perpetuating and publicizing a dispute because such actions constitute an admission of their own powerlessness. Thus, according to Bumiller, "[I]njured persons reluctantly employ the label of discrimination because they shun the role of the victim, and they fear legal intervention will disrupt the delicate balance between themselves and their opponents."[17] For example, in 1991 when law professor Anita Hill alleged that she had been sexually harassed several years earlier by Supreme Court nominee Clarence Thomas, Thomas's supporters in the U.S. Senate expressed disbelief that a victim of harassment would not immediately proceed with formal charges at the time the alleged harassment occurred. In fact, Hill's behavior was consistent with that of discrimination victims because her desire to end the injurious conduct did not necessarily outweigh her fear that her claim would lead to professional retaliation or otherwise adversely affect her career. Hill's allegations against Thomas did not stop his appointment to the Supreme Court, but they did spur a significant increase in the filing of sexual harassment claims nationwide, providing an indication that others who felt victimized were similarly wary about coming forward.[18]

When disputes occur within environments with dispute-processing mechanisms, such as in the employment context, they may be handled by a union shop steward or a company grievance committee rather than through litigation.[19] One study indicated that, particularly in poorer communities, people may resort to confrontational self-help to settle disputes—including the use of retaliatory property damage or even violence.[20]

## The Role of Lawyers

In order to push disputes toward actual civil litigation, people must seek the advice and assistance of lawyers. In effect, lawyers are "gatekeepers" who determine which cases enter the judicial process and which cases are stopped at the courthouse door. Lawyers play an important role in transforming disputes into legal cases. They must translate people's disputes into legal terminology in order to pursue cases in court. Not all disputes, however, can be translated into a form that courts will accept. For example, a student may not like the way a professor glares at him during class. The student may genuinely feel uncomfortable and believe that his classroom performance is being adversely affected. If the professor, informed of the student's discomfort, maintains her stern demeanor, the student may wish to pursue the matter with an attorney. However, a professor's stern visage in the classroom raises no *cause of action*, no plausible legal claim. Despite the student's genuine discomfort, courts will not process such a claim, and a lawyer will not pursue such a case.

In other instances, previous court cases prove that it would be pointless to translate specific disputes into legal cases. For example, if a man tried to institute a claim against a police department for refusing to hire him because of the length of his hair, the man might be genuinely and legitimately angered about a discriminatory criterion with little or no relation to his qualifications. Unfortunately for this man, a lawyer would explain that nothing could be accomplished by pursuing the case in court. Civil rights laws cover only specified categories of discrimination (e.g., race, color, national origin, etc.), and courts have already declared that law enforcement employers may discriminate against men because of the length of their hair.[21] Although lawyers can be creative in their arguments linking new kinds of claims to recognized legal concepts, some claims simply do not fit within the contours of contemporary legal principles.

Legal concepts in general are sufficiently malleable to make many arguments plausible. Because judges determine the course of the law, however, the lawyer must consider whether the particular judges who will decide the case will be amenable to new arguments. For example, because the U.S. Supreme Court was dominated by conservative Republicans in the 1990s, there was little incentive for lawyers to pursue new arguments for the expansion of the rights of criminal defendants. Thus, lawyers may discourage claimants from pursuing certain disputes. For many years, people with enough money could pay a lawyer to present almost any argument in court, but in the 1980s judges began to assess financial penalties on lawyers and litigants who brought frivolous claims. Lawyers now have reason to discourage clients and to decline disputes that do not fit with established legal principles.[22]

Lawyers' self-interest can also affect their willingness to transform disputes into legal cases. Because many lawyers charge more than one hundred dollars per hour for their services, the cost of legal fees will quickly outstrip any potential recovery in cases that concern a few thousand dollars or less. Although the claimant may have a "winning" argument, a lawyer may discourage the claimant because the case will not produce sufficient financial compensation for the attorney. In some instances, a client may still wish to hire the lawyer and may be willing to pay fees greater than the potential recovery because the client's motivations involve goals (e.g., revenge, vindication of principle, etc.) other than financial compensation. In contingency fee cases—most common in personal injury tort cases—lawyers receive a specific portion (usually 30 percent) of the recovery from a court victory or a negotiated settlement. If the injury was modest, the lawyer may discourage the client or may decline to accept valid legal claims because the potential recovery is inadequate to deserve an investment of the lawyer's time. In addition to calculations of lawyers' compensation, the litigant must consider court fees and litigation costs. Courts charge fees as high as $220, and litigants must also pay for the costs of expert witnesses, investigators, and other support personnel. These cost factors provide an additional deterrent to the pursuit of claims that may fail to produce significant financial rewards.

Sometime lawyers' financial calculations may clash with claimants' underlying motivations. In medical malpractice cases, for example, the claimant may hope that the doctor will lose his or her license to practice medicine. In discrimination cases, a victim may wish to be vindicated by having the world recognize that he or she unfairly suffered from illegal discrimination. Such personal goals rarely attract lawyers' enthusiastic support. Lawyers in private practice must pay monthly rent for their offices, pay salaries and benefits for their staff, and generate enough additional revenue for their own salaries. Not surprisingly, financial issues loom large for lawyers as they consider taking on specific cases. As a result, some claimants cannot find attorneys to present their claims in court.

The financial incentives that motivate lawyers have detrimental effects on poor and middle-class people. As a result, if legal services and access to courts' time and attention are regarded as valuable resources and services associated with a branch of government, these benefits flow disproportionately to wealthy individuals and businesses that can afford to take advantage of the judicial branch. Although a person or business willing and able to pay lawyers' hourly fees can secure assistance in pursuing civil litigation concerning any legally recognizable claim, less affluent people will have difficulty securing the assistance of counsel. If a less affluent person is injured in an airplane crash, lawyers will jump at the chance to share in the expected substantial recovery. Such cases may produce quick settlements that can reward a lawyer with hundreds of thousands of dollars for a few weeks' work. In ordinary cases of employment discrimination, property damage, and defective products—in which the financial rewards are uncertain and modest—lawyers are less likely to accept the cases. As discussed in chapter 3, free legal services for civil cases are available only to the poorest citizens and are confined to limited kinds of cases, so most low- and middle-income people experience difficulty in bringing their disputes to court.

## The Dispute Pyramid

It is evident from the foregoing discussion that civil litigation embodies only a small portion of the injuries occurring in society that could potentially enter

**Figure 5.1: Typical Dispute Pyramid for 1,000 Grievances Worth Approximately $1,000 or More.**

| | |
|---|---|
| Court Filings | 50 |
| Lawyers Consulted | -103- |
| Disputes | - - - - -449- - - - - |
| Claims | - - - - - - - - -718- - - - - - - - - |
| Grievances | - - - - - - - - - - - -1,000- - - - - - - - - - - - |

*Source:* Richard E. Miller and Austin Sarat, "Grievances, Claims, and Disputes: Assessing the Adversary Culture," *Law and Society Review* 15 (1980–81): 544. Reprinted by permission of the Law and Society Association.

the civil justice system. A picture of the dispute pyramid was developed by Richard Miller and Austin Sarat based on a survey of one thousand households in five states. Although this limited survey cannot offer a complete representation of disputes in American society,[23] it does provide a picture of the filtering processes that limit the number of claims that eventually reach the courts. Based on "middle-range" grievances worth approximately one thousand dollars or more, Miller and Sarat developed a typical dispute pyramid, illustrated in figure 5.1. The large number of grievances gradually shrinks as the dispute moves through each stage of the process toward the filing of a lawsuit. Typically, only 10 percent of disputants discuss their conflicts with lawyers, and only half of those discussions generate lawsuits.

The shape of the dispute pyramid changes for different kinds of cases because of the nature of claims and the relationships between disputants. For example, property disputes over real estate ownership are rarely amenable to compromise and therefore require a decision by a judge.[24] Out of one thousand discrimination grievances, fewer than three hundered were voiced to the offending party as claims, and fewer than one-third of the claims were satisfied voluntarily; only twenty-nine disputants sought an attorney's assistance; and only eight cases were actually filed in court.[25] The limited pursuit of such grievances may reflect the low status, lack of resources, and weak bargaining position of people who feel victimized by discrimination. In discrimination cases, as explained earlier, people may wish to avoid casting themselves in the role of "victims," thereby acknowledging their powerlessness.[26] By contrast, divorced couples apparently have few inhibitions about pursuing grievances concerning money, property, and other matters. Out of 1,000 post-divorce grievances, nearly 900 were voiced to the offending party as claims, only 100 were satisfied voluntarily by the offending parties, nearly 600 were brought to attorneys, and 451 were transformed into legal cases.[27] In such cases, there is little concern about preserving a future relationship so the parties pursue their grievances more freely and vigorously. Thus, the development of civil litigation varies according to the relationships, motivations, and resources of the disputants.

## Civil Litigation in American Society

The nature of civil litigation cases varies according to the historical moment and social environment in which people's interactions produce conflicts. For example, in a community of farmers, there may be disputes about property lines and the purchase or sale of agricultural equipment and products. Such disputes reflect the nature of interactions between people in that community. By contrast, business people in a large city may have disputes about financial investments, loans, and various kinds of commercial transactions since these subjects are the focus of their interactions.

Long-term studies of courts show the relationship between societal developments and litigation. A study of cases in the St. Louis, Missouri courts from 1820 to 1970 demonstrated the change in the nature of court cases as society changed.[28] In the early nineteenth century, litigation involved unpaid debt and real estate because the banking system was weak and the process of property acquisition on the western frontier led to many disputes. Commercial development and industrialization in the later nineteenth century gave rise to commercial contract litigation. At the close of the century, as legislatures began more extensive regulation of businesses, the need for judicial rulings concerning commerce declined. The twentieth century introduced a rise in tort cases, initially from injuries to industrial and railroad workers and subsequently from automobile accidents and other consequences of technological development. The twentieth century also witnessed an increase in family law cases, especially divorce, as lifestyles, family relationships, and norms for social behavior changed in a rapidly evolving society.[29]

Civil law and litigation developed in conjunction with changes in the relationships among private entities as American society became increasingly complex. People's interactions were previously focused on family members, neighbors, and others who shared a stake in maintaining stability in small communities and social networks. Disputes were shaped and moderated by a strong desire to preserve future relationships. In contrast, the close of the twentieth century finds many Americans lacking personal relationships with their neighbors while engaging in daily interactions (and transactions) with distant strangers and corporations via telephone and computer. The complex nature of modern interactions changes both the sources for dispute and the individual's sense of personal connection (or lack thereof) with transaction partners. If a neighbor sells someone a sick cow, there may be an incentive for both the buyer and seller to work out an arrangement to stop the incident from blossoming into a dispute. If a telemarketing firm in a distant state sells a consumer a defective product, it may be more difficult to process the resulting dispute without a threat of litigation. Thus, the existence of civil litigation as a potentially threatening expense, as well as actual litigation itself, may play a role in shaping contemporary disputants' interactions.

Contemporary litigation, however, often involves disputes between private entities and government, because government has become a dominant actor in the society of the twentieth century. A study of the federal courts found that "the presence of governmental activity is a central factor in an explanation of court filings in federal district courts."[30] Higher levels of court filings in specific districts are associated with the presence in those districts of government agencies involved in supervisory and regulatory activities that bring government into contact and conflict with citizens. The significant growth in civil case filings in the federal courts (e.g., from 87,321 in 1970 to 248,300 in 1995)[31] reflects the expansion of government regulation and benefit allocation into new spheres of American life and also the increased receptivity of the federal judiciary to cases of discrimination, prisoners' rights, and claims asserting individuals' constitutional rights.

The growth in the federal court caseload has often been cited as evidence of the purported "litigation explosion" burdening the court system.[32] Although it may be true that Americans increasingly expect, in Lawrence Friedman's terminology, "total justice," which allocates blame and dispenses compensation for perceived injuries,[33] the foregoing discussion of the dispute pyramid calls into question the extent to which these expectations actually translate into litigation. Moreover, the growth in federal case filings is potentially deceptive because of the attendant increase in the number of judges. During the twentieth century, the number of cases filed per judge peaked during the 1920s, declined dramatically during the 1930s and, after another dip during the 1950s, increased steadily thereafter, while remaining well below the peak levels of the 1920s.[34] In addition, the evidence from studies of state courts challenges the perception that contemporary American society is uniquely litigious:

> [I]t is clear that St. Louisans do not exhibit wanton litigiousness at any time during the twentieth century. In fact, both individuals and merchants were much more litigious before the Civil War than in any period since, and industrial litigants' rate of posting claims peaked during the formative years of the Industrial Revolution, approximately 1840 to 1865. If there has been a litigation explosion in St. Louis among any constituency, the blast was heard well over 100 years ago. . . . Recent hysteria regarding our litigation "problems" seems very much over drawn.[35]

The dire warnings from contemporary commentators about a litigation "crisis" may be attributable to excessive focus on federal court statistics, which are the most readily available and widely disseminated data on litigation, as well as increased media attention to large and unusual cases.[36] In 1992, the number of state civil cases concerning torts, contracts, and real estate actually declined.[37] Because the content and rate of civil litigation reflect developments in society, those who decry the perceived "explosion" of litigation may actually be objecting to underlying societal changes.

# THE PROCESSES OF CIVIL LITIGATION

Lawyers not only shape the client's underlying grievance in accordance with legal theories, they also guide the claim through the formal procedures of civil litigation. The federal and state court systems each have their own rules of procedure that dictate the form and timing of each step in the litigation process. In the federal system, each individual district court has its own additional rules for litigation within that district.[38] If litigants deviate from proper procedures, their claims may be dismissed by the court. Because the various rules of civil procedure include many technical requirements, it is difficult for people to present their own cases successfully without either the assistance of an attorney or detailed knowledge of legal processes and legal research techniques.

Cases are initiated by the plaintiff, the person or business that claims to have suffered a legally remediable injury, filing a *complaint*. The complaint lists the plaintiff's version of the facts underlying the injury, the law on which the claim is based, and a request for compensation or other remedy. In filing the complaint, the plaintiff must pay a filing fee ($120 in the federal courts) plus additional fees to have the complaint "served" or delivered to the defendant. Filing fees in state courts range from $20 in West Virginia and Puerto Rico to $220 in Cook County, Illinois.[39] The initial burden of court costs in addition to attorneys' fees deters speculative claims or claims worth little money. The costs also deter less affluent people who cannot afford the financial expense of litigation.

The complaint must be composed and phrased in accordance with court rules. Although the technical requirements for filing "pleadings" (i.e., the complaint and subsequent filings) make lawyers appear indispensable, in fact, many lawyers use standard fill-in-the-blank complaint forms or they simply copy sample complaints out of "form books" that are, unbeknownst to most lay people, available in law libraries.

The complaint must be filed in the proper court as specified by the rules of civil procedure, usually in the district in which the conflict occurred or in the district in which the defendant resides. Jurisdictional rules and requirements for "service of process" (delivery of papers to the defendant) shape and limit litigants' options. A plaintiff cannot always sue a defendant in the plaintiff's hometown courthouse. The intent of the rules is to prevent defendants from being harassed and disadvantaged by having to travel far from where they live or work to defend themselves. However, one consequence of these rules may be to limit the ability of plaintiffs with limited resources to sue certain defendants.

After the complaint is served, the defendant has a limited time period to respond with an *answer*. In the answer the defendant specifies which claims and facts will be accepted and which will be disputed. The defendant also has the opportunity to file a *counterclaim* by initiating an action against the plaintiff or to file a *cross-claim* by asserting that some other defendant should be held responsible in the matter. The defendant may also file an immediate *motion* for dismissal on the grounds that the case does not assert an officially recognizable claim or has been filed in the wrong court. A motion is a request for an immediate ruling by a judge on a matter related to the case. Motions may be used for a range of requests, from determining the admissibility of evidence to dismissing a case.

## Discovery and Strategic Interactions

After the answer is filed, the judge issues an order setting a timetable for *discovery*, the litigation process in which the parties investigate the case by obtaining relevant information from each other. Some judges set mandatory discovery deadlines in every case, but other judges consult the attorneys for mutual agreement on how long the discovery process will take—usually at least several months and in many cases several years. One reason that cases drag on for years is that lawyers and judges are socialized to accept procrastination as a normal component of litigation. Lawyers are accustomed to asking for "continuances" or extensions for the discovery deadlines, and many judges routinely grant such requests. These delays are frequently for the lawyers' convenience and do not satisfy the clients' desire for timely resolution of the case. The problem is so pervasive that a task force studying costs and delay in the federal courts has urged that judges require lawyers to show "good cause" before granting continuances.[40] Judges contribute to the problems of delay not only by readily acquiescing to both intentional and inadvertent stalling by attorneys, but also by failing to make timely rulings on discovery motions in which the litigants request decisions about whether certain evidence must be made available to the opposing side.[41]

The discovery process involves written requests for information directed to the opposing party (*interrogatories*), sworn testimony taken from witnesses in the presence of the two attorneys and a court reporter (*depositions*), and motions to dismiss the case or to contest the propriety of certain requests for information. In adversarial proceedings, there is no independent investigation by a neutral party. Each side must try to get necessary information from the other side's documents and witnesses. Lawyers often attempt to hide crucial information from the opposing party in order to gain an advantage; they also frequently try to swamp the opposition with requests for information as part of the "game playing" that infuses civil litigation. The lawyers may also appear before the judge on numerous occasions to argue about the admissibility of evidence or the misbehavior of opposing attorneys in improperly requesting information or harassing witnesses.

As a formal policy, judges universally declare that they expect cooperative, professional behavior from opposing attorneys, but lawyers frequently seek strategic advantages and personal satisfaction from complicating the discovery process. Since the 1980s, the federal courts have expanded the ability of judges to impose sanctions—such as attorneys' fees and court costs—on parties whose actions in litigation are intended "to harass or to cause unnecessary delay or needless increase in the cost of litigation."[42] The use of sanctions is very controversial because they are discretionary determinations by individual judges and are, therefore, not applied consistently. Moreover, the application of sanctions is perceived to favor defendants by deterring plaintiffs from asserting plausible but uncertain claims and arguments.[43] In a 5-to-4 decision in 1991, the Supreme Court endorsed the imposition of financial sanctions against clients as well as their lawyers for filing legal papers that are not "well-grounded in fact."[44] This ruling places clients at risk if their attorneys do not use good judgment in providing advice on whether a case is worth pursuing.

The discovery period initiates the process of strategic interaction between attorneys that frequently determines the outcome of the case—usually a negotiated settlement. By stalling, annoying, and hassling their opponents, lawyers hope to build pressure that will encourage compromise. When individuals sue corporations, for example, the larger entities can afford to keep the discovery process going and intentionally delay the case. This strategy is designed to make the plaintiff increasingly desperate for the claimed money, particularly if the plaintiff cannot pay for a long-term discovery process. Individual claimants also suffer greater psychological costs in keeping the litigation battle going:

> For businesses, government, and other organizations that use courts as part of their regular activities, psychological costs probably are not much of a problem, but for individuals who are rarely involved in court cases and who will be personally affected by the proceedings and outcome, the psychological load may be equal to or heavier than the financial one.[45]

Thus, the defendant seeks a surrender of the claim in a negotiated settlement by offering immediate payment of a much smaller amount than the plaintiff originally sought. The lawyers' fees generated by the discovery process can be a tremendous burden on individual litigants, especially if the judge permits continual delays. Lawyers can grow rich by representing corporate combatants who can afford to keep cases going in the hope that the opposition will become discouraged. Research on case outcomes has shown that "repeat players" with litigation experience and resources prevail more often than "one shotters" who are participating in one court case.[46] Thus, corporations and other organizational entities normally possess significant advantages when squared off against an individual in civil litigation.

Judges who aggressively control the civil litigation process will force lawyers *and* clients to meet repeatedly in settlement conferences throughout the discovery process in order to generate pressure on the parties to agree to a settlement.[47] Because lawyers engaged in civil litigation can become rich through prolonged litigation and may be obsessed with winning for egotistical reasons that predominate over the clients' real interests, many judges fear that lawyers will give their clients biased assessments of the prospects for victory of settlement. Thus, judges may insist that the actual litigants meet face to face in order to maximize the chances of settlement. If the parties hear first-hand the opposing side's settlement offers, they may be more likely to reach an agreement than if they rely solely on their lawyers' predictions about the prospects for more favorable results. In most cases, the continued conferences, discovery expenses, mediation by judges, and other elements in the process will eventually create sufficient pressures to produce settlements.

Figure 5.2 shows the outcomes for 762,000 tort, contract, and real estate cases filed in the nation's seventy-five largest counties in 1992. Negotiated settlements are the most frequent result in such civil cases (470,000) and far outnumber jury trials (12,000) as the final product of litigation. Default judgments occur when the defendant fails to respond or otherwise defend against the lawsuit and therefore the plaintiff automatically wins. Dismissals result when plaintiffs fail to present their claims in a manner consistent with prevailing law or fail to present sufficient evidence to make their claims plausible. Unlike dismissals, which may leave the door open for claims to be refiled using additional arguments and evidence, summary judgments formally terminate the case based on the initial pleadings when there are no disputes about the underlying factual circumstances and the evidence clearly shows one side must prevail. Some cases also result in trials conducted before a judge without a jury (bench trials), directed verdicts when the evidence indicates to the judge that one side must prevail, and arbitration

**Figure 5.2: Civil Case Processes and Outcomes: Tort, Contract, and Real Property Cases in the 75 Largest American Counties, 1992.**

| Tort, Contract, and Real Property Cases (762,000) | | | | | |
|---|---|---|---|---|---|

*Jury Trial* (12,000)

| Plaintiff wins (6,200) | Plaintiff loses (5,800) | | | | |
|---|---|---|---|---|---|

*Non-Jury* (750,000)

| Settle | Default | Dismiss | Transfer | Summary Judgment | Other* |
|---|---|---|---|---|---|
| (470,000) | (108,000) | (82,000) | (29,000) | (28,000) | (33,000) |

*"Other" category includes bench trials, arbitration awards, and directed verdicts.

*Source:* Carol J. DeFrances, Steven K. Smith, Patrick A. Langan, Brian J. Ostrom, David B. Rottman, and John A. Goerdt, "Civil Jury Cases and Verdicts in Large Counties," *Bureau of Justice Statistics Special Report* (July 1995): 1.

awards in courts that use alternative dispute resolution (ADR) procedures. As this chapter will discuss, ADR procedures are increasingly being used for processing civil cases.

## The Nature of Civil Litigation

Many people are amazed at how infrequently most lawyers who call themselves "litigators" actually conduct trials. In one major lawsuit concerning the deaths of dozens of people from a flood caused by a coal mining operation, the plaintiffs' lawyer, an experienced attorney for a major Washington, D.C., law firm, had twelve years of experience as a lawyer, but he had participated in only two jury trials.[48] Judges frequently say that the quickest way to facilitate a settlement is to set a firm trial date. Because so many lawyers prefer to avoid the extra expense and preparation required for trial, not to mention the risk that a trial might result in a clear victory for the opposition, settlements are frequently negotiated just before trial. A feigned willingness to take the case all the way through a trial can bluff and pressure the opposing side into accepting a compromise. Civil litigation can often be characterized as an elaborate—and expensive—game of "chicken," with each side waiting for the other to change its position as the trial date approaches.

The foregoing discussion of the civil judicial process demonstrates that civil litigation does not normally end in carefully considered judicial decisions. Instead of applying their knowledge and wisdom to determine the outcomes of disputes, judges serve either as uninvolved umpires presiding over the "game" of litigation or as mediators actively trying to encourage and often pressure the parties to settle their disputes prior to trial. The actual processes that underlie civil litigation raise questions about the appropriate role of judges in court cases. Whether or not judges should be actively involved in managing litigation or encouraging settlements, it is clear that they do not usually play the stereotypical role of decision maker, determining the outcomes of cases after bench trials or overseeing jury trials.

As indicated by figure 5.2, relatively few civil cases result in trials before judges or juries. Thus, civil litigation should be viewed as a process that structures litigants' interactions and applies pressure on disputants to negotiate settlements to their disputes. In its actual operations, the civil judicial process does not achieve "justice" in any abstract sense. A stereotypical conception of the civil judicial process might envision disputants asking an external decision maker (i.e., judge or jury) for an unbiased assessment of their rights and obligations in a conflict situation. The neutral decision maker's judgment would then be enforced by the courts' authority as a branch of the governing system. In reality, however, the civil justice process primarily serves to create an environment in which disputants engage in structured interactions under steadily increasing pressure until one or both parties agree to compromise because of resource pressures, uncertainty about a potential trial outcome, or even "arm twisting" by aggressive judges. The outcomes of civil litigation embody accommodations by one or both parties, so they do not necessarily vindicate meritorious claims or even satisfy the participants. Because the litigants "voluntarily" reach a negotiated settlement, it is difficult for them to complain about the outcome. The court system is thus saved from making any losing party unhappy.

Although this picture of civil judicial processes does not comport with idealized notions of courts and justice, these actual operations are a predictable consequence of courts' political nature. Case outcomes in civil litigation are produced not solely by law, but also by political processes: the assertion of parties' interests; the calculation of costs and benefits; the conflicts between parties with uneven resources and levels of information; and the negotiated compromises. These are precisely the processes that determine outcomes in legislatures, executive agencies, and other political forums. Legal doctrines and court procedures structure the political interactions underlying litigation in an environment different from those of other political forums. Nevertheless, the attributes of the outcome-producing processes are the same. Legislators develop compromises based on predictions of the number of votes a particular legislative proposal will garner. If the legislators who oppose the legislation appear to have a majority, proponents of the legislation feel pressured to compromise in order to attract additional supporters before the scheduled vote. Similarly, litigants develop settlements based on their predictions about the effects of existing legal doctrines and jury behavior on case outcome in a trial. The relative strength of the litigants' bargaining positions will be based on their respective beliefs about the probable outcome of a trial. Outcomes are also affected by the relative resource strength of each side with respect to possessing the time and money for continuing litigation if necessary.

## ALTERNATIVE DISPUTE RESOLUTION (ADR)

To decrease the costs associated with litigation, conserve judicial resources, and reduce delays in the judicial process, alternative mechanisms have been developed for processing disputes. Some mechanisms are incorporated into the judicial branch, and others are external alternatives for dispute processing.

### External Alternatives

Statutory alternatives to traditional litigation have placed in the hands of government agencies the initial responsibility for processing certain types of disputes. Under employment discrimination laws, for example, claimants frequently must file claims with the state antidiscrimination agency (e.g., Ohio Civil Rights Commission). These agencies investigate claims and attempt to mediate between the claimant and the alleged perpetrator to facilitate a voluntary resolution of the problem. If no resolution is produced, the case may be referred to the federal Equal Employment Opportunity Commission for further investigation and an attempt at mediation. If the conflict is not resolved, the agency or the individual may be permitted to file a lawsuit in federal court. Although agencies may succeed in resolving some cases, unresolved cases carry serious risks that discouraged claimants will abandon their claims because of the inevitable delays caused by two lengthy administrative proceedings and the drawn-out process of civil litigation. Scholars have criticized the American approach to discrimination cases because of these extra burdens on victims.[49] As indicated in the discussion of the dispute pyramid, people who believe that they have been victimized by illegal discrimination are much less likely to pursue their grievances than are other injured people.[50]

Neighborhood Justice Centers were developed in several cities to process disputes quickly and inexpensively using mediators drawn from the local community. The centers are intended to be forums for dispute-processing according to community values in an accessible, informal environment. The centers may handle disputes that might otherwise have been filed as either criminal or civil cases in the formal court system (e.g., property damage, etc.). Despite their good intentions, the centers serve to filter poor people's complaints out of the formal court system:

> The U.S. Solicitor General . . . said . . . Neighborhood Justice Centers have the potential of cutting off access to the court system to the poor, an "underclass" that looks to the courts as its only hope. The fact that most complainants in Neighborhood Justice Centers seem to be poor, females, and blacks seems to provide support for this fear.[51]

Decisions about which cases will receive the attention of the judicial process and which will be diverted to alternative forums may be biased in favor of the affluent or the influential. Poor people are generally unable to demand the same access and attention that the judicial system provides to disputants representated by privately retained attorneys.

One alternative mechanism allows disputants with sufficient resources to accelerate case processing by hiring an arbitrator, mediator, or "private judge." In other words, businesses and affluent individuals can voluntarily go outside the court system for commercial dispute-processing services. In California, in particular, many retired judges are hired to process disputes. The high cost of private dispute resolution, however, hinders its utilization by a broad range of citizens.[52]

## Small Claims Courts

The best-known and most widely utilized alternative to traditional litigation is the small claims court. Small claims courts were created to encourage quick, inexpensive, and informal resolution of disputes involving small amounts of money. Each state limits the value of claims that may be brought to small claims court, with maximum amounts ranging from a few hundred to a few thousand dollars. By presenting their own cases, claimants in small claims court are spared the expense of hiring attorneys. Local attorneys usually serve as referees, examining documentary evidence and listening to each side's case. This occurs in a relatively informal setting without the usual evidentiary and procedural rules that govern the civil judicial process. The hearings tend to be very brief, and decisions are usually rendered within a few days.

The primary complaint about small claims courts is that they are based on the erroneous premise that claims for small amounts necessarily arise from simple disputes. In fact, such disputes may involve complicated issues of fact and law. Because each case is generally alloted only minutes for presentation and is one of dozens of cases heard at the same session, the referees must simplify the issues involved in order to reach a quick decision.[53]

In addition, instead of helping the poor pursue their claims, small claims courts are frequently utilized by big businesses for inexpensive enforcement of debts against poor people. As summarized by Harry Stumpf, "far from providing a forum for the poor (i.e., individual, blue- or perhaps white-collar) litigant to afford him his day in court simply and inexpensively, these tribunals have largely become collection agencies for the 'haves' of our society against the 'have nots.' "[54] Businesses are frequently represented by attorneys in small claims proceedings, which increases companies' advantages over lay people. Creditors may automatically win their cases just by filing complaints because poor people have difficulty missing work, finding childcare, and otherwise arranging to appear in court. If one party files a claim and the other fails to appear without explanation, the initiating party can win a *default judgment* without presenting any arguments and evidence. Unlike white-collar workers and professionals, other workers frequently have less flexibility in their work schedules. People who do not own cars or do not have access to babysitters may be unable to make the arrangements necessary to contest small claims actions in court. Thus, collections agencies, landlords' associations, and other creditor organizations may succeed in their legal actions against poor and working-class debtors.

Small claims courts lack institutionalized mechanisms for enforcing judgments. Prevailing in small claims court may simply lead to additional court actions to enforce the judgment. Businesses that employ attorneys in small claims court to collect debts have the resources and experience to pursue additional actions. By contrast, an individual who prevails in small claims court can easily become discouraged and disillusioned on learning that winning in court does not necessarily mean receiving satisfaction or compensation.

The criticisms directed at small claims courts stem from the predictable results of political influences on judicial alternatives. Entities, such as businesses, with political and economic resources are in a better position than financially limited individuals to exploit the opportunities for quick, inexpensive litigation

offered by the small claims process. Moreover, the lack of institutionalized enforcement mechanisms is characteristic of other court reforms designed to benefit
marginal, politically weak individuals. Influential judicial decision makers are
frequently unwilling to provide the commitment and resources necessary to ensure
the success of innovations.[55]

## Court-Annexed Alternatives

Many courts have incorporated alternative procedures into their civil justice
processes. As described by a federal court study committee composed of judges
and lawyers, these alternatives are intended to encourage settlement *and* to help
prepare cases for trial:

> Alternative or supplementary procedures may enhance the operation of
> traditional civil judicial procedures, fostering the classic role of pretrial
> proceedings of helping prepare cases for trial or identifying grounds for
> settlement. In other cases, they may resolve disputes without recourse to
> traditional procedures. . . . In doing so, they provide litigants an opportunity
> to resolve their disputes without recourse to judges, thus enhancing access to
> justice.[56]

The range and organization of alternatives vary from courthouse to courthouse depending on the governing statutes and on individual judges' predilections.
In the federal court system, innovative judges have had significant autonomy in
designing alternative mechanisms and imposing them on litigants. Although many
of the alternatives use similar names, such as "arbitration" and "mediation,"
these alternatives are not always implemented in a similar manner.[57] The following
descriptions of alternatives utilized in various courthouses do not purport to
present a complete picture of ADR mechanisms but only to serve as illustrative
examples.

In the federal court in the Western District of Michigan, all civil cases seeking
one hundred thousand dollars or less are automatically referred to *arbitration*.
In the Northern District of California, arbitration is compulsory for all personal
injury, contract, and property damage cases seeking less than one hundred fifty
thousand dollars. Under the Michigan court's arbitration program, the judge
selects an experienced attorney to serve as the arbitrator for the case. In California,
the arbitration may be conducted by an individual or a three-attorney panel.[58]
Attorneys for both sides describe their evidence and present their arguments to
the arbitrator during a brief session. The arbitrator subsequently issues an opinion
on the case based on prevailing law and determines what the award should be
(if the plaintiff wins). The arbitrator's decision is not binding; it is merely informational. The arbitration process is supposed to provide the attorneys with information about the strength of their evidence and arguments. Presumably the party

that loses the arbitration session will be encouraged to make a settlement offer rather than risk losing the case in a real trial before a judge.[59]

Judges and magistrate judges in the Western District of Michigan can order any case into *mediation*. In the district's mediation process, each party is permitted to select one experienced attorney to serve on the mediation board. The two parties then mutually agree on another attorney to serve as the third member of the board. As in arbitration, the lawyers for each side present their arguments and evidence to the three-member panel. Unlike arbitration, however, the mediation board does not determine which party should win the case under prevailing law. Instead, the experienced attorneys on the board determine what amount of money should be acceptable to both parties to settle the case. The attorneys use their own litigation experience to weigh each side's chances of winning and to estimate the likely award. Even if a plaintiff presents a case that the board members believe will be unpersuasive to a judge or jury, the mediation board will recommend that the defendant offer a modest amount of money (e.g., $5,000) to settle the case. The mediators' argument to defendants who are confident of ultimate victory is that an immediate settlement will be less expensive than the ultimate court costs and attorneys' fees if the case goes to trial. Thus, if defendants are confident that a jury will side with them, but the discovery process and trial will cost twenty thousand dollars, these defendants will see the advantage of offering a five thousand dollar settlement—even if they strongly believe they are in the right. The mediation process focuses on a practical ''dollars and cents'' approach to disputes, without regard for perceptions of justice in the case.

The mediation process in Michigan state courts is backed by an incentive mechanism. Each side must inform the court whether they find the settlement amount acceptable. Suppose either or both parties reject a settlement unanimously recommended by the mediators. Then, at trial, the litigants must improve on the mediators' settlement amount by at least 10 percent, or they will be liable for their opponents' court costs and attorneys' fees from the moment that they rejected the recommended amount.[60] Thus, if the mediators believe that the case should settle for $100,000 and the plaintiff rejects that amount, the plaintiff must be awarded at least $110,000 at the subsequent trial or he or she will have to pay the defendants' costs. Alternatively, if the defendant turns down the settlement amount, defense attorneys must hold the plaintiff's award below ninety thousand dollars at trial. The incentive mechanism raises troubling questions. Do litigants have any right to demand that their dispute be heard before a judge in a real court without risking an extra financial penalty? In the hypothetical one hundred thousand dollars example, what if a jury subsequently awards the plaintiff eighty thousand dollars? The plaintiff's claim has been vindicated because a jury has found the defendant to be liable, yet, despite the meritorious claim, the plaintiff still faces the possible penalty of paying the opponents' costs. This mediation example shows how judges can increase the pressure for settlement in the civil justice process to levels that may directly coerce the litigants into compromising.

Litigants who face such penalties may feel forced to surrender their claims even though they were seeking vindication as well as compensation. The Federal Court Study Committee's 1990 report recognized the risks of coercion in such incentive mechanisms and recommended that "decisions about which incentives are permissible should be made by Congress and not left simply to local rules."[61] The federal court in the Western District of Michigan previously employed this sanctioning mechanism for parties that rejected mediation results, but the U.S. Court of Appeals ruled that district courts lack the authority to impose such rules.[62]

An innovation developed by Judge Thomas Lambros in the Cleveland federal court of the Northern District of Ohio is the summary jury trial.[63] This ADR method has been applied in the Western District of Michigan and in other federal courts around the country. In a summary jury trial, an actual jury of citizens hears a one-day trial in which attorneys for the two parties present their respective arguments. The jurors spend a brief period deliberating before rendering a verdict and recommending an award if the plaintiff is victorious. The jury's verdict and award are nonbinding and merely informational. As in the Western District of Michigan's arbitration process, the verdict serves to encourage the losing party to formulate a settlement rather than risk losing the case at another jury trial. If a lawyer believes that his or her case will be persuasive to a jury, the summary jury trial helps to verify or contradict counsel's expectations. As in arbitration and mediation, summary jury trials usually result in settlements. It is not clear whether these cases would have settled without the application of ADR methods, but it is believed that the ADR methods accelerate the settlement process and facilitate settlements in some cases that might otherwise have gone to trial. In addition, the use of formal, court-annexed procedures may, as in trials, make the litigants feel that their claims have received more serious attention than they would have been given in ordinary settlement negotiations.[64]

## Criticisms of Alternative Dispute Resolution

The utilization of ADR mechanisms undoubtedly encourages parties to settle disputes, but there are risks that the "encouragement" is in fact coercion that may improperly pressure people to surrender their claims. Richard Abel argues that the expansion of informal mechanisms for handling disputes, although ostensibly intended to improve the process, actually expands state control while disguising the existence of coercive mechanisms. Paraprofessionals—mediators, arbitrators, or small claims referees—replace citizen jurors as the final arbiters of case outcomes. The mechanisms neutralize conflict by forcing people to compromise their claims when justice might be better served by vindicating claims and thereby providing aggrieved parties with compensation for their losses.[65] As Christine Harrington has observed, "Substantive demands for social justice have been overshadowed by experimentation with techniques for alternative dispute resolution."[66]

In addition, ADR methods may actually increase the time and expense of litigation by forcing litigants to jump extra hurdles before they are permitted to have their cases heard in court. In the Western District of Michigan, the average number of days for termination of all cases is 309, yet the averages for cases entering arbitration and mediation are 403 days and 548 days, respectively. These delays burden litigants who must wait longer for their cases to be processed, but do not burden court resources since the ADR procedures are conducted by attorneys who either volunteer or receive modest compensation. Despite the apparent delays added by ADR methods, advocates of ADR argue that such figures do not consider the cases that settle prior to arbitration and mediation in which settlement was encouraged by the mere fact that litigants faced entering ADR processes.[67]

The implementation of multiple ADR methods may alter the role of the judge in the civil judicial process. The judge may become absorbed in administrative responsibilities, assigning and tracking cases through various ADR processes, and thereby diminish the time and resources he or she can apply to traditional judicial oversight and decision making.

Overall, one's assessment of the desirability of alternative dispute resolution will depend on fundamental beliefs about the purposes of the judicial branch: Should courts utilize ADR in order to process cases as efficiently as possible, or should courts remain freely available to claimants who seek traditional adversarial litigation and considered judicial decisions on case outcomes? Assessments of ADR also hinge on a determination of whether the risks of coercion outweigh the societal benefits of facilitating negotiated settlements while using a minimum of scarce judicial resources. Because ADR methods create new constraints and pressures on litigants in the structured environment of civil litigation, they merely enhance its predominant existing functions by further encouraging negotiated settlements. The continuing controversy surrounding ADR concerns whether these alternatives move the judicial process too far toward pressuring litigants to settle claims at all costs.

# TRIALS

As indicated in figure 5.2, relatively few cases are decided in either jury or bench trials. Generally, either party in a case can demand a jury trial, although some specific kinds of lawsuits can only be heard before a judge. Judges preside over most civil trials because the parties prefer a single, professional decision maker. If the issues or evidence are regarded as too technical or complex for ordinary citizens to understand, the parties will agree to a bench trial. For example, a lawsuit between two businesses concerning the provisions of a technical federal statute or involving evidence of complex financial transactions may be presented to a judge rather than to a jury.

As chapter 4 discussed in regard to criminal trials, there are significant questions about whether the American adversarial system produces or obscures facts. According to Judge Marvin Frankel, "Many of us trained in the learned profession of the law spend much of our time subverting the law by blocking the way to truth."[68] The risk that effective lawyering may overcome the facts of the case and thereby influence the outcomes is greatest in jury trials. Judges may be less impressed and overwhelmed by lawyers' courtroom performances. Because of their greater experience and understanding of legal tactics, judges can more effectively evaluate the substance of lawyers' presentations. By contrast, jurors may lack the knowledge and sophistication to recognize attorneys' strategic ploys.

Civil trials take place because the parties cannot agree on a settlement. This failure to agree may stem from the parties' mutual inability to decide what the case is worth. One party may anticipate a large damages award from a jury, while the opposing party feels confident that the jury will find no liability. Other cases may go to trial because one party is less concerned with the financial stakes than with the consequences of a settlement. An employer may fight employment discrimination suits to the very end, for example, for fear that if he or she agrees to a settlement, more employees will file suits. By fighting suits all the way through to trial, a business or individual sends a message to other potential litigants that they must be prepared to spend the time and money to pursue cases all the way. Litigants may also take cases to trial to seek vindication of the claims presented or because they want the courts to endorse a particular principle at issue. Some litigants may reject attractive financial settlements because they want a judge or jury to declare publicly, "Yes, you are in the right, and your opponent is in the wrong."

## Jury Trials

In jury trials, many factors affect the outcomes. Numerous studies have examined how different kinds of people perform as jurors. The studies are the basis for general conclusions that assist lawyers in determining what kinds of people might be most desirable as jurors for a particular case. Some findings about juror characteristics associated with personal attributes—such as the greater ability of educated people to remember and understand witnesses' testimony and judges' instructions[69]—probably reinforce lawyers' intuitive expectations. When clients can afford to hire outside consultants, lawyers frequently rely on psychologists to develop profiles of desirable and undesirable jurors. Relying on experimental studies with mock jurors, jury experts recommend that lawyers attempt to include or exclude jurors with certain demographic or personal characteristics. For example, in a lawsuit against a corporation for an allegedly defective product, people who work in similar businesses may be less likely to favor the arguments of the consumer. Jury experts may also supervise mock trials that enable lawyers to test their arguments in front of experimental jurors. When M.C.I. Communications (MCI) won $1.8 billion in a jury trial against its telephone company rival, American Telephone and Telegraph (AT&T), MCI's success was attributed to its lawyers' practice trials before mock juries, which provided feedback about the persuasiveness of strategic presentations of arguments and evidence.[70] Although some litigants attribute their success to scientific jury studies, psychologists cannot always utilize experimental jury studies to predict how actual juries will behave. In fact, one review of the literature on scientific jury selection has cautioned that "the approach can have a modest effect at best, and it can *decrease* as well as *increase* the probability of a favorable verdict."[71] In other words, lawyers must be wary of deferring to jury experts because of psychologists' imperfect abilities to assess and predict human behavior.

Although television, movies, and other media nearly always portray twelve jurors listening to testimony, many court systems actually use fewer jurors, especially in civil cases. The federal courts, for example, use six-member juries for civil cases and twelve-member juries for criminal cases. Twenty-three states use juries smaller than twelve in at least some of their civil cases.[72] A second common misconception about juries is that their verdict must be unanimous. In fact, although 95 percent of all juries reach complete agreement on the verdict,[73] states set their own rules for jury unanimity—with the exception that the Supreme Court has ruled that unanimity is required of six-member juries in criminal cases (the smallest permissible jury size).[74] In California, for example, the twelve-member jury in O.J. Simpson's murder case needed to reach a unanimous verdict, while in the civil lawsuit filed by the murder victims' familes, only nine of twelve jurors needed to agree in order to produce a verdict.

The use of small juries in civil cases can have several effects on case decisions. Smaller juries are less likely to offer broad representation from a community, so alternative perspectives are more likely to be missing from the jury deliberations.[75] There is a greater likelihood of "hung juries" in which the small jury divides and cannot reach agreement. In addition, there is often less consistency in jury decisions. When civil juries determine damage awards in tort cases, for example, "statistical analysis reveals that over two-thirds of the twelve-person juries will have average damage awards close to the community average, compared to just half of the six-person juries."[76]

Critics have claimed that citizen-jurors are not qualified to understand evidence and make proper decisions in complex civil cases that may concern, for example, financial disputes between corporations or defects in technologically sophisticated machinery. Scholars, however, blame court procedures for deficiencies in jurors' ability to understand and remember information:

> [C]ourts treat juries as passive recipients of information. . . . [T]hey often deny jurors an opportunity to learn in the courtroom. . . . Many judges thus prohibit jurors from taking notes or asking questions of witnesses—even

though these procedures appear to be useful and non-disruptive. And then, having erected these obstacles, the courts bemoan the jury's inability to overcome them. . . . Turning from the facts to the law, the ritual of instructing juries [by judges concerning how to make decisions] reveals the same kind of self-defeating pattern.[77]

Reforms have been initiated to help juries cope with complex cases. Numerous cases concerning the same issue—such as the thousands of lawsuits against asbestos manufacturers for producing materials that have caused lung diseases—have been consolidated into combined trials of representative cases. Other cases have "bifurcated" trials in which separate proceedings permit jurors to focus exclusively on a particular issue before moving on to decide the next issues in the case. This innovation is designed to avoid the confusion of hearing all of the evidence before making any decisions in complex cases involving multiple issues. Research with experimental juries indicates that changes in procedures will have consequences for case outcomes. In consolidated cases, for example, plaintiffs with weaker cases win larger awards when their cases are joined with others in lawsuits that present more compelling cases against the defendants.[78] In bifurcated cases, the process of making a focused decision on each issue leads to fewer verdicts finding defendant liability. However, when the bifurcated proceeding produces a verdict for the plaintiff, the jury's compensatory damage award is likely to be larger than one produced by a traditional, unitary trial.[79]

Juries in civil cases can have a significant impact on the distribution of resources in society. Large jury awards against corporations could force them out of business and put their employees out of work. Such awards also affect insurance premiums and have cumulative effects on the costs and availability of goods and services. Thus, there is significant newspaper attention to such major cases as the jury award of $10.53 billion to Pennzoil in its lawsuit against Texaco.[80] Observers note that "[i]t has become fashionable, especially among insurance companies and large corporations, to say that we have become a litigious society and the civil jury is partly to blame."[81] The opposing viewpoint asserts that businesses cause too many injuries to workers and consumers, and therefore civil juries act appropriately to compensate victims and deter further harmful conduct by making significant damages awards.[82] Prevailing plaintiffs are entitled to compensatory damages for the harm that they have suffered. They may also be awarded punitive damages, which can be very large amounts and are intended to punish the party at fault and deter others from engaging in similar conduct.

A study of civil verdicts in Chicago during the 1960s and 1970s indicated that the average jury award in personal injury cases was relatively small ($7,800) and that, adjusted for inflation, jury awards were remarkably stable over the entire time period.[83] In a study of jury trials in the seventy-five largest counties in 1992, it was discovered that the median jury award was $52,000 for tort, contract, and real property cases. However, juries awarded damages to plaintiffs in only 6,200 of the 762,000 cases filed, so it is difficult to say what a jury might have done in the "average" case since most cases settle before trial.[84] It is possible that the jury trial cases concerned more serious injuries or stronger evidence than the average civil case. There is some evidence of larger awards for more serious injuries, which may be attributable, in part, to juries' greater inclination to assess more damages against institutional entities with "deep pockets" and the ability to pay greater sums: "Corporations, hospitals, and governments were more likely to be found liable and they usually had to pay larger damage awards."[85]

As a result of these perceptions and trends, efforts have been made to limit juries' ability to make large damage awards. The U.S. Supreme Court has only reluctantly limited large awards by juries in civil cases. In one case presented to the Court, a woman was awarded $200,000 in compensatory damages and $840,000 in punitive damages when a local insurance agent failed to forward her premiums to an insurance company and the woman subsequently underwent expensive medical treatments without knowing that her insurance coverage had been canceled. The Supreme Court declined to declare the jury's award to be unconstitutionally excessive, even though it acknowledged that "the punitive damages award is more than 4 times the amount of compensatory damages, is more than 200 times the [claimant's] out-of-pocket expenses, . . . and . . . is much in excess of the fine that could be imposed for [criminal] insurance fraud."[86] In 1996, however, a narrow five-member majority overturned a two million dollar punitive damage award against the BMW car company based on a customer's claim about undisclosed paint damage on a newly purchased car.[87] The Court found the award to be "grossly excessive" in violation of the right to due process.

Due to infrequent judicial action limiting jury awards, legislation has been proposed throughout the country to limit the amount of money that civil juries can award to injury victims. The ultimate outcome of these reforms will, like the results of other reforms of the court system, reflect the interactions and respective political strengths of the groups seeking to advance their interests. In the face of a mounting public relations and lobbying campaign by insurance companies and businesses to limit jury awards, it remains to be seen whether trial lawyers who win large contingency fees in tort cases can persuade legislatures that society is best served by maintaining the present system of jury discretion. Because jury awards in civil litigation have such significant cumulative effects on the distribution of resources within society, it is likely that state legislatures and Congress will explore legislation that strikes a balance between compensating victims through the judicial process and lessening the economic and social costs of civil litigation.

## CONCLUSION

Civil litigation, like other aspects of the judicial process, is shaped by the interests and resources of the individuals and organizations who seek judicial assistance or find themselves involuntarily drawn into the dispute-processing procedures of the courts. Litigants' ability to raise claims, negotiate favorable settlements, or persevere through the many stages of the civil litigation process depends on both their access to legal resources and their motivation to pursue a particular case. Thus, certain segments of American society will be disadvantaged in the dispute-processing and policy-shaping forum of the civil litigation process. Because civil litigation can have such significant effects on the distribution of resources and responsibilities in American society, political interests will continue to use the judicial arena to pursue public policy goals. As the civil judicial process produces outcomes that shape the distribution of resources and power, legislatures and other political actors will respond to both cumulative policy influences and the judicial policy declarations produced by civil litigation.

## NOTES

1. Victor E. Kappeler, *Critical Issues in Police Liability* (Prospect Heights, IL: Waveland Press, 1993), p. 51.
2. Robert H. Mnookin and Lewis Kornhauser, "Bargaining in the Shadow of the Law: The Case of Divorce," *Yale Law Journal* 88 (1979): 950–97.
3. Randall Samborn, "Accelerating Caseloads Threaten to Swamp Courts," *National Law Journal*, 9 May 1994, p. A11.
4. "Chief Justice Recaps 1995 in Year-end Report," *The Third Branch* 28 (January 1996): 4–5.
5. Carol J. DeFrances, Steven K. Smith, Patrick A. Langan, Brian J. Ostrom, David B. Rottman, and John A. Goerdt, "Civil Jury Cases and Verdicts in Large Counties," *Bureau of Justice Statistics Special Report* (July 1995), p. 1.
6. Samborn, p. A11.
7. Bayless Manning, "Hyperlexis: Our National Disease," *Northwestern University Law Review* 71 (1977): 773.
8. See Richard E. Miller and Austin Sarat, "Grievances, Claims, and Disputes: Assessing the Adversary Culture," *Law and Society Review* 15 (1980–81): 544.
9. Marc Galanter, "Reading the Landscape of Disputes: What We Know and Don't Know (and Think We Know) About Our Allegedly Contentious and Litigious Society," *U.C.L.A. Law Review* 31 (1983): 12.
10. Ibid.
11. See Arthur Best and Alan R. Andreasen, "Consumer Response to Unsatisfactory Purchases: A Survey of Perceiving Defects, Voicing Complaints, and Obtaining Redress," *Law and Society Review* 11 (1977): 701–42.

12. William L.F. Felstiner, Richard L. Abel, and Austin Sarat, "The Emergence and Transformation of Disputes: Naming, Blaming, Claiming . . .," *Law and Society Review* 15 (1980–81): 635.

13. Galanter, "Reading the Landscape of Disputes," pp. 24–25.

14. Felstiner, Abel, and Sarat, "The Emergence and Transformation of Disputes," pp. 635–36.

15. Kristin Bumiller, "Victims in the Shadow of the Law: A Critique of the Model of Legal Protection," *Signs* 12 (1987): 421–39.

16. Ibid., p. 433.

17. Ibid., p. 438.

18. See Christopher E. Smith, "Politics and Plausibility: Searching for the Truth About Anita Hill and Clarence Thomas," *Ohio Northern University Law Review* 19 (1993): 697–757.

19. Galanter, "Reading the Landscape of Disputes," p. 17.

20. Suzanne R. Thomas-Buckle and Leonard G. Buckle, "Doing unto Others: Disputes and Dispute Processing in an Urban American Neighborhood," in *Neighborhood Justice: Assessment of an Emerging Idea*, eds. Roman Tomasic and Malcolm M. Feeley (New York: Longman, 1982), pp. 78–90.

21. *Kelly, Commissioner, Suffolk County Police Department v. Johnson*, 425 U.S. 238 (1976). See also *Willingham v. Macon Telegraph Publishing Co.*, 507 F.2d 1084 (5th Cir. 1975) (en banc).

22. Stephen Labaton, "Court Rethinking Rule Intended to Slow Frivolous Lawsuits," *New York Times*, 14 September 1990, p. B18.

23. Miller and Sarat, "Grievances, Claims, and Disputes," p. 533.

24. Ibid.

25. Ibid, pp. 544–45.

26. Bumiller, "Victims in the Shadow of the Law," pp. 433–35.

27. Miller and Sarat, "Grievances, Claims, and Disputes," pp. 544–45.

28. See Wayne V. McIntosh, *The Appeal of Civil Law: A Political-Economic Analysis of Litigation* (Champaign, IL: University of Illinois Press, 1990).

29. Ibid., pp. 47–76, 182–83.

30. Wolf Heydebrand and Carroll Seron, *Rationalizing Justice: The Political Economy at the Federal District Courts* (Albany, NY: State University of New York Press, 1990), p. 66.

31. "The Federal Civil Justice System," *Bureau of Justice Statistics Bulletin* (July 1987): 4; "The Chief Justice Recaps 1995 in Year-end Report," *The Third Branch* 28 (January 1996): 4.

32. Galanter, "Reading the Landscape of Disputes," pp. 5–11.

33. Lawrence Friedman, *Total Justice* (Boston: Beacon Press, 1985), pp. 3–5.

34. Heydebrand and Seron, *Rationalizing Justice*, pp. 128–32.

35. McIntosh, *The Appeal of Civil Law*, p. 184.

36. Galanter, "Reading the Landscape of Disputes," p. 10.

37. Samborn, p. A11.
38. See, e.g., *Rules of the United States District Court, Northern District of Ohio* (4 April 1984).
39. M.A. Stapleton, "County's Filing Fees Top Nation," *Chicago Daily Law Bulletin*, 26 December 1995, p. 1.
40. Brookings Institution Task Force on Civil Justice Reform, *Justice for All: Reducing the Costs and Delay in Civil Litigation* (Washington, D.C.: The Brookings Institution, 1989), pp. 21–22.
41. Ibid., p. 22.
42. Rule 11, Federal Rules of Civil Procedure.
43. *Report of the Federal Courts Study Committee* (2 April 1990), pp. 103–04.
44. *Business Guides v. Chromatic Communications* (1991), discussed in Linda Greenhouse, "Court Takes Up Drug Checks in Buses," *New York Times*, 27 February 1991, p. A13.
45. Henry Glick, *Courts, Politics, and Justice*, 2nd ed. (New York: McGraw-Hill, 1988), p. 126.
46. Marc Galanter, "Afterward: Explaining Litigation," *Law and Society Review* 9 (1975): 347. See also Marc Galanter, "Why the 'Haves' Come Out Ahead: Speculations on the Limits of Legal Change," *Law and Society Review* 9 (1974): 95–160.
47. For a description of assertive judicial behavior in the civil litigation process, *see* Christopher E. Smith, *United States Magistrates in the Federal Courts: Subordinate Judges* (New York: Praeger, 1990), pp. 90–93, 99–101.
48. Gerald M. Stern, *The Buffalo Creek Disaster* (New York: Random House, 1976), p. 279.
49. See Alan Freeman, "Antidiscrimination Law: The View From 1989," in *The Politics of Law*, rev. ed., ed. David Kairys (New York: Pantheon Books, 1990), pp. 121–50; Kristin Bumiller, *The Civil Rights Society: The Social Construction of Victims* (Baltimore: Johns Hopkins University Press, 1988).
50. Miller and Sarat, "Grievances, Claims, and Disputes," p. 544.
51. Roman Tomasic, "Mediation as an Alternative to Adjudication: Rhetoric and Reality in the Neighborhood Justice Movement," in *Neighborhood Justice: Assessment of an Emerging Idea*, eds. Roman Tomasic and Malcolm M. Feeley (New York: Longman, 1982), p. 229.
52. See Howard Abadinsky, *Law and Justice* (Chicago: Nelson-Hall, 1988), p. 221.
53. See Barbara Yngvesson and Patricia Hennessey, "Small Claims, Complex Disputes: A Review of the Small Claims Literature," *Law and Society Review* 9 (1975): 219–74.
54. Harry P. Stumpf, *American Judicial Politics* (New York: Harcourt Brace Jovanovich, 1988), p. 297–98.
55. See Malcolm M. Feeley, *Court Reform on Trial* (New York: Basic Books, 1983).
56. *Report of the Federal Courts Study Committee*, p. 83.

57. See Kathy L. Shuart, *The Wayne County Mediation Program in the Eastern District of Michigan* (Washington, D.C.: Federal Judicial Center, 1984); E. Allan Lind and John E. Sheppard, *Evaluation of Court-Annexed Arbitration in Three Federal District Courts* (Washington, D.C.: Federal Judicial Center, 1983).

58. Mark L. Krotoski, *Dispute Resolution Procedures in the Northern District of California* (1993), pp. 6–8 [information brochure distributed by the court].

59. Richard A. Enslen, "ADR: Another Acronym, or a Viable Alternative to the High Cost of Litigation and Crowded Court Dockets? The Debate Commences," *New Mexico Law Review* 18 (1988): 16–18.

60. *Report of the Advisory Group of the United States District Court for the Western District of Michigan Appointed Under the Civil Justice Reform Act of 1990* (21 November 1991), p. 102.

61. *Report of the Federal Court Study Committee*, p. 84.

62. *Tiedel v. Northwestern Michigan College*, 865 F.2d 88 (1988).

63. See M. Daniel Jacoubovitch and Carl M. Moore, *Summary Jury Trials in the Northern District of Ohio* (Washington, D.C.: Federal Judicial Center, 1982).

64. E. Allan Lind, Robert J. Maccoun, Patricia A. Ebener, William L. F. Felstiner, Deborah R. Hensler, Judith Resnik, and Tom R. Tyler, "In the Eye of the Beholder: Tort Litigants' Evaluations of Their Experiences in the Civil Justice System," *Law and Society Review* 24 (1990): 953–96.

65. Richard L. Abel, "The Contradictions of Informal Justice," in *The Politics of Informal Justice*, vol. 1, ed. Richard L. Abel (New York: Academic Press, 1982), pp. 267–320.

66. Christine B. Harrington, *Shadow Justice: The Ideology and Institutionalization of Alternatives to Court* (Westport, CT: Greenwood Press, 1985), p. 173.

67. *Report of the Advisory Group*, p. 101.

68. Marvin E. Frankel, *Partisan Justice* (New York: Hill & Wang, 1978), p. 17.

69. Reid Hastie, Steven D. Penrod, and Nancy Pennington, *Inside the Jury* (Cambridge, MA: Harvard University Press, 1983), p. 137.

70. Valerie P. Hans and Neil Vidmar, *Judging the Jury* (New York: Plenum Press, 1986), pp. 79–80, 87–88.

71. Diamond, "Scientific Jury Selection," p. 179.

72. DeFrances *et al.*, p. 12.

73. Saul M. Kassin and Lawrence S. Wrightsman, *The American Jury on Trial* (New York: Hemisphere Publishing, 1988), p. 214.

74. *Burch v. Louisiana*, 441 U.S. 130 (1979).

75. See Hans Zeisel and Shari Seidman Diamond, " 'Convincing Empirical Evidence' on the Six-member Jury," in *In the Jury Box*, eds. Lawrence Wrightsman, Saul M. Kassin, and Cynthia E. Willis (Newbury Park, CA: Sage Publications, 1987), pp. 193–208.

76. Hans and Vidmar, *Judging the Jury*, p. 167.

77. Kassin and Wrightsman, *The American Jury on Trial*, p. 213.

78. Kenneth S. Bordens and Irwin A. Horowitz, "Mass Tort Civil Litigation: The Impact of Procedural Changes on Jury Decisions," *Judicature* 73 (1989): 24–25.

79. Ibid., pp. 25–26.

80. Kassin and Wrightsman, *The American Jury on Trial*, p. 162.

81. Ibid.

82. See Richard L. Abel, "The Crisis Is Injuries, Not Liability," in *New Directions in Liability Law*, ed. Walter Olson (New York: Academy of Political Science, 1988), pp. 31–41.

83. Hans and Vidmar, *Judging the Jury*, p. 161.

84. Carol J. DeFrances, Steven K. Smith, Patrick A. Langan, Brian J. Ostrom, David B. Rottman, and John A. Goerdt, "Civil Jury Cases and Verdicts in Large Counties," *Bureau of Justice Statistics Special Report* (July 1995), p. 1.

85. Ibid., p. 162.

86. *Pacific Mutual Life Insurance Co. v. Haslip,* 499 U.S. 1, 23 (1991).

87. *BMW of North America, Inc. v. Gore,* 64 U.S.L.W 4335 (1996).

# Chapter 6

# Judicial Selection

Judges are powerful figures in the judicial process. Society gives them the authority to make important decisions in a broad spectrum of legal cases, ranging from disputes between individual citizens to public policy questions that may affect the entire country. In some cases, judges merely distribute benefits by deciding which party in a lawsuit will prevail. Frequently, one party wins money in the case and the other must pay. In other cases, judges' decisions determine whether individuals will lose their liberty through a prison term and sometimes even whether people will live and die. Individual judges also decide whether school systems are racially segregated, prisons are improperly over-crowded, and mental hospitals operate under unconstitutional conditions.

Who should be the judges? There are no easy answers to many of the questions that society directs to the judicial branch for consideration and decision. Whom do we trust to make decisions that will significantly affect people's lives? For example, which individuals in society possess the wisdom, knowledge, and other qualities needed to make difficult decisions in disputes concerning the legality of withdrawing medical treatment from an incapacitated, comatose person? Which individuals in society display the objectivity necessary to decide which parent should receive custody of the children when a marriage is dissolved? No human being fully possesses all of the qualities that society might desire in the ideal judge. Yet someone will be chosen to don the black robe and address the difficult legal issues that face the judiciary.

Before deciding which individuals will become judges, choices must be made about *how* judges will be selected. The choice of methods for selecting judges helps to determine what kinds of people become judges. Judicial selection processes may reflect traditional political practices within a state, or they may arise from conscious policy decisions about the qualities sought in judicial appointees. For example, many states retain judicial elections, in part, because political parties traditionally utilize judgeships to reward party loyalists. By contrast, other states have implemented merit selection procedures because they believe that better candidates for judicial positions will emerge from a reformed selection process. In merit selection processes, selection committees composed of lawyers and non-lawyers evaluate the qualifications of interested attorneys before recommending a short list of "most qualified" candidates to the governor for gubernatorial appointment. The various selection procedures utilized in the fifty-one separate federal and state court systems within the United States illustrate the competing values, interests, and consequences associated with the various methods for selecting judges. No matter what method a court system employs, politics plays a central role in determining which individuals will wear the black robes of authoritative judicial decision makers.

## UNDERLYING ISSUES AND PROBLEMS

### The Accountability and Independence of Judges

In democratic political systems, governmental policy makers are normally chosen through the process of competitive elections. If an individual is to be granted the authority to make decisions on behalf of the government, that individual must impress the voters with his or her professional experience, personality, and policy proposals. In subsequent elections, voters have the opportunity to replace government officials if those officials do not satisfy the citizenry's expectations. Thus, the electoral process permits the public to require *accountability* of government officials. Citizens maintain fundamental control over government and public policy by selecting desirable leaders and by rejecting officeholders who misuse power or fail to fulfill public expectations.

In the judicial branch, however, there are risks that the voters' power to hold judicial officers accountable for decisions may lead judges to follow public opinion rather than attempt to treat litigants as fairly as possible. When judges are afraid that they might lose their jobs by disappointing the public, they may be tempted to ignore the guiding language of constitutions and statutes; they may avoid controversial, difficult, or unpopular decisions rather than risk opposition from voters in the next election. For example, research indicates that state supreme court justices who face competitive reelection campaigns are less inclined than other judges to clash with public opinion by deciding against the imposition of capital punishment.[1] Elected judges' decisions may follow the wishes of the campaign contributors and political party leaders who help them win elections and stay in office. As a result, individuals and groups such as racial minorities, small religious sects, criminal defendants, and disabled people, who are unpopular or who lack political power, may not receive the protections guaranteed to them by state and federal laws. If judges simply seek to please the majority of voters with every judicial decision, society may suffer from the "tyranny of the majority,'' which the framers of the U.S. Constitution sought to avoid. Thus, in the judicial branch, traditional notions about accountability of democratic government officials clash with a need to ensure judicial *independence*. Unlike other government officials, judges need sufficient independence to make courageous decisions upholding freedom of speech, equal protection, and other rights—even for unpopular individuals.

The methods employed to select and remove judges in various judicial systems reflect choices concerning the appropriate emphasis to be placed on the competing goals of accountability and independence. In systems that emphasize accountability, judicial candidates campaign for office, and judges periodically face opponents in competitive political elections. In these states, judges are like any other elected officials who can be removed from office if voters are displeased with their decisions. By contrast, in the federal court system and state systems that emphasize judicial independence, judges are appointed to office by other government officials. These selection systems seek to ensure that judges have sufficient job security and insulation from electoral politics to permit them to make independent decisions.

In theory, democratic accountability is maintained in judicial appointment systems because the voters can oust the appointing officials, namely the president, governor, or legislature, if the electorate is unhappy with the judges. Thus, new elected officials in government would fill subsequent judicial vacancies with different appointees who would be more attuned to society's values. This indirect accountability mechanism simultaneously ensures that even appointed judges, as a group, do not move too far from the mainstream of society, and it insulates individual judges from direct political pressures that might interfere with their decision making.

## The Qualifications of Judicial Candidates

In addition to the issues of accountability and independence, the choice of a particular judicial selection procedure also affects the *qualifications* of the persons selected. Different kinds of candidates for judicial office will succeed in different selection systems. In electoral selection systems, candidates for judgeships get their names on the ballot either through self-promotion in primary and general elections or through connections to political parties. Both of these avenues to elected judgeships emphasize public image, loyalty to a political party, and other factors not related to the ''best'' qualifications for becoming a judge.

Judicial selection procedures in which judges are appointed by government officials provide an opportunity to carefully examine the qualifications of lawyers who might make good judges. This does not mean, however, that political considerations are eliminated from the selection process or that the ''most qualified'' candidate necessarily becomes the judge. Although it is obviously important that judgeships be filled by people with desirable characteristics and qualifications, there are fundamental reasons why no selection system can ever guarantee that the "best" candidates are chosen.

First, as subsequent sections of this chapter will discuss, political influences cannot be removed from judicial selection procedures. Every method of selecting judges requires that someone make decisions about the qualifications and desirability of candidates. The particular actors who make these decisions may vary from context to context, but whether they are voters, political party leaders, governors, or merit selection committees, the decision makers always have interests, values, and biases that affect their views about which individuals should become judges.

Second, there can never be a consensus about which candidates for judicial office are "best" qualified. Thus, even if decision makers in a given selection process consciously decided to focus solely on selecting the "most qualified" judge, they would disagree about which qualities are "best" and which candidates possesses them. A Democrat is likely to think that other Democrats would make the best judges because of their shared viewpoints about controversial issues that are presented to courts for decision. A Republican is likely to view other Republicans as the best judges for the same reasons.

A social scientist who studies judicial selection developed a list of the qualities associated with good judges.[2] The list could garner almost universal agreement on its choice of attributes that a good judge must have:[3]

1. Neutrality as to the Parties in Litigation
2. Fair-mindedness
3. Being Well Versed in the Law
4. Ability to Think and Write Logically and Lucidly
5. Personal Integrity
6. Good Physical and Mental Health
7. Judicial Temperament
8. Ability to Handle Judicial Power Sensibly

Consider this list of desirable attributes. How easy would it be to decide which judicial candidate possesses these attributes? How does one assess "judicial temperament"? Is it best to have an assertive judge who closely supervises all court proceedings, aggressively demands respect, and chastises lawyers who do not meet expected standards for preparation and behavior? Or, is it best to have a quiet judge who refuses to be drawn into arguments with attorneys and who earns respect through sensitive, thoughtful interactions with lawyers, witnesses, and others in the courtroom? People may agree that judges should have "judicial temperament," but they will not always agree on what that term means and on which candidates exhibit that quality. Similarly, assessments of ambiguous qualities such as "fair-mindedness" and "neutrality" vary according to the values and experiences of the governors or merit selection committee members who scrutinize judicial candidates.

The criterion of "ability to handle judicial power sensibly" offers an especially good illustration of the difficulty of seeking a consensus on the "best" qualified candidate for a judgeship. In 1990, for example, five members of the U.S. Supreme Court concurred in an opinion that asserted that a lower court judge could facilitate an increase in local property taxes in Kansas City, Missouri, in order to ensure that the school system had enough money to fund a plan to end racial segregation in the schools.[4] Four other members of the Supreme Court objected strenuously to what they labeled an improper "expansion of power in the federal judiciary beyond all precedent."[5] The justices of the Supreme Court are deeply divided about the proper use of judicial power. Are either of the two groups of justices on the Supreme Court—the five justices in the majority or the four dissenting justices—unqualified because they do not understand the sensible use of judicial power? The application of any criteria for the qualifications of judicial candidates inevitably comes down to a matter of judgment. Furthermore, because perceptions of the qualifications of judicial candidates may vary, depending on the values and viewpoints of the people making the selection, no selection procedure can completely ensure that the "best" qualified individuals will be chosen.

In addition to the problems of agreeing on which personal qualities are most desirable in a judge, there is also disagreement about what kinds of experience best prepare one for a judgeship. Should a judicial candidate have years of experience as a practicing attorney before becoming a judge? If so, how many years? What kind of legal practice—corporate, criminal, or civil—best qualifies one to be a judge? Perhaps people who were law professors at universities would be most qualified, because they have become exceptionally knowledgeable by studying law and teaching it to others. Obviously, there are no easy answers to questions about the "best" qualifications. It remains a matter of judgment.

In determining which experiences provide the best preparation for a good judge, one might presume that previous experience as a judge would help qualify a candidate for service in another court. Indeed, candidates for appellate judgeships frequently point to their experience as trial court judges to demonstrate that they are more qualified than other lawyers to serve on the appellate courts. However, although it may appear that prior judicial experience makes one better qualified to be a judge, studies of the U.S. Supreme Court challenge that assumption. People are often surprised to learn how many leading justices on the nation's highest court were never judges in any court before their Supreme Court appointments. The Chief Justice of the United States, William Rehnquist, had no prior experience as a judge before being appointed to the Supreme Court in 1971. The same was true of Earl Warren, who served as chief justice from 1953 to 1969, as well as many twentieth-century associate justices. A survey of scholars who study the Supreme Court found that many of the justices that history regards as "great" did not have prior experience as judges.[6]

Although society benefits when capable individuals become the judges who make difficult and important decisions affecting people's lives, no method of judicial selection can ensure that the ''most qualified'' candidates are chosen. The inevitable effects of political considerations and the impossibility of agreeing on criteria for qualification prevent even merit selection systems from completely achieving their stated purposes.

## Demographic Representation

Because the judicial system constitutes a branch of the government, there are legitimate concerns that all citizens should receive equal treatment in judicial processes and legal decisions. Historically, the judiciary, like other institutions in American society, has been composed almost exclusively of affluent, middle-aged, white males. Were these individuals chosen because they were wiser, more knowledgeable, and more just than other people? Clearly not. As discussed in chapter 3, the homogeneous nature of the judiciary reflected the fact that women and minority group members were denied opportunities to attend universities and enter the legal profession. In 1873, for example, the Supreme Court agreed that the state of Illinois could prohibit women from becoming attorneys because, according to Justice Miller, ''[t]he natural and proper timidity and delicacy which belongs to the female sex evidently unfits it for many of the occupations of civil life.''[7] Indeed, women and racial minorities were prevented from voting for most of American history, and thus they had no hope of pushing the government toward considering them for important positions, such as judgeships. The U.S. Constitution was not amended to guarantee women the right to vote until the passage of the Nineteenth Amendment in 1920. Although racial discrimination in voting was outlawed by the Fifteenth Amendment in 1870, many cities and states still practiced such discrimination until Congress began to supervise their elections after the passage of the Voting Rights Act of 1965. The exclusivity of the judiciary as a domain of affluent white males was merely a reflection of the monopolization of political power that affected institutions throughout American society.

The underrepresentation of the nation's majority group—women—was highlighted in 1991 when the appointment of a fourth woman to the Minnesota Supreme Court created the first American appellate court with a female majority.[8] The Minnesota court was especially unusual because only fifty-nine women had ever served on state supreme courts and very seldom were there even two women serving on the same court simultaneously.[9]

Hypothetically, the gender, age, religion, and other demographic characteristics of a judge should not matter as long as the judge follows the law in making decisions. Indeed, most judicial decisions advancing legal equality for women and minority groups were made by white male judges. However, the absence of diversity in the judiciary has had detrimental effects on the quality of justice in court decisions.

For most of American history, the judicial process was intentionally manipulated by white judges, prosecutors, and police officers in order to maintain control

over African-Americans and to permit whites to avoid sharing political power.
African-Americans knew that if the police arrested them, they were likely to be
convicted by all-white judges and juries, whether or not there was any evidence
of their guilt. At the same time, white citizens knew that they were not likely
to be punished by the legal system for crimes perpetrated against African-
Americans. After studying the American judicial system in the 1940s, a prominent
sociologist observed that discriminatory practices by unrepresentative judiciaries
lead to a breakdown in the beneficial functions of law for encouraging stability
and equality within society:

> If there is a deficiency of legal protection for [African-Americans], white
> people will be tempted to deal unfairly with them in everyday affairs. [Whites]
> will be tempted to use irregular methods to safeguard what they feel to be their
> interests against [African-Americans]. They will be inclined to use intimidation
> and even violence against [African-Americans] if they can count on going
> unpunished. When such patterns become established, the law itself and its
> processes are brought into contempt, and a general feeling of uncertainty,
> arbitrariness, and inequality will spread.[10]

This situation was not so different in many northern cities in which all-white
judiciaries demonstrated their biases against minorities.

Representativeness of the judiciary by gender, race, and ethnicity—or the lack
thereof—can have two significant effects on the judicial system. First, decisions
by homogeneous, white judiciaries may be less sensitive to the diversity of American society than legal decisions produced by court systems with demographically
diverse judges. For example, one study found that white judges were more lenient
toward white criminal defendants and demonstrated a greater inclination to
sentence African-American defendants to prison.[11] By contrast, African-
American judges treated white and African-American defendants evenhandedly in
deciding whether to incarcerate them.[12] Research has shown that female appellate
judges in the federal courts tend to be more receptive than their male counterparts
to individuals' claims in employment discrimination and search and seizure
cases.[13]

Second, the respect and obedience granted to the court system by the citizenry
may be affected by the representativeness of the judiciary. Thus, according to
scholars who study the courts, diversity among judges "can result in a strength-
ened judiciary whose presence can reassure certain segments of the population
of the neutrality and fairness of the judicial process."[14] Moreover, greater representativeness creates "a bench which fosters public confidence and which is
sensitive to the diverse perspectives necessary for a 'just' judiciary."[15] When
the ranks of judges include people from the broad spectrum of groups composing
American society, citizens have greater willingness to trust, accept, and obey
judicial decisions.

Concerns about diversity in the judiciary can affect judicial selection in several ways. First, merit selection procedures may explicitly include increased diversity among judges as one goal. When President Carter created nominating commissions to screen applicants for federal appellate judgeships, his executive order pointedly encouraged each panel "to make special efforts to seek out and identify well-qualified women and members of minority groups as potential nominees."[16] Second, in electoral judicial selection systems, political parties may use representativeness as one criterion for deciding which candidates should run under the party banner. If parties want to gain the electoral support of certain constituencies, such as African-American voters in urban areas, they may seek to recruit judicial candidates with whom those voters can identify. In addition, governors may advance diversity in the judiciary in gubernatorial appointment systems or in electoral systems in which governors can fill unexpected judicial vacancies by appointment.

Another important element in judicial selection, especially for appellate courts, is the geographic representativeness of judges on a court covering a broad jurisdiction. In federal appellate courts, which are divided into circuits covering several states each, the president and U.S. senators who control the judicial appointment process are keenly aware that each state in a circuit wants to be represented by at least one judge on the appellate court. Thus, for example, in the Sixth Circuit, which includes Michigan, Ohio, Kentucky, and Tennessee, if a judge from Tennessee dies or retires, there will be significant political pressure to preserve the "Tennessee seat" on the court by appointing a replacement from that state. Similarly, in elections for state supreme courts, political parties frequently try to make sure that they draw candidates from various large cities and regions rather than just from one city or region. On the U.S. Supreme Court, a traditional concern for geographic balance formerly affected presidential appointments. For example, when William O. Douglas was appointed to the Supreme Court by President Franklin Roosevelt, the President's advisors were concerned about whether Douglas would be regarded as a westerner because he had grown up in Washington state or as an easterner because he had taught at Yale Law School.[17] Recent presidents have been much less concerned about geographic balance on the Court and have focused instead on appointees' philosophical orientations. Thus, in 1993, two of the nine justices on the Supreme Court came from a single small state, Arizona (Chief Justice William Rehnquist and Justice Sandra Day O'Connor) and a third Arizonan, Secretary of the Interior Bruce Babbitt, was a finalist to fill an additional spot on the Court.[18]

Another aspect of representativeness concerns the partisan composition of courts. In a speech prior to the 1988 presidential election, Justice Harry Blackmun issued a warning that the election of another Republican president could make the Supreme Court become "very conservative well into the twenty-first century."[19] From 1991 to 1994, there were eight Republicans and one Democrat on the Supreme Court, a partisan composition that is skewed in favor of a political party that can claim the affiliation of only one-third of the population.[20] From 1987 to 1990 and then after 1994, there were seven Republicans and only two Democrats. Although a court's reputation for neutrality could be tarnished if it became too closely identified with one political party, concerns about excessive partisanship rarely affect judicial selection procedures. Political parties' dedicated efforts to fill the judiciary with their own loyalists are accepted without notice because the public frequently does not know or soon forgets judges' specific political party affiliations. The black robe of judicial office tends to obscure and inhibit popular awareness that all judicial officers are selected through political processes. Occasionally, judicial officers are selected in order to increase representativeness or, alternatively, to enable a president or governor to cultivate bipartisan support. For example, President Dwight Eisenhower, a Republican, appointed William Brennan, a Democrat, to the Supreme Court in 1956. Eisenhower adopted "the political wisdom of designating, especially in an election year, a Democrat. . . . [in order to maintain] the non-political or bipartisan atmosphere in which Ike felt most comfortable."[21] Republican President Richard Nixon appointed Democrat Lewis Powell to the Supreme Court in 1971 because he wanted to fulfill his campaign pledge to appoint a southerner by identifying a respected, conservative nominee who would not be opposed by Democratic senators.

Each system employed to select state and federal judges represents a different mix of choices concerning the relative importance of accountability, independence, qualifications, and representativeness. Proposals to change existing judicial selection procedures frequently stem from reformers' notions that one or more of these underlying issues should receive greater attention. Thus, for example, the continuing efforts in many states to initiate merit selection procedures reflect a view that the qualifications of judicial candidates deserve greater emphasis and that the electoral accountability of judges should be diminished.

## JUDICIAL SELECTION IN THE STATE COURTS

In the first years after the adoption of the U.S. Constitution, states selected judges by empowering state legislatures to make judicial appointments or by permitting legislatures to veto gubernatorial appointments. The appointment procedures stemmed, in part, from colonial familiarity with the manner in which kings of England had fired judges whose legal decisions did not conform to the rulers' desires. Thus, judicial selection procedures in the American states emphasized judges' independence from the state executive's control. By the 1820s, however, many states had adopted the practice of electing trial judges, and in the following decades, most states began to hold elections for appellate judgeships as well.[22] The movement toward judicial elections was part of a larger populist revolt against state legislatures because they were perceived to be under the control of political parties and business enterprises and to be unresponsive to the general public.[23]

Many state constitutions were rewritten to limit the power of state legislatures and to increase the power of governors. The introduction of judicial elections reflected an increased emphasis upon the accountability of the judiciary to the public.

In the twentieth century, concerns about the qualifications and competence of judicial officers led to the creation of merit selection procedures designed to remove judicial selection from the influence of partisan politics. In 1940 Missouri became the first state to adopt merit selection procedures. As a result, such procedures are often modeled on the "Missouri Plan." Although other states have subsequently followed Missouri's lead by implementing the merit selection method, many states still emphasize the accountability of judges by retaining judicial elections. Other states emphasize judges' independence by empowering the governor or the state legislature to make judicial appointments. None of the mechanisms for selecting judges, including merit selection, have removed the influence of politics. Although they operate differently in each selection method, political factors always affect the process. As a result, different kinds of individuals emerge as judges through each different process for judicial selection.

## An Overview of Selection Procedures

Because of numerous variations in the states' methods of selecting judges, including the use of different methods of selecting judges for different courts in the same state, it is difficult to categorize many states as adhering to one particular system. For example, New York has partisan elections for judgeships except for judges on the state's highest court, who are appointed by the governor and confirmed by the state senate.[24] In Kansas, seventeen of the state's thirty-one judicial districts use merit selection while the remaining fourteen districts employ partisan elections to choose trial judges.[25] Unlike other states' merit selection systems, which emulate the Missouri Plan, Connecticut's merit selection system gives the legislature, rather than the governor, the power to appoint judges from a list of nominees recommended by a judicial nominating commission. In Illinois and Pennsylvania, judges run in uncontested retention elections after their initial partisan election. Governors in Massachusetts and Delaware have formal authority to make judicial appointments, but they voluntarily rely on nominations from selection committees. In Rhode Island, the legislature appoints justices to the state supreme court, but the governor appoints other state judges. The primary selection method in each state is listed in figure 6.1, but as the foregoing examples demonstrate, some states use different procedures for judgeships in different courts.

## Partisan Elections

Political parties and their leaders exert significant influence over the selection of judges in partisan elections. Party leaders may use judgeships as rewards

**Figure 6.1: Methods of Selecting State Judges for General Jurisdiction Courts, Intermediate Appellate Courts, and Courts of Last Resort.**

*Partisan Elections*

| | |
|---|---|
| Alabama | New York (trial and intermediate appellate) |
| Arkansas | North Carolina |
| Illinois | Pennsylvania |
| Indiana (trial) | Tennessee (trial and last resort) |
| Kansas (some counties) | Texas |
| Mississippi | West Virginia |

*Nonpartisan Elections*

| | |
|---|---|
| Arizona (trial: small counties) | Nevada |
| Florida (trial) | North Dakota |
| Georgia | Ohio |
| Idaho | Oklahoma (trial and intermediate appellate) |
| Kentucky | Oregon |
| Louisiana | South Dakota (trial) |
| Michigan | Washington |
| Minnesota | Wisconsin |
| Montana | |

*Gubernatorial Appointments*

| | |
|---|---|
| California | New Jersey |
| Maine | New York (last resort) |
| New Hampshire | Rhode Island (trial) |

*Legislative Appointments*

| | |
|---|---|
| Rhode Island (last resort) | Virginia |
| South Carolina | |

*Nominating Commissions ("Merit Selection")*

| | |
|---|---|
| Alaska | Massachusetts |
| Arizona | Missouri |
| Colorado | Nebraska |
| Connecticut | New Mexico |
| Delaware | Oklahoma (last resort) |
| Florida (appellate) | South Dakota (last resort) |
| Hawaii | Tennessee (intermediate appellate) |
| Indiana (appellate) | Utah |
| Iowa | Vermont |
| Kansas (most counties) | Wyoming |
| Maryland | |

*Source: The Book of the States, 1994–1995 ed. (Lexington, KY: Council of State Governments, 1994), pp. 190-92.*

for lawyers' loyal service to the party. Lawyers who have served as campaign managers, fund raisers, or candidates for other political offices can forge personal connections in local and state political parties, laying the groundwork for future judicial campaigns. The selection of candidates for judicial office is not based on ideal criteria for selecting the "most qualified" judge but focuses on such factors as who can raise the most campaign money, who has worked diligently for the party, and who can win an election against the opposing party's candidate. Although there are usually primary elections, which permit several candidates to seek a party's nomination, party leaders may determine which lawyer will become the nominee by providing endorsements and organizational resources for favored candidates. Because of their influence, party leaders may be able to pressure lawyers interested in a particular judgeship to step aside in deference to favored candidates and to work more diligently for the party in order to "earn" an opportunity to run for judicial office. After the party's nominee is selected, organizational resources can be devoted to an open campaign on behalf of the candidate.

Political parties utilize judicial elections not simply to reward loyal lawyers, but also to reward other party loyalists with jobs in the courthouse. Traditionally, judges appoint many bailiffs, court clerks, secretaries, law clerks, and other support personnel. Thus, judgeships have been significant sources of political patronage. In 1990 the U.S. Supreme Court decided that elected officials cannot discriminate against low-level government workers who belong to an opposing political party in hiring and promotions.[26] In earlier cases, the Court had prohibited the firing of low-level government employees because of their political party affiliations.[27] Such discriminatory employment decisions were found to violate employees' and applicants' First Amendment rights to freedom of political belief and association. Although these Supreme Court decisions make it more difficult for elected judges and local party leaders to practice overt political patronage in hiring courthouse employees, party loyalists frequently continue to be favored for such positions.

In the view of lawyers' organizations and political reformers, the use of partisan elections for judicial selection connects judges too intimately with political parties and electoral politics. Judges are too closely aligned with and indebted to their political party leaders. Thus, there is a perceived risk that judges' decisions will be affected by partisan loyalties, or at least that they will appear in the public eye to be too closely connected to politicians. To many people, close connections between judges and local politics violate the image of the judicial branch as "legal" rather than "political." In other words, partisan elections make judges accountable to political parties and voters, but such selection procedures do not ensure that judges will be sufficiently independent and neutral in their decision making.

In addition, critics of partisan judicial elections argue that such mechanisms do not adequately emphasize qualifications. Judges are chosen because of service to political parties, with insufficient regard for their qualifications, experience, and personal attributes.

## Nonpartisan Elections

In order to emphasize the accountability of judges to the citizenry and sever the intimate connections between political parties and judicial candidates, many states implemented nonpartisan elections of judges. In theory, voters cast their ballots for the most qualified candidate without regard for political affiliation. Moreover, political parties no longer control judicial selection as a means of perpetuating political patronage. In practice, however, nonpartisan elections do not remove the influence of politics or political parties.

In many states with nonpartisan elections, political parties remain deeply involved in the selection of judges. Frequently, the parties select and support favored candidates, but alter their campaign activities. Although the formal political party organization may not officially run the campaign, leaders and members of a political party become actively involved in the formation and operation of "independent" campaign committees. In some states, political parties provide funding for "nonpartisan" judicial campaigns, although candidates are precluded from advertising their political affiliations. In Ohio, for example, political parties hold primaries to select nominees and then campaign on behalf of judicial candidates. The nominally nonpartisan election procedures merely require that candidates' party labels be removed from the ballots for the general election. Party leaders still retain the power to reward loyalists with judicial nominations.

Although political parties usually seek to influence the selection of appellate court judges, depending on local political traditions and party strength, the parties may not be involved in all nonpartisan campaigns for local judgeships. Sometimes other organized interests, namely local bar associations, may be significantly involved in selection of nominees. Lawyers' organizations will influence judicial elections by publicizing their endorsements of particular candidates.[28] When voters know very little about the candidates in a nonpartisan judicial election, the endorsement of a local bar association may be highly influential. The influence of bar association endorsements reflects the public's deference to lawyers on matters of law and judicial administration. Voters presume that lawyers are most knowledgeable about which candidates are best qualified to become judges; and, indeed, lawyers are likely to be most familiar with the professional performance of their peers in the legal profession. Lawyers, however, do not always agree about what makes someone "most qualified" to become a judge. In 1988, for example, an American Bar Association committee was deeply split over whether Judge Robert Bork, a U.S. Supreme Court nominee, should be labeled "well qualified" or "not qualified."[29] In 1991, twelve members of the ABA committee said Supreme Court nominee Clarence Thomas was "qualified," two members labeled Thomas "not qualified," and no committee members declared him to be "highly qualified."[30] Moreover, not all lawyers belong to bar associations. Thus, local and national bar associations represent the views of *some* lawyers, most frequently those who represent businesses and affluent individuals rather than those who represent the less fortunate or those who practice law to pursue social change. The substitution of bar association influence for political party influence in local nonpartisan elections does not ensure that the "best" candidates are selected; it merely forces judicial candidates to seek the support of a different political interest group.

Nonpartisan judicial elections pose problems for voters seeking to make informed choices about candidates. Judicial candidates are forbidden by the Code of Judicial Conduct from "announc[ing] his [or her] views on disputed legal or political issues."[31] Because they cannot discuss their views on specific issues that may be of interest to the voting public, such as crime and civil rights, judicial candidates primarily advertise their experience and credentials and make general assertions about being "tough on crime." They may criticize their opponents for specific decisions, for lack of experience, or for questionable ethics, but such criticisms are often muted because the Code of Judicial Conduct, adopted by most states, requires judicial candidates to "maintain the dignity appropriate to judicial office."[32] By launching overt political attacks—the staple of campaigns for other elective offices—judicial candidates run the risk of incurring sanctions from state supreme courts and other professional bodies that monitor lawyers' and judges' conduct. They may also alienate voters by appearing to be too "political" and lacking dignified judicial temperament.

Because of the limitations on judicial campaigning, successful candidates do not win simply because they are better qualified. Candidates for judicial office win elections for a variety of *political* reasons. They may win because they gained the endorsement of the local bar association or because an effective political party organization has supported their nonpartisan campaign. Lawyers who have held other elective offices, such as former prosecutors or city council members, frequently enjoy a huge advantage in nonpartisan elections because they have name recognition among the electorate. In Michigan, several former governors won nonpartisan elections to the state's supreme court because they had better state-wide name recognition than did the other lawyers running for the high courts. Wealthy candidates or successful fund-raisers enjoy similar advantages because of their ability to win name recognition through campaign advertising. Thus, nonpartisan elections do not achieve the twin goals of eliminating politics from judicial selection and ensuring that judges are selected because of their qualifications.

Candidates with a common or well-known last name may also win simply by attracting votes from an uninformed or disinterested electorate. Ohio voters, for example, are known for electing officials, including state supreme court justices, with the last name of Brown. In Washington, an unknown solo practitioner named Johnson defeated the incumbent chief justice of the state supreme court in a primary election without conducting any campaign at all.[33]

The drawbacks of nonpartisan elections illuminate the primary benefit of partisan elections. Voters have difficulty getting useful information about candidates in nonpartisan elections. In partisan elections, by contrast, despite their lack of familiarity with individual candidates, voters possess one crucial piece of information about every candidate: the party label. Even if voters are unfamiliar with the individuals running for judicial office, when the party label appears, a voter can make informed guesses about which candidate is likely to share his or her values and viewpoints. If a voter is a Democrat, he or she can guess that the Democratic judicial candidate's views concerning discrimination, crime, and other issues are similar to the voter's own views. Republican voters can make the same assessments about Republican judicial candidates. Based on the national political parties' platforms on various issues, independent voters can use party labels to decide which Republican, Democratic, or independent candidate to choose. Thus, voters are better able to select judges whose views they want represented in court when they have some concrete information about the political beliefs and affiliations associated with the party label.

The effectiveness of judicial elections, both partisan and nonpartisan, for maintaining accountability is undercut by two important factors. First, because judicial campaigns cannot focus on issues, voters must cast their ballots based on party labels, bar association endorsements, or name recognition. As a result, incumbent judges are rarely defeated unless they become embroiled in highly publicized controversies. Incumbents gain name recognition through daily newspaper and broadcast news coverage of their decisions. Because legal cases capture public attention but do not usually attract public opposition, incumbent judges gain easy reelection. In nonpartisan systems, the public frequently loses any awareness of the judge's original political party identification. Thus, voters simply endorse the well-known incumbent at each election as long as they cannot think of a compelling reason to remove him or her from office.

Second, the usefulness of judicial elections is diminished because of the power of governors to make interim appointments when judges resign, retire, or die in office. Governors use this appointment power to place party loyalists into judgeships. Once on the bench, these appointees enjoy the name recognition benefits of incumbency and continue to win reelection. Studies of judicial selection indicate that the judiciaries in many states with judicial elections are overwhelmingly composed of judges who were originally appointed by the governor, state supreme court, or chief administrative judge. In addition, interim appointments provide a crucial point of entry for judges from racial minority groups who are otherwise frequently unsuccessful in gaining judicial positions.[34] Such appointments may also diminish diversity, as in New York City, where the legislature created "temporary judgeships" to be filled by appointees, ostensibly to provide additional help for the regular elected judges.[35] Eventually these "acting judges," many of whom had served for more than ten years, outnumbered the elected judges 123 to 88 in the boroughs of Manhattan, the Bronx, and Brooklyn. While 27 percent of the elected judges came from minority groups, reflecting the diversity of New York City, only 11 percent of the "acting judges" were African-American or Hispanic.[36] In this instance, judicial appointments that circumvent the electoral process have diminished demographic representativeness on the New York trial bench.

Judicial elections create opportunities for voter participation in selecting and removing judges, but in practice voters actually have limited control because they have little information about judicial candidates and because many candidates have the benefits of incumbency through interim appointments.

## Gubernatorial and Legislative Appointments

A few states retain gubernatorial or legislative appointments as the formal mechanism for selecting judges. In the states with electoral systems, governors play a significant role by appointing judges to fill vacancies that arise between elections. Although governors usually favor members of their own political parties for judicial appointments, their selections may be influenced by various individuals and groups. Bar associations sometimes play a formal role in screening potential appointees. Local political party officials, state legislators, interest groups, and personal associates of the governor can also be particularly influential. A study of gubernatorial appointments in California found that ''[a]ppointees . . . of [Democratic Governor] Pat Brown relied upon personal political contacts with the governor, while business connections were important to [Republican Governor Ronald Reagan's] appointees, and local political and state legislator support were more central to the appointees of [Democratic Governor] Jerry Brown.''[37]

If governors wish to emphasize the qualifications of appointees, they may establish advisory committees to recruit and recommend potential nominees. For example, as governor of California, Ronald Reagan relied on judicial selection advisory boards in each county, composed primarily of prominent attorneys, businessmen, and civic leaders.[38] Although the use of advisory committees provides a mechanism for explicit consideration of the qualifications of judicial candidates, the process still ultimately results in the appointment of judges who share the governor's political party affiliation and/or ideological orientation.

Legislators from the governor's political party can have significant influence over the choice of appointees, especially if the gubernatorial appointments require legislative approval. Governors may defer to the preferences of key legislators when there are judicial vacancies in those legislators' districts. If the legislature itself possesses the appointment power, party affiliation and personal connections also influence the selection. Moreover, both governors and legislators can offer judicial appointments as rewards to former legislators and other loyal political allies.

Although service and loyalty to a political party play important roles in determining which lawyers will become judges under both appointment systems and electoral selection procedures, this does not mean that judges are necessarily incompetent party hacks. Political parties, governors, and legislators have an interest in ensuring that judges are adequately capable of fulfilling judicial responsibilities. Incompetent judges embarrass the political parties, governors, or legislators who helped to place them on the bench. The public may hold the selecting authorities responsible for the judges' behavior. Thus, the decision makers have an incentive to ensure that new judges are competent. This does not mean that the decision makers emphasize candidates' qualifications over their political credentials. It does mean, however, that there are pressures on decision makers to ensure that judicial nominees meet minimum qualifications for judicial service.

## Merit Selection

The primary trend in contemporary reforms of judicial selection procedures is away from electoral or appointment systems and toward so-called merit selection processes. Although many states have adopted merit selection procedures, other states have opted to retain greater participation and control by voters, political parties, and elected officials. The states that retain traditional judicial selection methods place greater formal emphasis on the accountability of judges than on judicial candidates' qualifications. In a state-wide referendum in 1987, for example, Ohio voters rejected a proposed merit selection plan in favor of retaining their nominally nonpartisan election system. The Ohio electorate apparently feared that, despite the inclusion of a retention election in the proposed procedures, a merit selection system would effectively prevent citizens from participating in the selection of judges. The public's fears were enhanced by an effective public relations campaign mounted by labor groups in opposition to a competing campaign by the Ohio Bar Association and the League of Women Voters, the groups supporting merit selection.[39]

The Missouri Plan, implemented in 1940, became the model for the states that subsequently adopted merit selection programs. The Missouri Plan involves four primary steps designed to emphasize the qualifications of appointees and to reduce the role of partisan politics. First, the governor forms a selection committee, which is responsible for collecting and screening applications from individuals seeking judicial appointments. Second, the committee recommends a list of three nominees. Third, the governor appoints one of the recommended nominees to the vacant judgeship. The final step requires the judge to stand for a retention election after one year in office. The citizens' opportunity to maintain accountability in the judiciary involves a simple "yes" or "no" vote for retaining the judge, usually without any campaigning or opposition from other judicial candidates.

The Missouri Plan attempts to reduce partisan politics while emphasizing qualifications and accountability. It is not possible, however, to remove the political influences that affect the decisions of those who appoint people to authoritative, policy-making positions in the American governmental system. The Missouri Plan simply restructures the political interactions that influence the so-called merit appointments to the judiciary. Moreover, because of the continuing and inevitable role of politics in judicial selection, political factors undermine the effectiveness of the scheme's emphasis on qualifications and accountability. As a result, one study of merit selection found that:

[T]he Missouri Plan does not consistently produce obviously superior judges in terms of quality education, cosmopolitan backgrounds, previous judicial experience or nonpartisan careers. Indeed, not only are the judges not decidedly superior in this regard, . . . they often appear indistinguishable from the [judges selected through other procedures].[40]

A well-known study of judicial selection in Missouri demonstrated that the Missouri Plan merely altered, but could not eliminate, political influences affecting the appointment of judges.[41] Political considerations did not directly determine the selection, but politics did affect an earlier stage in the procedures—the appointment of merit committee members. Thus, by winning the political battle over the composition of the selection committee, political interests could influence the selection of judges by applying their own values and criteria to the screening and recommending of nominees. In Missouri, the plaintiff bar—lawyers representing people who initiate lawsuits against businesses and individuals—battled the defense bar—lawyers who defend against lawsuits on behalf of insurance companies and corporations—over which group would dominate the selection committee. Moreover, there were overtones of traditional partisan political conflict because of the plaintiff lawyers' affiliation with the Democratic party and the defense lawyers' affiliation with the Republican party. The political interests that prevailed over the committee's composition could then influence the selection of judges. Thus, the purported emphasis on nominees' qualifications was limited, because the merit criteria for selecting judges were interpreted in light of the values and interests of the committee members. If plaintiff lawyers on the committee believed that judges should be sensitive to the interests of aggrieved plaintiffs, the committee members could ensure that the judicial appointees possessed plaintiff rather than defense experience or gave some other indication of sympathy to plaintiffs' interests. Conversely, defense lawyers on the committee could similarly stress their values in selecting nominees. In a separate study of judicial selection, one scholar summarized the way merit selection produces partisan results:

In merit plan systems, the partisan nature of the process by which judicial nominating commissions are staffed, the political dynamics of intracommission deliberations, and the partisan role of the governor in making final selections combine to result in the placement of partisans on the bench. The result of these informal aspects of . . . merit selection is as much partisanship on the bench as one observes in the formally partisan selection systems.[42]

The effectiveness of accountability under the Missouri Plan is questionable because so few judges are ever removed from office through retention elections. Judicial retention elections have been criticized for generating low voter turnout, presenting no issues to the public, and providing no meaningful choices on the ballot. If voters cannot think of a compelling reason to remove a judge—and judges' actions usually go relatively unnoticed—they have no reason to vote against him or her in a retention election. A study of judicial retention elections in ten states over a twenty-year period confirmed their relative ineffectiveness as an accountability mechanism. Out of 1,864 elections, judges were removed from office only 22 times, or in 1.2 percent of the elections.[43] Thus, judges appointed to office are seldom removed through retention elections.

Although judges are seldom removed through retention elections, these elections place pressure on judges to perform conscientiously. A survey of judges found that many believe that they must impress the public with their performances in order to retain their positions. For other judges, however, retention elections lead them to consciously avoid controversial rulings. By contrast, a third segment of judges believed that they simply needed to maintain good relationships with local attorneys and bar associations in order to succeed in retention elections.[44]

Judges, however, are not immune from removal through retention elections. In the most notable example, three justices of the California Supreme Court lost their seats in 1986 when interest groups critical of the court's decisions on capital punishment mobilized and spent nearly eight million dollars on a successful public relations campaign to oust the justices.[45] It is very unusual, however, for political interest groups or political parties to take such an active interest in judicial retention. It is generally difficult for political interests to identify and publicize an issue such as capital punishment, which can capture the public's attention and motivate people to vote in such elections.

## The Results of Judicial Selection Systems

All of the methods of selecting judges provide opportunities for involvement by political interests. In election systems, both partisan and nonpartisan, political parties play an important role in selecting and supporting candidates. Governors have formal influence over the selection of judges in appointment and merit systems, but they also participate significantly in electoral systems because of their power to make interim appointments. In merit selection systems, political parties and interest groups can seek representation on selection committees in order to influence the appointment of judges. Although each state's adoption of a specific selection system reflects a particular mix of concerns relating to accountability, qualifications, and independence of judges, all selection systems yield similar results.

Judges throughout the United States remain overwhelmingly male, white, middle-aged, and politically well-connected. For example, out of three hundred state supreme court justices nationwide in 1985, only twenty-three were female and, outside of Hawaii, only nine were members of racial minority groups.[46] By 1992, there were still only thirty-nine women on state supreme courts plus three additional female judges on the court of last resort for the District of Columbia.[47] Although these figures represented a great increase in representativeness compared to 1960 when three lonely female judges prevented white males from completely monopolizing all state supreme courts, these numbers still fall far short of reflecting the demographic composition of American society. The Minnesota Supreme Court attained a unique distinction in 1991 by becoming the first appellate court with a female majority, but few other courts are even close to representation of women in proportion with the American population.[48]

A study of the background characteristics of state supreme court justices found only slight variations, regardless of methods of judicial selection, in the kinds of people selected to be judges. Legislative appointment systems, for example, were notable for placing former legislators with fewer than fifteen years of legal experience into judgeships,[49] but other aspects of the appointees' backgrounds were not markedly different from those of appointees produced by other selection systems. The education, employment, and other characteristics of judges in election, appointment, and merit systems were remarkably similar. The study's authors observed only one notable difference: a tendency for merit selection procedures to provide fewer appointments for religious minorities.[50] This finding may reflect the fact that "merit" is in the eyes of the beholder, and therefore the biases of selection committee members may color their evaluations of candidates' qualifications. As the researchers concluded, "Since the credentials of merit selection judges are not superior to nor substantially different from those of other judges, the claims for merit selection and the need for bar leaders to have special influence in order to guarantee the selection of superior judges are questionable."[51]

Although merit selection procedures constitute the selection system of choice in the largest number of states, there is continued experimentation aimed at developing judicial selection methods that will simultaneously advance the desired goals of accountability, qualifications, and independence. In 1988 New Mexico carried its experimentation one step beyond the usual merit selection procedures by forcing merit selected judges to run in an initial *partisan* election after their first appointment and then to run in standard retention elections for subsequent terms in office.[52] The introduction of one partisan election into the merit selection process is an obvious attempt to increase voter participation and judicial accountability without sacrificing the perceived benefits of higher judicial qualifications derived from merit selection procedures.

## JUDICIAL SELECTION IN THE LOWER FEDERAL COURTS

The design of the federal judiciary places a premium on judges' independence. Article III of the U.S. Constitution provides that judges shall serve "during good Behavior," which essentially means service for life as long as the judges do not commit crimes or ethical improprieties that would warrant impeachment. Judges' salaries are also protected against reduction during their service on the bench.

The framers of the Constitution sought to ensure that federal judges would possess sufficient independence to make decisions without being influenced by the executive or legislative branches or by any other political actors or institutions. This independence and insulation from political control has been especially important for protecting individual liberties under the Bill of Rights. Since the 1950s, federal judges have frequently made courageous decisions to protect the rights of criminal defendants, racial minorities, small religious sects, and others who are unpopular and lack political power.

Judicial independence was incorporated as a component of the "checks and balances" in the constitutional system, both by insulating judges from partisan influence and by providing the executive and legislative branches with shared responsibilities for determining the composition of the judiciary. As chapter 9 will show in regard to judicial selection for the Supreme Court, because of the publicity surrounding the appointment of new justices, the public is aware that the president and the Senate have authority over appointments to the nation's highest court. By contrast, the selection of district and circuit court federal judges, who are also nominated by the president and confirmed by the Senate, rarely receives much public attention. Normally, the Senate automatically endorses most judicial appointees whose names are put forward by the president with the backing of their homestate senators. In some instances, however, the president and the Senate clash over the desirability and qualifications of specific nominees. In these instances, the two branches both try to influence the future course of federal law, court decisions, and judicial policy by defining the appropriate political and ideological composition of the judiciary. The Senate Judiciary Committee, in particular, plays a pivotal role in the appointment of judges by conducting hearings to examine each nominee and then by making a recommendation to the full Senate about whether the nominee ought to be confirmed.

## The Selection of Nominees

Usually a lawyer needs strong connections to a political party, a U.S. senator, or the president in order to receive an appointment to the federal judiciary. As with judicial appointments in state systems, federal judgeships are rewards for lawyers' loyalty and service to political parties or to politicians. Because federal judges have secure tenure in office, notable prestige in the legal profession, and significant power over public policies and other issues, many lawyers aspire to the federal judiciary, and some hopefuls even mount campaigns to cultivate the necessary political connections. A journalistic description of the career of Judge Roger Miner illustrates how political contacts produce judicial appointments:

In early 1980, [Judge Roger Miner] was just a local trial judge in upstate New York; [his wife] was an influential Republican operative lucky enough to pick the right horse in the presidential race, serving as Ronald Reagan's state vice chairman. Within nine months of [Reagan's inauguration as president], Roger had himself a judgeship on the federal district court; four years later, he was elevated to the powerful federal appeal bench in [New York City]. . . . In October 1987, when the nominations of Robert Bork and Douglas Ginsberg to the Supreme Court were going up in flames, [Mrs. Miner] became a virtual campaign committee for her husband. . . . "It really isn't fair that I get this attention [for seeking a promotion for my husband]," [Mrs. Miner] complains. "Most judges do their campaigning themselves."[53]

Traditionally, senators have had significant influence over the selection of appointees. If a district court vacancy occurred in a state with a senator from the same political party as the president, the president would defer to the senator's judgment about the best nominee. Thus, senators have been able to help their political allies become federal judges. Similarly, the Senate Judiciary Committee has maintained a procedure for permitting homestate senators to veto potential nominees. *Senatorial courtesy* generally leads the Senate to confirm nominees supported by their homestate senators. This courtesy is based not on friendship but on the practice of reciprocal cooperation when other senators seek confirmation for favored judicial candidates from their own states.

Since the 1950s, the American Bar Association has utilized a committee to evaluate and rate nominees for the federal judiciary. The committee's ratings for individual candidates receive national publicity, and senators seize the ABA ratings either to tout controversial nominees if the rating is favorable, or to oppose such nominees if the candidate is labeled "not qualified" by the committee. Because the ABA committee has traditionally been composed of conservative, business-oriented attorneys, it has tended to work most closely with Republican presidents.[54] However, presidential administrations have chosen to ignore the ABA committee at moments when they were displeased with ratings given to some of their nominees. The dissatisfaction expressed by these presidents reflects, in part, the fact that the ABA has attempted to diversify the membership of the committee in the past two decades. The committee's traditional conservatism has been moderated by this diversification. The change in membership has led to disagreements within the committee about the qualifications of some appointees, such as unsuccessful Supreme Court nominee Judge Robert Bork.

Elliot Slotnick's study of the ABA committee's evaluations of judicial nominees during 1979 and 1980 indicates that "the variables most associated with ABA rankings tended to be demographic and legal career variables, not education or political activity."[55] In other words, the committee's ratings were significantly associated with nominees' age, race, place of birth, gender, and income rather than simply with their "professional qualifications." Indeed, the study indicated that "the strongest possible relationship which emerged . . . was that between the ABA rating and the candidate's white male status."[56] Slotnick's empirical study of the ABA committee's ratings indicates the presence of bias in the evaluations of judicial nominees. As Slotnick observed:

The correlations do demonstrate convincingly, however, that the ABA and its Standing Committee on Federal Judiciary do not approach the judicial selection process in a political vacuum. Rather, like all groups active in the political process, the ABA and its standing committee are composed of individuals responding to political events from a value structure and perceptions of self and societal interests not necessarily shared by all interested parties.[57]

The Senate Judiciary Committee holds hearings to question each candidate for judicial office before voting on whether to recommend that the full Senate confirm the nominee. For district and circuit court nominees, the Judiciary Committee's staff and the F.B.I. conduct background checks on the candidates. If no major problems are discovered, the committee's hearing usually amounts to a brief introduction of the candidate by a homestate senator followed by a short period of general questions from the few committee members in attendance. The committee's unanimous vote to endorse the nominee is subsequently echoed by the entire Senate in granting official confirmation. The full committee will normally undertake detailed questioning of candidates only when the committee staff members or interest groups provide damaging information concerning extremist views, ethical improprieties, or questionable affiliations or conduct. Traditionally, the chairperson of the Judiciary Committee has been a powerful figure who can force the president and other members of the Senate to accept his preferred candidates for judgeships in his state and circuit by threatening to oppose or delay the confirmation process for other nominees. If a presidential election is approaching and the Judiciary Committee is controlled by senators from the opposition's party, the chairperson will usually stop conducting confirmation hearings for pending nominees in the hope that the White House will be captured and a new president will fill the remaining vacancies with like-minded partisans.

## Judicial Selection in the Carter Era

During the 1970s, President Jimmy Carter attempted to reform the selection of federal judges by introducing merit selection procedures. The Carter administration created judicial nominating commissions composed of lawyers and lay members to solicit applications in each circuit, screen interested candidates, and make recommendations to the president. The Carter reforms had two primary purposes. First, the Carter administration sought to reduce partisan political influences over the selection process by introducing merit procedures that would place more emphasis on judicial nominees' qualifications. Second, the reforms were intended to create more opportunities for qualified nontraditional candidates to receive consideration for federal judgeships. The Carter administration was particularly interested in providing opportunities for female and minority candidates, because traditional partisan processes of judicial appointment consistently led to the appointment of politically well-connected white males. The Carter administration instructed each nominating commission to give special consideration to female and minority candidates in order to increase representativeness of the federal judiciary.[58] Carter's desire to increase representativeness coincided with his political interests, because women and minority voters are strong constituencies in the Democratic party.

Because senators could not be expected to surrender their traditional involvement in the selection of district judges, Carter could not impose merit selection on the appointment process for federal trial judges. Instead, he strongly encouraged senators to initiate merit selection procedures for federal judicial vacancies occurring in their home states. Some senators implemented such procedures, and some did not.

Carter's reforms advanced some of his intended goals. In several instances, experienced lawyers without strong political connections received appointments to the federal bench. In addition, Carter appointed more women and minority judges than did any previous president. Over 98 percent of the appointees by previous presidents were male. Minority judges comprised 9 percent of the appointees of one previous president—Gerald Ford.[59] During Carter's four-year term, more than 15 percent of his appointees were female, and more than 21 percent were minority group members.[60] This was the federal judiciary's peak of demographic representativeness prior to the beginning of the Clinton administration in the 1990s.

Carter's role in the diversification of the federal judiciary was enhanced by the creation of more than 150 new judgeships in 1978. Thus, Carter had the opportunity to add diversity through a bloc of appointees, rather than merely by replacing judges one by one as they died or retired. Congress is normally reluctant to create new judgeships unless its dominant party also controls the White House. In the late 1970s, the Democrat-controlled Congress created the new judgeships because a Democratic president would have the opportunity to fill them with Democratic appointees.

Studies of the federal courts indicate that Carter pursued the goal of representativeness without compromising the goal of appointing qualified individuals. In fact, one scholar concluded that the female and minority appointees generally had stronger qualifications than the white males who received judicial appointments.[61]

Although Carter's selection procedures advanced the goal of increased representativeness and maintained an emphasis on appointees' qualifications, his merit selection procedures did not eliminate the influence of partisan considerations. The nominating commissions were overwhelmingly composed of Democrats and, not surprisingly, over 90 percent of the appointees were Democrats as well. Thus, as in the Missouri Plan for state judicial selection, political considerations did influence the composition and deliberations of Carter's merit selection committees.[62] Moreover, there were situations in which the committees' recommended nominees did not receive appointments because senators and other political actors successfully lobbied the president on behalf of politically-connected candidates.[63]

## Judicial Selection in the Reagan Era

When President Ronald Reagan took office in 1981, he abolished Carter's judicial nominating commissions and undertook a systematic strategy to change the composition of the federal judiciary. Although Republican senators maintained influence over appointments for district judgeships and some senators retained merit selection procedures for federal judicial vacancies in their home states, the Reagan administration gave significant authority for selecting and screening potential judicial nominees to political appointees in the Justice Department and the White House. These officials initiated what one scholar has labeled "the most systematic ideological or philosophical screening of judicial candidates since the first Roosevelt administration."[64] The Reagan administration made a determined effort to ensure that all nominees possessed a conservative judicial philosophy and, moreover, shared the administration's opposition to controversial issues such as abortion and affirmative action. On several occasions, Republican political leaders were distressed that the Reagan administration rejected outstanding Republican lawyers and law professors who were "too moderate." By contrast, Democratic senators found themselves vigorously opposing several nominees appointed for their extremely conservative views and lacking legal experience or otherwise demonstrating questionable qualifications or behavior. For example, one unsuccessful Reagan appointee generated opposition by saying that civil rights advocates were "unAmerican" and "Communist-inspired."[65] The Reagan administration also made the first concerted effort to appoint young judges, many only in their thirties, in order to ensure that these conservative jurists would remain on the bench to influence law and public policy for decades after Reagan's departure from office.[66] During Reagan's eight years in office, over half of all federal judges gradually took senior status, retired, resigned, or died. Thus, Reagan employed his strategy for making the federal judiciary more conservative by appointing 368 district and circuit judges.[67]

Because the Reagan administration was primarily interested in appointees' political ideologies, there was no emphasis on maintaining representativeness in the federal judiciary. Less than 8 percent of Reagan's appointees were female and less than 7 percent were members of minority groups.[68] In contrast to the Carter administration, the Reagan administration generally disregarded representativeness as a goal in judicial selection. This is illustrated by the fact that less than 2 percent of Reagan's appointees were African-Americans. Despite the significant increase in the number of African-American attorneys qualified for judicial appointments because discriminatory barriers to higher education had been removed over the course of three decades, Reagan appointed a smaller percentage of African-American judges than any of his predecessors, Republican or Democrat, in the preceding twenty-five years. The Reagan administration did, however, achieve its primary goal of appointing judges who would alter the development of law and judicial policies by producing conservative decisions in the federal courts.[69]

## Judicial Selection in the Bush Era

The Bush administration emulated the Reagan era in thoroughly screening judicial candidates to ensure that they were sufficiently conservative and loyal to the Republican party's positions.[70] Out of Bush's first sixty-nine nominees to federal judgeships, 93 percent were white, 88 percent male, and 64 percent had net incomes over five hundred thousand dollars.[71] Ultimately, the Bush administration emphasized appointing more women judges. Nearly 20 percent of Bush's appointees were female, a percentage that exceeded even that of the Carter administration.[72]

Unlike the Reagan administration, which had officials devoting their time to judicial selection, the Bush administration gave the responsibility for investigating and screening candidates to attorneys in the Justice Department. This reorganization of the judicial selection process frustrated many political supporters who believed that Bush was not working efficiently to nominate Republicans for vacant judgeships. During the Bush era, it took an average of three hundred eighty-five days from the vacancy date for the administration to select a nominee, and an additional average of one hundred thirty-nine days for the Senate to confirm nominees.[73] It is possible that the Bush administration lacked any sense of urgency about filling judicial vacancies because it believed, in light of the president's popularity in the immediate aftermath of the Persian Gulf War, that the president was likely to be reelected for a second term. When Governor Bill Clinton won the 1992 presidential election, Bush left office without having filled nearly one hundred judicial vacancies—judgeships that would then be filled by Clinton-appointed Democrats.[74] Bush had, in fact, made nominations for half of these vacancies, but the Democrat-controlled Senate Judiciary Committee slowed the confirmation process due to a dispute with the president about access to F.B.I. reports on nominees' backgrounds.[75]

## Judicial Selection in the Clinton Era

President Clinton used his judicial appointment power to make an unprecedented effort to increase demographic diversity among federal judges. Nearly 32 percent of Clinton's district court appointees were women, a proportion far exceeding Bush's record-setting 20 percent. In addition, more than 25 percent of Clinton's appointees were African-Americans, more than 8 percent were

Hispanic, and Asian and Native American appointees each comprised 1 percent. As a result, only 39 percent of Clinton's appointees were white males, a figure far below those of his predecessors (Bush, 73 percent; Reagan, 85 percent; Carter, 68 percent).[76]

Clinton's emphasis on broadening opportunities for members of historically excluded groups did not mean that his administration reduced the quality of appointees for federal judgeships. If qualitative ratings from the traditionally conservative ABA are used as a common reference point, Clinton's female and minority appointees earned the ABA's highest rating ("highly qualified") in the same or higher proportion as all nominees, white males and otherwise, by the Reagan and Carter administrations. If all of Clinton's nominees are taken into consideration, the proportion of Clinton appointees receiving the ABA's highest rating exceeds that of all other presidential administrations since the ABA began evaluating judicial nominees.[77]

The Clinton administration's selection process differed from that of its immediate predecessors in several ways. Clinton returned to the Reagan administration's practice of having several attorneys devote themselves to the process of investigating and nominating judicial candidates. Unlike Reagan, however, Clinton told Democratic senators that there would be no ideological screening process for potential judicial nominees. Clinton's nominees were overwhelmingly drawn from Democrats (89 percent), but the administration did not insist that nominees share the President's views on specific policy issues. Although several women in the Bush administration had been key decision makers in the judicial selection process, Clinton was the first president to place responsibility for judicial selection in offices that were headed by women.[78]

## Federal Judicial Selection and the Possibility of Reform

The continuing emphasis on political and ideological criteria for selecting judicial appointees perpetuates the long-standing concerns that inadequate attention is given to the qualifications needed by a good federal judge. After studying judicial selection, one scholar developed a set of recommendations to improve the selection procedures.[79] These recommendations explicitly recognize that the process of selecting federal judges will inevitably involve political considerations and political actors. Instead of trying to remove the influence of politics, as advocates of merit selection unsuccessfully seek to do, these recommendations attempt to reshape political interaction in the judicial selection process to ensure that decision makers have complete information and that opposing political interests have the opportunity to present their views. When nominations are made, for example, interest groups could be notified and given time to conduct their own investigations of the candidates as well as an opportunity to present their conclusions to the Judiciary Committee.[80] In addition, the Senate Judiciary Committee could increase the staff devoted to investigating appointees' backgrounds and qualifications, and the committee could seek to ensure that adequate time is spent evaluating each candidate.[81] Moreover, the ABA should not be permitted to maintain its special role in the appointment process unless it "stop[s] rating virtually all nominees as 'qualified' and provide[s] explanations for its unfavorable ratings."[82] These changes may help to make the selection process more thorough and visible.

## ALTERNATIVE JUDICIAL SELECTION PROCEDURES

### United States Magistrate Judges

As described in chapter 2, U.S. magistrate judges serve as assistants to federal district judges. The magistrate judges are important, however, because they are authoritative judicial officers in their own right. They can undertake virtually any judicial task carried out by district judges, including presiding over complete civil trials with the consent of litigants, except for the trials and sentencing of felony criminal defendants.[83] Because the magistrate judges are selected through procedures that differ from those used to select regular federal judges, the magistrate judges provide an instructive basis of comparison, illuminating the inherently political nature of judicial selection, regardless of method.

Prior to 1979, magistrate judges, or U.S. magistrates, as they were called prior to their title change in 1990,[84] were appointed directly by the judges of the district court in which the specific magistrate judge would work. After serving an eight-year term as a full-time magistrate judge or a four-year term as a part-time magistrate judge, the magistrate judge could be reappointed or terminated at the discretion of the district judges. In 1979, as part of the Carter administration's efforts to introduce merit selection procedures into the judiciary and to increase representativeness among judicial officers, Congress mandated that district judges use citizen selection committees to advertise magistrate judge positions, solicit and screen applicants, and recommend nominees to the judges. Research into the magistrate judge selection process indicates that the introduction of merit procedures merely restructured interactions among decision makers but did not eliminate the role of politics in the appointment process.[85] In different districts, judges appointed distinctive types of selection committees which, depending on their composition, either catered to the judges' preferences, diligently searched for the "best" candidate, or engaged in battles reflecting the divisions between the judges of the district court.[86] In the end, the continuing control of district judges over the final selections yielded nearly identical percentages—both before (59.1 percent) and after (59.8 percent) the introduction of merit procedures—of magistrate judges who were former district court law clerks and Assistant U.S. Attorneys (and, therefore, close associates of the judges.)[87] Although more women and minority group members became magistrate judges in some districts, the overall consequence of introducing merit selection procedures was to reduce the appearance of impropriety that previously existed when district judges appointed favored assistants to authoritative judicial positions.

## Administrative Law Judges

The judicial selection process that puts the greatest emphasis on the nonpolitical qualifications of appointees is the appointment process for Administrative Law Judges, who are, in fact, not part of the federal judiciary at all. An Administrative Law Judge (ALJ) presides over quasi-judicial proceedings in executive branch agencies. In the Social Security Administration, for example, ALJs hold hearings to determine whether claimants are entitled to disability payments from the agency. Although agency proceedings do not follow all of the formal procedures used in federal courts, the ALJ can hear testimony, examine medical evidence, and listen to arguments by attorneys, much the same as a regular judge but in the limited, specific context of a particular executive agency. Decisions by ALJs can be appealed to the federal courts. The ALJs constitute a gigantic, invisible judiciary in the executive branch of the federal government. There are more ALJs in the federal government than there are judges in the federal courts. In fact, disregarding the ALJs in the other twenty-nine federal agencies that have such judges, the ALJs in the Social Security Administration alone outnumber all the judges in the federal court system.[88]

The development of merit selection for ALJs was influenced by political considerations. Political choices had to be made, for example, between the agencies' desire to appoint candidates who were experts in their specialized areas of law and the ABA's goal of locating the best overall candidates with general litigation experience.[89] Ultimately, the merit selection process that was implemented required candidates to have seven years of general litigation experience, including two years of recent experience in specific areas of administrative law.[90] When positions are advertised, candidates begin a grueling application process.[91] The government rates each candidate's judicial qualifications by interviewing judges and lawyers who are familiar with the applicant. The applicant takes a written test, writing a sample ALJ opinion based on sample materials from a hypothetical case. The written test is followed by a personal interview with a panel composed of a Chief Administrative Law Judge, a Civil Service Commission representative, and a private attorney. Applicants who pass each stage of the process are placed on a register of eligible candidates. When a vacancy occurs, the top three candidates, based on overall scores plus any additional veterans' preference points for past military service, are re-interviewed by a Chief Administrative Law Judge who recommends one nominee to the head of the executive agency.

Although the selection process includes subjective, discretionary decisions by those who evaluate the writing samples and conduct the interviews, these procedures place more emphasis than do other selection systems on relevant legal experience and performance. The process has apparently succeeded in eliminating evidence of partisan political influences over the selection of ALJs, because the appointees include a remarkably even mix of Republicans, Democrats, and independents.[92]

Could a similar process be developed and implemented to reduce the openly political considerations that underlie the appointment of federal judges? No. Unlike the narrow role of the ALJ, which requires knowledge, experience, and judicial qualifications directed at a single, specific area of law, federal judges must decide cases covering a diverse range of legal issues. As a result, there could never be a consensus on precisely what experiences, knowledge, and personal qualities make someone best qualified to be a federal judge. Moreover, because federal judges have such significant power over controversial social issues and public policies, political actors, including the president, the Senate, and political parties, would not willingly surrender their power, through the current appointment process, to influence important judicial decisions, public policy, and the development of federal law. As one scholar has observed, many kinds of potential judicial selection reforms "would be contrary to our political tradition and would be specially inapposite at a point when there is widespread recognition of the policy-making role of our courts. Our courts and judges cannot be isolated and sanitized from public policy."[93]

## Lay Judges

An alternative approach to judicial selection would be to reconceptualize the qualifications for becoming a judge. Must someone have a law degree in order to be qualified? Most lawyers would answer, "Yes," and the general public presumes that lawyers know best about judicial matters. However, several states still use lay judges for lowest level courts, such as Ohio's Mayor Courts, which primarily handle traffic offenses in small towns. Although there are examples of outrageous statements and decisions by lay judges, it is not difficult to find comparable counter-examples of such statements and decisions by lawyer-judges. A law school education does not guarantee that a lawyer-judge will be wise or unbiased. A study of lay judges concluded that their decisions are not necessarily bad and, in fact, are very similar to decisions by judges trained in law.[94]

Although most lay judges work in the lowest state courts, frequently in rural areas, handling minor misdemeanors and traffic offenses, occasionally the question arises of whether nonlawyers should be considered for appointment to higher courts with more authority for significant decisions. In his autobiography, Justice William O. Douglas describes telling President Franklin Roosevelt that the U.S. Constitution does not require that justices on the Supreme Court be lawyers. According to Douglas, Roosevelt might have appointed a nonlawyer to the Supreme Court if he had lived to finish his fourth term in office.[95] In 1976

Governor Cecil Andrus of Idaho asked the Idaho Judicial Council, the state's judicial nominating commission, to consider recommending a lay person for appointment to the Idaho Supreme Court. Predictably, lawyers and others strenuously objected to the notion that a lay person could be qualified to serve on the state's highest court, and Andrus ultimately appointed a lawyer.[96] Although no lay person has been appointed to an appellate court in modern times, these examples raise the question of whether lay people should be considered for such appointments.

A lay person would have a very difficult time serving as a judge in a trial court. The nature of the trial judge's job in overseeing trials requires specific knowledge of legal procedures, rules of evidence, and other subjects taught in law school. An appellate judge has different responsibilities than a trial judge. Unlike trial judges, who frequently must respond immediately to motions concerning the admissibility of evidence and other matters, appellate judges spend weeks or months studying legal cases and writing careful opinions. An intelligent lay person could study cases and, like an appellate judge, seek previous cases and other relevant information in libraries in order to write a thoughtful opinion. The appellate judge does not necessarily need to spout detailed knowledge about technical rules of law off the top of his or her head.

Moreover, the kinds of cases presented in appellate courts and especially in supreme courts frequently elicit decisions based on personal values and predictions of the social consequences of judicial policies rather than on legal knowledge. For example, when the Supreme Court addressed whether or not life support systems could be removed from a comatose person with severe, irreversible brain damage,[97] knowledge of the Constitution and federal law was of limited utility. The decision had to be made based on the justices' concepts of fundamental personal rights and the power of state governments to make decisions for individuals. An intelligent lay person could participate in such decisions as well as a legally-trained judge and, indeed, the lay person might be able to contribute valuable insights that could be ignored when decisions are left entirely to lawyers. As discussed in chapter 3, legal education has a narrowing effect on the thinking of lawyers, which may limit their capacities to analyze difficult issues outside the technical constraints of legal reasoning.

The best evidence that a lay person could serve effectively on the Supreme Court may be the fact that the justices of the Supreme Court, lawyers one and all, frequently diverge into dramatic disagreements. If judges, who share a common legal education, cannot agree on the answers to these difficult questions, what would be wrong with permitting nonlawyers to participate? Some people assert that nonlawyers cannot be judges because they do not know legal precedents. In fact, Chief Justice William Rehnquist has written that "[t]here is simply no demonstrably 'right' answer to the question involved in many of [the Supreme Court's] difficult cases."[98] Judicial officers' values and attitudes influence their decisions and their willingness to follow or ignore case precedents.

The political reality is that even if a daring president (or governor) appointed a lay person to an appellate court, the legislature—an institution in which lawyers, although not a numerical majority, represent the dominant occupational group[99]— would never approve. The action would clash so directly with the public's belief that judges must be lawyers that the appointing official would probably incur significant political opposition and damage. Moreover, because the power of the courts depends so much on public acceptance of the legitimacy of judges as knowledgeable and authoritative in a "legal" rather than "political" sense, the judicial branch might be harmed by the introduction of lay judges on appellate courts. People might come to view the courts as merely political institutions. Although courts are in fact political, the public's belief in, acceptance of, and obedience to law may depend on the continuation of the popular view that only lawyer-judges can make decisions consistent with law and justice. The real value of legal education may lie in providing judges with the skills to write their decisions in the form of legal opinions that *sound* solidly grounded in established principles, whether the actual decision reverses precedent, upholds prior decisions, or breaks new ground.

## JUDICIAL SALARIES

In 1989 federal judges asserted that it would no longer be possible to recruit qualified judicial appointees if Congress did not agree to raise federal judges' salaries. Chief Justice William Rehnquist, in an unprecedented press conference, labeled the judges' salary concerns "the most serious threat to the future of the Judiciary and its continued operations that I have observed."[100] At the time of the press conference, federal district judges were paid annual salaries of $89,500, circuit judges received $95,000, and Supreme Court justices earned $110,000 with $5,000 extra for the chief justice. All of these salaries were more than three times greater than the $28,704 median salary earned by managerial and professional workers nationwide, and the judges' salaries placed them in the top 7 percent of family incomes nationally.[101] Congress eventually approved pay raises for federal judges in excess of 30 percent, which moved these judicial officers' compensation even farther beyond the average salaries of other Americans. The federal judges' dire warnings and successful lobbying efforts to gain a pay increase highlight some questions seldom considered by the public and policymakers. How much should judges be paid? Do judicial salaries affect the quality of lawyers available for appointment to the bench? What do judges' salary expectations reveal about the judges' views of themselves and about their awareness of daily life in American society?

### The Attractiveness of Judicial Office

It is difficult to say just how much judges should be paid. As public servants paid from limited governmental budgets, they cannot expect to be paid as much as private attorneys who work for profit-seeking law firms. Moreover, how does one place a value on the tremendous power, prestige, autonomy, and job security enjoyed by judges? These attributes of judicial office must be extremely valuable, because there are always many lawyers seeking to obtain appointments to or nominations for state and federal judgeships. The fact that 73 percent of federal judicial appointees took a pay cut averaging nearly $70,000 in order to become judges indicates that there must be substantial nonfinancial benefits from judgeships.[102] In 1994, the salaries of state court trial judges ranged from $63,000 in Montana to $113,000 in New York, with higher salaries for state appellate judges.[103] Despite the fact that most state judicial salaries lag behind federal judicial salaries, there has never been any indication that political parties, governors, and other decision makers in state judicial selection processes have trouble finding capable, interested candidates.

In their lobbying efforts directed at Congress in 1989, the federal judges made clear that their reference group for determining their salary expectations was highly paid attorneys in private practice in major cities. The judges' information booklet on the salary issue emphasized that federal judges' qualifications and experience make them comparable to partners in urban law firms who make $300,000 or more per year.[104] The judges asserted that because their salaries lagged so far behind the highest paid private practitioners, it would soon be difficult to find qualified lawyers willing to become federal judges. The implication of the judges' assertion is that the current method of appointing federal judges succeeds in selecting qualified judges and that there is a shortage of lawyers qualified to become federal judges.[105] It is obvious, however, that the intensely political process of appointing federal judges focuses on attorneys' *political qualifications* rather than on any ideal qualifications. A variety of lawyers with divergent educational backgrounds, legal experiences, and judicial philosophies serve in the federal judiciary. The one thing that they have in common is their political links to the president's political party or to homestate senators at the time they were appointed.

The judges' lobbying campaign provided few examples of judges leaving the bench because of dissatisfaction with salaries and no evidence that salaries prevented new judges from being recruited. There are more than seven hundred federal judges, yet no more than five or six judges voluntarily leave the bench each year.[106] The judges portrayed the salary issue as a "crisis" as part of a political strategy to pressure Congress to increase salaries. Similarly, their characterization of the federal judicial selection process as emphasizing appointees' qualifications and producing qualified judges distorted the procedures' true emphasis on political factors. Certainly most federal judges work very hard and do a creditable job of processing a burdensome caseload. Their accomplishments are evidence of the abundance of capable lawyers among the more than 800,000 attorneys in United States who are available to fill the 825 federal judgeships. The quality of the federal judiciary does not indicate that the selection process places a premium on identifying the "most qualified" candidates.

## Implications for Judicial Behavior

One important issue underlying every judicial selection process, state and federal, is the question of whether the judges produced by those processes understand the people and the society that will be affected by their decisions. In states that emphasize judicial accountability through electoral selection procedures, there are incentives for judges to remain in touch with society in order to gain and retain office. The job security that elected judges enjoy through the power of incumbency diminishes their need to remain connected to society, but the periodic elections provide greater contacts between the judges and the public than do the appointive systems in other states and in the federal judiciary.

Because judges' decisions are inevitably shaped by their values, attitudes, and experiences, it is important for them to understand how disputes arise in society and how judicial decisions touch people's lives. Even Chief Justice Rehnquist, whose judicial decisions have been characterized as unsympathetic to individual litigants,[107] has acknowledged that judges must possess knowledge about how people are affected by social forces in society.[108] In pursuing their pay raises, however, the appointed federal judges provided disturbing evidence that they are isolated from American society and from the people affected by their decisions. The federal judges' report to Congress advocating immediate and substantial pay raises emphasized a quotation from an anonymous judge: "The long term financial sacrifice for my family is too much. I cannot sentence them to a lifetime of genteel *poverty*" [emphasis supplied].[109] In addition, at his highly publicized press conference, Chief Justice Rehnquist issued a plaintive plea: "[The government] should offer [judges] enough so that they will be able to educate their kids."[110] Both of these statements say more about the judges' views of society than about their own suffering from salary dissatisfaction. As one analysis of judicial salaries concluded:

> For anyone earning at least $89,500 annually, a sum that is over four times greater than that of the median salary for full-time American workers, to speak about living in poverty is outrageous. This characterization not only ignores the fact that millions of Americans are unemployed, homeless, and lacking medical insurance, but it bespeaks an absence of sensitivity to the harsh realities of life in American society and the undeniably privileged position enjoyed by citizens who receive the relatively high salaries of federal judges.[111]

After winning their raises, district judges' salaries moved from $89,500 to $129,500 by 1992. Circuit judges' salaries were raised to $137,300, associate Supreme Court justices received $159,000, and the chief justice was paid $166,200.[112] Despite the raises, judges continued to pursue additional salary increases on a regular schedule by repeating their same arguments to Congress. For example, in his year-end report for 1995, Chief Justice Rehnquist said "unless a solution is found to deal adequately with the issue of judicial salary erosion, it will be difficult to attract outstanding lawyers to the bench and retain them.''[113]

It appears that the prestige, privilege, and power of judicial office can insulate judges from contact with the social forces shaping our society. The quoted statements of the federal judges indicate that perhaps these judicial officers, whose salaries place them near the top of American society, have little understanding of poverty or of the struggles facing most Americans in trying to educate their children. It is difficult to know whether the appointive system fosters this insulation from social forces by selecting at the outset elite lawyers removed from society. Alternatively, giving federal judges such independence and autonomy gives them little reason to be concerned with the daily lives of their fellow citizens.

## CONCLUSION

Various state and federal court systems employ a variety of methods for selecting judges. Each of these methods—partisan elections, nonpartisan elections, appointments, and merit selection—emphasizes a different mix of the underlying values promoted in the selection of judges—accountability, independence, and qualifications. Every selection method employed is influenced by politics. Even methods designed to eliminate political influences merely manage to reshape, rather than remove, political influences. For example, nonpartisan elections are frequently influenced by political parties and governors' interim appointments of loyal partisans to vacancies that arise between elections. Merit selection procedures simply shift the focus of political competition to the committee authorized to screen candidates and recommend appointees to the governor. While politics is often treated as a ''dirty word'' when associated with the judiciary, some elements of politics may actually be quite beneficial. For example, the use of partisan political elections helps inform voters when selecting candidates because the visible party label provides a clue about candidates' values and policy preferences.

In the federal system, partisan politics is evident in the processes for presidential nomination and senate confirmation of judges. In addition, interest groups, including the American Bar Association, seek opportunities to provide information and arguments that may influence the judiciary's composition.

This chapter began with a discussion of the goals of accountability, independence, qualifications, and representativeness that underlie various methods of selecting judicial officers. The chapter concludes with a question about whether judicial selection systems produce judges sensitive to daily life in American society. Because all judicial selection procedures are influenced by political interactions and produce similarly elite, politically well-connected judges, perhaps the search for the ''best'' selection system distracts the public from the equally important goal of keeping judges not merely accountable to society, but actually *connected to society*. If judges lack connections to society, their decisions may be insensitive to the social conditions generating the legal issues brought before them in court. Moreover, judges may be unable to accurately anticipate the consequences of their decisions on people's lives. For example, because the public may not benefit from insulating comfortable, policy-making elites, such as judges, from contact with immediate social problems, judges may be better connected to society if their salaries are not increased too high above the salaries of other citizens. Society must be concerned not only with the issue of who will be the decision makers, but also with the question of what factors and conditions will enhance or diminish the quality of judicial officers' decisions. As the next chapter will discuss, judges' decisions are influenced by their values and policy preferences, elements shaped by their knowledge, experiences, and philosophies.

## NOTES

1. Melinda Gann Hall, "Justices As Representatives: Elections and Judicial Politics in the American States," *American Politics Quarterly* 23 (1995): 485–503; Paul Brace and Melinda Gann Hall, "Studying Courts Comparatively: The View From the American States," *Political Research Quarterly* 48 (1995): 5–29.
2. Sheldon Goldman, "Judicial Selection and the Qualities that Make a 'Good' Judge," *The Annals of the American Academy of Political and Social Science* 462 (1982): 112–24.
3. Ibid., pp. 113–14.
4. *Missouri v. Jenkins*, 495 U.S. 33 (1990).
5. *Missouri v. Jenkins*, 495 U.S. 33, 58 (1990) (Kennedy, J., concurring in judgment and concurring in part).
6. Albert Blaustein and Roy Mersky, "Rating Supreme Court Justices," *American Bar Association Journal* 58 (1972): 1183–86.
7. *Bradwell v. State of Illinois*, 83 U.S. (16 Wall.) 130, 141 (1873).
8. David W. Allen and Diane E. Wall, "Minnesota: Where Women Justices Are a Majority," *Judicature* 77 (1993): 162.
9. David W. Allen and Diane E. Wall, "Role Orientations and Women State Supreme Court Justices," *Judicature* 77 (1993): 156.
10. Gunnar Myrdal, *An American Dilemma: The Negro Problem and Modern Democracy* (New York: Harper & Row, 1944), p. 524.
11. Susan Welch, Michael Combs, and John Gruhl, "Do Black Judges Make a Difference?" *American Journal of Political Science* 32 (1988): 131–33.
12. Ibid.
13. Sue Davis, Susan Haire, and Donald R. Songer, "Voting Behavior and Gender on the U.S. Courts of Appeals," *Judicature* 77 (1993): 129–33.
14. Goldman, "Judicial Selection," p. 119.

15. Elliot Slotnick, "Lowering the Bench or Raising it Higher?: Affirmative Action and Judicial Selection During the Carter Administration," *Yale Law and Policy Review* 1 (1983): 273.

16. Elliot Slotnick, "Federal Appellate Judge Selection: Recruitment Changes and Unanswered Questions," *The Justice System Journal* 6 (1981): 285.

17. William O. Douglas, *Go East, Young Man* (New York: Random House, 1974), p. 462.

18. Sheldon Goldman, "Judicial Selection Under Clinton: A Midterm Examination," *Judicature* 78 (1995): 277.

19. The Hon. Harry Blackmun, Speech to the Eighth Circuit Judicial Conference, St. Louis, Missouri, 15 July 1988.

20. Everett Ladd, *The American Polity*, 2nd ed. (New York: W.W. Norton, 1987), p. 491.

21. Henry Abraham, *Justices and Presidents: A Political History of Appointments to the Supreme Court* (New York: Oxford University Press, 1974), p. 245.

22. Kermit L. Hall, *The Magic Mirror: Law in American History* (New York: Oxford University Press, 1989), p. 104.

23. Ibid., pp. 103–5.

24. Council of State Governments, *The Book of the States* (Lexington, KY: Council of State Governments, 1994), p. 191.

25. David A. Crynes, "The Electoral Connection and the Pace of Litigation in Kansas," *Judicature* 78 (1995): 243.

26. *Rutan v. Republican Party of Illinois*, 497 U.S. 62 (1990).

27. *Elrod v. Burns*, 427 U.S. 347 (1976); *Branti v. Finkel*, 445 U.S. 507 (1980).

28. Charles H. Sheldon, "The Role of State Bar Associations in Judicial Selection," *Judicature* 77 (1994): 300–305.

29. David M. O'Brien, *Storm Center: The Supreme Court in American Politics*, 2nd ed. (New York: W.W. Norton, 1990), p. 75.

30. Neil A. Lewis, "Thomas to Win High Court Seat, Senators Predict," *New York Times*, 14 September 1991, pp. 1, 7.

31. *Code of Judicial Conduct*, Canon 7(B)(1)(c).

32. *Code of Judicial Conduct*, Canon 7(B)(1)(a).

33. Lou Cannon, "A Blue-Collar Judge on Washington State's Top Court," *Washington Post National Weekly Edition*, 26 August-1 September 1991, p. 15.

34. Barbara Graham, "Do Judicial Selection Systems Matter?" *American Politics Quarterly* 18 (1990): 316–36.

35. Joseph P. Fried, "Wide Use of Unelected Judges Prompts Voting-Rights Inquiry," *New York Times*, 19 July 1994, pp. B1, B3.

36. Ibid., p. B1.

37. Philip L. DuBois, "State Trial Court Appointments: Does the Governor Make a Difference?" *Judicature* 69 (1985): 28.

38. Ibid., p. 22.
39. John D. Felice and John C. Kilwein, "Strike One, Strike Two . . .: The History of and Prospect for Judicial Reform in Ohio," *Judicature* 75 (1992): 193–200.
40. Henry R. Glick, "The Promise and Performance of the Missouri Plan: Judicial Selection in the Fifty States," *University of Miami Law Review* 32 (1978): 527.
41. See Richard A. Watson and Rondal G. Downing, *The Politics of Bench and Bar* (New York: Wiley, 1969).
42. Philip L. DuBois, *From Ballot to Bench: Judicial Elections and the Quest for Accountability* (Austin, TX: University of Texas Press, 1980), p. 248.
43. William K. Hall and Larry T. Aspin, "What Twenty Years of Judicial Retention Elections Have Told Us," *Judicature* 70 (1987): 344, 347.
44. Larry T. Aspin and William K. Hall, "Retention Elections and Judicial Behavior," *Judicature* 77 (1994): 313.
45. See John T. Wold and John H. Culver, "The Defeat of the California Justices: The Campaign, the Electorate, and the Issue of Judicial Accountability," *Judicature* 70 (1987): 348–55.
46. Henry R. Glick and Craig F. Emmert, "Selection Systems and Judicial Characteristics: The Recruitment of State Supreme Court Judges," *Judicature* 70 (1987): 231.
47. Allen and Wall, "Role Orientations," p. 157.
48. David Margolick, "Women's Milestone: Majority on Minnesota Court," *New York Times*, 22 February 1991, p. B16.
49. Glick and Emmert, "Selection Systems and Judicial Characteristics," p. 232.
50. Ibid., pp. 233–35.
51. Ibid., p. 235.
52. Dixie K. Knoebel, "The State of the Judiciary," in *The Book of the States*, 1990–1991 ed. (Lexington, KY: Council of State Governments, 1990), p. 200.
53. "Campaigning for the High Court," *Time*, 2 July 1990, p. 61.
54. Robert A. Carp and Ronald Stidham, *The Federal Courts*, 2nd ed. (Washington, D.C.: Congressional Quarterly Press, 1991), p. 104.
55. Elliot E. Slotnick, "The ABA Standing Committee on Federal Judiciary: A Contemporary Assessment—Part 2," *Judicature* 66 (1983): 392.
56. Ibid.
57. Ibid., p. 393.
58. Slotnick, "Federal Appellate Selection," p. 285.
59. Sheldon Goldman, "Reagan's Judicial Legacy: Completing the Puzzle and Summing Up," *Judicature* 72 (1989): 322, 325.
60. Ibid.

61. Sheldon Goldman, "Should There Be Affirmative Action for the Judiciary?," *Judicature* 62 (1979): 492–93.

62. See Peter Fish, "Merit Selection and Politics: Choosing a Judge of the United States Court of Appeals for the Fourth Circuit," *Wake Forest Law Review* 15 (1979): 635–54.

63. See E. M. Gunderson, " 'Merit Selection': The Report and Appraisal of a Participant Observer," *Pacific Law Journal* 10 (1979): 638–706.

64. Sheldon Goldman, "Reagan's Second Term Judicial Appointments: The Battle at Midway," *Judicature* 70 (1987): 326.

65. Herman Schwartz, *Packing the Courts: The Conservative Campaign to Rewrite the Constitution* (New York: Charles Scribner's Sons, 1988), p. 92.

66. Ibid., pp. 90–95.

67. Carp and Stidham, *The Federal Courts*, p. 110.

68. Goldman, "Reagan's Judicial Legacy," p. 322.

69. See, e.g., C. K. Rowland, Donald Songer, and Robert A. Carp, "Presidential Effects on Criminal Justice Policy in the Lower Federal Courts: The Reagan Judges," *Law and Society Review* 22 (1988): 191–200.

70. Neil A. Lewis, "Bush Travels Reagan's Course in Naming Judges," *New York Times*, 10 April 1990, p. A1; Ruth Marcus, "Using the Bench to Bolster a Conservative Team," *Washington Post National Weekly Edition*, 25 February–3 March 1991, p. 31.

71. "Rich, White and Male," *Time* 12 November 1990, p. 23.

72. Sheldon Goldman, "Bush's Judicial Legacy: The Final Imprint," *Judicature* 76 (1993): 287.

73. Ibid., p. 286.

74. Ibid., p. 284.

75. Ibid.

76. Goldman, "Judicial Selection Under Clinton," p. 281.

77. Ibid., p. 285.

78. Ibid., p. 279.

79. David M. O'Brien, *Judicial Roulette* (New York: Priority Press, 1988), p. 98.

80. Ibid.

81. Ibid.

82. Ibid.

83. See Christopher E. Smith, *United States Magistrates in the Federal Courts: Subordinate Judges* (New York: Praeger, 1990), pp. 15–28.

84. See "Judiciary Fares Well in Legislation Passed by 101st Congress," *The Third Branch* 11 (November 1990): 5.

85. See Christopher E. Smith, "Merit Selection Committees and the Politics

of Appointing United States Magistrates,'' *The Justice System Journal* 12 (1987): 210–31.

86. Ibid., pp. 216–25.

87. Christopher E. Smith, ''Who Are the U.S. Magistrates?'' *Judicature* 71 (1987): 147.

88. Donna P. Cofer, *Judges, Bureaucrats, and the Question of Independence* (Westport, CT: Greenwood Press, 1985), p. 14.

89. Thomas C. Mans, ''Selecting the 'Hidden Judiciary': How the Merit Process Works in Choosing Administrative Law Judges (Part I),'' *Judicature* 63 (1979): 66–68.

90. Ibid., p. 71.

91. Ibid., pp. 71–73.

92. Thomas C. Mans, ''Selecting the 'Hidden Judiciary': How the Merit Process Works in Choosing Administrative Law Judges (Part II),'' *Judicature* 63 (1979): 133.

93. Goldman, ''Judicial Selection and the Qualities that Make a 'Good' Judge,'' p. 123.

94. See D. Marie Provine, *Judging Credentials: Nonlawyer Judges and the Politics of Professionalism* (Chicago: University of Chicago Press, 1986), pp. 108–21.

95. William O. Douglas, *The Court Years* (New York: Random House, 1980), p. 281.

96. Dennis C. Colson, ''Would a Lay Justice Be Just?'' *Idaho Law Review* 13 (1977): 351–71.

97. See *Cruzan v. Missouri*, 110 S. Ct. 2841 (1990).

98. William H. Rehnquist, *The Supreme Court: How It Was, How It Is* (New York: William Morrow, 1987), p. 291.

99. Roger H. Davidson and Walter J. Oleszek, *Congress and Its Members*, 2nd ed. (Washington, D.C.: Congressional Quarterly Press, 1985), p. 110.

100. Statement of Chief Justice William Rehnquist in press release provided by the Administrative Office of the United States Courts, 15 March 1989.

101. See *Bureau of Labor Statistics News* (31 January 1989): Table 6; U.S. Department of Commerce, *Money Income of Households, Families, and Persons in the United States: 1986,* June 1988: Table 19.

102. Committee on the Judicial Branch of the Judicial Conference of the United States, *Simple Fairness: The Case for Equitable Compensation of the Nation's Federal Judges* (1988), p. 24.

103. Council of State Governments, *The Book of the States*, p. 200.

104. See Committee on the Judicial Branch, *Simple Fairness*, pp. 71–74.

105. See Richard Posner, *The Federal Courts: Crisis and Reform* (Cambridge, MA: Harvard University Press, 1985), pp. 39–42.

106. Committee on the Judicial Branch, *Simple Fairness*, p. 35.

107. See Sue Davis, *Justice Rehnquist and the Constitution* (Princeton, NJ: Princeton University Press, 1989), pp. 41–65.

108. Lois Forer, *Money and Justice: Who Owns the Courts?* (New York: W.W. Norton, 1984), p. 77.

109. Committee on the Judicial Branch, *Simple Fairness*, p. 31.

110. Remarks of Chief Justice William Rehnquist, Washington, D.C. Press Conference, 15 March 1989, C-SPAN broadcast.

111. Christopher E. Smith, ''Federal Judicial Salaries: A Critical Appraisal,'' *Temple Law Review* 62 (1989): 864.

112. Stephen L. Wasby, *The Supreme Court in the Federal Judicial System*, 4th ed. (Chicago: Nelson-Hall, 1993), p. 90.

113. ''Chief Justice Recaps 1995 in Year-end Report,'' *The Third Branch* 28 (January 1996): 3.

# Chapter 7

# Judicial Decision Making

Litigants bring their disputes to courts because they have certain expectations about the nature of judicial decision making. They expect judges to make considered judgments after thorough, neutral, and fair examinations of all relevant arguments and evidence. If people genuinely believed that judges were wholly biased or unfair, no disputant would spend the time and money to pursue a claim through the judicial process. A loss of faith in the fair and proper exercise of judicial decision making might lead people to refuse to enter into contractual relationships, to feel helpless when their legal rights are infringed, or, in the worst case scenario, to turn to self-help justice to seize disputed property and seek revenge against opponents. Thus, without the public's confidence, courts could not fulfill their functions for maintaining stability in society.

Public confidence in the judiciary is maintained through the use of symbols that perpetuate the myth that judicial decision making is neutral and objective. Judges wear black robes and sit on elevated benches, apart from the citizens who come to them. The public must stand in deference as the judge enters and leaves the courtroom. The physical environment of the courtroom, frequently characterized by high ceilings, marble columns, wood paneling, and other visible symbols such as the scales of justice, reinforces the judicial branch's image as a serious institution that deserves public respect and obedience. The formal, solemn environment of the court, with its robed decision makers and traditional procedures, is more akin to religious institutions and ceremonies than to any other governmental setting in American society. Moreover, the use of "law" as the purported basis of decision making reinforces the symbolic elements and reassures the public that judges are different from other authoritative decision makers (such as legislators and other elected officials whose decisions are affected by greed, self-aggrandizement, and partisan political interests). The imagery is designed to convey the impression that judges are society's learned elders whose special knowledge of law enables them to make neutral and just decisions.

Are judges really neutral, unbiased decision makers whose special knowledge of law provides clear answers to the difficult questions brought to courts for resolution? Of course not. Beneath the black robes are human beings who were placed in their authoritative judicial positions through the operation of the political system. Like other people in American society, judges possess values, attitudes, biases, and political interests that affect their decisions. Judges' knowledge of law provides them with tools to create decisions that will appear proper and legitimate to the public. In some instances, established law may provide examples and principles for assessing a dispute and dictating an outcome. In other cases, legal knowledge merely supplies techniques for rationalizing and justifying judges' personal preferences so that the public will perceive and accept the judges' decisions as based on law.

Many lawyers and judges strenuously object to any characterization of judicial decision making that equates judges' behavior with that of other actors in the political system. They argue that judges employ established courtroom procedures for the thorough consideration of evidence. Unlike politicians who pursue their own self-interest, judges must follow precedents established in prior legal cases. Despite the heartfelt sincerity that may underlie such arguments, one should not blindly accept lawyers' and judges' perceptions of the judicial process. They are actors in the system who are socialized through their legal education to accept and defend an idealized image of the judicial system. Moreover, they benefit from the public's deference to and respect for legal institutions. As Harry Stumpf observed, lawyers and judges "can hardly be faulted for packaging and marketing a product that is in such large demand by the public."[1] The public wants to believe that the judiciary is the repository of wisdom and justice. The public wants to believe that there is one governmental institution capable of neutral decision making. If it were otherwise, a loss of public confidence might detract from the courts' dispute-processing and stability-enhancing functions in society. Thus, the judiciary's defenders merely reinforce the valuable social functions that derive from the courts' public image.

How do we know that judicial decision making is influenced by personal characteristics and political factors rather than merely by neutral, legal principles? Systematic analyses of judicial decisions reveal the judicial inconsistency and creativity that are indicative of some judges' ability to determine case outcomes without regard for established legal precedents. Moreover, the theories and methodologies of social science have enabled scholars to identify factors associated with particular judges' decisions.[2] Although most research on judicial decision making focuses on federal courts, the factors that influence judges' decisions apply to both state and federal judges. One study concluded, for example, that federal appellate judges tend to make different decisions concerning criminal and civil liberties cases, depending on whether the judges were appointed by

Republican or Democratic presidents.[3] Democratic appointees are much more likely to decide in favor of criminal defendants and individuals claiming that their rights have been violated.

If the outcomes of judicial cases were determined by established principles of law, then there should not be systematic disparities in judicial decisions, such as those existing between judges with different political affiliations. However, differences in judges' decisions are understandable when we remind ourselves of the political nature of judicial selection processes, which produce very different kinds of judges during different political eras. The Democratic party's constituency includes people concerned with affirmative action and issues of gender and racial equality. Thus, it is no surprise that more than 60 percent of President Clinton's appointees to federal district judgeships were female, members of minority groups, or both.[4] This appointment pattern also produces judges whose life experiences, priorities, and values are likely to be different than those of Republican appointees, who were predominantly white males during the Bush (73 percent) and Reagan (85 percent) administrations.[5]

This chapter will discuss research into judicial decision making to illuminate the personal and political factors that actually influence the outcomes of legal cases. For some people, the recognition that judges do not make decisions strictly in accordance with neutral legal principles may generate dismay and cynicism about the judicial process. The notion that judges' decisions evince biases and political interests clashes with Americans' idealistic beliefs in the neutral principles that are presumed to underlie the judicial system. A recognition that judicial decision making is a form of human behavior similar to human decision making in other contexts need not, however, completely destroy one's reliance on the judicial system.

Although judges determine case outcomes under the guise of legal decision making, judicial officers are not free to make decisions simply to suit their wishes. Numerous constraints, supplied by the individual decision makers themselves and imposed by the external political environment, serve to limit and create boundaries for the range of possible decisions. These constraints include judges' views about their proper roles, state judges' concerns about being reelected, and judges' anticipation of adverse public reactions to decisions. As James Gibson concluded after a thorough review of the social science literature on judicial decision making, "Judges' decisions are a function of what they prefer to do, tempered by what they think they ought to do, but constrained by what they perceive is feasible to do."[6]

How does the external political environment affect judicial decision making? Developments in the political system determine the composition of the judiciary. In the federal courts, Republican presidents appoint Republicans as judges and Democratic presidents appoint Democrats. In many state courts, competitive elections, including visible and hidden participation by political parties, determine who will be judges. The composition of the judiciary, in turn, shapes the decisions and outcomes produced by the judicial branch. Although political elites from certain demographic groups (i.e., whites, males, and the affluent) dominate the judiciary, the links between the judicial branch and the political system help judicial decisions reflect changes and trends in American society and thereby provide a mechanism for law to develop in accordance with evolving societal values. For example, research on death penalty decisions by state supreme court justices has found that electoral conditions can be influential factors as judges seek to avoid clashing with public viewpoints, which determine their fates in future elections.[7]

The fact that judges' decisions are shaped by personal and political factors does not mean that the judiciary cannot fulfill its valuable social functions of processing disputes, developing public policies, and providing stability in society. As one commentator observed about the U.S. Supreme Court, judges' self-consciousness about striving to make good decisions distinguishes the judicial process from decision making in other governmental institutions:

> The justices' constitutional interpretations owe more to political ideologies than they pretend. But far more than the Congress, far more than any recent president, justices reach decisions by searching their consciences, carefully sifting facts and law, trying to do right as they see the right.[8]

Legislative decisions are frequently motivated by legislators' explicitly political self-interest in satisfying constituents and thereby gaining reelection. Judicial decision making, by contrast, is implicitly infused with politics because political developments determine the composition of the judiciary, and individual judges inevitably apply their values, attitudes, and policy preferences in making decisions. Although the influence of political factors over judicial decision making has led to many biased decisions favoring the interests of political elites,[9] judges have sometimes helped society combat racial discrimination and social ills neglected by the other branches of government.[10]

## LEGAL REASONING AND CASE PRECEDENTS

The United States inherited the common law legal system from Britain. Under the common law, judges are important decision makers who use case precedents to decide the issues presented to them. By contrast, in civil law systems, such as those in France and Germany, judges' decisions are guided by detailed statutes enacted by the legislature. Under the common law system, by identifying previous judicial decisions that address the legal issue at hand, the judge applies principles and reasoning already established by other judges to determine the outcome of a given case. Thus, traditional judicial decision making has been characterized as a three-step mechanical process.[11] First, the judge determines the facts underlying the dispute and locates prior cases with analogous factual situations. Second, the judge draws the relevant legal principle from the prior case or cases. Finally, the judge applies the legal precedent to the current case to yield the appropriate result. When the steps of traditional judicial decision making are described, the process appears very simple. Moreover, it appears that judges do not impose their own values or biases but apply established principles to contemporary disputes. Under this formal process, judges appear to have the very limited role of referees in individual disputes, not that of creators of new law or developers of public policy.

In reality, however, every case presents the opportunity for judges to interpret facts or law in light of their own values, attitudes, and biases. The three-step process is not as simple as it first appears, because judges make choices about how to assess the facts of the case. Was the collision between the automobiles an unavoidable accident, the result of one driver's negligence, or the result of misbehavior by both drivers? The answers to such questions are not simple or obvious but require judges to draw from their experiences and perceptions to comprehend factual situations. Moreover, after making a choice about how to view the facts, judges may face an array of precedents based on closely related but differing cases. Rather than act passively and permit a particular precedent to dictate the outcome of the case, the judge's own sense of the appropriate outcome may influence his or her characterization of the facts and choice of case precedent. By employing case precedents as the purported bases for decisions, judges convey the impression that they are following established law when in fact they may be setting new precedents. The flexibility in decision making granted to judges in the common law system permits them to change the governing law through case decisions. According to Edward Levi, "[N]ot only do new situations arise, but in addition people's wants change. The categories used in the legal process must be left ambiguous in order to permit the infusion of new ideas."[12]

In comparing the current case to previous cases, the judge has the option of *distinguishing* the case by asserting that it is somehow different from previous cases in order to decide the case without regard for previous decisions. For example, in a 5-to-4 decision, the U.S. Supreme Court determined that police officers had improperly questioned a suspect outside of the presence of his attorney while driving him to the police station. The police officers elicited incriminating statements from the suspect by saying that it was a shame that the missing girl (whom he was suspected of abducting and murdering) would not receive a Christian burial because her body would not be found in the winter weather. As a result, the suspect's statements were excluded from evidence and he was granted a new trial (at which he was subsequently convicted for murder).[13] By contrast, three years later without any change in the Court's composition, the justices found no improper questioning when, while driving a suspect to the station, one officer said that it would really be a shame if a handicapped kid stumbled on the gun that the suspect was believed to have hidden near a special education school.

In response to the officer's words, the suspect made incriminating statements.[14] Four justices (Burger, White, Blackmun, Rehnquist) believed that there was no police interrogation in either case. By contrast, three justices (Brennan, Marshall, Stevens) believed that improper interrogation was involved in both cases because police officers made apparently calculated statements to an isolated defendant, which succeeded in producing incriminating admissions. The 6-to-3 decision of the second case hinged on the fact that two justices (Powell, Stewart) distinguished the first situation from the second. They provided the crucial votes for the five-member majority in the first case because they believed that comments directed to the suspect constituted interrogation. Subsequently, they provided the deciding votes in the second case by distinguishing the new situation as merely a conversation between police officers, which just happened to elicit incriminating statements. By distinguishing the facts in the second case from those in the first, the justices were able to apply a different legal rule and thereby produce a different result. Obviously, the authority to interpret and characterize factual meaning in a case can give judges tremendous influence over case outcomes.

At the appellate level, in particular, judges may also *reverse* the case precedent by declaring that previous cases were wrongly decided. Thus, the judges can create their own opportunities to decide cases as they wish. It is much more difficult for trial judges to create new legal rules by explicitly nullifying old rules because their decisions may be reviewed and rejected by appellate courts above them. As a result, the common law process of legal reasoning actually provides judges with great flexibility for infusing case decisions with their own values and biases.

For example, the Supreme Court decided cases in 1987 and 1989 that forbade the use of victim impact testimony in death penalty sentencing hearings.[15] Many prosecutors like to use victim impact testimony, which focuses on the murder's impact on surviving family members and friends, in an effort to persuade a jury to recommend execution. However, the Court said testimony could only focus on the nature and details of the crime itself and the defendant's personal qualities and prior record. In 1991, after the appointment of Justice David Souter, the Supreme Court reversed these precedents and declared that victim impact testimony may be used.[16] Such reversals instantly establish new legal rules and occur as a result of new appointments to a court or as individual judges change their views about a particular issue.

## Avoiding Precedents

Judges may also ignore precedents with which they disagree. If no higher appellate court subsequently requires a judge to apply a particular precedent, the judge is essentially free to apply or not apply previous decisions. In one well-known example, Chief Justice Warren Burger created a test to determine whether government policies or programs comport with the First Amendment's requirements about the separation of church and state. In the 1971 case of *Lemon v. Kurtzman*,[17] Burger enunciated a three-part test, known as the *Lemon* test, to determine whether the government's actions favored any religions or caused excessive entanglement of government and religion. The test was subsequently applied in other First Amendment Establishment Clause cases, but as Louis Fisher notes, "[T]his three-prong test is frequently waived or ignored by the courts."[18] Most notably, Chief Justice Burger, the author of the test, ignored the test himself in order to declare that no constitutional problems arise when state legislatures pay Christian ministers to lead prayers at each legislative session. As Justice William Brennan noted in dissent, "most law students applying the *Lemon* test would find the practice of legislative prayer unconstitutional."[19] Chief Justice Burger apparently recognized that the application of his test would lead to a result that he did not desire—the elimination of legislative prayer. Thus, he ignored his own precedent in order to ensure that the case outcome would fit with his preferences. During the same term and in subsequent terms, the Supreme Court utilized the *Lemon* test again and again to decide other First Amendment religion cases.[20] It remained available for them to use in cases to achieve the outcomes that they desired.

The common law decision-making process is so flexible that judges, especially at the appellate level, can alter the precedents that they claim to be following. The process of writing a legal opinion provides the opportunity to rationalize the outcome preferred by the judge. Although opinions are supposed to explain how precedents govern the current case, judicial opinions frequently do nothing more than selectively cite, freely reinterpret, or mischaracterize prior cases to provide rationalizations for new results. In 1991, for example, Justice Antonin Scalia wrote a majority opinion that changed the standard for assessing whether conditions inside prisons violated the Eighth Amendment prohibition against cruel and unusual punishments. In *Wilson v. Seiter* (1991), the Supreme Court examined a prisoner's claim that living conditions inside an Ohio prison violated the Eighth Amendment.[21] In reviewing the Supreme Court's relevant precedents, Scalia emphasized a case concerning alleged deprivation of medical care from a prisoner,[22] a death penalty case concerning a malfunctioning electric chair,[23] and a case in which a guard shot an inmate during a prison uprising.[24] He used these precedents to justify a new standard that required prisoners to show that prison officials were deliberately indifferent to bad conditions; simply showing that living conditions were terrible and inhumane would no longer be sufficient. Justice Byron White, in a dissenting opinion, noted that Scalia chose to rely on precedents that did not concern the issue at hand—living conditions in prison. Although the Supreme Court decided two precedents concerning living conditions and neither of those precedents required a showing of deliberate indifference, Scalia ignored one of the precedents completely[25] and dismissed the other precedent[26] as having been superseded by the case in which the officer shot the prisoner. Scalia demonstrated the flexibility of the common law decision-making process by ignoring or dismissing precedents most relevant to the case in order to use precedents that were more favorable to the new direction he sought to move the law.

## Limitations on Judicial Decision Making

Because, in the words of one scholar, case precedents "do not yield single correct solutions,"[27] judges have tremendous freedom in determining the outcomes of cases. Does anything prevent judges from deciding whatever they wish to decide, regardless of established precedents and legal principles? Although chapter 10 will discuss the limitations on judges' decisions in greater detail, a few of the constraints can be noted here.

Lower court judges cannot freely ignore and rewrite precedents, because their decisions may be reversed by higher appellate courts. The judges can ignore precedents, but their opinions must then include persuasive rationalizations to convince higher courts that the precedents should indeed be reversed or changed. For example, a federal district judge in Alabama declared that, notwithstanding twenty years of Supreme Court decisions to the contrary, the Constitution actually permits a state to authorize voluntary, organized prayer in the public schools. Unfortunately for him, his interpretation of the Constitution was not found persuasive by the Supreme Court in 1985, so his decision was reversed, and his desire to deviate from precedent was held in check.[28]

Judges on lower courts may vehemently disagree with established precedents, as illustrated by the federal district judge who ridiculed Supreme Court precedents that force prisoners to prepare their own cases by using prison law libraries. The judge wrote that merely providing prisoners with law libraries "makes about as much sense as furnishing medical services through books like: *Brain Surgery Self-Taught, or How to Remove Your Own Appendix*, along with scalpels, drills, hemostats, sponges and sutures."[29] Despite his disagreement with the Supreme Court, the threat of subsequent reversal on appeal led the judge to rule against the prisoners and follow the precedent that he found so objectionable.

Because there is no court above the U.S. Supreme Court, the justices on the Court have the greatest freedom to ignore or change precedents. The same is true of state supreme court justices with respect to issues that exclusively concern state law. Any particular justice's ability to advance preferred decisions is limited by the fact that courts of last resort are deliberative bodies of five, seven, or nine judicial officers. Thus, the support of a majority of justices is needed for any decision. In group decision making, the justices limit each other by developing compromises in order to form stable majority coalitions.

The links between the political system and the judiciary can constrain judges' decisions. In state court systems in which judges are elected, judges may be cautious about ignoring precedents or being overly creative in decision making for fear that a controversial decision will generate opposition among voters at the next election. For example, in the contemporary era of public support for capital punishment, research by Paul Brace and Melinda Gann Hall found that "[V]otes upholding death sentences are more likely in politically competitive states with elected judges."[30] Moreover, the judges most likely to clash with the public's support for capital punishment are Democrats with long terms in office who, therefore, are apparently both less susceptible to removal from office by voters and philosophically inclined to have extra concerns about protecting individuals' rights.[31]

In the federal system, the congressional threats to limit court jurisdiction or to initiate constitutional amendments may constrain judges' decisions. State legislatures can pose similar threats to state judiciaries. Judicial officers may limit their own decisions for fear that legislative action or public referenda may limit their jurisdiction and authority. Moreover, in statutory interpretation cases, Congress can directly reverse judicial decisions by passing clarifying legislation that defines a statute's meaning differently than did the interpretation by the judges. For example, Congress enacted the Civil Rights Act of 1991 to nullify seven decisions issued by the Supreme Court in 1989 that altered the meaning of civil rights statutes and diminished the likelihood that discrimination victims could prevail in lawsuits.[32] In addition, the range of judicial decisions is constrained over time by the president's power to replace departing federal judges with new judicial officers who have differing views when the president's political supporters disagree with trends in federal court decisions. Finally, judges may limit their own decision making either because they possess a limited view of a judge's proper role or because they are concerned that a particular decision, despite its desirability, will generate excessive opposition and resistance from other governing institutions and from the public. Judges' education and socialization as lawyers may also lead to self-restraint if they believe strongly in the formal legal ideal of adherence to case precedents.

Judges have significant ability to make decisions and then justify those decisions with persuasive rationalizations in judicial opinions. This ability is not absolute, however, because the structure of the court system and the relationship between the judicial branch and the larger political system constrain the range of potential decisions.

## SOCIAL SCIENCE RESEARCH ON JUDICIAL DECISION MAKING

Analyses of judicial opinions focus on the consistency, or lack thereof, of the reasoning presented to justify particular decisions. As the foregoing discussion of judicial opinions indicates, judges' strategic manipulations of case precedents may not constitute coherent, consistent legal theories. Such analyses are useful for debunking the myth that judges always follow established legal principles in deciding cases. An examination of substantive consistency in judges' reasoning does not, however, reveal what factors influence their decisions. Thus, judicial scholars have applied social science research methods to judges' decisions in a systematic effort to develop a more complete understanding of the underlying factors and processes that are part of judicial decision making.

In 1948 C. Herman Pritchett provided the groundbreaking study of the Supreme Court, applying empirical social science methods to the study of judicial decisions.[33] Pritchett systematically examined patterns in the decisions of Supreme Court justices in the 1930s and 1940s. As in the work of many scholars who followed him, the focus of Pritchett's research is on the judicial officers' votes favoring one party or the other, not on the reasoning behind the judicial opinions. The research presumes that by identifying patterns in judges' decisions, one can discover factors associated with, and potentially influential over, judicial decision making. In Pritchett's original study, the patterns of justices' decisions indicated that the justices were divided between liberal and conservative blocs on civil liberties and economic issues. Thus, scholars infer that the justices' personal attitudes or values were key factors influencing their decisions.

As subsequent researchers applied more sophisticated analytical techniques to patterns of judicial decisions, complex models have been developed to explain judicial decision making. In this research, scholars attempt to identify and determine the relative strength of the independent variables—such as judges' attitudes, values, and backgrounds—which combine to determine the dependent variable—a particular judicial decision. Empirical research into judicial decision making may suggest that one can predict particular case outcomes by knowing which factors affect each judge. Thus, for example, social science research may reveal that Republican appellate judges—who were previously prosecutors in rural areas in western states—are likely to decide most cases against criminal defendants and thus produce decisions much different than those issued by Democratic judges—who were previously defense attorneys in northeastern cities.

As this hypothetical example illustrates, the findings of judicial research can be consistent with intuitive perceptions about factors that influence political behavior. Such perceptions might include the expectation that contemporary Republicans are more conservative than Democrats and that rural prosecutors are more conservative than urban public defenders. By systematically identifying such factors, social science research reinforces the conclusion that judicial decision making is a form of political behavior, influenced by the kinds of human factors (e.g., values, attitudes, experiences, etc.) that people already recognize as affecting citizens' votes, politicians' policy preferences, and other forms of political behavior.

Social science research has been useful in providing systematic analysis of judges' decisions and for demonstrating that judicial decision making is a form of human political behavior. Students encountering such research must, however, keep two warnings in mind. First, the identification and measurement of independent variables does not prove absolutely that such factors affect judicial decisions in a particular way. Judicial scholars identify factors strongly *associated* with particular patterns of judges' decisions. In other words, these are factors that are present in conjunction with certain kinds of decisions at rates much higher than one would expect if their relationship was merely accidental. Thus, prior experience as a prosecutor may be highly associated with decisions against criminal defendants, but we cannot say that prior experience as a prosecutor *causes* a judge to decide cases against defendants. Statistical techniques that associate particular factors with specific decisions lead scholars to draw inferences about the influence of those factors over judicial decision making. Social scientists' predictions about judicial behavior rest on statistical probabilities, not on absolute certainty. Second, one must be wary of reducing judicial decision making to a simple set of factors. Although judges' attitudes or values may influence decisions, case outcomes are also affected by a variety of other forces that may be present in differing combinations in individual cases. Thus, fact patterns in individual cases, judges' role orientations, and other complex factors also influence decisions and prevent simplistic conclusions about particular personal characteristics and their relation to a specific decision.

## Judges' Personal Attributes

Studies of judicial decision making have found that judges' personal attributes are highly associated with particular kinds of decisions. Although the influence of particular personal attributes and social background characteristics may change from generation to generation,[34] several personal attributes have been identified as useful in predicting contemporary judicial decisions. One of the most obvious is political party affiliation. Because judges gain their positions through the operations of the political system, they arrive on the bench with political experiences, beliefs, and values that led them to identify with and work for their particular political party. It is not surprising to find that political parties' positions on public policy issues are reflected in the case decisions of their partisans in black robes. Republican judges and Democratic judges frequently differ on civil liberties and other issues, with the Democrats making more liberal decisions.[35] C. Neal Tate's statistical studies of Supreme Court justices' decisions from 1946 to 1986 found that "partisanship is by a significant margin the most powerful personal attribute influencing the decision making of postwar Supreme Court justices."[36]

The identification of political party affiliation as a factor in judicial decision making does not explain why and how this and other personal attributes influence judges' decisions. According to James Gibson, "[M]ost background variables can be understood as indirect surrogates for attitudes and values."[37] Thus, the political party affiliation itself does not necessarily motivate specific judicial decisions. Instead, judges who share a common party identification frequently also share common beliefs and values that manifest themselves in judicial decisions similar to those made by fellow partisans. Although this explanation appeals to popular intuition, the complexity of judicial decision making and the difficulties involved in systematically analyzing judges' decisions are illuminated by the fact that there may be alternative explanations for the connection between party affiliation and certain judicial decisions. For example, Tate posits that political party identification may serve—consciously or unconsciously—as a shorthand decision-making cue for judicial officers as they confront specific issues.[38] As a cue, party identification may be a time-saving device that permits judges to decide issues quickly based on their partisan policy orientation without resolving all of the specific, complex value choices contained in the legal case. As Tate observes:

> [T]he party identifications of citizens help them to orient themselves to a complicated political environment in which it is impossible for them to make a coldly rational choice on every political decision they face. There is no reason why Supreme Court justices, though they are probably more sophisticated political decision makers than the average citizen, would not also use the shorthand decision-making tool represented by political party identification.[39]

Another personal attribute found to have statistical significance in particular judicial decisions is prior experience as a prosecutor.[40] As Gibson noted, ''The causality may be exactly the opposite of that which is typically postulated. . . . [because] prosecutorial experience may not cause attitudes, but may instead be caused by attitudes (e.g., self-selection).''[41] Do future judges become more conservative because of their experiences as prosecutors fighting crime, or do they become prosecutors on the way to becoming judges because they were conservative to begin with? Such questions are not easily answered.

Other personal attributes have been associated with particular judicial decisions. As with the party affiliation and prosecutorial experience, it is not always easy to discern precisely how and why these factors influence judicial decision making. In regard to the federal judiciary, for example, some scholars have examined the factor of presidential appointment to find differences in decisions by judges appointed by different presidents.[42] Because President Reagan's administration made a concerted effort to appoint judges who would make conservative decisions on a range of specific issues, his appointees have been found to be more conservative than other Republican judges on civil rights and civil liberties issues.[43]

Party affiliation, identity of appointing president, and prior prosecutorial experience are ''especially useful predictors'' of judicial decisions on civil liberties and economics cases in the federal courts.[44] Other personal attributes of judges have been examined with mixed results as to their association with particular judicial decisions. For example, studies comparing the sentencing decisions of white and African-American judges have led to mixed results. Most studies find little difference between the two sets of judges. However, some studies find that white judges treat African-American defendants more harshly, and others find that both white and African-American judges treat African-American defendants more harshly than white defendants.[45] It appears obvious from these mixed results that factors other than the judge's race must also influence sentencing decisions. Religious affiliation may influence judicial decisions on particular issues[46] as, for example, when Catholic judges decide abortion cases differently than Protestant judges.[47] Although these other personal attributes may emerge in specific kinds of decisions, most differences among judges are better predicted by party affiliation.

## Judges' Attitudes and Values

The personal attributes of judges should be understood as representing or reflecting underlying attitudes and values, which affect judicial decision making. Psychologists and public opinion specialists would determine the nature and strength of individuals' attitudes through the analysis of interviews or surveys containing questions carefully designed to elicit revealing responses. It is very difficult, however, to identify and measure attitudes and values because judges do not give forthright interviews to clarify their beliefs, preferences, and biases. Judges have an interest in maintaining the public's belief in neutral judicial decision making according to legal principles. Moreover, ethical expectations limit judges' willingness to discuss issues with researchers or with the news media. By discouraging judges from revealing their attitudes on issues, society perpetuates its naive expectation that the judges can overcome their humanness and be completely open-minded and unbiased when considering issues in court.

Many scholars have built on Pritchett's original empirical research by measuring consistent policy preferences in judges' decisions as a means of identifying underlying attitudes and values.[48] In this research, judges are classified according to a liberal/conservative scale. Because individual judges tend to show consistency in their decisions, the patterns of past decisions on freedom of speech, civil rights, or other specific case categories provide a basis for predicting how judges will decide similar subsequent cases. According to scholars who pursue this research, "If we can ascertain judicial attitudes, these will reflect an overall ideology motivating the judge. From an understanding of the ideology, we can gain explanations and make predictions about judicial behavior."[49]

Obviously, there is a problem of circular reasoning involved in using judicial decisions as the basis for discerning the existence of attitudes used to predict judicial decisions. Thus, researchers have sought to find an independent source for the identification of judicial officers' attitudes. Research using media characterizations of Supreme Court appointees' ideological orientations found that justices' decisions generally matched the values that they apparently brought to the Court with them.[50] From their initial findings, the researchers concluded that "the ability of the attitudinal model to explain justices' voting behavior indicates that [other] influences are minimal."[51] Subsequent research found media characterizations of judicial appointees' ideological values as useful predictors of Supreme Court justices' civil liberties and economics decisions since the 1950s. But this independent source for attitude identification was less useful for earlier appointees.[52] Although there is general agreement among social scientists about the importance of judicial officers' attitudes and values in shaping decisions, scholars continue to refine methods and models for identifying these attitudes and explaining how they impact courts and cases.

Lawrence Baum asserts that Supreme Court justices follow their attitude-based policy preferences in deciding cases:

> [J]ustices' policy preferences, which can be summarized in ideological terms, are perhaps the most important factor influencing their behavior. . . . [D]ifferences among the justices stem chiefly from their preferences, and the basic direction that most justices take on the Court seems to reflect the attitudes about policy issues that they bring to the Court.[53]

Scholars' conclusions about the importance of policy preferences do not contradict the previously discussed research that identified judges' political party affiliations as "the most powerful political attribute influencing [judicial] decision making."[54] Party identification is simply a separate indicator of values and policy preferences. Thus, it is not surprising that analyses of judges according to ideological differences evident in their policy preferences frequently correspond with classifications of judges according to their party identification.

The recognition that judges' values and policy preferences are important elements underlying judicial decisions has not ended the search for better understanding of judicial decision making. Judges' attitudes and values are not the only influential factors in judicial decision making. Moreover, the impact of attitudes and values may vary depending on the structure and the political environment of the court. For example, lower court judges cannot freely pursue their preferences because their decisions may be reversed on appeal. In appellate court cases, including those heard by the U.S. Supreme Court, other factors shape and limit the expression of judges' attitudes and values.

## Legal Factors and Facts in Cases

Although judicial decisions, especially at the appellate level, may reveal patterns of consistent policy preferences that demonstrate the judges' attitudes and values, those attitudes and values are not the sole determinants of case outcomes. According to Gibson, "[J]udges' attitudes specify the substantive objectives— what they prefer to do—but that is not all there is to the process of decision making. Some sort of decision-making process or framework or formula must also be established."[55] Judges must develop decision-making processes to assess and weigh relevant information in light of rules, procedures, and external constraints on judicial decision making.[56] One study, for example, found that federal district court judges follow legal rules to avoid conflicts with the president in cases concerning presidential power over foreign affairs.[57] By contrast, these judges applied their values and policy preferences more freely when the president's domestic policies were challenged.[58] This difference may reflect judges' perceptions of external constraints on their relative effectiveness in each issue area. When it comes to foreign affairs, there is a tradition of judicial deference to the president, and judges have little ability to enforce their decisions if the president does not acquiesce to an adverse decision.

Judges may also follow legal precedents rather than policy preferences when faced with the prospect of reversal by higher courts. The hierarchy of the courts presents an external constraint on judges' decision making. For example, one study indicated that judges on the U.S. Courts of Appeals tend to follow the Supreme Court's lead in deciding economic cases, such as labor and antitrust issues, whether or not those outcomes fit their own policy preferences.[59] Lower court judges, in particular, can adhere to traditional conceptions of judicial decision making by restraining personal preferences and adhering to precedents established by higher courts. It is not that these judges lack values and policy preferences, but rather that the political environment in which they make decisions constrains their ability to freely advance their preferences. Specifically, the fact that the hierarchical structure of the court system makes decisions subject to review and reversal by appellate courts makes lower court judges adhere to precedent. Research on federal district and circuit judges' adherence to Supreme Court decisions indicates that lower court judges are very likely to follow precedents of Supreme Court decisions that are clear and not complex, are supported by strong majorities, and address cases whose litigants and facts are similar to those facing the lower courts.[60]

Scholars have identified facts in cases that may elicit the expression of judges' attitudes and values. Some research has identified fact patterns, which can lead to predictions about decisions in subsequent cases containing the same facts.[61] Other researchers have examined the influence of factual circumstances unrelated to the details of the case—such as the race[62] or social status of the defendant[63]— to show that legally irrelevant facts can elicit the expression of judges' biases and thereby influence decisions.

A primary premise underlying research into facts in case decisions has been the judges' need to rely on cues, because they do not have the time and resources to assess all the information contained in each case. In other words, the factual circumstances in cases offer shortcuts to help the judges select policy preferences (or biases) to express in the case decisions. Research on the Supreme Court, for example, has shown that certain justices, who could not be classified according to a clear policy preference on search and seizure cases, utilized factual cues in cases (e.g., "Did the contested search take place inside someone's home?") in order to reach decisions.[64]

Judicial decisions are also affected by the nature and forms of arguments presented to judges. Although judges' values and the court's political environment significantly influence judicial decisions, the nature of issues to be decided by judges, as well as the available reasoning to support different options, are produced by each side's advocates. Lawyers' arguments are especially likely to influence judges who do not possess strong ideological values with respect to a specific issue. As Lee Epstein and Joseph Kobylka found in their study of the Supreme Court's decisions on capital punishment and abortion,

> [B]eneath the Court-based and environmental factors that stimulate doctrinal change by the Supreme Court lurk arguments made by the attorneys and interes[t] [groups] that sponsor and support constitutional litigation. . . . [T]here is substantial evidence that the less ideologically driven justices take these arguments seriously and account for them in explaining the positions they take.[65]

## Small Group Processes

Appellate court judges do not make decisions on their own, but instead work with other judges in deciding cases. Appellate courts are referred to as "collegial courts" because the judges must work together and interact with colleagues in order to produce decisions. No single judge can decide a case without attracting support for his or her position from other judges on the court. Thus, the interactions among judges become an important influence on judicial decision making.

The dynamics of the appellate judges' interactions will depend on a number of factors. For example, the size of the court will affect interactions. On most intermediate appellate court panels, there are only three judges. Thus, any particular judge who can convince one other judge to join an opinion can control the outcome of a case. By contrast, the nine-member U.S. Supreme Court provides a different environment for interactions, because a justice can prevail only by shaping an opinion to attract at least four other justices. The resources and decision-making processes in a court will also affect interactions. If there is a burdensome caseload, judges may not have time to discuss cases or to read each other's opinions carefully. Therefore, they may make quick collective decisions after hearing oral arguments, then go off to their individual chambers to write their respective portions of pending opinions without further discussion and persuasion.

Walter Murphy's classic analysis of interaction among Supreme Court justices drew from the notes of retired justices to describe how they attempted to persuade, flatter, bargain, and otherwise engage in strategic behavior to influence their colleagues' decisions.[66] Other studies have examined how chief justices serve as leaders within the Court to influence the decisions of other justices.[67]

When Justice William Brennan retired from the Supreme Court in 1990, news media accounts of his career described how he used his leadership and interpersonal communication skills to influence other justices over the course of three decades.[68] Thus, the personality and communication skills of particular judicial officers may permit them to advance their policy preferences by persuading or otherwise inducing colleagues to join them in case decisions.

Because judges' deliberations take place in secrecy, it is difficult to know precisely how small group processes influence decisions. Judges only rarely reveal details of their interactions with their colleagues.[69] Even if judges were willing to describe their discussions and deliberations, researchers would have to be skeptical of the descriptions because the judges' accounts could be self-serving—attempting to preserve the judicial branch's image as an institution based on law rather than on human interests and interactions. Scholars must piece together details of judges' interactions from anonymous comments during limited interviews with judges,[70] historical descriptions provided by former law clerks and other court personnel,[71] notes from retired judges' personal papers,[72] and evidence of interactions inferred from shifts in a particular judge's decisions.[73] Journalistic accounts of interactions between judges, such as the description of the Supreme Court in the best-selling book *The Brethren*,[74] substantiate the notion that small group processes affect judicial decisions, although scholars are reluctant to accept all of the details described by journalists for fear that journalists' conclusions are not supported by a sufficiently systematic examination of evidence. Although questions remain concerning precisely how judges' interactions influence judicial decision making, chapter 9 will discuss additional research documenting the effects of small group processes on the decisions of justices on the U.S. Supreme Court.

## Role Orientations

The interpretation of facts and expression of values in judicial decisions are also affected by judges' role orientations. The basic premise of role theory is that individuals act differently within their institutional context than they do in relative isolation. According to a leading theorist, a role consists of "behaviors that are characteristic of persons in a context."[75] Thus, a judge's role is a pattern of behavior determined by the judge's expectations, the normative expectations that others have for the judge, and other factors that inform the judge's conception of a judicial officer's function in the judicial system.[76] In other words, judges' role conceptions limit the expression of what judges want to do (i.e., their policy preferences) because judges also seek to do what they think they *ought to do* according to their beliefs about the proper role and behavior for judicial officers. Sometimes, by fulfilling their conceptions of their judicial role—what they believe judges ought to do—judicial officers decline to advance their actual policy preferences. In Gibson's words, "the basic function of decisional role orientations is to specify which variables can legitimately be allowed to influence decision-making, and in the case of conflict, what priorities to assign to different decision-making criteria."[77]

Judges' role orientations have been studied on state supreme courts,[78] state trial courts,[79] federal courts of appeals,[80] and the U.S. Supreme Court.[81] One well-known study examined the U.S. courts of appeals and found that federal appellate judges viewed themselves as "innovators," "realists," or "interpreters."[82] Innovators felt obligated to make new laws and to influence public policies whenever a case presented the opportunity to do so. These judges did not view their judicial roles as limiting their ability to express policy preferences, but instead believed that judges should seek to "launch new ideas."[83] Interpreters, by contrast, believed that judges should be limited to interpreting the law in the context of specific cases.[84] Therefore, these judges restrained the expression of their policy preferences in order not to usurp the authority of the legislative and executive branches by broadly influencing public policy. On the U.S. Supreme Court, this role orientation was illustrated by four justices who said that a Texas statute designed to prevent illegal alien children from attending school was "senseless" and "folly" and that they would never adopt such a harsh policy themselves.[85] However, these justices dissented from the majority's decision to declare the statute unconstitutional because they believed that judges should not interfere with educational policy enacted by legislatures.[86] Realists took a middle position in which they were careful to avoid improper influence on public policy. Although these judges were willing to restrain policy preferences if they felt that a decision on a particular issue should be limited, they would make broad decisions on other issues that they felt required judicial action.[87]

Judicial role orientations are a potentially significant constraint on the expression of judges' policy preferences. By assessing a case and formulating a decision while constantly asking, "Is it appropriate for a judge to do this?" judges restrain and alter the expression of their attitudes and values. Appellate judges' conceptions of their appropriate roles can also affect the way they screen cases to determine which ones deserve thorough consideration.[88] Role orientations do not prevent or negate the expression of judges' preferences. The role concept merely provides a filter through which values and biases are shaped. The attitudes of judges with limited judicial role conceptions (e.g., interpreters) may still be detectable in their decisions, but their decisions will not reflect the clearest and most forceful expression of underlying policy preferences.

## AN EXAMPLE OF EMPIRICAL RESEARCH: JUSTICE STEPHEN BREYER'S FIRST TERM

The foregoing discussion of research into judges' decision making describes the theories and approaches of social scientists who study judicial behavior. Many of the most useful and precise analyses of judicial decision making rely on complex quantitative methods, including regression analysis. For those unfamiliar with the methods of empirical research, it can be difficult to fully visualize and grasp the way scholars use statistical equations and other social science methods to measure and test identifiable factors that underlie judicial decisions. The following analysis of Justice Stephen Breyer's first term on the U.S. Supreme Court provides a straightforward look at how social science approaches analyze judicial decision making as a form of human behavior. Because this example is based on only one year's worth of decisions on one court, it cannot clearly identify all factors underlying judicial decision making on the Supreme Court. Other studies have accomplished that task through the use of larger case samples and more sophisticated methods. In illustrating how social scientists study judicial behavior, this simple example is intended to demonstrate the kinds of questions that social scientists ask, the kinds of hypotheses they explore, and to offer an example of empirical methods employed by judicial scholars.

Traditional legal analyses of a justice's first term on the Supreme Court normally focus on how the justice voted on each type of issue that faces the Court and how the justice crafted opinions on specific issues. Legal analyses of Justice Antonin Scalia's first term, for example, focused on the legal theories espoused by Scalia in his opinions: "[Scalia's] dedication to the doctrine of separation of powers may be his strongest present doctrinal commitment, aside from his rejection of affirmative action. Compromise of his principles on the basic structure of government under his view of the Constitution is unlikely."[89] Such traditional legal analyses frequently presume that justices are consistent in their decisions, that their decisions are based on adherence to coherent legal theories rather than on attitudes and policy preferences, and that justices' opinions are straightforward presentations of their genuine views. The judicial decision maker is also analyzed in isolation, without adequate attention to court processes and the judicial environment in which decisions are made. From a political scientist's perspective, traditional legal analysis often overlooks the influence of justices' backgrounds, small group processes, role orientations, and the other elements of judicial decision making that are explored through social science.

A traditional legal analysis of Justice Breyer's first term on the Court might discuss his opinions and explore, for example, how Breyer analyzed procedures for convicted criminal offenders to raise claims concerning their constitutional rights.[90] A social science analysis of Breyer's first term, by contrast, might begin with an examination of how Breyer's opinion-writing productivity compared with that of other justices. As chapter 8 will discuss in greater detail, the process of determining which judicial officer will write the appellate court's opinion involves small group processes and strategic interactions. Table 7.1 shows that Chief Justice William Rehnquist and the other senior justices assigned Breyer eight majority opinions. As chapter 9 will show, the chief justice—when in the majority—makes the opinion assignments. Otherwise, the senior justice in the majority

**Table 7.1: Number of Opinions Authored, 1994 Supreme Court Term.**

|  | Majority Opinions | Majority Votes[1] | OAR | Concurring Opinions | Dissenting Opinions[2] | Total Opinions Authored[3] |
|---|---|---|---|---|---|---|
| Rehnquist | 11 | 69 | 15.94% | 1 | 4 | 16 |
| Stevens | 9 | 56 | 16.07 | 5 | 19 | 33 |
| O'Connor | 10 | 69 | 14.49 | 10 | 7 | 27 |
| Scalia | 8 | 66 | 12.12 | 9 | 7 | 24 |
| Kennedy | 10 | 76 | 13.15 | 4 | 1 | 15 |
| Souter | 9 | 66 | 13.63 | 3 | 6 | 18 |
| Thomas | 8 | 61 | 13.11 | 7 | 8 | 23 |
| Ginsburg | 7 | 68 | 10.29 | 4 | 8 | 19 |
| **Breyer** | **8** | **67** | **11.94** | **2** | **6** | **16** |
| Average | 8.89 | 66.44 | 13.38 | 5.0 | 7.3 | 21.22 |

1. The number of times a justice voted in the majority (including concurring votes).
2. Opinions are counted as dissents whether the justice dissented in part or in whole.
3. Majority opinions + concurring opinions + dissenting opinions.

*Source:* Christopher E. Smith, Joyce A. Baugh, and Thomas R. Hensley, "The First-Term Performance of Justice Stephen Breyer," *Judicature* 79 (1995): 76.

decides which justice in the majority will write the opinion for the Court. In addition, although any justice is free to write either concurring opinions based on different reasoning than the majority's or dissenting opinions, Breyer only rarely seized the opportunity to present his views through such opinions.

Breyer also had the second lowest Opinion Assignment Ratio (OAR), a measure developed by Elliot Slotnick to determine whether justices are equally productive as opinion writers.[91] The OAR indicates the percentage of cases in which a justice wrote the opinion for the Court (based on the number of cases in which the justice was a member of the majority). A justice who seldom agrees with the majority might naturally write fewer opinions for the Court. The OAR standardizes the assessment of justices' relative productivity. Thus, for example, although Justice John Paul Stevens wrote fewer majority opinions (9) than did Chief Justice Rehnquist (11) because Stevens was a member of the majority in fewer cases (56 versus 69), his OAR indicates that he wrote proportionally more opinions for the Court than did Rehnquist. In other words, Stevens' 9 opinions are a higher percentage of the 56 cases in which he voted with the majority than is Rehnquist's 11 opinions as a percentage of his 69 majority votes. In regard to Justice Breyer, his OAR indicates he received proportionally fewer assignments than almost any other justice during his first term on the Court. His OAR of 11.94 was lower than all other justices except for Justice Ginsburg.

How important is a justice's level of productivity as the author of opinions for the Court? What might these productivity figures indicate about decision making on the Supreme Court? Breyer's low number of opinion assignments fits a hypothesis about the behavior of first-term justices that was developed from previous research on the Supreme Court. According to this hypothesis, new justices experience a "freshman effect" as their senior colleagues decline to burden them with opinion assignments until the experienced justices are confident that the new justices are familiar and comfortable with Supreme Court procedures.[92] Thus, new justices may be given fewer opportunities to assert their views and to shape the justifications for the Court's decisions by writing majority opinions. If there really is a "freshman effect" that influences the opinion-writing opportunities of new justices, it would show that small group processes influence the distribution and content of work in the Supreme Court.

Another element of the "freshman effect" hypothesis is the purported reluctance of new justices to join either the liberal or conservative voting blocs. Supposedly, new justices tend to stay in the middle of the Court by initially refusing to commit to either end of the ideological spectrum. This reluctance or inability to adopt a strong, consistent viewpoint is regarded as a component of the bewilderment that new justices experience while learning how to interact with other justices. Like several other justices who published retrospective assessments of their experiences as new justices, Justice William O. Douglas commented on the bewilderment and uncertainty experienced by newcomers to the Court: "It is always difficult, and especially so for a newcomer, to withdraw his agreement to one opinion at the last minute and cast his vote for the opposed view. A mature Justice may do just that; a junior is usually too unsure to make a last-minute major shift."[93]

As illustrated in tables 7.2 and 7.3, when agreement scores are averaged together, Breyer agreed with the Supreme Court's most liberal bloc of justices

Table 7.2: Interagreement in Split Decisions[1] of the Full Supreme Court, 1994 Term (percent).

|           | SC   | TH   | RE   | KE   | OC   | BR   | SO   | GN   | ST   |
|-----------|------|------|------|------|------|------|------|------|------|
| Scalia    | —    | 85.1 | 78.7 | 72.3 | 59.6 | 48.9 | 42.6 | 44.7 | 23.4 |
| Thomas    | 85.1 | —    | 76.6 | 66.0 | 57.4 | 42.6 | 36.2 | 34.0 | 12.8 |
| Rehnquist | 78.7 | 76.6 | —    | 72.3 | 68.1 | 53.2 | 46.8 | 44.7 | 25.5 |
| Kennedy   | 72.3 | 66.0 | 72.3 | —    | 61.7 | 63.8 | 57.4 | 63.8 | 46.8 |
| O'Connor  | 59.6 | 57.4 | 68.1 | 61.7 | —    | 68.1 | 66.0 | 46.8 | 36.2 |
| **Breyer** | **48.9** | **42.6** | **53.2** | **63.8** | **68.1** | —    | **76.6** | **78.7** | **59.6** |
| Souter    | 42.6 | 36.2 | 46.8 | 57.4 | 66.0 | 76.6 | —    | 68.1 | 66.0 |
| Ginsburg  | 44.7 | 34.0 | 44.7 | 63.8 | 46.8 | 78.7 | 68.1 | —    | 72.3 |
| Stevens   | 23.4 | 12.8 | 25.5 | 46.8 | 36.2 | 59.6 | 66.0 | 72.3 | —    |

1. Includes only 47 nonunanimous cases in which all nine justices participated.

*Source:* Smith, Baugh, and Hensley, "The First-Term Performance of Justice Stephen Breyer": 75.

**Table 7.3: Indicies of Interagreement, Supreme Court, 1994 Term.**

| | |
|---|---|
| Thomas, Scalia, Rehnquist, Kennedy | = 75.2% |
| **Breyer**, Souter, Ginsburg | = 74.5 |
| **Breyer**, Souter, Ginsburg, Stevens | = 70.2 |
| Scalia, Thomas, Rehnquist, Kennedy, O'Connor | = 69.8 |
| Souter, Ginsburg, Stevens | = 68.8 |

*Source:* Smith, Baugh, and Hensley, ''The First-Term Performance of Justice Stephen Breyer'': 76.

(i.e., Souter, Ginsburg, Stevens) in 70 percent of nonunanimous cases. He was a relatively consistent member of the Court's most liberal voting bloc. Does this mean that Breyer did not experience the socialization difficulties and learning processes of the ''freshman effect,'' or alternatively, did the highly conservative and polarized Court (conservative versus liberal) lack a ''middle'' for the new justice to join? It will take more research to fully assess Breyer's judicial philosophy and role in the Court.

Although the validity of the ''freshman effect'' hypothesis has been questioned by several scholars,[94] it provides a simple, understandable example of how social scientists empircally examine judicial officers' decision-making behavior rather than simply read judges' opinions—as lawyers and law professors often do. As this brief example demonstrates, social scientists' empirical analyses attempt to question and explore the human and political factors that influence judicial decisions.

## CONCLUSION

Research on judicial decision making, as much as any other scholarly research on the courts, refutes the notion that judges merely follow established legal principles in determining the outcomes of cases. Although the questions presented to judges are phrased in legal terms and structured by the judicial process, the factors that influence their decisions are the same kinds of factors that influence decisions by other human beings. To reiterate the conclusion from Gibson's review of relevant research: ''Judges' decisions are a function of what they prefer to do, tempered by what they think they ought to do, but constrained by what they perceive is feasible to do.''[95] Thus, judges' policy preferences are motivated by attitudes and values, shaped by role orientations, and limited by views concerning whether particular decisions can be effectively implemented in the political system. The combination of these factors within a particular case produces the judicial decision.

Recognition of the complex human attributes and interactions that influence judicial decision making helps to illuminate the political nature of the judicial process. Judges are similar to other political actors in advancing their policy preferences within the constraints of the political contexts in which their decisions are made and subsequently implemented. The structural differences between legislative and judicial institutions lead to differences in the factors influencing decision making in the respective institutions. Decision making in legislatures, for example, is explicitly political because legislators' votes are frequently intended to please constituents, generate campaign contributions, or otherwise advance legislators' overriding goal of gaining reelection. By contrast, judicial decision making is implicitly political because the developments in the political system determine the composition of the judiciary and because individual judges' decisions are determined by a complex combination of factors, both personal (e.g., attitudes, values, policy preferences) and structural (e.g., precedents, likelihood of reversal on appellate review). Despite the institutional differences that produce different factors and processes underlying legislative and judicial decisions, judges' decisions are best viewed as the product of the same human and political factors that shape decisions in legislatures, executive branch agencies, and other sites of authoritative decision making. Just as decisions by members of Congress are influenced by interactions with their colleagues, by perceptions about feasible policies and public reactions to legislative initiatives, and by views about the proper roles of legislators,[96] judges' decisions are influenced by a similar set of factors within the context of the judicial branch. Thus, judicial decision making does not constitute a unique, mechanical process undertaken by learned judges who follow "the law." Instead, judicial decision making fits neatly into a widely accepted definition of "politics"—activities affecting the "authoritative allocation of values for society" by human actors and institutions that manifest values, biases, and interests.[97]

Not only does judicial decision making itself involve a political process, the authority and discretion possessed by judges increase the importance of the connections between the judiciary and the governing political system. In particular, because "the law" does not dictate how judges should decide cases, the selection of judges is of great importance to political interests who wish to advance their policy preferences and values. Within the boundaries of the political environment, judges have significant ability to make decisions based on personal values and policy preferences. Thus, in order to influence case outcomes and public policies produced by the judicial branch, political parties and interest groups remain actively involved in the judicial selection processes that place judges on the bench. As described in chapter 6, all the methods employed by state and federal court systems for the selection of judges—including merit selection procedures—create opportunities for political interests to affect judicial decision making by influencing the composition of the judiciary.

## NOTES

1. Harry P. Stumpf, *American Judicial Politics* (New York: Harcourt Brace Jovanovich, 1988), p. 42.
2. See Jeffrey A. Segal and Harold J. Spaeth, *The Supreme Court and the Attitudinal Model* (New York: Cambridge University Press, 1993).
3. See Christopher E. Smith, "Polarization and Change in the Federal Courts: *En Banc* Decisions in the U.S. Courts of Appeals," *Judicature* 74 (1990): 133–37.
4. Sheldon Goldman, "Judicial Selection Under Clinton: A Midterm Examination," *Judicature* 78 (1995): 281.
5. Ibid.
6. James L. Gibson, "From Simplicity to Complexity: The Development of Theory in the Study of Judicial Behavior," *Political Behavior* 5 (1983): 9.
7. Melinda Gann Hall, "Justices as Representatives: Elections and Judicial Politics in the American States," *American Politics Quarterly* 23 (1995): 485–503.
8. Stuart Taylor, "Season of Snarling Justices," *Akron Beacon Journal*, 5 April 1990, p. A11.
9. For example, in *Plessy v. Ferguson*, 163 U.S. 537 (1896), the Supreme Court endorsed racial discrimination against African-Americans by permitting segregation to be imposed by law. In *Hammer v. Dagenhart*, 247 U.S. 251 (1918), the Supreme Court prevented Congress from combatting the exploitation of child laborers by factories, mining interests, and other industrial enterprises.
10. Most famously, in *Brown v. Board of Education*, 347 U.S. 483 (1954), the Supreme Court took a significant stand against racial discrimination by declaring that racial segregation in the public schools violated the U.S. Constitution. The decision itself did not transform American society, because racial discrimination continued to exist in many forms. The Court's decision did, however, lead to individual judicial decisions combatting racial discrimination in specific school systems and spur the mobilization of civil rights advocates who succeeded in pushing other governmental institutions to act against discrimination.
11. Edward H. Levi, *An Introduction to Legal Reasoning* (Chicago: University of Chicago Press, 1948), pp. 1–2.
12. Levi, *An Introduction to Legal Reasoning*, p. 4.
13. *Brewer v. Williams*, 430 U.S. 387 (1977).
14. *Rhode Island v. Innis*, 446 U.S. 291 (1980).
15. *Booth v. Maryland*, 482 U.S. 496 (1987); *South Carolina v. Gathers*, 490 U.S. 805 (1989).
16. *Payne v. Tennessee*, 501 U.S. 808 (1991).
17. *Lemon v. Kurtzman*, 403 U.S. 602 (1971).

18. Louis Fisher, *American Constitutional Law* (New York: McGraw-Hill, 1990), p. 713.
19. *Marsh v. Chambers*, 463 U.S. 783 (1983).
20. See, e.g., *Mueller v. Allen*, 463 U.S. 388 (1983); *Edwards v. Aguillard*, 482 U.S. 578 (1987).
21. *Wilson v. Seiter*, 501 U.S. 294 (1991).
22. *Estelle v. Gamble*, 429 U.S. 97 (1976).
23. Louisiana ex rel. *Francis v. Resweber*, 329 U.S. 459 (1947).
24. *Whitley v. Albers*, 475 U.S. 312 (1986).
25. *Hutto v. Finney*, 437 U.S. 678 (1978).
26. *Rhodes v. Chapman*, 452 U.S. 337 (1981).
27. Martin Shapiro, "Toward a Theory of Stare Decisis," *The Journal of Legal Studies* 1 (1972): 134.
28. *Wallace v. Jaffree*, 472 U.S. 38 (1985).
29. *Falzerano v. Collier*, 535 F.Supp. 800, 803 (D.N.J. 1982).
30. Paul Brace and Melinda Gann Hall, "Studying Courts Comparatively: The View From the American States," *Political Research Quarterly* 48 (1995): 24.
31. Ibid.
32. Bob Cohn, "A Turnabout on Civil Rights," *Newsweek*, 4 November 1991, p. 32.
33. See C. Herman Pritchett, *The Roosevelt Court: A Study in Judicial Politics* (New York: Macmillan, 1948).
34. S. Sidney Ulmer, "Are Social Background Models Time-Bound?" *American Political Science Review* 80 (1986): 957–67.
35. See, e.g., Smith, "Polarization and Change in the Federal Courts," pp. 135–37; Sheldon Goldman, "Voting Behavior on the U.S. Courts of Appeals Revisited," *American Political Science Review* 69 (1975): 491–506; Stuart Nagel, "Political Party Affiliation and Judges' Decisions," *American Political Science Review* 55 (1961): 843–50.
36. C. Neal Tate, "Personal Attributes as Explanations of Supreme Court Justices' Decision Making," in *Courts in American Politics*, ed. Henry R. Glick (New York: McGraw-Hill, 1990), p. 273.
37. Gibson, "From Simplicity to Complexity," p. 25.
38. Tate, "Personal Attributes as Explanations," p. 274.
39. Ibid.
40. Tate, "Personal Attributes and Explanations," pp. 270–73; C. Neal Tate, "Personal Attribute Models of the Voting Behavior of U.S. Supreme Court Justices: Liberalism in Civil Liberties and Economic Decisions, 1946–1978," *American Political Science Review* 75 (1981): 355–67.
41. Gibson, "From Simplicity to Complexity," p. 25.
42. See C. K. Rowland, Robert A. Carp, and Ronald Stidham, "Judges' Policy Choices and the Value Basis of Judicial Appointments: A Comparison of Support for Criminal Defendants among Nixon, Johnson, and Kennedy Ap-

pointees to the Federal District Courts,'' *Journal of Politics* 46 (1984): 886–902.

43. Steve Alumbaugh and C. K. Rowland, "The Links Between Platform-Based Criteria and Trial Judges' Abortion Judgments," *Judicature* 74 (1990): 153–62; C. K. Rowland, Donald Songer, and Robert Carp, "Presidential Effects on Criminal Justice Policy in the Lower Federal Courts: The Reagan Judges," *Law and Society Review* 22 (1988): 191–200; Ronald Stidham and Robert Carp, "Judges, Presidents, and Policy Choices: Exploring the Linkage," *Social Science Quarterly* 68 (1987): 395–403.

44. Gibson, "From Simplicity to Complexity," p. 23.

45. Samuel Walker, Cassia Spohn, and Miriam DeLeone, *The Color of Justice: Race, Ethnicity, and Crime in America* (Belmont, CA: Wadsworth, 1996), pp. 168–70.

46. Stuart Nagel, "Ethnic Affiliations and Judicial Propensities," *Journal of Politics* 24 (1962): 92–110.

47. Alumbaugh and Rowland, "The Links Between Platform-Based Appointment Criteria and Trial Judges' Abortion Judgments," pp. 160–61.

48. See, e.g., Glendon Schubert, "Judicial Attitudes and Voting Behavior: The 1961 Term of the United States Supreme Court," *Law and Contemporary Problems* 28 (1963): 100–142; Glendon Schubert, *The Judicial Mind: The Attitudes and Ideologies of Supreme Court Justices, 1946–1963* (Evanston, IL: Northwestern University Press, 1965); Harold J. Spaeth, "An Analysis of Judicial Attitudes in the Labor Relations Decisions of the Warren Court," *Journal of Politics* 25 (1963): 290–311; Joseph Tanenhaus, "Supreme Court Attitudes Toward Federal Administrative Agencies, 1947–1956: An Application of Social Science Methods to the Study of Judicial Process," *Vanderbilt Law Review* 14 (1961): 482–502.

49. Charles H. Sheldon, *The American Judicial Process: Models and Approaches* (New York: Dodd, Mead & Co., 1974), p. 48.

50. Jeffrey Segal and Albert Cover, "Ideological Values and the Votes of U.S. Supreme Court Justices," *American Political Science Review* 83 (1989): 557–65.

51. Ibid., p. 563.

52. Jeffrey A. Segal, Lee Epstein, Charles M. Cameron, and Harold J. Spaeth, "Ideological Values and the Votes of Supreme Court Justices Revisited," *Journal of Politics* 57 (1995): 812–23.

53. Lawrence Baum, *American Courts: Process & Policy*, 2nd ed. (Boston: Houghton Mifflin, 1990), pp. 299–300.

54. Tate, "Personal Attributes and Explanations," p. 273.

55. Gibson, "From Simplicity to Complexity," p. 15.

56. Ibid.

57. Craig Ducat and Robert Dudley, "Federal District Judges and Presidential Power During the Postwar Era," *Journal of Politics* 51 (1989): 98–118.

58. Ibid.

59. Donald R. Songer, "The Impact of the Supreme Court on Trends in Economic Policy Making in the United States Courts of Appeals," *Journal of Politics* 49 (1987): 830–41.

60. Charles A. Johnson, "Law, Politics, and Judicial Decision Making: Lower Federal Court Uses of Supreme Court Decisions," *Law and Society Review* 21 (1987): 325–40.

61. See Fred Kort, "Quantitative Analysis of Fact-Patterns in Cases and Their Impact on Judicial Decisions," *Harvard Law Review* 79 (1966): 1595–1603.

62. See, e.g., Joan Petersilia, *Racial Disparities in the Criminal Justice System* (Santa Monica, CA: Rand Corporation, 1983).

63. See, e.g., Stevens H. Clarke and Gary G. Koch, "The Influence of Income and Other Factors on Whether Criminal Defendants Go to Prison," *Law and Society Review* 11 (1976): 57–92.

64. Jeffrey A. Segal, "Supreme Court Justices as Human Decision Makers: An Individual-Level Analysis of Search and Seizure Cases," *The Journal of Politics* 48 (1986): 938–55.

65. Lee Epstein and Joseph Kobylka, *The Supreme Court and Legal Change* (Chapel Hill, NC: University of North Carolina Press, 1992), p. 310.

66. See Walter F. Murphy, *Elements of Judicial Strategy* (Chicago: University of Chicago Press, 1964).

67. David J. Danelski, "The Influence of the Chief Justice in the Decisional Process of the Supreme Court," *American Court Systems*, 2nd ed., Sheldon Goldman and Austin Sarat, eds. (New York: Longman, 1989), pp. 486–99.

68. See, e.g., David A. Kaplan, "A Master Builder," *Newsweek,* 30 July 1990, pp. 19–20.

69. See Stuart Taylor, "Blackmun Provides a Peek at the People Under Those Robes," *New York Times*, 25 July 1988, p. B6.

70. See H. W. Perry, Jr., "Deciding to Decide in the U.S. Supreme Court: Bargaining, Accommodation, and Roses." Paper presented at the annual meeting of the American Political Science Association, 1986.

71. See, e.g., Linda Greenhouse, "Name-Calling in the Supreme Court: When the Justices Vent Their Spleen, Is There a Social Cost?" *New York Times*, 28 July 1989, p. B10.

72. See D. Marie Provine, *Case Selection in the United States Supreme Court* (Chicago: University of Chicago Press, 1980).

73. See Christopher E. Smith, "Bright-Line Rules and the Supreme Court: The Tension Between Clarity in Legal Doctrine and Justices' Policy Preferences," *Ohio Northern University Law Review* 16 (1989): 119–37.

74. Bob Woodward and Scott Armstrong, *The Brethren*, (New York: Simon & Schuster, 1979).

75. Bruce J. Biddle, *Role Theory* (New York: Academic Press, 1979), p. 56.

76. Joel B. Grossman, "Role Playing and the Analysis of Judicial Behavior:

The Case of Mr. Justice Frankfurter,'' *Journal of Public Law* 11 (1962): 294.

77. James L. Gibson, ''The Role Concept in Judicial Research,'' *Law & Policy Quarterly* 3 (1981): 303.

78. John T. Wold, ''Political Orientations, Social Backgrounds, and Role Perceptions of State Supreme Court Judges,'' *Western Political Quarterly* 27 (1974): 239–48.

79. James L. Gibson, ''Judges' Role Orientations, Attitudes and Decisions: An Interactive Model,'' *American Political Science Review* 72 (1978): 911–24.

80. See J. Woodford Howard, *Courts of Appeals in the Federal Judicial System* (Princeton, NJ: Princeton University Press, 1981).

81. Grossman, ''Role Playing and the Analysis of Judicial Behavior,'' pp. 285–309.

82. J. Woodford Howard, ''Role Perceptions and Behavior in Three U.S. Courts of Appeals,'' *Journal of Politics* 39 (1977): 916–38.

83. Ibid., p. 920.

84. Ibid.

85. *Plyler v. Doe*, 457 U.S. 202, 242 (1982) (Burger, C.J., dissenting).

86. Ibid.

87. Howard, ''Role Perceptions and Behavior,'' p. 921.

88. Victor E. Flango, ''Case Selection in the Georgia and Illinois Supreme Courts,'' *The Justice System Journal* 12 (1987): 384–405.

89. Michael King, ''Justice Antonin Scalia: The First Term on the Supreme Court—1986–1987,'' *Rutgers Law Journal* 20 (1988): 67.

90. See *O'Neal v. McAninch*, 115 S. Ct. 992 (1995).

91. Elliot Slotnick, ''Judicial Career Patterns and Majority Opinion Assignment on the Supreme Court,'' *Journal of Politics* 41 (1979): 643.

92. See Eloise Snyder, ''The Supreme Court As a Small Group,'' *Social Forces* 36 (1958): 232–38.

93. William O. Douglas, *The Court Years, 1939–1975* (New York: Random House, 1980), p. 45.

94. See Edward Heck and Melinda Hall, ''Bloc Voting and the Freshman Justice Revisited,'' *Journal of Politics* 43 (1981): 852–60; Albert Melone, ''Revisiting the Freshman Effect Hypothesis: The First Two Terms of Justice Anthony Kennedy,'' *Judicature* 74 (1990): 6–13.

95. Gibson, ''From Simplicity to Complexity,'' p. 32.

96. See John C. Wahlke, Heinz Eulau, William Buchanan, and Leroy C. Ferguson, *The Legislative System: Explorations in Legislative Behavior* (New York: John Wiley, 1962).

97. David Easton, *The Political System* (New York: Knopf, 1960), p. 129.

# Chapter 8

# Appellate Processes

I t would be possible to have a judicial system in which trial court decisions are final. If litigants receive a complete hearing in front of a judge or jury, why should they have the opportunity to present their arguments again in front of different judges? Presumably the decision of the trial judge or the jury under a judge's supervision has as much validity and basis in law as any subsequent decision by other judges. The overwhelming majority of American trial judges are lawyers who were trained in accredited law schools. Moreover, appellate judges do not necessarily have any special qualifications that make them better suited than trial judges to decide appeals. Many appellate judges are less experienced than the trial judges whose work they review. The appellate judges simply had the necessary political connections or success to gain appointment or election to a higher court. Indeed, several notable justices on the U.S. Supreme Court, including Chief Justice Earl Warren, Chief Justice William Rehnquist, Justice William O. Douglas, and Justice Felix Frankfurter, had never served as judges before being appointed to the nation's highest court. Why should trial judges' decisions be less reliable than those of similarly trained lawyers who happen to serve on appellate courts? Although a hypothetical judicial system could lack an appeal process, appellate courts, the higher courts in the hierarchies of American court systems, are important components of the American judicial system because they serve different functions for society than do trial courts.

## THE FUNCTIONS OF APPEALS

The appeal process is an important buffer against adverse reactions by disappointed litigants. Martin Shapiro argues that the "appeal allows the loser to continue to assert his rightness in the abstract without attacking the legitimacy of the legal system or refusing to obey the trial court."[1] The appeal process, in

effect, *maintains the stability and legitimacy of the courts' dispute-processing functions*. Thus, the appeal process is a kind of psychological safety valve for losers that provides them with additional time and opportunity to accept an adverse outcome. Moreover, the opportunity for appeal keeps the loser's attention focused on legal mechanisms for dispute processing within the judicial system and thereby avoids the chaos that may follow if losing litigants rejected court decisions and took matters into their own hands. According to Shapiro:

> [T]oo abrupt a termination [of conflicts] may be counterproductive of true conflict resolution. Appeal, whether actually exercised, threatened, or only held in reserve, avoids adding insult to injury. The loser can leave the courtroom with his head held high talking of appeal and then accept his loss, slowly, privately, and passively by failing to make an appeal.[2]

Appeals courts also serve to *supervise judicial decision making and outcomes in trial courts* that are scattered throughout a geographic area. Appellate courts can correct errors made by trial courts. Moreover, because the appellate process involves lengthy written and oral arguments on specific issues, deliberative discussion by several judges, and thoughtful written opinions, appellate judges are removed from the hurly-burly and theatrics of the trial process, which can force trial judges to make quick, and perhaps unwise, decisions. Trial judges must frequently make instantaneous decisions about whether evidence and arguments are being properly presented to a jury. Such quick decisions are necessary to keep the trial moving in an orderly fashion. Appellate judges, by contrast, have time to undertake more careful deliberations and to craft thorough explanations of decisions concerning difficult issues.

In addition, the appellate courts are centralizing forces that *promote uniform decision making in the judicial branch*. Thus, uniform laws govern human behavior throughout a jurisdiction, and people can expect equitable results from trial courts in a particular court system. This uniformity can also help link far-flung areas of the country. Without a national appellate process embodied in the federal circuit courts of appeals and the U.S. Supreme Court, local and regional differences in political cultures and social values would lead courts in various parts of the United States to interpret the Constitution and other laws in very different ways. For example, if southern courts had been sufficiently independent to endorse the legality of racial discrimination in the 1960s when the rest of American society was rejecting such official policies, the country would have been deeply divided. Because the federal courts of appeals and the U.S. Supreme Court were available to reverse decisions endorsing discrimination and thereby pull the regional trial courts in a unified direction, the country remained bound by the appellate courts' interpretations of the Constitution. In effect, appellate courts unify and stabilize American society and its existing governing system.

Although federal district courts produce different results in some cases, depending on the attitudes and values of the various judges, the appellate courts can ensure that the judges follow the same dispute-processing procedures, and appellate supervision can control the range of differences in decisions produced by trial courts. However, appellate courts cannot provide complete control and supervision over the lower courts. Because of their limited resources, appellate courts can decide only a finite number of cases.

Although intermediate appellate courts generally have *mandatory jurisdiction* that requires them to decide the cases presented to them, they may permit oral arguments and complete consideration only for selected cases. Other cases are decided summarily based on the lawyers' written submissions. Many appellate courts of last resort, which possess *discretionary jurisdiction* that allows them to choose cases selectively, focus their attention on cases that are of great interest and importance to their judges. Although appellate courts may not ensure that all judicial decisions are completely uniform, they do exert a unifying influence over a broad range of issues. The unifying influence of the appellate process may be necessary to maintain public support for and acquiescence to judicial authority. If all trial judges could create laws in their own jurisdictions, the citizenry would be less likely to accept and obey any resulting judicial pronouncements that were inconsistent with and unconnected to the law in other locales. The public's belief that American society is governed by ''law'' might be seriously threatened.

In adding uniformity to judicial decisions, appellate courts do not merely ensure that citizens are treated equitably by courts and that the judicial system conveys the appearance of consistency. Courts of appeals use conflicts between disputants as vehicles for *judicial policy making that will affect the entire jurisdiction*. Appellate courts provide the judicial branch with its most far-reaching opportunities to enunciate values, establish policies, and distribute resources in society. As scholars who study appellate courts have observed, ''Often the substance of a case shifts on appeal, and while the litigants remain the same, the judicial system permits a case to undergo significant transformation as it moves within the appellate process.''[3]

Cases may be transformed into policy-making vehicles either through the preferences of the judges or through the explicit intentions of the litigants' attorneys. One study of U.S. Supreme Court cases presented on behalf of needy people by Legal Services lawyers indicated that ''[t]he [Legal Services] Program's appellate challenges were a result of attorneys' casework, not of a strategy to bring about specific policy changes.''[4] Individual claimants' cases happened to present issues with broad implications for public policy in the eyes of the justices. In other instances, interest groups provide legal representation for individuals because these groups seek to persuade appellate courts to utilize the sponsored cases as bases for enunciating public policies.[5] In some instances, appellate judges may look for specific cases that will provide useful vehicles for the development of the judges' preferred policy positions. For example, after the addition of Justice Anthony Kennedy, President Reagan's final appointee to the Supreme Court, a slim five-member majority asked the attorneys in a civil rights case to reargue the case by emphasizing the question of whether the Court should invalidate a precedent established twelve years earlier. The precedent was the basis for discrimination suits against private individuals and businesses.[6] Although ultimately the five-member majority merely altered the precedent and did not reverse it, the justices' desire to use the case for their own policy interests is evident in the fact that none of the litigants had asked them to reconsider the civil rights precedent. The appellate process, as Shapiro has noted, concerns the development and enunciation of broad rules and policies for society rather than merely the processing of disputes between litigants:

> [W]hile in form [appellate courts] may be engaged in finally resolving one particular dispute between two particular litigants, their principal role may be to provide uniform rules of law. Naturally such rules must be based on considerations far broader than the concerns of the two litigants, essentially on considerations of public policy that may have little to do with the particular litigation.[7]

As indicated by the foregoing descriptions of appellate functions, "Appellate institutions are more fundamentally related to the political purposes of central regimes than to the doing of individual justice."[8] If the judicial system's function was merely to process disputes, trial courts alone could handle that task by structuring an environment for negotiated settlements and issuing decisions in unsettled cases. The purposes of the appellate process are directed at larger issues concerning the creation, maintenance, and acceptance of societal rules and institutions. Thus, appellate courts help unify Americans under a single political governing system.

## THE NATURE OF APPEALS

In the American system, appeals are generally focused on one or more particular issues of law or procedure that the appellant (the litigant who initiates the appeal) asserts were handled incorrectly by the trial court. Appellate courts do not conduct trials. Although appellate courts may hear oral arguments from attorneys concerning the narrow questions at issue in the appeal, lawyers do not present evidence and witnesses as they do in trial courts. The appellate court is obligated to accept the factual record as developed from the presentation of evidence during the trial. The appellate judges may, however, disagree with the inferences drawn from the facts by the trial judge.[9] If the appeal is based on a claim that after the trial important new evidence was discovered that casts doubt on the trial's outcome, the appellate court will not decide whether the new evidence should change the judge's or jury's verdict, but will merely decide whether the new evidence casts sufficient doubt on the trial outcome to warrant a new trial. Thus, appellate courts do not determine questions of guilt and innocence in criminal cases or of liability in civil cases. They merely evaluate selected issues concerning the conduct and results of the trial and decide whether errors were committed. In the course of focusing on narrow issues, however, appellate courts may create broad public policies. In the famous case that led to the nationwide establishment of a right to appointed counsel for indigent criminal defendants, Clarence Earl Gideon's appeals through the Florida appellate courts did not seek a judicial declaration that he was innocent of the crime for which he had been convicted and imprisoned. Instead, the appeal focused on the narrow issue of whether the Sixth and Fourteenth Amendments to the U.S. Constitution required the trial judge to appoint an attorney to represent Gideon.[10]

Although the appeal may specifically allege that, for example, the prosecutor or jurors took improper actions, in effect all appeals assert either that the trial judge made direct errors in applying established law and procedure or that the judge failed to control the substantive errors committed by other actors during the trial. Because trial judges are umpires who enforce court rules, reversal on appeal often amounts to a declaration that the trial judge made an error. Although trial judges do not generally wish to have cases reversed on appeal, sometimes it cannot be avoided because appellate courts' decisions effectively create new rules that were not in existence at the time that the trial occurred. In the right to counsel case, for example, the trial judge followed established law in declining to appoint an attorney to represent the defendant, Mr. Gideon. When the case reached the Supreme Court, however, a majority of justices changed the interpretation of constitutional law by creating a new rule requiring legal representation for indigent defendants facing incarceration for felony charges.[11] Gideon received a new trial (and was acquitted of all charges in the second trial) because the Supreme Court created a new policy that could not have been anticipated by the trial judge.

Appellate courts do not seek to ensure that each trial court proceeding was perfect. Appellate courts will not usually consider any asserted errors unless the errors were sufficiently significant to affect the outcome of the case. Moreover, under many jurisdictions' rules of procedure, litigants must raise objections to errors at trial and thereby give the trial judge an opportunity to correct any errors. In some instances, if the litigant does not object to an asserted error at trial, he or she forfeits the opportunity to raise the issue on appeal. This prevents litigants from waiting to see whether they have won or lost at trial before they begin to state their objections to judges' decisions on evidence and other matters. In effect, if the asserted error was not sufficiently important to cause a litigant to complain when it happened, appellate courts do not wish to spend time examining it merely because the litigant is now unhappy after losing. This is not a practice designed to ensure that court decisions achieve justice. Its purpose is to advance the efficient administration of the courts. It creates pressure on attorneys to identify errors and raise them in order to protect the litigants' interests. Clients' appeals may be irrevocably damaged if their attorneys make mistakes in raising objections at trial. The practice of precluding appeals on some issues relieves the appellate courts of potential burdens by limiting the range of possible appeals that may emerge from a trial. In reality, the existence of such a practice acknowledges that significant errors may not be reviewable on appeal even if they have led to improper outcomes.

Cases filed with appellate courts fall under those courts' mandatory or discretionary jurisdiction. Intermediate appellate courts have mandatory jurisdiction over most cases. In other words, the judges on the intermediate appellate courts must consider these cases and issue decisions for each case. The decisions may merely be announcements of a brief, a summary affirmation of the trial court's decision after a panel of appellate judges has reviewed the records of the case and the lawyers' written arguments. Alternatively, lawyers may be permitted to make oral arguments, and the judges may discuss the case and circulate draft opinions among panel members before publishing a formal written opinion detailing the reasoning underlying their decision. By contrast, under discretionary jurisdiction for courts of last resort, litigants cannot file appeals directly. They must file petitions asking the appellate court to accept their cases. The judges can choose to hear those cases they regard as most interesting and important, and they can decline to hear cases they do not wish to consider. When a court declines to accept a case, it leaves intact the last lower court decision. Technically, the higher court does not endorse the lower court's decision. The higher court merely leaves the lower court decision intact because it does not deem the issue in the case sufficiently important to receive a hearing. The division of jurisdictional responsibilities for appellate courts provides litigants with opportunities to appeal most cases through the intermediate courts' mandatory jurisdiction but leaves the courts of last resort free to reserve their resources and deliberations for selected cases with significant policy consequences.

Unlike trial court judges who supervise procedures that produce negotiated settlements in the overwhelming majority of cases, appellate judges must actually make decisions in most cases. In some cases, the parties may "settle" after trial for terms different from those set by the trial verdict in order to avoid the expense of an appeal or the risk of an adverse appellate decision. With few exceptions, the cases before the appellate courts have already been through the entire gamut of trial processes and have subsequently moved to the appellate stage precisely because the disputants have been unable to reach a settlement despite the pressures imposed on them by the judicial process. In many cases, appellate judges merely decide not to hear a case or summarily affirm a lower court decision. In reaching these decisions, the judges (or their staff) must read and assess the issues and arguments presented in written documents filed with the court. By contrast, a trial judge can create an environment in which to process disputes through negotiated settlements by forcing the parties to meet in periodic conferences without the judge ever closely examining the competing arguments and evidence. In cases given complete review at the appellate level, the judges—depending on their caseload pressures—may have the luxury of reading and analyzing written arguments before listening to oral arguments during which they may freely ask questions. Afterward, they can discuss the case with other judges, compose draft opinions to elicit criticisms and suggestions from colleagues and law clerks, and spend whatever time they deem necessary—often several months—crafting an opinion that will persuasively justify their decision. Caseload pressures force some appellate courts to rely more heavily on law clerks for summarizing written arguments prior to hearing or for preparing preliminary drafts of opinions.

## THE DECISION TO APPEAL

Many factors can influence a litigant's decision to appeal. These factors may reflect the litigant's interests, the attorney's interests, or both. After losing at the trial, many litigants claim that they will pursue an appeal, but some reconsider the decision and accept their losses. A key factor influencing the decision is the cost of pursuing a case in the appellate process. Litigants have frequently expended considerable time, money, and emotion on a trial. Even with a continued psychological desire to seek vindication in a higher court, the financial costs of filing an appeal may be daunting. Attorneys' fees can mount rapidly because of the considerable effort required in researching and writing appellate briefs and preparing oral arguments. In addition, the prospect of continuing the dispute for an extended period of time may deter potential litigants who wish to begin putting the dispute behind them. For example, during the mid-1960s, when many southern federal district judges resisted recognition of civil rights, relatively few appeals were filed in such cases despite the fact that appellate judges reversed nearly half of the trial judges' decisions.[12] Despite the likelihood of success, financial or other personal reasons apparently deterred civil rights litigants from filing appeals.

The decision to appeal may also be influenced by the attorney's assessment of the prospects for victory in the appellate court. If the case is based on a contingency fee, the attorney may be especially reluctant to pursue an uncertain appeal that may yield further expenditures but no compensation. If the client can afford to pay the attorney's fees, however, the attorney may be willing to pursue the case as long as the client is willing to foot the bill. Attorneys must evaluate the composition of the court of appeals and the trends in the court's decisions on related issues in order to predict whether there is a reasonable likelihood of success.

The decision to appeal may be based on goals that extend beyond the resolution of the underlying dispute. For example, interest groups may seek to attain policy goals by pursuing cases through trial and appellate levels.[13] With few exceptions, cases must be heard at the trial level before they can move to the appellate level. Because interest groups frequently adopt ''test cases'' to change established interpretations of constitutional and statutory law, these groups expect to push their arguments through every court that will hear the case. Their goal is to persuade the highest court possible to establish a new policy through a judicial decision. When a parent challenged Alabama's law requiring public schools to provide opportunities for teachers to lead willing students in prayer, the federal district judge, who was drawn from the local environment of Alabama politics, rejected arguments that such prayers violate the First Amendment's insistence on the separation of church and state. Only when the case was pursued through the U.S. Court of Appeals and the U.S. Supreme Court did the parent and the interest groups that supported him achieve their objective of gaining judicial declarations outlawing the school prayers implemented by the Alabama statute.[14]

Because appellate courts exercise supervisory authority over the decisions of trial courts, even litigants who attain their policy objectives through victory at trial must plan to present their arguments again in appellate courts in case the losing side decides to appeal. There is a risk that the appellate court may rule that the trial court erred, so the victor at the trial level cannot feel confident of ''victory'' until the case has completed its journey through the judicial process. Interest groups may pursue appeals that are unlikely to succeed simply to demonstrate to their constituents that they are willing to keep fighting for policy objectives. Even when previous favorable court decisions have not led to concrete policy changes, interest groups may continue to pursue appellate litigation if only to attain reinforcing judicial declarations that preserve and advance their policy objectives. Such was the case in school desegregation litigation—many judicial decisions against discrimination were not fully implemented. Despite the practical ineffectiveness of such decisions, particularly in communities with organized resistance to desegregation, civil rights lawyers continued to seek favorable declarations from courts.[15]

After trial, people convicted of criminal offenses have everything to gain and nothing to lose by filing appeals. Indigent prisoners are eligible for waiver of court fees for appeals, and they are also entitled to free representation by appointed attorneys during their initial appeal.[16] However, most convicted criminal offenders, whose convictions are based on negotiated guilty pleas, have few bases for filing appeals. These offenders have admitted their guilt and, in effect, accepted the fact that they will be subjected to a negotiated range of criminal punishments. Although they may claim that they did not enter their pleas voluntarily or their lawyers provided ineffective assistance of counsel, they have relatively few legal grounds for appeal.

Convicted offenders—whether convicted after trial or through a guilty plea—may challenge their convictions in the courts through traditional *habeas corpus* petitions. Such petitions are used to seek federal court review of constitutional claims that have been rejected in the state appllate courts during the investigation and adjudication of a criminal case. These actions begin in trial courts but may eventually move to appellate courts after trial judges reject the prisoners' claims. In 1991 the U.S. Supreme Court acted to reduce the burden of *habeas corpus* petitions on the federal courts by limiting state prisoners' ability to file such actions. In 1996 Congress created further limitations.[17]

## COPING WITH RISING CASELOADS IN APPELLATE COURTS

Rising caseloads have taxed the resources of appellate courts. In the federal appellate courts, for example, the number of appeals filed grew from 27,946 in 1982 to 50,224 in 1993.[18] Many state appellate courts have experienced similar caseload increases since the 1960s.[19] For example, an examination of caseload data for thirty-eight states from 1973 to 1983 showed a 107 percent increase in civil case appeals and a 114 percent increase in criminal case appeals.[20] The rapid rise in appeals strains appellate courts' capabilities for processing cases. As a result, federal and state court systems have initiated various strategies to cope with the increased demands on judicial resources. A study of state appellate courts found that these courts have coped with rising caseloads in a number of ways: adding more judges; creating an intermediate appellate court; dividing appellate courts into panels; adding more law clerks; adding more staff attorneys; and curtailing the publication of opinions.[21] In addition, courts may limit the number of cases accepted for oral argument and, especially in the federal system, the creation of new specialized appellate courts can reduce the burdens on the regular appellate courts. As described in chapter 2, the federal system's specialized appellate courts remove many cases concerning patents, duties on imports, veterans' benefit claims, and other issues from the regular circuit courts. Justice Antonin Scalia of the U.S. Supreme Court advocates the creation of an additional appellate court for Social Security disability claims in order to keep them from burdening the regular federal courts.[22] There are risks, however, that specialization may lead to routinized or otherwise unequal treatment of separated categories of cases. Various problems have arisen regarding the consequences of the other strategies introduced to cope with burdensome caseloads. Each new strategy affects the manner in which cases are processed as well as the outcomes produced by appellate courts.

### Additional Appellate Judges

By adding additional judges, appellate courts increase their capacity to decide cases because there are more judicial officers to share the responsibilities for case screening and opinion writing. Very few states have recently increased the number of judges on their courts of last resort. Between 1970 and 1984, a few states increased the size of their highest courts from three or four judges to five judges (i.e., Delaware, Wyoming) or from five or six judges to seven judges (i.e., Maine, Montana), but most high courts have remained fixed in size at five, seven, or nine judges.[23] Because many courts of last resort sit only *en banc* (i.e., as an entire group) there may be only modest benefits in increasing the number of judges to share in writing opinions. Indeed, an increase in size may actually have detrimental effects, adding more viewpoints and more disagreements and dissenting opinions that can slow the processing of cases. A smaller body of judges may work together more efficiently. In a study of Rhode Island's five-member Supreme Court, one justice said he "would not like to see his court expanded to seven [justices], despite the need for a reduction in individual case loads, because 'more [justices] means more disagreement.' "[24] Thus, the benefits of adding judges apply primarily to intermediate appellate courts, which generally utilize several different three-judge panels in order to process many cases simultaneously. Many states made significant increases in their numbers of intermediate appellate judges since the 1970s. For example, California increased the number of its intermediate appellate judges from forty-eight to eighty-eight, and Florida increased its judges from twenty to fifty-seven.[25] The federal judiciary's case-processing capacity has also been increased in this manner. The number of judges on the federal circuit courts of appeals increased from 87 in 1969 to 167 in 1991.[26]

The federal court system and fifteen state court systems increase their case-processing capacities by utilizing retired judges and trial judges as visiting panel members on intermediate appellate courts.[27] The utilization of temporary judicial officers from outside the appellate court produces limited benefits because of the need to ensure that regular appellate judges constitute a majority on each panel and because such borrowing diminishes the resources of lower courts.

Although adding judges may increase the number of panels that can process cases on an intermediate appellate court, there are drawbacks to this strategy for coping with rising caseloads. First, states may be reluctant to undertake the expense of increasing the judicial payroll by adding judges and the staff personnel that each new judge needs. In addition, new judges may require additional courtrooms, chambers, computers, and other expensive facilities. Second, the creation of new judgeships inevitably places extra influence on the composition of the judiciary in the hands of the political interests that control the judicial selection mechanisms at a given moment. An increase in federal appellate judgeships permits the political party that controls the presidency to appoint its partisans to these influential, policy-making positions. Thus, for example, when there is a Republican in the White House, Democratic members of Congress will be reluctant to create many new judgeships. Third, although the intermediate appellate court may increase its case-processing capacity, the court of last resort's ability to monitor intermediate appellate decisions may diminish. The fixed size of most courts of last resort prevents them from keeping up with the increased output of the courts below them. The highest court may experience increasingly severe backlogs or may begin to lose its capacity to shape clear judicial policies and ensure uniform decisions in the lower courts. For example, there are indications that the U.S. courts of appeals have gained increased influence on policy making because the Supreme Court has less ability and inclination to supervise the federal lower courts that received additional judgeships in the 1970s and 1980s:

> [The U.S. Supreme Court] supervises the [federal] intermediate appellate courts to an even lesser extent than it did in the 1960s. Thus, the importance of the courts of appeals in defining circuit precedent and policy has continued to grow. The Supreme Court appears to prefer to review certain types of cases, but even among the preferred types it disturbs very few decisions of the courts of appeals.[28]

## Creating Intermediate Appellate Courts

Several states still lack intermediate appellate courts and must rely for appeals exclusively on their courts of last resort: Delaware, Maine, Mississippi, Montana, Nevada, New Hampshire, Rhode Island, South Dakota, Vermont, West Virginia, and Wyoming.[29] Not surprisingly, these are less populous states in which fewer lawsuits are filed and appealed than in other states. Some states have only recently created intermediate appellate courts (e.g, Virginia, 1985; Nebraska, 1991) to reduce the burdens on their courts of last resort. In 1987 North Dakota created a temporary court of appeals utilizing retired judges and trial court judges. The state legislature authorized the court to hear appeals from 1987 to 1990, but subsequently extended the court's tenure through 1996. Obviously, the creation of an intermediate appellate court is a significant structural change designed to increase a court system's case-processing capacity. As with the addition of judges in other contexts, the creation of new courts affects judicial outcomes by introducing new authoritative decision makers drawn from the currently prevailing political interests.

The intermediate court will increase opportunities for litigants to be heard by a small panel of appellate judges (usually three members). A new intermediate appellate court reduces the significant burden of mandatory jurisdiction cases that fall on courts of last resort when they are the only appellate courts. However, the corresponding increase in the highest appellate court's discretionary authority to decline to hear cases may make it much more difficult for litigants to have their appeals heard by the larger deliberative body (usually five, seven, or nine members) on courts of last resort. Because many courts of last resort meet in larger groups than the three-member panels typical of intermediate appellate courts, the highest courts create a greater likelihood of divergent viewpoints that may produce more thorough examination, discussion, and deliberation concerning the litigants' competing arguments. Thus, the creation of an intermediate appellate court can change the decision-making processes in appellate cases by making three-member panels, with their more limited opportunities for discussion and interaction, the final decision makers for many cases.

In the federal system, there has been significant opposition to a proposal to create a new "super" intermediate appellate court with a rotating composition of current federal judges as a new institution between the circuit courts and the Supreme Court. A "super" intermediate appellate court could reduce the Supreme Court's burden and increase the court system's capacity to provide unified answers on issues that cause disagreement within and among the circuit courts. There are serious questions about which federal judges would serve on the court, what effect the new court would have on the Supreme Court's role, and how the new court would affect the existing circuit courts.[30] The introduction of an intermediate appellate court will inevitably increase a court system's capacity to process cases, but such restructuring can also affect judicial outcomes by altering the manner in which cases are processed.

## Dividing Appellate Courts into Panels

Court systems can increase their appellate case-processing capabilities by dividing *en banc* courts into panels. Appellate courts can hear several cases simultaneously by dividing the judges into smaller groups. As of 1989, thirteen state courts of last resort divided into panels to hear some of their cases.[31] Some commentators have argued that judicial reformers should seriously consider whether the U.S. Supreme Court might benefit by emulating the practices of European courts of last resort that are split into multiple deliberative bodies.[32] However, this proposal may violate the U.S. Constitution because Article III of the Constitution says "[T]he judicial power of the United States shall be vested in *one* Supreme Court . . ." (emphasis supplied). If appellate courts were divided into small panels, the potential problems for uniform decisions and of biased decision making within smaller groups of judges would be more easily remedied in courts of last resort, because the relevant judicial officers would be more closely in touch with each panel's decisions and could easily schedule reargument in front of the entire court for problematic cases.

The idea of increasing resources by dividing into smaller panels has been pushed to its furthest extreme in two states. In Wisconsin a single appellate judge can hear appeals in certain categories of minor cases.[33] In New Jersey's intermediate appellate court, cases may be heard by two-judge panels. Because of the potential problems posed by such small panels, scholars who have studied state appellate processes have concluded that New Jersey's innovation is not desirable for other court systems unless it is accompanied by adequate safeguards:

> [T]he [two-member panel] technique may not be appropriate elsewhere unless other procedures are also in place. In New Jersey, the quality of appellate review is maintained by two important safeguards. First, written decisions in every

appeal explain the court's reasons for the outcome. Second, the several layers of screening (experienced staff review plus scrutiny by judges) ensure that only appropriate cases are heard by two-judge panels.[34]

In addition, a third judge can be brought in whenever the two panel members disagree.[35]

## Adding Law Clerks and Staff Attorneys

An increase in staff assistance can add to a court's case-processing capacity. Thus, many appellate courts have hired additional law clerks and staff attorneys to assist their judges. These assistants help judges by screening cases, conducting research, or writing draft opinions. Generally, "staff attorneys function very much like law clerks" except that they are not attached to specific judges.[36] A study of several state appellate courts described the roles of staff attorneys: "In Florida, . . . a staff attorney and the clerk of court screen briefed appeals to identify routine, one-issue cases for expedited submission. . . . [S]taff attorneys screen briefed appeals and prepare draft opinions (Arizona) or memoranda (New Jersey) in appeals of at least moderate complexity."[37] Federal Judge Richard Posner has raised concerns about the use of staff attorneys because they are not sufficiently socialized by and loyal to particular judges:

> There can be no assurance that the staff attorney will share the outlook and values of the judge, and he will not have a chance to acquire that outlook and those values. . . . by working continuously with the same judge for a substantial period of time [as a law clerk does].[38]

Both law clerks and staff attorneys perform important roles in providing judges with information about cases prior to oral arguments. As described by J. Woodford Howard:

> Prior to oral argument most [federal appellate] judges seldom do more than scan pertinent portions of the record called to their attention by clerks or counsel, a technique increasingly systematized in several circuits to streamline appeals. To prepare for oral argument, all but a handful of circuit judges rely upon bench memoranda prepared by their law clerks, plus their own notes from reading briefs. . . . For their perceptions of issues prior to decision, circuit judges are increasingly dependent upon the homework of others.[39]

After oral argument, many judges assign to law clerks or staff attorneys the responsibility for producing a draft opinion.

Although judges' assistants, especially law clerks, may have little prior legal experience, the accelerating delegation of duties to law clerks and staff attorneys makes these subordinate decision makers increasingly influential. For example, law clerks can sometimes persuade judges to change their minds about case decisions. In a documentary film on the U.S. Supreme Court, an on-camera conversation between Justice John Paul Stevens and one of his law clerks reinforced the recognition of law clerks' influence:

> Justice Stevens: [pointing to law clerk] "One [case] that you convinced me to change my mind on, you remember? You convinced me once, but then I think I got unconvinced."
> Law Clerk: "Then you got reconvinced again."
> Justice Stevens: "Reconvinced. . . . We went back and forth on it several times."[40]

According to Thomas Marvell, "The most important influence of law clerks [is] a subtle modifying of judges' overall outlooks, rather than directly affecting decisions in specific cases."[41] The law clerks and staff attorneys also affect the wording and reasoning in judges' opinions by commenting on draft opinions and by writing draft opinions themselves.[42] Although judges need assistance with their tasks, there are risks that subordinates may impart too much influence on court outcomes that are supposed to be produced by the judges selected through state and federal judicial selection processes.

Reliance on staff assistance creates risks that instead of spending time making considered judgments about disputes and policy issues, judicial officers in appellate courts will become, in Judith Resnik's terminology, "managerial judges" who function as administrators supervising the work of assistants.[43] Indeed, in his study of several U.S. circuit courts of appeals, Howard found that "[j]udges increasingly spent their time supervising decision making by others, including central staff attorneys responsible to the chief judge and the circuit council as a whole, rather than deciding [cases] themselves."[44]

## Modified Appellate Processes

Many courts have modified their traditional procedures to increase their case-processing efficiency. Cases are screened by judges, law clerks, and staff attorneys in order to dismiss unwanted cases that fall under appellate courts' discretionary jurisdiction. In some cases, screening procedures may also lead to summary decisions based entirely on the written briefs submitted by the opposing attorneys. Thus, time-consuming oral arguments are reserved for only a portion of the caseload. In addition, the judges may write and publish opinions in only a portion of cases and thereby issue terse, conclusory decisions (e.g., "trial court order affirmed") in other cases.

The emphasis on screening out less important cases creates risks that underprivileged litigants will have fewer opportunities to be heard in appellate courts.

Research on the federal courts indicates that prisoners' petitions, Social Security appeals, and criminal appeals are more likely than other cases to be decided summarily.[45] Similarly, studies show that criminal cases are less likely to receive full consideration in state appellate courts.[46] The unequal treatment of different kinds of cases may reflect what one state judge claims is a pervasive judicial bias in favor of giving complete attention to commercial, corporate, and other cases involving large sums of money and prominent, influential litigants.[47] The acceptance and rejection of cases for hearing may be determined by the values and predispositions of the judges involved in the screening process.[48]

In 1990 the federal circuit courts' rates of granting litigants the opportunity to present oral arguments varied. Overall, less than half of intermediate appellate courts' cases were decided after oral arguments. While the Fifth Circuit (covering Texas, Louisiana, and Mississippi) led the circuits by hearing arguments in 69.9 percent of its cases, other circuits' rates of granting oral argument ranged as low as 24.2 percent in the Second Circuit (covering New York, Connecticut, and Vermont).[49] The elimination of oral arguments creates risks that the judges will make decisions without complete information. Oral argument provides the opportunity for judges to ask questions and to hear colleagues' questions and comments to the attorneys. A judge may feel perfectly comfortable making a decision based on the written submissions alone, yet his or her colleagues' concerns raised during oral argument may reveal insights and concerns that were not recognized by the judge when merely reading the appellate briefs.

According to Marvell, "The most drastic way to reduce time spent on [appellate] opinions is to decide cases without [writing opinions]."[50] By curtailing the writing and publishing of opinions, appellate courts create several problems:

> The court may seem arbitrary, and losing parties cannot tell whether the judges gave their arguments sufficient attention. The act of writing opinions is an important part of the decision process since tentative ideas may not survive the test of putting them in writing. Finally, opinions are absolutely necessary under common law tradition whenever the decisions create new law or change existing law.[51]

Although it is sometimes presumed that judges fail to write opinions only in routine or unimportant cases, research indicates that "a significant number of unpublished decisions of the courts of appeals appear to involve cases which are nonroutine, sometimes politically significant, and which...present the judges...with an opportunity to exercise substantial discretion in their decision making."[52] As in the screening of cases for oral argument, selectivity regarding cases that receive full written opinions can result in unequal treatment of particular categories of cases. In criminal appeals, for example, death penalty and drug cases may be more likely than other kinds of cases to receive written opinions.[53] Thus, by foregoing the normal appellate procedure of writing judicial opinions when deciding cases, appellate judges can adversely affect the decision-making process, the litigants' acceptance of outcomes, and the judicial system's dissemination of new rules and policies. Lawyers are frequently distressed by these developments because, in Howard's words, "[C]ourt expediency appear[s] to override the needs of litigants and the traditions of oral advocacy."[54]

## APPELLATE DECISION MAKING

One distinctive feature of the appellate process is that courts are "collegial courts" in which decisions are rendered by groups of judges rather than by a single judge. Some influential decisions in the appellate process are made by single individuals, such as staff attorneys' recommendations about which cases to summarily dismiss and law clerks' characterizations of cases that provide information for judges prior to oral argument, but formal judicial decisions after complete review are made either by panels of appellate judges or by an appellate court sitting *en banc*. The factors that influence appellate decisions have been a significant focus for research by scholars because the appellate process is different from other components of the judicial process.[55] It is relatively easy to see why decision making in appellate courts differs from that in trial courts. Because judges interact with one another and must garner support from a majority of the panel or court in order to produce a decision, appellate decision making is influenced by factors that do not affect trial court decision making in which a single judge or jury determines outcomes. For example, appellate judges with notable powers of leadership or persuasion may influence the decisions of colleagues. In addition, procedures for discussing and voting on cases may influence outcomes. State supreme courts, for example, differ in their discussion and voting procedures. In some courts, the senior justice leads discussions, and subsequent voting is conducted according to seniority. In others, the discussion leader varies from case to case, and voting is done in order of reverse seniority.[56] As a result, those who speak first may have the opportunity to shape the terms and tone of the discussion, and those who vote last may have the opportunity to cast their votes strategically when they see which way the decision is going.

   Although appellate judges can disagree with their colleagues, most appellate decisions are unanimous. For example, federal circuit judges dissent on average in fewer than 10 percent of cases.[57] The relative lack of visible disagreement in appellate courts may be influenced by a variety of factors. Elected state judges may suppress dissenting views for fear of adverse electoral consequences if they are seen as out of step with the dominant views and values of the electorate.[58] On three-member appellate panels, judges may be reluctant to dissent because of the extra work of writing dissenting opinions in a losing cause. Moreover, dissenters may feel psychologically outnumbered and may therefore accommodate the majority on three-member panels. As researchers noted in one study,

"The intrinsic loneliness of dissent on the circuits may well act as a deterrent to a single judge who faces the possibility of lone disagreement with a majority of judges."[59] In addition to these factors that may influence the decisions of individual judges, the appellate process also contains decision points and processes that provide opportunities for individual judges to steer and shape appellate decisions according to their own preferences and values.

## Panel Assignments

When a case is accepted by an appellate court, a key element that determines the outcome of the case is the composition of the panel that will actually hear the case. Although many appellate decisions are unanimous, there are many issues that elicit disagreements between judges on courts of appeals. Because there is ample evidence that political party affiliations are associated with judges' appellate decisions in certain categories of cases,[60] the outcomes of federal civil rights, criminal, and other cases may depend on whether the panel that hears the case is composed of three Democrats, three Republicans, two Democrats and a Republican, or two Republicans and a Democrat. Courts of appeals produce so many decisions that the U.S. Supreme Court and other courts of last resort do not have the resources or inclination to review all appellate decisions. Moreover, most cases are not taken to courts of last resort after decisions in intermediate appellate courts. Therefore, panel decisions are final in most appellate cases and, for example, Democrat-controlled panels can make "liberal" decisions in civil rights and other cases even when the conservative Republican majority on the court of last resort might have made different decisions. Thus, the initial determination about which judges will sit on the appellate panel for a particular case can significantly affect the case outcome.

The potential for judges' political interests and policy preferences to affect the formation of appellate panels was illustrated by the controversy that emerged in the Fifth Circuit U.S. Court of Appeals during the 1960s. The Fifth Circuit covered the southern states and was the focus of many legal battles over civil rights and racial discrimination. A judge who strongly supported the maintenance of racial segregation created a stir within the circuit when he complained that he was never assigned to sit on panels that were considering civil rights cases.[61] Although liberal judges were overrepresented on such panels for a variety of benign reasons, such as the ill health of several conservative judges, careful study of assignment patterns in the Fifth Circuit shows that race relations cases were steered to liberal-dominated panels for several years in the early 1960s.[62] Howard explains the manipulation of panel assignments as not merely advancing liberal judges' policy preferences but also ensuring that the appellate court's image, effectiveness, and cohesion would be maintained by preventing segregationist judges from making decisions that would clash with the ongoing development of the Supreme Court's civil rights precedents. The dominant judges "sacrific[ed] an *internal* rule of the game—random rotation—to meet *external* obligations of compliance with national law''[63]:

> [L]iberals appeared to shuffle the panels to keep the circuit in line with national policy. . . . No sooner had the court settled its own policies toward desegregation then enforcing those policies in a hostile community erupted into an acute national disturbance. . . . [T]he leadership [on the court] apparently maintained a degree of panel management not so much to control doctrine as to compose internal conflict over civil rights enforcement and an incipient law explosion.[64]

Most appellate courts have opted for random assignment systems in order to avoid any perception that judicial outcomes are being manipulated for political purposes. However, assignments are not necessarily completely random. Panel assignments may be adjusted to ensure that senior court members preside over a certain number of panels or to permit judges to trade assignments for their own personal convenience.[65] Because the chief judge of an appellate court (or the chief justice of a state supreme court that splits into panels) may control the administration of the court, cases can sometimes be steered to particular judges with special expertise on the legal issues involved.

## En Banc Hearings

When a case raises an issue that is entirely new, exceptionally controversial, or likely to produce broad policy consequences, appellate courts may decide to hear the case *en banc* with all of the appellate judges participating. *En banc* cases in the federal intermediate courts can permit a rehearing of panel decisions with which nonpanel judges disagree or of cases in which two or more panels reached contradictory decisions concerning the same or similar issues. *En banc* decisions can be definitive by leaving no doubts about whether particular panel decisions were correct. Moreover, *en banc* decisions carry the authoritative force of the appellate court as a whole rather than of only a portion of the court. On the other hand, *en banc* cases diminish the court's ability to hear multiple cases simultaneously because they are time consuming and require the attention of all of the judges.

Unlike state supreme courts and the other federal circuits—which have, at most, nine to fifteen judges and can therefore sit as complete courts—the Ninth Circuit U.S. Court of Appeals cannot readily hear cases *en banc* because it is composed of twenty-eight judges. In order to avoid problems of scheduling and decision making posed by such an unwieldy number of judges, the Ninth Circuit randomly draws the names of eleven judges to constitute the panel for each *en banc* case. Thus, the ''luck of the draw'' determines the composition of the panel and influences the case outcome.

By strategically requesting *en banc* review of cases, judges can seek to advance their values and preferences. Because *en banc* cases are generally, in Howard's words, "reserved for policy making and head-on collisions,"[66] a circuit judge might seek to change judicial policies by requesting *en banc* hearings with the intention of reversing undesirable panel decisions. Even if the judge's preferred position did not prevail in the *en banc* decision, the fact that the appellate court heard the case *en banc* may attract the high court's attention to the importance of the issue and lead to a further review—and possible reversal—by the justices of the court of last resort.[67] When the composition of an appellate court changes, judges may seek to alter prior decisions with which they disagree, in the belief that the majority on the appellate court is now composed of like-minded judges. Indeed, President Reagan's appointees to the U.S. Courts of Appeals were accused of using *en banc* requests too frequently simply to try to overturn established decisions by now-departed appointees of previous presidents.[68] Because Reagan was president for eight years, he had an especially powerful impact on the composition of federal courts by making judicial appointments for a longer period than any president since Eisenhower in the 1950s. Although studies cast doubt on assertions that Reagan appointees were unique in utilizing *en banc* review,[69] these judges were best situated to produce desired outcomes for cases on which they agreed with each other because of their numerical dominance in several circuits. Regardless of the extent to which any particular judges use *en banc* review to advance their preferences, the strategy remains a viable means of challenging panel decisions and signalling the Supreme Court about the importance of an issue.

## Opinion Assignments

Appellate outcomes are shaped by opinion assignment decisions. The judge assigned to write the opinion in a case can develop the content and reasoning of the new precedent. By shaping the meaning of the court's decision, the judge can influence how the case will affect society as a judicial policy and how it will affect future decisions as a precedent. Thus, assignments to write appellate opinions can be distributed strategically to advance the assigning judges' policy preferences. It is possible, for example, that if a chief justice has the authority to assign opinions, such assignments may be made so as to reward allied judges with desirable assignments and burden opposing judges with unimportant, uninteresting, or otherwise undesirable assignments. This distribution of work might create pressure or incentives for judges to agree more frequently with the chief justice's views in order to improve the quality of their workload.[70]

There are two general methods of assigning opinion-writing responsibilities on appellate courts: random assignment prior to oral argument and assignment by chief or senior judges after oral argument.[71] In the federal courts of appeals, opinions are assigned by the senior judge on the panel or by the chief judge. Assignment practices in state supreme courts are as follows: random assignment prior to conference (27); random assignment after consideration of the case (8); assignment at discretion of chief justice (10); assignment by chief or senior justice in majority (4); assignment by consensus of majority coalition (1).[72] Under rotation or random assignment systems, if the assigned judge is in the minority after oral argument, the opinion will generally be written by the justice in the majority who is most interested in the issue. Judges may also swap assignments to fit their respective areas of interest.[73]

In his study of federal circuit courts, Howard found that "in principle, these judges were strongly attached to panel [assignments by random] rotation . . . [but] [o]pinion assignments, by contrast, the judges saw as more purposive and specialized."[74] Although federal judges prefer to distribute decisions throughout the judicial body to avoid dominance by particular judges, the elements of specialization and seniority influence the opinion-writing assignments.[75] According to Howard, "[B]eneath an umbrella of equalized work, nevertheless, significant sprinklings of specialization occurred, especially in the Fifth Circuit, by virtue of seniority, judicial strategies, and affinities between particular individuals and subjects."[76] Senior judges on panels make opinion assignments and therefore have the opportunity to write opinions themselves in the cases they regard as most interesting or important. Conversely, senior judges can assign less interesting or less important opinions to other judges. Judges may be able to obtain desired opinion assignments by requesting them or by showing more interest in the cases.[77]

## CONCLUSION

As the foregoing discussion indicates, judges are especially important in the appellate process. At the trial level, most outcomes are shaped by the interactions and decisions of the litigants' lawyers in a structured environment supervised by the trial judge. By contrast, outcomes in the appellate process are produced by the decisions and interactions of the judges and their assistants. Thus, the political factors that influence the selection of appellate judges are particularly important forces in shaping the values and policy preferences that will be applied in deciding appeals.

Although judges are the most influential actors in the appellate process, no single judge can necessarily control outcomes, because a majority coalition must be formed on a panel or on an entire appellate court in order to produce a decision. Thus, judicial officers' strategic interactions, as well as their values and policy preferences, shape appellate courts' outcomes. In this way, factors that influence appellate decisions are different than those that shape trial court cases in which a single judge or jury serves as the primary decision maker. In effect, an appellate court's internal give-and-take politics between judges can affect case decisions in conjunction with the external political factors (e.g., politics of judicial selection, legislature's design of appellate courts' structures and processes, etc.) that are always inescapable influences over the judicial branch.

# NOTES

1. Martin Shapiro, *Courts: A Comparative and Political Analysis* (Chicago: University of Chicago Press, 1981), p. 49.
2. Ibid.
3. Richard J. Richardson and Kenneth N. Vines, "Review, Dissent and the Appellate Process: A Political Interpretation," *Journal of Politics* 29 (1967): 602.
4. Susan E. Lawrence, "Legal Services Before the Supreme Court," *Judicature* 72 (1989): 268.
5. See, e.g., Karen O'Connor and Lee Epstein, "The Rise of Conservative Interest Group Litigation," *Journal of Politics* 45 (1983): 479–89.
6. Stuart Taylor, "Court, 5–4, Votes to Restudy Rights in Minority Suits," *New York Times*, 26 April 1988, pp. 1, 11.
7. Shapiro, *Courts*, p. 56.
8. Ibid., p. 52.
9. Thomas B. Marvell, *Appellate Courts and Lawyers* (Westport, CT: Greenwood Press, 1978), p. 158.
10. Anthony Lewis, *Gideon's Trumpet* (New York: Random House, 1964), pp. 7–10.
11. *Gideon v. Wainwright*, 372 U.S. 335 (1963).
12. J. Woodford Howard, *The Courts of Appeals in the Federal Judicial System* (Princeton, NJ: Princeton University Press, 1981), p. 37.
13. See Lee Epstein, "Courts and Interest Groups" in *The American Courts: A Critical Assessment*, eds. John B. Gates and Charles A. Johnson (Washington, D.C.: Congressional Quarterly Press, 1991), pp. 335–71.
14. *Wallace v. Jaffree*, 472 U.S. 38 (1985).
15. Stephen Wasby, "Civil Rights Litigation by Organizations: Constraints and Choices," *Judicature* 68 (1985): 347.
16. *Douglas v. California*, 372 U.S. 353 (1963).
17. See *McCleskey v. Zant*, 499 U.S. 467 (1991) (prisoner cannot submit more than one *habeas corpus* petition unless there is a good reason why all claims were not raised in the first petition), discussed in Linda Greenhouse, "Supreme Court Puts Sharp Cuts On Repeated Death-Row Appeals," *New York Times*, 17 April 1991, p. A1; *Coleman v. Thompson*, 501 U.S. ____, 111 S. Ct. 2546 (1991) (failure to follow state court procedures bars state prisoners from filing *habeas corpus* petitions in federal court), discussed in Linda Greenhouse, "Court Again Curbs Federal Appeals by State Inmates," *New York Times*, 25 June 1991, p. A1; Richard C. Reuben, "New Habeas Restrictions Challenged," *American Bar Association Journal* (July 1996), p. 22.
18. Administrative Office of the U.S. Courts, *Annual Report of the Director of the Administrative Office of the U.S. Courts* (Washington, D.C.: Government Printing Office, 1993), p. 3.

19. See, e.g., Bureau of Justice Statistics, "State Court Caseload Statistics," *Bureau of Justice Statistics Special Report* (February 1983), p. 6.
20. Bureau of Justice Statistics, "The Growth of Appeals," *Bureau of Justice Statistics Bulletin* (February 1985), p. 2.
21. Thomas B. Marvell, "State Appellate Court Responses to Caseload Growth," *Judicature* 72 (1989), 282–91.
22. Stuart Taylor, "Scalia Proposes Major Overhaul of U.S. Courts," *New York Times*, 15 February 1987, p. 1.
23. Thomas B. Marvell and Paul M. Dempsey, "Growth in State Judgeships, 1970–1984: What Factors Are Important?," *Judicature* 68 (1985): 276.
24. Edward N. Beiser, "The Rhode Island Supreme Court: A Well-Integrated Political System," in *American Court Systems*, eds. Sheldon Goldman and Austin Sarat (San Francisco: W. H. Freeman, 1978), p. 476.
25. Marvell and Dempsey, "Growth in State Judgeships," p. 276; David B. Rottman, Carol R. Flango, and R. Shedine Lockley, *State Court Organization—1993* (Washington, D.C.: U.S. Government Printing Office, 1995), pp. 352–57.
26. Committee on the Judicial Branch of the Judicial Conference of the United States, *Simple Fairness: The Case for Equitable Compensation of the Nation's Federal Judges* (1988), p. 17; Kathleen Maguire and Ann L. Pastore, *Sourcebook of Justice Statistics—1993* (Washington, D.C.: U.S. Government Printing Office, 1994), p. 550.
27. Marvell, "State Appellate Court Responses to Caseload Growth," p. 285.
28. Sue Davis and Donald R. Songer, "The Changing Role of the United States Courts of Appeals: The Flow of Litigation Revisited," *The Justice System Journal* 13 (1988–89): 339.
29. *BNA's Directory of State Courts, Judges and Clerks,* 2nd ed. (Washington, D.C.: Bureau of National Affairs, 1988), pp. 47, 139, 172, 191, 196, 201, 204, 236, 276, 282.
30. Richard H. Winters, "An Intercircuit Panel of the United States Courts of Appeals: The Costs of Structural Change," *Judicature* 70 (1986): 31–40.
31. Marvell, "State Appellate Court Responses to Caseload Growth," p. 285.
32. See, e.g., Robert L. Stern, "Remedies for Appellate Overload: The Ultimate Solution," *Judicature* 72 (1988): 103–10.
33. Marvell, "State Appellate Court Responses to Caseload Growth," p. 286.
34. Joy A. Chapper and Roger A. Hanson, *Intermediate Appellate Courts: Improving Case Processing* (Williamsburg, VA: National Center for State Courts, 1990), p. 22.
35. Marvell, "State Appellate Court Responses to Caseload Growth," p. 286.
36. Marvell, *Appellate Courts and Lawyers*, p. 98.
37. Chapper and Hanson, *Intermediate Appellate Courts*, p. 59.
38. Richard Posner, *The Federal Courts: Crisis and Reform* (Cambridge, MA: Harvard University Press, 1985), p. 113.

39. Howard, *Courts of Appeals in the Federal Judicial System*, p. 198.
40. "This Honorable Court: Inside the Marble Temple" (documentary film broadcast 12 September 1989 on PBS), quoted in Christopher E. Smith, *Judicial Self-Interest: Federal Judges and Court Administration* (Westport, CT: Praeger, 1995), p. 106.
41. Marvell, *Appellate Courts and Lawyers*, pp. 95–96.
42. Ibid., p. 96.
43. See Judith Resnik, "Managerial Judges," *Harvard Law Review* 96 (1982): 376–448.
44. Howard, *Courts of Appeals in the Federal Judicial System*, p. 279.
45. Ibid., pp. 279–80.
46. See Thomas Y. Davies, "Gresham's Law Revisited: Expedited Processing Techniques and the Allocation of Appellate Resources," *The Justice System Journal* 6 (1981): 372–404.
47. Lois G. Forer, *Money and Justice: Who Owns the Courts?* (New York: W.W. Norton, 1984), p. 108.
48. See S. Sidney Ulmer, "Selecting Cases for Supreme Court Review: An Underdog Model," *American Political Science Review* 72 (1978): 902–10.
49. Thomas E. Baker, *Rationing Justice on Appeal: The Problems of the U.S. Court of Appeals* (St. Paul, MN: West Publishing, 1994), pp. 109–10.
50. Marvell, "State Appellate Court Responses to Caseload Growth," p. 287.
51. Ibid.
52. Donald R. Songer, "Criteria for Publication of Opinions in the U.S. Courts of Appeals: Formal Rules Versus Empirical Reality," *Judicature* 73 (1990): 313.
53. See David W. Neubauer, "Unpublished Opinions Versus Summary Affirmation: Criminal Appeals in Louisiana," *The Justice System Journal* 10 (1985): 173–92.
54. Howard, *Courts of the Appeals in the Federal Judicial System*, p. 278.
55. See, e.g., Sheldon Goldman and Charles M. Lamb eds., *Judicial Conflict and Consensus: Behavioral Studies of American Appellate Courts* (Lexington, KY: University Press of Kentucky, 1986).
56. Melinda Gann Hall, "Opinion Assignment Procedures and Conference Practices in State Supreme Courts," *Judicature* 73 (1990): 210.
57. See, e.g., ibid., pp. 194–96.
58. Melinda Gann Hall, "Constituent Influence in State Supreme Courts: Conceptual Notes and a Case Study," *Journal of Politics* 49 (1987): 1117–24.
59. Richardson and Vines, "Review, Dissent and the Appellate Process," p. 611.
60. See, e.g., Donald R. Songer and Sue Davis, "The Impact of Party and Region on Voting Decisions in the United States Courts of Appeals, 1955–1986," *Western Political Quarterly* 43 (1990): 317–34.

61. Jack Bass, *Unlikely Heroes* (New York: Simon and Schuster, 1981), pp. 231–47.
62. Burton M. Atkins and William Zavoina, ''Judicial Leadership on the Court of Appeals: A Probability Analysis of Panel Assignment in Race Relations Cases on the Fifth Circuit,'' *American Journal of Political Science* 18 (1974): 701–11.
63. Howard, *Courts of Appeals in the Federal Judicial System*, p. 246.
64. Ibid., pp. 241, 244.
65. Ibid., p. 233.
66. Ibid., pp. 218–19.
67. Burton M. Atkins, ''Decision-Making Rules and Judicial Strategy on the United States Courts of Appeals,'' *Western Political Quarterly* 25 (1972): 631.
68. Stephen Wermiel, ''Full-Court Review of Panel Rulings Becomes Tool Often Used by Reagan Judges Aiming to Mold Law,'' *Wall Street Journal*, 22 March 1988, p. 70.
69. Michael E. Solimine, ''Ideology and En Banc Review,'' *North Carolina Law Review* 67 (1988): 29–76. See also Christopher E. Smith, ''Polarization and Change in the Federal Courts: *En Banc* Decisions in the U.S. Courts of Appeals,'' *Judicature* 74 (1990): 133–37.
70. Melinda Gann Hall and Paul Brace, ''Order in the Courts: A Neo-Institutional Approach to Judicial Consensus,'' *Western Political Quarterly* 42 (1989): 397.
71. Marvell, *Appellate Courts and Lawyers*, p. 105.
72. Hall, ''Opinion Assignment Procedures and Conference Practices in State Supreme Courts,'' p. 212.
73. Marvell, *Appellate Courts and Lawyers*, p. 105.
74. Howard, *Courts of Appeals in the Federal Judicial System*, p. 234.
75. Ibid., pp. 235, 247–55.
76. Ibid., p. 255.
77. Marvell, *Appellate Courts and Lawyers*, p. 106.

# Chapter 9

# United States Supreme Court

The U.S. Supreme Court stands as the literal and symbolic pinnacle of the American court system. The Supreme Court can hear cases concerning federal statutes and the U.S. Constitution brought from both the federal and state court systems. As the ultimate interpreters of the U.S. Constitution, the justices on the Supreme Court have significant influence on the development of public policy on many different issues.

Because of its important role, the Court is the focus of actions and reactions by other political actors and institutions. The appointment of a new justice, for example, frequently generates a flurry of partisan political activity as various interests attempt to ensure that the Court's composition will favor their policy preferences. In 1993, President Clinton appointed Judge Ruth Bader Ginsburg to replace retiring Justice Byron White. Clinton appointed Ginsburg because of the President's political calculations that Ginsburg's reputation as a moderate appellate judge would satisfy Republican partisans while her record as an advocate for gender equality would appeal to his Democratic constituency. The Senate Judiciary Committee questioned Ginsburg thoroughly concerning her judicial philosophy, her views about court-influenced public policies, and her actions in previous legal and judicial offices. Ginsburg was also questioned closely about her positions on abortion and capital punishment because her vote could have a significant impact on Supreme Court decisions concerning such controversial issues. Like other nominees, Ginsburg selectively declined to answer certain questions, claiming that she should not prejudge issues that might come before the Court. However, she actually expressed positions on certain issues that could produce litigation. For example, she was the first Supreme Court nominee to publicly announce during confirmation hearings that she recognized a woman's constitutional right of choice concerning abortion.[1]

Whenever the president appoints a new nominee to the Supreme Court, the public has the opportunity to see the political processes that influence the composition of the high court. Although defenders of a nominee, including the president's advisors and senators from the president's party, frequently accuse opponents of improperly criticizing the nomination for "political" reasons, the entire nomination process involves politics. The president selects the nominee for political reasons, and the senators' questioning of the nominee flows from partisan political interests and policy preferences. The visible interactions by interest groups, senators, and the news media that are unleashed in reaction to new appointments demonstrate to the public that the Supreme Court is the focus of political battles by partisan interests seeking to influence the Court's future decisions. Outside the nomination process, the political aspects of the Supreme Court, including its decision-making processes and its interactions with other branches of government on policy matters, are less frequently recognized.

## THE SUPREME COURT IN AMERICAN POLITICAL HISTORY

The Supreme Court has always played an important role in the political development of the United States. The nature of the issues presented to the high court for decision reflected the emergence of problems and debates at each new stage in the country's political, social, and economic development. In these stages of American history, the attitudes and values represented among the Court's justices affected the distribution of power among the nation's institutions and the policies pursued by government.

When defending the new governing system created by the U.S. Constitution, Alexander Hamilton described the judiciary as the weakest and "least dangerous" branch of government.[2] The Constitution vests the Supreme Court with the "judicial power of the United States" and the authority to decide cases and controversies arising under the laws and Constitution of the United States.[3] At the time the Constitution was written, no one anticipated how powerful the Supreme Court's influence over public policies would eventually become. In fact, the Supreme Court was initially regarded as so weak and unimportant that some appointees declined to serve on it. According to David O'Brien, "[I]n its first decade (1790–1800), the Court had little business, frequent turnovers in personnel, no chambers or staff of its own, no fixed customs, and no clear institutional identity."[4] The formation of the Court's institutional identity was hampered by the justices' individual responsibilities for riding through assigned circuits to hear appeals in various regions of the country. Through the mid-nineteenth century, the justices met together as the entire Supreme Court in Washington, D.C., for only a few weeks each year.[5]

## Institutional Definition: 1790 to 1865

During the first era in Supreme Court history, from the ratification of the Constitution through the Civil War, the Court's decisions focused on defining and strengthening the American government. The pivotal actor who helped establish the Supreme Court as an authoritative institution was John Marshall, who served as Chief Justice for more than thirty years (1801–1835). Marshall brought his Federalist values to the Court and applied his vision of a strong national government to decisions that shaped the nation's governing institutions. Within the Supreme Court, Marshall helped establish regularized procedures, such as the filing of written arguments by attorneys, while forging unanimous decisions that solidified the Court's institutional voice.[6] During Marshall's tenure, the Court issued decisions that formed the basis for the significant policy-making authority that would be exercised by justices in subsequent decades.

In *Marbury v. Madison*[7] Chief Justice Marshall wrote a unanimous opinion in which the justices declared that the Supreme Court possesses the power of *judicial review* (i.e., the authority to determine the constitutionality of actions undertaken by other branches of government.) Although this power is not explicitly granted to the judiciary by the Constitution, the Supreme Court simply declared a congressional enactment unconstitutional. Over time, the judicial branch's authority to review and strike down actions by the states, the president, and Congress became an accepted component of the constitutional governing system. If the Supreme Court had been composed of justices who did not share Marshall's vision of an authoritative high court and strong national government, the distribution of power among the nation's governing institutions may have developed in a different manner.

During the Marshall era and the subsequent Civil War years, the Supreme Court clarified the extent of judicial power, the substance of presidential and congressional authority, and the distribution of power between states and the federal government. The Court's constitutional interpretations defining the distribution of authority among the branches of government helped establish a workable, stable system of government. These particular interpretations were not commanded by the Constitution. Instead, justices necessarily applied their political values in giving meaning to the Constitution's provisions, many of which are phrased in an ambiguous fashion.

Because the justices apply their political values in constitutional interpretation, they have difficulty keeping the Court removed from political and policy controversies when large or influential segments of society possess differing values. For example, the Court became embroiled in the country's most divisive political controversy—the battle over the legality of slavery. In the 1857 case of *Dred Scott v. Sandford*,[8] the Supreme Court inflamed regional anger and moved the country closer to the Civil War by favoring pro-slavery interests in a decision that thwarted Congressional attempts to legislate against slavery. The case demonstrated that the Supreme Court had moved beyond its ineffectual infancy and had become an important influence on public policy and a catalyst for political reactions by actors and institutions throughout American society.

## Commerce and Social Welfare: 1865 to 1937

After the Civil War, the United States underwent a social transformation. The country changed from an agrarian society to one with an increasingly industrialized and commercialized economy. People began to move from farms to cities in order to work in the emerging manufacturing industries. Railroads and telegraphs drastically expanded societal capacity for transportation and communication. The automobile, radio, and telephones further accelerated the process of linking a far-flung country's people and enterprises into one large national economy. These transforming processes led to new kinds of social, legal, and political problems as legislatures attempted to regulate powerful business interests and to address the social problems attendant to urbanization. The Supreme Court was called on to determine whether state legislatures and Congress possessed the legal authority to address the new problems facing the rapidly changing society. For most of this historical era, the Supreme Court impeded governmental efforts to address the emerging economic and social welfare issues. A majority of justices valued free enterprise principles, and their decisions interpreting the Constitution reflected this inclination to prevent government regulation of business. They used the ambiguous right to "due process" as the basis for applying their political values to establish a right to be free from governmental interference with economic decisions. The justices' political orientation generally superseded any arguments presented by state and federal governments that citizens needed protection from the harms generated by industrialization and urbanization. Among the Court's most famous and representative decisions during this era were *Hammer v. Dagenhart* (1918),[9] which declared unconstitutional congressional efforts to halt the exploitation of child workers in factories and mines, and *Lochner v. New York* (1905),[10] which refused to permit a state to protect workers' health by limiting the number of working hours of bakery employees to sixty hours per week. In the 1930s, after political attacks on the Court by the administration of President Franklin Roosevelt, a majority of justices ceased their opposition to governmental regulation, and Roosevelt was subsequently able to replace the last justices from this era with his own appointees as the holdovers began to retire.

Because judicial decision making is influenced by the attitudes and values of judges, it is no surprise that Supreme Court justices during this era interpreted the Constitution to support the interests of business. Supreme Court justices apply their political values to shape law and policy, but they are not necessarily closely connected to political changes affecting the dominant values of American society. Justices on the Supreme Court serve "during good behaviour,"[11] which can effectively mean for life, and therefore the composition of the Court does not change immediately in conjunction with political changes in American society. Because periodic elections select the president and determine the composition of Congress, those branches of government will be more sensitive to and more accurately reflect trends in American society. As described by Archibald Cox, the Supreme Court's justices during the early twentieth century were too removed from problems affecting the rapidly changing society:

> All of the Supreme Court justices who participated in the consideration of *Lochner v. New York* were born in the 1830s and 1840s. They grew up in an America ignorant of large-scale industrial organization, urban squalor, and the helplessness of the individual in dealing with organized wealth. The ideas they expressed were not unsuited to their early years [when the United States was an agrarian society]. Probably most law must lag slightly behind the march of change.[12]

At certain historical moments, the institutional design of the Supreme Court may lead it to reflect political values and policy preferences of prior decades and thereby slow the rate at which governmental policies can change to reflect new societal developments.

## Civil Rights and Liberties: 1937 to the 1990s

Although the Supreme Court is generally given credit for having "protected and expanded the constitutional rights of [minority groups members], as well as of individuals generally,"[13] the justices' actions to protect civil rights and liberties seldom occurred prior to recent decades. For most of American history, the Supreme Court's interpretations of the Constitution provided few protections for individuals' rights. Up until the second half of the twentieth century, the Court endorsed discrimination against racial minorities[14] and women.[15] Because the justices' decisions are guided by their personal attitudes, biases, and policy preferences, it is not surprising that the Supreme Court has often endorsed society's contemporary prejudices rather than advanced the protection of individuals' rights. As illustrated by the Supreme Court's endorsement of the wholesale incarceration of Japanese-Americans in concentration camps during World War II,[16]— a policy for which the United States government later apologized to its victimized citizens and offered compensation to the survivors—the justices of the Supreme Court do not always possess an extraordinary capacity to separate themselves from social forces affecting American society.

The Supreme Court's initial interpretation of the Bill of Rights limited constitutional protections to infringements by the federal government.[17] Thus, until the twentieth century, state and local governments did not have to respect freedom of speech and other federal constitutional rights. It was not until 1925 that the Supreme

Court began to apply individuals' constitutional rights against state infringement,[18] and most rights were not activated against the states until the 1950s and 1960s. This expansion of rights' applicability occurred when the Court interpreted the Fourteenth Amendment right to "due process" as including many of the individual rights contained in the Bill of Rights (e.g., speech, religion, etc.).

Since the 1940s, the Supreme Court has focused much of its attention on civil liberties. Through decisions in the 1950s and 1960s, the Supreme Court influenced public policy decisions on racial discrimination, criminal defendants' rights, freedom of speech, abortion, and a variety of other controversial issues. During this era, the Supreme Court initiated a rapid expansion of the scope of the constitutional rights of individuals. This recognition of broader rights effectively limits governmental policies that collide with these rights. Thus, the Court has had significant impact on programs and policies of city, state, and federal governments. For example, when the Court decided in 1963 that indigent criminal defendants facing incarceration were entitled to a "right to counsel" under the Sixth Amendment,[19] city and state governments throughout the country had to create new positions and spend public funds to provide attorneys for indigent defendants. Supreme Court decisions since the 1950s have had similarly significant effects on school desegregation, prison reform, police procedures, and other public policy issues.

The Supreme Court's influence over public policy through its declarations on constitutional rights generates opposition from other political actors and institutions. As a result, Republican presidents Richard Nixon, Ronald Reagan, and George Bush used their appointment power to nominate new justices who would limit the scope of individuals' rights and thereby alter the Supreme Court's influence on public policy. For example, President Reagan's appointees possessed values and policy preferences substantially different from their predecessors during the 1950s and 1960s. These new justices initiated a trend toward shrinking the breadth of individuals' rights. The Court relaxed established requirements for informing criminal suspects of their rights,[20] permitted greater state regulation over women's choices about abortion,[21] and restricted well-established laws prohibiting employment discrimination,[22] among other actions advancing conservative political values. This does not mean that the new justices were reducing the Supreme Court's influence on public policy. It merely means that the values supported by the Supreme Court's emerging majority led the Court to advance different policy preferences.

These new developments reflected the American electorate's preference for conservative Republican presidents during the 1970s and 1980s. Thus, the Court's new policy-making direction was linked to changing social developments and political values in American society. The Court's changing values did not, however, represent a precise reflection of the distribution of political preferences among American voters. The Court's composition changes in conjunction with electoral events (i.e., presidential elections, senate elections) affected the officials involved in selecting and confirming judicial nominees. However, quirks in the timing of judicial retirements and appointments can prevent the Court from mirroring American society. In this case, the Republican presidents' appointees may have had an especially significant impact because a lack of retirements (or deaths) among the justices prevented the lone Democratic president from the 1970s and 1980s, Jimmy Carter, from making any Supreme Court appointments during his term in office from 1977 to 1981.

## THE SELECTION OF JUSTICES

In appointing new justices to the Supreme Court, presidents seek to advance dual political purposes: advancing their partisan policy preferences in future Court decisions and pleasing political supporters with a nominee who will be popular or impressive in the eyes of fellow partisans. There are no "best" or "most qualified" candidates for Supreme Court vacancies because each president seeks to fulfill different political criteria. Perhaps the only time that a justice was appointed because he was universally recognized as the nation's most outstanding judge was in 1932 when Benjamin Cardozo was appointed. A broad-based lobbying campaign was undertaken by faculty members at prestigious law schools, business and labor leaders, liberal politicians, and conservative officials to persuade President Hoover to appoint Cardozo, a respected judge on the New York State Court of Appeals.[23] While diverse interests pressed Cardozo's name on Hoover, his actual appointment still hinged on political considerations rather than on his qualifications alone. Hoover ultimately appointed Cardozo to gain the cooperation and support of senators whom he needed to please in order to pursue his legislative goals.[24]

The particular political criteria applied by the appointing president will vary according to the president's political interests at the moment that a Supreme Court vacancy arises. Some presidents appoint loyal supporters of their policy preferences. Others attempt to please specific political constituencies with nominees from particular geographic regions or demographic groups. President Clinton undoubtedly anticipated political benefits from his decision to appoint Ruth Bader Ginsburg, thereby doubling the Court's representation of women.

It is easy to identify the political connections that underlie virtually every appointment simply by examining the backgrounds of justices. Byron White, a Kennedy appointee, for example, held important positions in John F. Kennedy's campaign for the presidency. Thurgood Marshall's appointment as the first African-American on the Supreme Court was a component of President Lyndon Johnson's efforts to advance racial equality. John Paul Stevens, a moderate, respected but little-known Republican judge, was selected by President Gerald Ford, in part because of Ford's desire to avoid the political risk that the Senate would delay the confirmation process of a controversial nominee until the election year of 1976.[25] President Ronald Reagan made a campaign pledge to appoint a woman to the Supreme Court in an attempt to attract women voters. Justice Sandra Day O'Connor's appointment was the result of that pledge.[26] Through the appointment of Antonin Scalia to the Supreme Court, President Reagan enjoyed the dual benefits of claiming credit for the appointment of the first Italian-American justice and for placing a leading political conservative on the high court. Similar political considerations could be detected by examining the backgrounds of Supreme Court justices throughout history.[27]

The recognition that political considerations influence the choices of Supreme Court nominees should not, however, denigrate the qualifications of the justices. Although some appointees have ultimately been inconsistent and unimpressive, the Supreme Court has benefitted from the presence of numerous experienced, intelligent, and creative justices—both liberals and conservatives. Because presidents seek to appoint experienced, capable justices, the qualifications and credentials of nominees are important considerations. It would cause great political embarrassment if partisan opponents on the Senate Judiciary Committee could publicly establish that a nominee was truly unqualified or incapable of serving as a justice. Indeed, President Nixon suffered political damage when one of his allies in the Senate, Senator Roman Hruska of Nebraska, was reduced to arguing on behalf of an unsuccessful Nixon appointee that: "Even if he is mediocre there are a lot of mediocre judges and people and lawyers. They are entitled to a little representation, aren't they, and a little chance? We can't have all Brandeises, Cardozos, and Frankfurters, and stuff like that there."[28]

President Bush generated political fallout for the Republican Party with his nomination of Clarence Thomas, a young appointee with limited legal experience who spent most of his career working in the Reagan administration and had only one year of experience as a federal appellate judge. Bush appointed Thomas, a staunchly conservative African American, to replace retiring liberal Thurgood Marshall with the hope that some senators would not dare vote against his nomination for fear of being blamed for returning the high court to its previous all-white status. Not one member of the American Bar Association's committee rated Thomas as "highly qualified" to serve on the Supreme Court. During the confirmation hearings, questions about Thomas's inexperience and qualifications were compounded by accusations that he had sexually harassed a female subordinate while serving as an official in the Reagan administration. Thomas was ultimately confirmed by the narrowest of margins, 52 to 48. In the aftermath of Thomas's confirmation, women candidates and voters mobilized in the 1992 elections. Five women won election as Democratic senators, and several of Thomas's senate supporters had difficult campaigns.[29]

Because there are some political risks associated with the appointment of an unimpressive nominee to the Supreme Court, presidents generally include a concern for qualifications among their political considerations in selecting nominees. For example, one could examine the previously mentioned justices as well as many others and identify their impressive legal qualifications: Justice White was a Rhodes Scholar, Yale Law School honors graduate, and experienced Denver attorney; Justice Marshall argued many cases before the Supreme Court as an attorney and served as a federal appellate judge and as Solicitor General of the United States; Justice Stevens was a federal appellate judge; Justice O'Connor was a state legislator and a state appellate judge; and Justice Scalia was a prominent law professor and federal appellate judge. Political considerations determine the ultimate selection of Supreme Court justices, but presidents examine candidates' experience and other qualifications to increase the likelihood that the nominees will gain confirmation by the Senate and will subsequently have an effective impact on the work of the Court. In contrast to the problems experienced by Presidents Nixon and Bush, for example, President Clinton opted for a safer course of action by appointing two experienced, moderate appellate judges to the Supreme Court, Ruth Bader Ginsburg and Stephen Breyer. Clinton knew that they were respected by Democrats and Republicans alike and, therefore, would not generate political controversies.

## Actors in the Process

The actual selection of a Supreme Court nominee is normally influenced by the president's closest advisors who help to formulate a list of candidates possessing desirable legal and political qualifications. Because of the importance of the appointment, both for its political and public policy implications and for its effects on the president's place in history, the president personally makes the final selection of the nominee. For other federal judgeships, the president may defer to the choices of allied senators and other political supporters, but with a Supreme Court nomination there is the utmost concern that the nominee will fulfill the president's political purposes. In the past, presidents frequently nominated political supporters with whom they were well-acquainted. Franklin Roosevelt, Harry Truman, and Lyndon Johnson, for example, included close associates among their nominees to the Supreme Court. Since the 1970s, however, presidents have appointed justices with whom they were not personally well acquainted after receiving recommendations from trusted advisors. President Bush, for example, met David Souter for the first time the very day he decided to appoint Souter to the Supreme Court. Souter, a former judge on the New Hampshire Supreme Court, had been recommended to Bush by John Sununu, the President's chief of staff and a former governor of New Hampshire, and by Republican Senator Warren Rudman of New Hampshire. Bush reportedly made his final choice between Souter and Edith Jones, a federal judge from Texas, shortly before the scheduled press conference to announce the nomination and just after he had met briefly with each candidate.[30] President Clinton chose Ruth Bader Ginsburg, who originally was not among his favored finalists, after lobbying by Democratic

Senator Daniel Patrick Moynihan of New York led him to take a closer look at her record and qualifications.[31]

The selection of Supreme Court nominees is sometimes influenced by lobbying from justices on the Supreme Court. As described by Henry Abraham:

> We know, for example, that Chief Justice Taft was not at all reluctant in expressing his thoughts to presidents Harding, Coolidge, and Hoover . . .; that his successor, Hughes, followed a similar course of action with Hoover and F.D.R.; . . . that President Kennedy apparently consulted with Chief Justice Warren and Justice Frankfurter in 1962 regarding Arthur J. Goldberg . . .; that President Johnson approached Warren concerning his successor as Chief Justice; and that Justice Rehnquist urged President Reagan to nominate Sandra Day O'Connor in 1981.[32]

In addition, interested candidates will attempt to organize political lobbying campaigns on their own behalf by having their supporters in the president's political party urge the president to appoint them.[33]

As in the federal judicial selection process described in chapter 6, the American Bar Association's evaluation committee has played a role in rating Supreme Court nominees since the 1950s. Although presidents have occasionally ignored the ABA committee, the committee has continued to issue evaluations of nominees. A positive ABA rating can help to deflect opposition—so much so that Justice Powell once lobbied the committee to lower its standards in order to give a favorable rating to a former law clerk who was appointed to be a federal appellate judge.[34] There are concerns, however, that it is improper to give a private interest group a formal role in the judicial nomination processes.[35] The uncertain value of the ABA's rating system was illuminated by the divisions on the committee that evaluated Judge Robert Bork's 1987 nomination and Judge Clarence Thomas's 1991 nomination. Ten committee members judged Bork to be ''well-qualified,'' but four members found him ''not qualified.'' Thomas was rated merely ''qualified'' by twelve committee members and ''not qualified'' by two committee members, with no members giving him the highest qualification rating.[36] Should politicians and the public defer to the judgments of legal professionals when those professionals cannot agree among themselves about which nominees are qualified to become Supreme Court justices? It is clear that there are no precise, universally agreed on merit criteria for determining whether nominees are qualified to serve as judicial officers. Thus, it is not surprising that political considerations play such an important role in the selection process.

Interest groups focus their efforts on the nomination process for Supreme Court justices because the composition of the high court has a significant effect on judicial policy making. When Justice O'Connor was evaluated by the Senate Judiciary Committee, leaders of anti-abortion groups testified in opposition to her appointment because they believed that she had not adequately proven that she agreed with their position. At Justice Souter's hearings, representatives from pro-choice groups testified against the nomination because they believed that he might contribute to the reversal of Supreme Court precedents recognizing abortion choices as an element of the right to privacy. The greatest mobilization of interest groups occurred in reaction to the unsuccessful nomination of Judge Robert Bork. Civil rights groups, labor unions, women's organizations, and pro-choice interest groups mobilized their supporters to lobby members of the Senate to oppose the Bork nomination. A long list of witnesses from these groups testified against Bork because his academic writings over two decades indicated that, among other things, he opposed the recognition of a right to privacy, and he was initially opposed to the passage of antidiscrimination laws. Conservative interest groups mobilized to support Bork. For example, the National Conservative Political Action Committee spent more than $1 million to lobby on Bork's behalf.[37] The conservatives attempted to portray Bork as a moderate jurist whose views were similar to those of other justices.

The level of interest group activity is primarily a function of the political circumstances surrounding the nomination. If the nominee is outspoken and controversial, like Bork, there is a greater likelihood that political interests will be mobilized in opposition. By contrast, Souter had no discernible record on controversial issues, so there was relatively little lobbying organized against his nomination. Outspokenness alone, however, does not generate political mobilization. Justice Scalia, a law professor like Bork, had written extremely strident articles in which he called the Supreme Court's affirmative action decisions "an historic trivialization of the Constitution" and "an embarrassment to teach."[38] Yet Scalia's nomination generated relatively little mobilized opposition, and he was confirmed easily. The difference between Bork's nomination and Scalia's stems from their respective predicted effects on the composition of the Court and the development of judicial decisions. Scalia, a conservative, replaced Warren Burger, another conservative, and therefore did not change the ideological balance of power on the Court. By contrast, the conservative Bork was nominated to replace Lewis Powell, who despite an overall record of conservatism on many issues,[39] served as a crucial moderate vote on a sharply divided Court on such issues as affirmative action[40] and abortion.[41] Unlike Scalia's earlier appointment, the timing of Bork's nomination would have dramatically shifted the balance of power and the trends in decision making on the Supreme Court. Ultimately, President Reagan was able to gain the confirmation of a conservative justice, Anthony Kennedy, but one with a less strident voice.

A crucial element in the Bork nomination was the extensive questioning of the nominee by the Senate Judiciary Committee. For several days, Bork answered detailed questions about his academic writings, his decisions as an appellate judge, and his judicial philosophy. Although Bork claims that political considerations improperly undermined his confirmation,[42] one scholar has observed that "[u]ltimately Bork was defeated because of his controversial views and his association with the legal-policy goals of the New Right.''[43] During Bork's detailed testimony concerning specific cases and legal issues, ''he had contradicted much of what he had stood for and for which he was nominated.''[44]

David Souter received similar scrutiny from the members of the Judiciary Committee because he was perceived as a conservative judge replacing William Brennan, one of the most liberal justices in the Supreme Court's history. It is apparent, however, in the aftermath of the Bork controversy, the Senate Judiciary Committee will thoroughly question all Supreme Court nominees instead of letting some, such as Scalia, sail through with little questioning, debate, or discussion. It is equally apparent that presidents and their advisors learned from Bork's experience to advise and even prepare nominees to present their views in moderate ways to avoid controversy. Both Souter and Thomas studied the Bork confirmation hearings for weeks while preparing for their own questioning.[45] Moreover, there are strong indications that Thomas, in particular, prepared his testimony to distance himself from the conservative views that he espoused both prior to appointment and in the judicial opinions he authored after his confirmation.[46] Ruth Bader Ginsburg and Stephen Breyer also presented themselves to the Judiciary Committee as moderate jurists who would not answer specific questions about many issues. Their nominations created less risk of controversy because, with the exception of their pro-choice views on abortion, their long-established, moderate records as federal judges reassured senators from both political parties.[47]

Although Bork's supporters have charged that the detailed questioning by the Judiciary Committee constituted interference with the president's prerogative to appoint whomever he or she chooses, other commentators have argued that the Senate was finally doing its job properly, scrutinizing nominees before confirming them or rejecting them. Bork was not unique in being rejected by the Senate. More than two dozen prior Supreme Court nominees had been rejected over the years, and indeed, whenever a president makes a Supreme Court appointment during his final year in office—especially when the opposing party controls the Senate—confirmation rates have been very low (27 percent).[48] The Senate, however, was inconsistent in scrutinizing nominees prior to Bork's confirmation hearings.

## Selection, Court Composition, and Judicial Policy Making

The selection of Supreme Court justices creates an opportunity for political reactions to Court decisions. The president, who is elected by the voters, has the authority to select new justices. When voters select a new president, different values will be reflected in Supreme Court appointments made during that presidency. The composition of the Supreme Court will not precisely reflect the electorate's current value preferences, but because the appointment and confirmation processes are under the control of elected officials, over time the Court's composition will be shaped by developments in electoral politics. Despite the life tenure granted to justices, the Supreme Court's composition and decision making over several decades evolve in the direction of American society's political trends.

Two factors diminish this connection between the Court's composition and the political evolution of American society. First, presidents cannot always accurately predict how a nominee will decide cases. President Eisenhower was reported to have labeled his appointments of Chief Justice Earl Warren and Justice William Brennan as the "greatest mistakes" of his presidency because their decisions were much more liberal than he expected. President Nixon selected a safe, moderately conservative nominee in Harry Blackmun, but Nixon could never have predicted that Blackmun's views would gradually become more liberal. Some of Justice White's decisions have been more conservative than President Kennedy probably would have expected. President Bush probably did not anticipate either David Souter's relative liberalism or Clarence Thomas's extreme conservatism.[49]

Second, the appointment of justices is determined by the quirks of history that affect the timing of departures from the Supreme Court and the election of new presidents. For example, although he was president for only two years, Gerald Ford had the opportunity to appoint a new justice because of the retirement of Justice William O. Douglas in 1975. By contrast, Jimmy Carter did not have the opportunity to appoint a justice during his four-year term. Because of the timing of justices' retirements, Ronald Reagan was able to appoint three new justices and elevate the Court's most conservative justice, William Rehnquist, to chief justice over the course of eight years. Bill Clinton was able to make two appointments during his first two years in office.

The policy outcomes produced by the Supreme Court are significantly affected by the timing of small, fateful events.[50] When Lyndon Johnson was president, for example, he attempted to replace the retiring chief justice, Earl Warren, with Justice Abe Fortas, a close Johnson associate. Simultaneously, Johnson sought to fill Fortas's associate justice position with an undistinguished political crony from Texas. Because Johnson was a lame duck president nearing the end of his term, Republican senators sought to delay the nominations in the hopes that a new Republican president would fill the pending Supreme Court vacancies. The nomination of Fortas was derailed by revelations of questionable ethical behavior, and Johnson did not have sufficient political power to push his nominees successfully through the confirmation process.[51] If Johnson had nominated a respected, moderate Democratic judge or senator instead of his political associates, he might have prevented his successor, Richard Nixon, from making one or possibly two of his four appointments to the Supreme Court. As a result of Johnson's miscalculation, Nixon had an unusually significant influence on the composition of the Court and on important policy decisions by the justices. For example, in two education cases during the early 1970s, the four Nixon appointees comprised the bulk of slim five-member majorities that limited district courts' ability to order school desegregation in large metropolitan areas[52] and to order equalization in funding between rich and poor school districts.[53] Had it not been for the historical quirks and political miscalculations surrounding the timing of the retirements of Chief Justice Warren and Justice Fortas, public education in the United States might be dramatically different, with equal funding for all school systems in each state and school desegregation implemented throughout metropolitan areas instead of merely within individual city boundaries.

It is interesting to speculate about the judicial decisions that might have been different if not for small historical events. If Iran had not hurt President Carter politically by holding Americans hostage at the U.S. Embassy in Tehran and John Anderson had not mounted an independent presidential campaign that siphoned liberal voters away from Carter, Ronald Reagan might not have won the 1980 presidential election.[54] Carter would then have appointed the replacement for Justice Stewart, and some of the elderly liberal justices (i.e., Brennan, Blackmun, and Marshall) might have retired in order to permit Carter to appoint their replacements. Instead, the timing of retirements produced a 1992 Court composed of eight Republicans and only one Democrat—a political composition unrepresentative of the American political system, because only one-third of Americans identify themselves as Republicans.[55] By 1996, the composition had shifted only slightly to seven Republicans and two Democrats. This does not necessarily mean that the justices' decisions will be out of step with American society, but it does indicate that the Supreme Court's composition and decisions do not precisely reflect the values and preferences of the American public.

## CASES BEFORE THE SUPREME COURT

As described in chapter 5, American society is a bubbling caldron of grievances and disputes involving individuals and organized entities. Relatively few disputes pass through the necessary stages to become cases filed in court. Of those cases that do enter the judicial system, only a small minority are processed through a trial to receive a formal judicial decision. Most are dismissed or settled through negotiation. Out of the small number of cases that receive judicial decisions, even fewer are selected for hearing by an appellate court. The tiny number of cases that are subsequently accepted for hearing by the U.S. Supreme Court might be analogized to selected grains of sand on the beach when their numbers are considered in light of the total number of disputes or potential legal cases that arise every year in American society. Thus, when angry litigants frequently claim that they will take their cases "all the way to the Supreme Court," they are engaging in wishful thinking. Only a tiny number of cases make it past all the hurdles in the judicial system and are selected for hearing by the high court.

There are two primary underlying factors that limit the number of cases heard by the justices. First, because the Supreme Court is a body of nine people who, as a group, hear and decide each case and write detailed opinions to justify case outcomes, the structure of the Supreme Court ensures that the justices can hear only a small number of cases each year. The process of producing Supreme

Court opinions is extremely time-consuming, so the Court's resources can be applied only to selected cases.

Second, the justices have nearly complete discretion to choose the cases that they wish to hear and, conversely, to decline other cases. Thus, the justices have significant control over their own workload. The Constitution gives the Supreme Court *original jurisdiction* over cases involving states, ambassadors, and "other public Ministers and Consuls."[56] Thus, such cases can be filed in the Supreme Court, which serves as both the initial and final decision maker. Hypothetically, the Supreme Court can act as the trial court in cases involving these parties. In reality, however, because of jurisdiction subsequently granted to other courts, the Supreme Court reserves its original jurisdiction power only for legal cases between two or more states.[57] The Supreme Court's *appellate jurisdiction*, in which litigants have a right to have their cases considered by the Supreme Court, is limited to reviews of the handful of cases in which special three-judge district courts grant or deny injunctions under specified statutes.[58] Both categories of cases arise infrequently. The overwhelming majority of cases arrive at the Supreme Court through petitions for a *writ of certiorari*, which is simply a legal action requesting the Supreme Court to call up the case from a lower court. The Supreme Court has complete discretion to grant or deny these petitions. If the writ is granted, the Supreme Court has agreed to consider and decide the case. If the writ is denied, the last lower court decision, usually from a state supreme court or a federal circuit court of appeals, remains intact. Virtually 99 percent of the Supreme Court's docket arrives through the certiorari process.[59]

Since 1980, the Supreme Court has received more than 4,000 petitions each year, but it typically accepted only 150 or so for complete hearing and decision.[60] In the late 1980s, the justices appeared to heed the call of Justice Scalia, who urged the federal judiciary to reserve its considered judgments for a smaller number of select cases.[61] As part of this trend, even though the number of annual petitions climbed to nearly 7,000, the Supreme Court decided only 82 cases with full opinions during the 1994–95 term and only 75 cases during their 1995–96 term.[62] In addition to the cases that receive complete review, some cases receive a *summary disposition*. The justices decide these cases based on the written arguments alone. Table 9.1 illustrates the Supreme Court's caseload and decision making productivity during recent years.

**Table 9.1: U.S. Supreme Court Productivity.**

|                  | *1977–78* | *1982–83* | *1988–89* | *1994–95* |
|------------------|-----------|-----------|-----------|-----------|
| Cases on Docket  | 4,731     | 5,079     | 5,657     | 6,996     |
| Full Opinions    | 153       | 174       | 156       | 82        |

*Source:* Administrative Office of the U.S. Courts, *Annual Reports of the Director*, 1979, 1983, 1989. Table A-1; "Chief Justice Recaps 1995 in Year-end Report," *The Third Branch* 28 (January 1996): 5–6.

**Table 9.2: The Supreme Court's Expanding Caseload.**

| Term | Cases Filed |
|---|---|
| 1957–58 | 1,646 |
| 1962–63 | 2,399 |
| 1967–68 | 3,105 |
| 1972–73 | 3,720 |
| 1977–78 | 4,731 |
| 1982–83 | 5,079 |
| 1988–89 | 5,657 |
| 1994–95 | 6,996 |

*Sources:* Gerhard Casper and Richard A. Posner, *The Workload of the Supreme Court* (Chicago: American Bar Foundation, 1976); Administrative Office of the U.S. Courts, *Annual Report of the Director*, 1979, 1983, 1989; "Chief Justice Recaps 1995 in Year-end Report."

The Supreme Court, like other federal courts, has witnessed a dramatic increase in the number of cases filed over the years. Table 9.2 shows the growth in the number of case filings. In the 1950s, there were fewer than 2,000 petitions filed. The subsequent increase in case filings stems from several factors. Over the past three decades, many more interest groups have come to view the Supreme Court as a receptive forum for public policy initiatives. In addition, because the Supreme Court became active in the mid-1950s and thereafter in identifying and protecting the constitutional rights of individuals, many more individual claimants seek the justices' assistance. In particular, the Supreme Court receives large numbers of petitions from prisoners who wish to challenge their criminal convictions or the severity of their punishments. Increased regulatory activity by Congress and executive branch agencies has generated additional litigation. Moreover, Congress has written many new statutes that provide Americans with opportunities to file lawsuits concerning civil rights and other matters in federal courts.

Computerized word-processing systems and increases in the number of law clerks who assist the justices have led to modest increases in the Court's capacity for producing opinions in recent years, but the number of cases decided each year in the 1980s was only a few dozen more than the number decided in the 1950s. The drastic increase in petitions has forced the justices to turn down many more cases than in prior decades and has created greater pressures on the Court's review and selection processes.

## The Selection of Cases

Petitioners must pay a fee of two hundred dollars when filing their cases with the Supreme Court and an additional one hundred dollar fee if their cases are accepted for review.[63] Since the late 1950s, about half of the petitions have been filed *in forma pauperis*, meaning that the petitioners request that the fees be waived because they are too poor to pay. The percentage of such petitions has increased so that in 1994–95 they constituted 69 percent of the 6,996 petitions filed. Most of these petitions are from prisoners. Except for the paupers' petitions which are filed *pro se* (i.e., the litigant initiates the case without the benefit of an attorney), the petitions and accompanying briefs must meet precise requirements for printing, number of pages, and even the color of the outside binding. If petitions do not comply with the Supreme Court's procedural rules, the Supreme Court Clerk's office returns them to the petitioners.

The thousands of petitions are reviewed by the justices' law clerks, outstanding recent graduates from top law schools who spend a year working for a justice, normally after only one year of prior experience working for another federal judge. These inexperienced lawyers bear the important responsibility of evaluating petitions to determine which cases merit review by the Supreme Court. The petitions are analyzed by the law clerks who then write short memoranda to the justices describing the cases, evaluating their importance, and recommending whether the Supreme Court should hear the cases. The law clerks' jobs are made more difficult by the fact that they must constantly review certiorari petitions while they also do research and writing to assist the justices in preparing written opinions in cases that have been heard and decided. The *pro se* petitions are difficult to assess because they are often handwritten by prisoners with meager education, little understanding of the law, and limited ability to identify and assert appropriate constitutional claims. There is a risk that the law clerks, who have little practical legal experience to begin with, will mischaracterize or overlook important issues, especially in petitions submitted by poor, uneducated claimants who do not have attorneys.

The risks that law clerks will not give petitions thorough and equal evaluations have been increased by the formation of a "cert pool" in which the law clerks of eight justices divide responsibilities for reviewing petitions. Although petitions were previously evaluated by nine sets of law clerks, since the formation of the "cert pool," each petition is evaluated by only one law clerk in the pool plus the law clerks of the one justice, Stevens, who remained outside the pool.[64] The justices themselves rarely read the petitions. Instead, they rely on their clerks' memoranda in deciding whether to hear a case. A study of certiorari memoranda by Chief Justice Fred Vinson's law clerks found that although Vinson's clerks generally tried to anticipate his preferences in their recommendations, they evinced a liberal orientation in their case selection recommendations, and the Chief Justice generally followed their suggestions.[65] It is possible that because the clerks' values and policy preferences are at least subtly embodied in their memoranda, the clerks may influence the justices' decisions concerning some cases.

The chief justice influences the decision process by making a preliminary assessment of the cases' worthiness. The chief justice prepares a "discuss list" of cases worthy of consideration by the other justices and a separate list of cases to be summarily rejected. Although the chief justice's initial recommendations frequently determine which cases will be discussed, other justices can add cases to the discuss list based on policy preferences, assessments of pending conflicts in the lower courts, and other factors.[66] During their weekly conferences, the justices go over the discuss list to determine which cases they will hear. The Supreme Court follows the *Rule of Four* requiring that at least four justices must vote to hear a case in order for it to be accepted.

What determines which cases the justices will select for complete hearing? As with other aspects of judicial decision making, the certiorari decisions are influenced by a variety of legal, political, and human factors.

## Jurisdictional Rules

The Supreme Court utilizes several jurisdictional doctrines to determine which cases are appropriate for consideration and decision.[67] These concepts are common as entry criteria throughout the levels of American court systems, but many of the most famous debates about their applicability concern Supreme Court cases. Litigants must have *standing* to pursue their cases. That is, they must be parties who have suffered some harm or otherwise have sufficient interest in presenting the case to the Court. Questions of standing can become complicated, when, for example, interest groups want to initiate cases, people want to file environmental actions for damage to forests and rivers, taxpayers oppose particular governmental programs, and circumstances arise in which someone wishes to initiate a legal action despite questions about whether he or she has in fact suffered documentable harm. The parties in the case must be actual adversaries. Litigants may not undertake a friendly, contrived test of a legal precedent. The Court will not issue advisory opinions in friendly test cases or at the request of public officials. The dispute must be ripe as a present dispute, not anticipating a possible future conflict. The controversy must be current when it reaches the Supreme Court. Disputes that are already over are moot and will generally not be considered by the Court.

In addition, the Court will not decide political questions, which are properly left to other branches of government. Obviously many kinds of issues presented concern politics. However, political questions are those that the judicial branch regards as within the exclusive province of some other government branch. For example, during the Vietnam War in the 1960s and 1970s, several lawsuits were filed challenging the legality of the war because Congress had never exercised its constitutional power to "declare war," and President Nixon unilaterally expanded American military action from Vietnam to Cambodia. Although two justices, William O. Douglas and Potter Stewart, believed that such lawsuits raised appropriate questions for the Court to consider, the other justices overrode them and declared that issues concerning wars are "political questions" that are exclusively under the control of Congress and the president.[68] As a practical matter, justices recognize that there are certain circumstances in which their judicial orders are likely to have little effect or in which basic issues concerning governmental powers must be worked out through the interactions of other governmental branches. If the Supreme Court ordered Congress and the president to stop fighting a war, would the other branches and the people of the United States respect and obey the Court's decision? Most justices apparently believe that this is not worth testing. Thus, justices employ the political question doctrine to avoid involving the courts in decisions concerning wars. In the past, the doctrine was also used to avoid judicial participation in issues concerning the design of legislative election districts, but during the 1960s the Supreme Court changed course, removed the political question label, and decided cases to force states to create districts of equivalent size.[69]

Although these jurisdictional premises may appear to provide guidance for which cases to accept, these rules can be altered and manipulated at the discretion of the justices. The rules provide justifications that permit the Supreme Court to avoid cases that they do not wish to take, but the rules can be modified by the justices if they really desire to hear a case. For example, the Supreme Court heard the original abortion case, *Roe v. Wade*,[70] despite the fact that the case was technically moot because the baby had already been born. The Court recognized that the nine-month human gestation period might mean that any pregnant woman's case would become moot before it reached the high court, yet the issue was not moot for Ms. Roe and other women who might become pregnant and be denied the opportunity to obtain an abortion. Thus, the justices ignored the mootness issue by asserting that the abortion question should be decided because it would arise again and again. In addition to creating exceptions for these rules, the justices actually determine when the rules apply; therefore, they have discretionary power to choose the circumstances in which they will say that they are bound by the rules. For example, the Court defines which cases fall under the political question doctrine. It is unclear what issues other than governmental war powers currently qualify as political questions, but the justices retain the ability to apply this label to other issues that they may wish to avoid.

In addition to the general jurisdictional rules, the Supreme Court's own formal procedural rules provide guidance in determining which cases should be accepted. Rule 17 officially lists factors that the Supreme Court will consider in deciding whether to hear a case.[71] Under Rule 17, justices emphasize their interest in cases that embody conflicting decisions between appellate courts, both state and federal, and that raise new questions of federal law. The Rule reflects the Supreme Court's interest in reserving its resources for unsettled questions of far-reaching importance and for contradictory case decisions addressing such issues. Rule 17 does not dictate which cases the Supreme Court will accept or reject. The actual certiorari decisions are completely at the discretion of the justices.

## Empirical Research on Case Selection

Social scientists have studied the Supreme Court's selection of cases for insight into why the Court selects some cases and not others. The original research by Joseph Tanenhaus and his associates found that "cues" in the cert petitions were utilized by the justices and their law clerks to determine which cases to accept. In particular, the Tanenhaus research found that the Supreme Court was most likely to accept a case when the United States government was one of the parties.[72] In addition, this study of cases in the 1950s found the Supreme Court favored cases involving dissension (i.e., concurring opinions or dissenting votes) in the lower court and those that concerned civil liberties or economic issues.[73] Other scholars found this theory of "cues" valid in later periods of Supreme Court history.[74] Subsequent studies have confirmed that conflicting decisions attract the attention and interest of the justices.[75] Although some scholars have persuasively challenged the notion that the justices actually look for cues in the petitions,[76] other researchers argue that cues may offer important information to law clerks and justices even if they are not utilized for a cursory sorting of petitions.[77]

Recent research into other relevant factors associated with accepted cases has found that cases in which *amicus*—or "friend of the court"—*briefs* (written arguments submitted by interested parties not involved in the case) are filed are also more likely to be accepted for hearing.[78] With the agreement of the justices or the parties to the case, outside parties may be permitted to submit written briefs presenting additional arguments for the Supreme Court to consider. Such third-party contributions are frequently utilized by interest groups in their attempts to persuade the justices to favor the groups' policy preferences. The presence of these written submissions from interested outsiders at the early stage of the Court's consideration of certiorari petitions may signal the justices that the case involves a substantial controversy worthy of their attention.

Although the use of cues may help justices and law clerks sift through the thousands of petitions, the justices' policy preferences undoubtedly figure in their determinations about which cases to accept. The justices do not, however, freely apply their preferred values to the underlying cases to determine the cases' worthiness. Research on certiorari voting has detected certain strategies used by the justices in their attempts to advance policy positions they prefer.[79] Justices sometimes vote to hear cases that set undesirable precedents that they wish to reverse or to affirm in order to strengthen a valued precedent.[80] The justices may be concerned, however, that not enough of their colleagues will favor reversal of the prior case decision. Without adequate opposition among the justices, the undesirable precedent might receive the Supreme Court's endorsement. Thus, a justice may vote *not* to hear a case that he or she considers important, because the Supreme Court majority might subsequently make a policy decision that this particular justice will find objectionable. The voting on certiorari petitions is

influenced not just by the individual justices' assessments of the cases' importance, but also by their predictions as to how a majority of justices will ultimately
decide the case.

Studies indicate that justices engage in relatively little interaction during the
consideration of certiorari petitions.[81] The justices apparently have insufficient
time and interest to persuade their colleagues to accept a particular case. With
the constant flow of cases, justices know that issues of interest will arise again,
even though there may not be four members of the Court willing to hear the
issue. In extreme instances, a justice may threaten to write a dissenting opinion
criticizing the Court for failing to accept a particular case. The threat of such
an opinion may persuade other justices to hear a case—either because they are
moved by the intensity of their colleague's feelings or because they wish to avoid
a public display of conflict within the Court. By changing their position and
agreeing to hear a case, justices make only a modest accommodation. They are
still free to decide the merits of the case as they wish—perhaps in a manner
opposed by the justice who was originally intent on hearing the case. Dissent
from a denial of certiorari may also signal the legal community that one or more
justices would be interested in the underlying issue and that future cases relating
to that issue may have a greater chance for acceptance if the arguments presented
to the Supreme Court are shaped in a particular manner.

## DECIDING THE CASES

After cases are accepted for consideration by the justices, there are two procedures
for deciding them. Most accepted cases receive complete review through full
written briefs and oral arguments. Other cases, which receive summary dispositions based on written submissions alone, are sometimes handled with a one- or
two-sentence conclusion that frequently sends the case back to the lower court
for reconsideration in light of a recent Supreme Court decision. Other summary
dispositions receive *per curiam* rulings in which the opinion comes from the
Court and not from any particular justice. A *per curiam* opinion may indicate
that the outcome is obvious and that the parties should immediately comply with
judicial directives. Such an opinion may also show that the Court is divided and
the justices can agree on only a limited conclusion.[82] By the beginning of the
1990s, the Court's use of *per curiam* opinions had declined markedly in contrast
to preceding decades, and such opinions were increasingly focused in cases with
decisions based on filings without oral argument.[83]

In *in forma pauperis* cases that are accepted for complete review, the justices
appoint an attorney to represent the petitioner. In 1963 when the Supreme Court
made its famous decision that indigent criminal defendants facing incarceration
are entitled to the assistance of counsel,[84] the justices appointed future Supreme
Court justice Abe Fortas, one of the nation's top lawyers, to represent the penniless

prisoner. Clearly, a majority of the Court's members were eager to set a new precedent, so they ensured that the case would be argued by a top-flight attorney.[85]

Other litigants must secure their own representation. It can be extremely expensive to bring a case before the Supreme Court. Attorneys' fees will run, at a minimum, into the tens of thousands of dollars to carry a case through all the various levels of the state or federal court systems and to the Supreme Court. Thus, many individuals are represented by attorneys from organized interest groups when those litigants' claims can serve as vehicles to advance the groups' policies.

The federal government is represented before the Supreme Court by the Solicitor General of the United States, the third-ranking officer in the Department of Justice. Over the years, the office has been held by a number of well-known lawyers and legal scholars, including Thurgood Marshall, Robert Bork, and Harvard professors Archibald Cox and Erwin Griswold. Traditionally, the Solicitor General's office has had a special relationship with the Supreme Court. Briefs and petitions from the Solicitor General's office have been held in such high esteem for their careful, thoughtful analyses of legal issues that the justices have often deferred to the Solicitor General's arguments. This deference is indicated, at least in part, by the fact that the federal government's participation in cases has emerged as the most consistent ''cue'' for predicting when the Supreme Court will accept a case. Unlike other parties, the Solicitor General's Office has been permitted to submit amicus briefs whenever it wishes and may even present oral arguments in cases in which the U.S. government is not a litigant. The Solicitor General traditionally maintained the office's reputation and special relationship with the Supreme Court by maintaining a degree of independence from the attorney general and the president. In several instances, when presidents and cabinet officers wanted the Solicitor General to present overtly partisan or otherwise questionable arguments to the Supreme Court, Solicitor Generals have succeeded either in dissuading the executive branch from these questionable legal tactics or in signaling the Supreme Court that the Solicitor General disagreed with the arguments by, for example, presenting but declining to sign the written briefs on behalf of the U.S. government.

## Oral Arguments

After final written briefs are submitted, the case is scheduled for oral argument during the Supreme Court's annual term from October through June. Oral arguments usually occur from October through April so that justices can finish writing their judicial opinions in May and June. Normally, the attorneys for each side are given thirty minutes to present their arguments to the Court. As the Court's docket has grown, the time allotted for oral argument has decreased. In the nineteenth century, when the Supreme Court heard fewer cases, each side was given several hours to present its case. Although attorneys prepare formal arguments to present to the Court, the justices frequently interrupt to ask questions and challenge arguments. If a contemporary attorney ever succeeded in presenting a prepared half-hour argument without interruption, it would probably indicate that the attorney will lose the case because the justices showed little interest in that side of the argument.

The justices' questions are not intended merely to test the attorneys' arguments. Frequently the justices use questions to attorneys as a means of persuading their colleagues of the merits of a particular argument. If a justice knows that a particular policy position or argument will attract a colleague to that justice's preferred outcome, the justice may formulate a question simply to elicit a persuasive response from the attorney. Although individual justices have frequently already decided on their preferred case outcome after reading the written briefs, they may use the question period to probe the attorneys' minds for additional arguments and justifications to make their case opinions more complete and compelling. In one example in 1989, a five-member majority on the Court requested that a case be reargued in order to consider whether a civil rights precedent should be reversed.[86] It was clear from the previous decisions and policy preferences of several justices that they objected to the precedent because they felt it improperly regulated the behavior of private individuals and businesses.[87] During oral argument, however, Justice Scalia, one of the justices who had requested the reargument, indicated that the attorney had not provided him with sufficient justifications to render an opinion in support of his policy preference. After pressing for additional useful arguments, Scalia dismissed the attorney in frustration, saying, ''If that is all you have, you have nothing.''[88]

Although it varies from case to case, some justices ask very few questions while others frequently challenge the attorneys during oral argument. Because the Supreme Court is a collegial body in which the justices must work together to reach decisions, it is possible that interactions during oral arguments may influence decisions, not merely through persuasive answers to specific questions but also through the human emotions generated by conflict among the justices. For example, Justices Scalia and Ginsburg, both former law professors, are notable for their vigorous participation in oral argument. Some people have accused them of dominating oral argument and interrupting their colleagues' efforts to ask questions. Indeed, Chief Justice Rehnquist has interrupted Scalia's questioning in order to move an attorney's presentation back to the issues of interest to the other justices.[89] During a rare interview concerning behind-the-scenes interactions on the Supreme Court, Justice Blackmun described the effects of Scalia's domineering manner during oral argument:

[Justice Scalia] is and always will be the professor at work. . . . He asks far too many questions, and he takes over the whole argument of the counsel, he will argue with counsel. . . . Even [Justice O'Connor], who asks a lot of questions, a couple of times gets exasperated when [Scalia] interrupts her line of inquiry and goes off on his own. She throws her pencil down and [says,] ''umh, umh.''[90]

Similarly, unnamed sources inside the Court were quoted in news reports as saying that several justices have complained to Chief Justice Rehnquist about Justice Ginsburg's penchant for interrupting her colleagues.[91] Observers speculate that such interactions can adversely affect a justice's influence on his or her colleagues, but it is difficult to know the precise impact of such interpersonal conflicts.[92]

## Decision-Making Processes

After oral arguments, the justices make preliminary decisions during conferences. The justices meet in private sessions on Wednesdays and Fridays to vote on *certiorari* petitions and to decide cases heard during oral arguments. No one except the justices is permitted in the room. Historically, the Supreme Court's conferences have been among the most "leakproof" meetings in government. Because of their universally supported tradition of secrecy prior to the issuing of a formal opinion, the justices can discuss and argue freely about cases without fear that outsiders will learn any details of the discussions.

The chief justice plays an influential role in the conferences by characterizing each case and presenting his views first. The opportunity to speak first creates the greatest possibility of influencing the views of undecided justices, because the chief justice can forcefully argue for a particular outcome before alternative positions have been presented. In addition, the authority to characterize the facts and issues in the case creates the possibility that it can be summarized in a fashion favorable to a particular outcome. When the Supreme Court was considering its monumental decision against school segregation in *Brown v. Board of Education*, for example, Chief Justice Earl Warren placed on the defensive any justices who might have considered supporting continued segregation. According to the leading study of the decision making underlying the *Brown* decision, Warren initiated the discussion by saying that "[s]egregation . . . could be justified only by belief in the inferiority of [African-Americans]; any of the [justices] who wished to perpetuate the practice, [Warren] implied, ought in candor to be willing to acknowledge as much.''[93] Warren's forceful characterization of the issue may have contributed to the attainment of his goal: a unanimous decision.

The chief justice is also influential in guiding the course of discussion and debate among justices. Some chief justices, such as Harlan Stone in the 1940s, do not attempt to shape the course of discussion. This creates the risk that conference discussions will drag on and on, and that interpersonal animosities among justices will escalate during the extended expression of conflicting views. Other chief justices attempt to move on to other cases after preliminary views have been clarified. Thus, the conference is concluded in a timely manner without aimless debate in which justices may become angry but fail to persuade one another. The second approach creates risks that some justices will be dissatisfied with the opportunity for discussion, especially if they disagree with the chief justice's decision to close debate on a particular case.

Scholars who study the roles of the justices in conference have identified two leadership styles. First, there are "social leaders" who can encourage discussion, yet are sensitive enough to avoid overt conflict. Second, there are "task leaders" who focus on the case decision itself, regardless of the risks of conflict.[94] Although the chief justice may or may not assume one or both of these styles, the titular leader of the Court is well positioned to influence the conference's decision-making processes through these roles:

> Although his task leadership is not primarily derived from his office, the fact that he speaks first in conference tends to maintain such leadership if he has an independent claim to it. Also his control of the conference process puts him in a favorable position to exercise social leadership, for he can minimize exchanges which contribute toward negative feelings among Court members and perform other activity which favorably disposes his associates toward him.[95]

After a preliminary vote on the merits of the case, the chief justice, if a member of the majority, will assign one justice to write the opinion. Recent research on the strategic use of opinion assignments indicates that, although Chief Justice Rehnquist keeps important opinions for himself as a means of advancing his values and policy preferences, he does not fully exploit his opportunities to assign opinions to other justices in a manner that maximizes the advancement of his preferred positions.[96] In other words, he has spread opinion-writing assignments among the justices without providing special opportunities for the justices most closely aligned with his conservative views. If the chief justice is not in the majority, the senior justice in the majority makes the opinion assignment. During a career spanning more than thirty years (1965–90), Justice William Brennan developed the practice of the senior dissenter assigning opinions to other dissenters as a means of organizing dissenting justices to speak with a unified voice in opposition to the majority.[97] The authority to assign opinions can ultimately affect both the decision and the reasoning in a case. If the chief justice or senior majority justice wishes to establish a strong, clear precedent, he or she may assign the opinion to the most outspoken member of the majority. If he or she fears that some members of the majority are wavering, he or she may avoid a strident opinion that might drive less committed justices over to the other side. A less committed member of the majority may receive the assignment to write the opinion with the hope that the justice's position will strengthen in the course of researching and writing. In effect, it is hoped that the author will persuade him- or herself about the merits of the decision while writing the justifications on behalf of the entire majority. Moreover, a less committed member, or a member who crafts an opinion strategically, may be able to develop justifications that appeal to wavering members of the opposing side. Thus, in drafting a majority opinion, the justices may be able to increase the size of their majority.

When circulating drafts of dissenting opinions, the successful persuasion of less committed members of the majority may even turn decisions around so that the original dissenters prevail as a new majority. For example, studies show that marginal justices are likely to write dissenting opinions in closely divided five-to-four decisions, but that extremist justices write dissents criticizing comfortable majorities.[98] Thus, the tone of dissenting opinions is moderated in close cases to attract less strongly committed members of the majority. When it appears impossible to create a new majority by "stealing" one vote, dissenters make forthright statements of their values and policy preferences in the hope that justices will draw from their ideas in future cases.

Contemporary Supreme Court justices assert that they persuade one another regarding case decisions during the process of writing and circulating draft opinions. After the preliminary decision about a case in conference, the justices return to their chambers and, with the assistance of their law clerks, begin to draft opinions explaining the reasoning behind their preferred outcomes. In addition to the majority opinion, which is assigned, a concurring or dissenting opinion may be written by any other justice. A member of the majority may write a concurring opinion to advance alternative reasons that may offer better justifications for the majority view. Justices who disagree with the preliminary outcome may write dissenting opinions to persuade members of the majority to switch sides. When published after the case decision and opinions are finalized, dissenting opinions frequently lay the groundwork for future Court decisions that might move in a different direction when the composition of the Court changes or if individual justices change their minds. Many notable dissenting opinions have later become the majority position—sometimes long after the death of the opinion's author—when the values of society and some newly appointed justices move the Supreme Court to different conclusions. In 1896, for example, the first Justice John Harlan (his grandson, also named John Harlan, served on the Supreme Court during the 1950s and 1960s) was a lone dissenting voice warning that government-sponsored racial discrimination and segregation violated the Fourteenth Amendment's Equal Protection Clause and would ultimately harm society.[99] Fifty-eight years later in 1954, his forward-thinking views were vindicated when a unanimous Supreme Court helped turn American society against racial discrimination by declaring school segregation unconstitutional.[100]

It is difficult for researchers to know precisely how interactions and opinion writing strategies affect the decisions of the justices in each case. Information about the interactions behind specific cases is sometimes discernible through the rare forthright interview with a justice, through the personal papers of past justices (if their notes were sufficiently detailed), or through law clerks' anonymous comments to reporters and scholars. It is possible in other cases, however, to detect the influence of persuasion in opinion writing. In *Enmund v. Florida*,[101] for example, the driver of a getaway car was sentenced to death under the felony murder rule for a homicide committed by his accomplices during a robbery.

Because there was no evidence of his participation in the actual killing, a slim five-member majority on the Supreme Court disallowed the death sentence in an opinion by Justice White, which concluded:

> For purposes of imposing the death penalty, Enmund's criminal culpability must be limited to his participation in the robbery, and his punishment must be tailored to his personal responsibility and moral guilt. Putting Enmund to death to avenge two killings that he did not commit and had no intention of committing or causing does not measurably contribute to the retributive end of ensuring that the criminal gets his just deserts.[102]

Justice O'Connor wrote a vigorous opinion on behalf of the four dissenters in which she objected to the new rule limiting the death penalty to killers and their actively participating accomplices.

In a subsequent case a few years later, *Tison v. Arizona*,[103] Justice O'Connor wrote an opinion for a slim five-member majority which, contrary to the rule in *Enmund,* approved the death penalty for two young men who helped their father escape from prison and then accompanied him as he brutally murdered four people. Although O'Connor objected vigorously to the *Enmund* decision, her *Tison* opinion purported to accept *Enmund* as established precedent, but proceeded to approve the execution of accomplices who show "reckless disregard for human life"[104] even if they do not participate in any actual killing. Instead of establishing a clear link between the defendant's action and the homicide as the basis for the death penalty, O'Connor's rule permits prosecutors, judges, and juries to use discretion in imposing capital punishment on accomplices. Why did O'Connor not directly reverse *Enmund* instead of subtly subverting the *Enmund* rule, since it was obvious from her original dissenting opinion that she thought *Enmund* was wrongly decided? Apparently O'Connor and the *Enmund* dissenters needed a fifth vote to create a new majority and reinstate death sentences for accomplices who do not participate directly in homicides. The justice available to be persuaded was Justice White. If O'Connor had attempted to reverse *Enmund*, she would have been less likely to win over Justice White, because White would have been forced to admit that the rule he himself created in *Enmund* was erroneous. Rather than force White to repudiate his own work, O'Connor attracted him to the new majority by purporting to support *Enmund* while erasing its effect through the creation of the ambiguous standard in *Tison*. The opinion-writing process provides ample opportunity for justices to strategically change, ignore, and abolish precedents in order to appeal to specific colleagues whom they wish to persuade.

Because the justices' interactions and strategic opinions have so much influence on Supreme Court decisions, personal animosities among justices may affect their case decisions. Historically, there were some notable "wars" between justices—as when Hugo Black and Robert Jackson engaged in a bitter feud in the

1940s and 1950s and when Felix Frankfurter's professorial manner alienated several of his colleagues.[105] During the late 1980s, President Reagan's appointees began to assert themselves as an emerging conservative majority, and commentators detected an increase in pointed, personal barbs aimed at individual justices on a Court deeply divided between liberals and conservatives. One long-time Court observer characterized the era as "the season of snarling justices."[106] For example, after the emerging majority drastically weakened an antidiscrimination statute, Justice Blackmun wrote: "One wonders whether the majority still believes that race discrimination—or, more accurately, race discrimination against nonwhites—is a problem in our society, or even remembers that it ever was."[107] The following year, Justice Scalia fired back at the liberals in a case concerning racial discrimination in jury selection: "Justice Marshall's dissent rolls out the ultimate weapon, the accusation of insensitivity to racial discrimination—which will lose its intimidating effect if it continues to be fired so randomly."[108] In another case, Justice Blackmun came very close to admitting that criticisms in an opinion by Justice Kennedy had made him angry: "[N]othing could be further from the truth, and the accusations could be said to be as offensive as they are absurd."[109] Such strong language, if taken to heart by the justices, may inhibit cooperative and persuasive interactions.

The foregoing opinion assignment strategies and tactical interactions are part of the small group processes discussed in chapter 7 that are characteristic of decision making in appellate courts. In addition, Supreme Court decision making is influenced by the individual and environmental factors that generally influence all judicial decision making. Policy preferences, characteristics, attitudes, and role conceptions of the decision makers all affect judicial decisions. Studies of the Supreme Court, in particular, have permitted scholars to examine the influence of these factors through systematic evaluation of patterns within justices' decisions on particular issues.[110] For example, scholars have evaluated the ideological values of Supreme Court nominees through news media analyses of their decisions, and subsequently compared their liberal or conservative orientations with their case decisions. For cases concerning economic and civil liberties issues, there are strong correlations between nominees' ideological values and their subsequent behavior in deciding such cases.[111] The influential interactions and strategic opinion writing undertaken by justices stem from these values, policy preferences, and other individual elements.

The justices' decisions are also influenced by factors in the political environment outside the Court's chambers. As chapter 10 will discuss, the Supreme Court's decisions may be influenced by perceived threats from other branches of government, by anticipation of adverse public reaction, and by other constraints—because the Court is a part of, not separate from, the political governing system. For example, Congress may redraft statutes to reverse the Court's statutory interpretation decisions with which it disagrees. Congress can also initiate constitutional amendments which, if ratified by state legislatures or constitutional conventions, can nullify the Court's decisions interpreting the Constitution. While Congress has rarely succeeded in initiating the constitutional amendment process, the Supreme Court's justices are aware that such power exists if any of their decisions are too extreme or controversial. Similarly, the Court's decisions may be shaped by concerns for public reactions. In 1992, Justices O'Connor, Kennedy, and Souter helped preserve a right of choice for abortion because they claimed to be concerned with the public's respect for the Court's image as a legal rather than political institution. This image would be tarnished if the controversial *Roe v. Wade* precedent were overturned after defining law and policy for nineteen years.[112]

## THE ROLE OF THE SUPREME COURT IN THE AMERICAN GOVERNING SYSTEM

Modern characterizations of the Supreme Court's role in American society frequently emphasize the Court's special responsibilities for upholding the Bill of Rights and enforcing protections for individuals and political minorities, including religious, racial, and other groups who suffer from policy choices made by majoritarian interests in the elected branches of government.[113] Since the 1950s, the Supreme Court has earned this image by making courageous decisions against racial discrimination, religious discrimination, and other practices that violate people's constitutional rights. Is the Supreme Court really a policy leader pulling American society toward fulfillment of the progressive principles embodied in the Constitution? By examining the Supreme Court's actions throughout American history, one can see that the Supreme Court is neither a consistent protector of constitutional rights nor a guiding teacher leading the nation toward the fulfillment of democratic, egalitarian ideals.

For most of American history, the Supreme Court did little to protect the rights of individuals or politically weak minorities. Over the Court's history, the justices have reflected the biases of their backgrounds and social eras. Thus, for example, the Supreme Court protected slavery when a majority of the American public was turning against it,[114] endorsed racial segregation,[115] and approved the arbitrary incarceration of innocent Japanese-Americans when other Americans feared them during World War II.[116] Because justices of the Supreme Court are drawn from the same political and social environment that produces the leaders of the other branches of government in each era of American history, it is no surprise that the justices lack a unique capacity to defend ideals and principles. As human beings, the justices interpret constitutional principles in ways that reflect the values, policy preferences, and political forces of the age in which they live. Thus, the long-term role of the Supreme Court has frequently been to endorse policies advanced by the majority political coalition dominating the national government at a given time.[117] Public opinion research indicates that the Supreme Court's decisions are generally as majoritarian as those of other branches of government.[118] Because the Supreme

Court maintains the image of a "legal" rather than a "political" institution, its endorsement of policies created and maintained by Congress, the president, and state legislatures may lend extra legitimacy to those policies in the eyes of the public.

The Supreme Court has never been an independent legal institution supervising the activities of the political branches of government. Indeed it is intimately connected to the political system. The Court is shaped by developments in the political system, as when presidents appoint new justices with different political viewpoints in order to fill a Court vacancy created by a death or retirement of a current justice. The Court also participates, often unwittingly, in changes in the larger political system. For example, the Supreme Court has played a role in the major political conflicts and electoral realignments that have dramatically altered the country's political development.[119] The Supreme Court's endorsement of slavery in the *Dred Scott* case increased regional divisiveness in the 1850s. Along with other political actors and institutions, the Supreme Court failed to lead the nation by asserting constitutional principles and inadvertently accelerated the onset of the bloody Civil War, which ultimately resolved the mounting political polarization.

The Supreme Court's image as the independent protector of individual rights stems primarily from its decisions since the mid-1950s. Although the Supreme Court deserves credit for establishing protections for racial minorities and other individuals, it may simply have been on the leading edge of societal viewpoints moving in that direction.[120] Moreover, the effects of some Supreme Court decisions, particularly the school segregation cases, were primarily symbolic because of the Court's relative weakness in enforcement and implementation. As chapter 10 will show, there are significant limitations on the judiciary's ability to ensure compliance with its directives. Thus, the Supreme Court's racial discrimination decisions were often symbolic endorsements that may have helped to legitimize and mobilize other political actors. One can seriously question whether American society's significant shift away from racial discrimination came in the aftermath of the 1954 *Brown v. Board of Education* decision or not, in fact, until Congress passed comprehensive antidiscrimination laws in the 1960s. Congressional action may not have been taken if the Supreme Court had not, at least symbolically, pushed the country away from segregation, but the Court was not a solitary policy leader, singlehandedly changing the social landscape. The Supreme Court's role as guardian of individual rights has been further diminished by the changing composition of the Court during the 1980s. The Court does not and cannot have a fixed role as guardian of individual rights because changes in the composition of the Court determine whether individual rights are a priority for the justices on the Court at any given moment.

## CONCLUSION

This discussion of the Supreme Court's larger role in American society is not meant to denigrate the Court's important contributions to positive developments in American society. One cannot assume, however, that the Supreme Court actually fulfills its idealized image as an independent, courageous guardian of the Bill of Rights. Because the Supreme Court is a political institution composed of human beings drawn from a complex social environment, the nation's highest court inevitably acts within the governing system as a political component influenced by and interacting with other political actors and social forces.

## NOTES

1. Joyce A. Baugh, Christopher E. Smith, Thomas R. Hensley, and Scott Patrick Johnson, "Justice Ruth Bader Ginsburg: A Preliminary Assessment," *University of Toledo Law Review* 26 (1994): 1–34.
2. Alexander Hamilton, "Federalist, No. 78," in *Courts, Judges, and Politics*, 4th ed., eds. Walter F. Murphy and C. Herman Pritchett (New York: Random House, 1986), p. 15.
3. U.S. Constitution, Article III, sec. 1 and 2.
4. David O'Brien, *Storm Center: The Supreme Court in American Politics*, 2nd ed. (New York: W.W. Norton, 1990), p. 136.
5. Ibid., pp. 136–40.
6. Ibid., pp. 140–43.
7. *Marbury v. Madison*, 5 U.S. 137 (1803).
8. *Dred Scott v. Sandford*, 60 U.S. 393 (1857).
9. *Hammer v. Dagenhart*, 247 U.S. 251 (1918).
10. *Lochner v. New York*, 198 U.S. 45 (1905).
11. U.S. Constitution, Article III, sec. 1.
12. Archibald Cox, *The Court and the Constitution* (Boston: Houghton Mifflin, 1987), p. 136.
13. Lucius J. Barker and Jesse J. McCorry, Jr., *Black Americans and the Political System* (Cambridge, MA: Winthrop, 1976), p. 176.
14. *Plessy v. Ferguson*, 163 U.S. 537 (1896) (state-mandated separation of people according to racial categories found to be acceptable under the Constitution).
15. *Goeseart v. Cleary*, 335 U.S. 464 (1948) (states permitted to forbid women from working in taverns unless they were the wives or daughters of male tavern owners).
16. *Korematsu v. United States*, 323 U.S. 214 (1944).
17. *Barron v. Baltimore*, 32 U.S. (7 Pet.) 243 (1833).
18. Freedom of speech was recognized as protected against state and local government action in 1925. *Gitlow v. New York*, 268 U.S. 652 (1925). One previous decision had protected property rights against state government interference, but that decision directly benefitted a corporation rather than individual citizens. *Chicago, Burlington Railroad Co. v. Chicago*, 166 U.S. 266 (1897).

19. *Gideon v. Wainwright*, 372 U.S. 355 (1963).
20. *Duckworth v. Eagan*, 492 U.S. 195 (1989).
21. *Webster v. Reproductive Health Services*, 492 U.S. 490 (1989).
22. *Patterson v. McLean Credit Union*, 491 U.S. 164 (1989).
23. Henry J. Abraham, *Justices & Presidents: A Political History of Appointments to the Supreme Court*, 2nd ed. (New York: Oxford University Press, 1985), pp. 201–02.
24. Ibid., pp. 202–03.
25. Ibid., p. 324.
26. Ibid., pp. 334–35.
27. For brief biographical descriptions of all justices who have served on the Supreme Court, see *The Supreme Court at Work* (Washington, D.C.: Congressional Quarterly, 1990), pp. 127–208.
28. Abraham, *Justices and Presidents*, pp. 16–17.
29. Christopher E. Smith, *Critical Judicial Nominations and Political Change* (Westport, CT: Praeger, 1993), pp. 123–52.
30. Richard Lacayo, "A Blank Slate," *Time*, 6 August 1990, pp. 16–18.
31. See Neil Lewis, "Rejected as Clerk, Now Headed for the Bench," *N.Y. Times*, 15 June 1993, p. A1.
32. Henry J. Abraham, *The Judiciary: The Supreme Court in the Governmental Process*, 8th ed. (Dubuque, IA: William C. Brown Publishers, 1991), p. 48.
33. "Campaigning for the High Court," *Time*, 2 July 1990, p. 61.
34. Stephen L. Wasby, *The Supreme Court in the Federal Judicial System*, 3rd ed. (Chicago: Nelson-Hall, 1988), p. 110.
35. Ibid.
36. Timothy Phelps and Helen Winternitz, *Capitol Games* (New York: Hyperion, 1992), pp. 140–41.
37. O'Brien, *Storm Center*, p. 108.
38. Antonin Scalia, "The Disease as Cure," *Washington University Law Quarterly* (1979): 147–48.
39. Janet L. Blasecki, "Justice Lewis Powell: Swing Voter or Staunch Conservative," *Journal of Politics* 52 (1990): 530–47.
40. *Regents of the University of California v. Bakke*, 438 U.S. 265 (1978).
41. *City of Akron v. Akron Center for Reproductive Health*, 497 U.S. 502 (1983).
42. Robert H. Bork, *The Tempting of America: The Political Seduction of Law* (New York: Free Press, 1990), pp. 9–10.
43. O'Brien, *Storm Center*, p. 111.
44. Ibid., p. 109.
45. David Shribman, "Souter's Progress: How Nominee Won In His Classic Clash With Capital Culture," *Wall Street Journal*, 3 October 1990, p. A1; Ruth Marcus, "Haven't We Met Before? If You Like the Souter Hearings,

Then You Love the Thomas Replay,'' *Washington Post National Weekly Edition*, 23–29 September 1991, p. 14.

46. Joyce A. Baugh and Christopher E. Smith, ''Doubting Thomas: Confirmation Veracity Meets Performance Reality,'' *Seattle University Law Review* 19 (1996): 455–96.

47. Neil Lewis, ''Ginsburg Deflects Pressure to Talk on Death Penalty,'' *New York Times*, 23 July 1993, p. A1; Neil Lewis, ''Taking Initiative, Nominee Defends Conduct As Judge,'' *New York Times*, 13 July 1994, p. A1.

48. Wasby, *The Supreme Court in the Federal Judicial System*, p. 128.

49. Christopher E. Smith and Kimberly A. Beuger, ''Clouds in the Crystal Ball: Presidential Expectations and the Unpredictable Behavior of Supreme Court Appointees,'' *Akron Law Review* 27 (1993): 115–39.

50. See Christopher E. Smith, '' 'What If. . . .': Critical Junctures on the Road to (In)Equality,'' *Thurgood Marshall Law Review* 15 (1989–90): 1–25.

51. Abraham, *Justices and Presidents*, p. 286.

52. *Milliken v. Bradley* 533 U.S. 267 (1974).

53. *San Antonio Independent School District v. Rodriguez*, 93 S. Ct. 1278 (1973).

54. Richard Kolbe, *American Political Parties: An Uncertain Future* (New York: Harper & Row, 1985), p. 209.

55. Everett Carll Ladd, *The American Polity*, 2nd ed. (New York: W.W. Norton, 1987), p. 491.

56. U.S. Constitution, Article III, sec. 2.

57. Abraham, *The Judiciary*, p. 19.

58. Ibid., p. 21.

59. O'Brien, *Storm Center*, p. 197.

60. Wasby, *The Supreme Court in the Federal Judicial System*, pp. 193–94.

61. Stuart Taylor, ''Scalia Proposes Major Overhaul of the U.S. Courts,'' *New York Times*, 16 February 1987, pp. 1, 12.

62. Joan Biskupic, ''Justices Show a Propensity For Letting Others Decide,'' *Congressional Quarterly*, 7 July 1990, p. 2131; ''Chief Justice Recaps 1995 in Year-end Report,'' *The Third Branch* 28 (January 1996): 5–6; Linda Greenhouse, ''In Supreme Court's Decisions, A Clear Voice, and a Murmur,'' *New York Times*, 3 July 1996, p. A12.

63. O'Brien, *Storm Center*, p. 199.

64. Wasby, *The Supreme Court in the Federal Judicial System*, pp. 207–08.

65. Saul Brenner and Jan Palmer, ''The Law Clerks' Recommendations and Chief Justice Vinson's Vote in Certiorari,'' *American Politics Quarterly* 18 (1990): 68–86.

66. Gregory Caldeira and John Wright, ''The Discuss List: Agenda Building in the Supreme Court,'' *Law and Society Review* 24 (1990): 807–36.

67. See O'Brien, *Storm Center*, pp. 200–212; Wasby, *The Supreme Court in the Federal Judicial System*, pp. 170–87.

68. *Mora v. McNamara*, 389 U.S. 934 (1967).
69. *Baker v. Carr*, 369 U.S. 186 (1962).
70. *Roe v. Wade*, 410 U.S. 113 (1973).
71. See Wasby, *The Supreme Court in the Federal Judicial System*, pp. 209–10.
72. Joseph Tanenhaus, Marvin Schick, Matthew Muraskin, and Daniel Rosen, "The Supreme Court's *Certiorari* Jurisdiction: Cue Theory," in *American Court Systems*, 2nd ed., eds. Sheldon Goldman and Austin Sarat (New York: Longman, 1989), pp. 158–65.
73. Ibid.
74. Virginia Armstrong and Charles A. Johnson, "Certiorari Decision Making by the Warren and Burger Courts: Is Cue Theory Time Bound?" *Polity* 15 (1982): 141–50.
75. S. Sidney Ulmer, "The Supreme Court's Certiorari Decisions: Conflict as a Predictive Variable," *American Political Science Review* 78 (1984): 901–11.
76. D. Marie Provine, *Case Selection in the United States Supreme Court* (Chicago: University of Chicago Press, 1980), pp. 77–83.
77. H.W. Perry, Jr., "Agenda Setting and Case Selection," *The American Courts: A Critical Assessment*, eds. John B. Gates and Charles A. Johnson (Washington, D.C.: Congressional Quarterly, 1991), p. 273.
78. Gregory Caldeira and John Wright, "Organized Interests and Agenda Setting in the U.S. Supreme Court," *American Political Science Review* 82 (1988): 1109–27.
79. See Saul Brenner and John F. Krol, "Strategies in Certiorari Voting on the United States Supreme Court," *Journal of Politics* 51 (1989): 828–40.
80. Robert L. Boucher, Jr. and Jeffrey A. Segal, "Supreme Court Justices as Strategic Decision Makers: Aggressive Grants and Defensive Denials on the Vinson Court," *Journal of Politics* 57 (1995): 824–37.
81. See H.W. Perry, Jr., *Deciding to Decide: Agenda Setting in the United States Supreme Court* (Cambridge, MA: Harvard University Press, 1991).
82. Wasby, *The Supreme Court in the Federal Judicial System*, pp. 204–05.
83. Stephen L. Wasby, Steven Peterson, James Schubert, and Glendon Schubert, "The Per Curiam Opinion: Its Nature and Functions," *Judicature* 76 (1992): 29–38.
84. *Gideon v. Wainwright*, 372 U.S. 335 (1963).
85. See Anthony Lewis, *Gideon's Trumpet* (New York: Random House, 1964).
86. Stuart Taylor, "Court, 5-4, Votes to Restudy Rights in Minority Suits," *New York Times*, 26 April 1988, pp. 1, 11.
87. *Runyon v. McCrary*, 427 U.S. 160, 205 (1976) (White, J., dissenting).
88. Linda Greenhouse, "Justices Seem Unswayed by Civil Rights Debate They Sought," *New York Times*, 13 October 1988, p. A23.
89. O'Brien, *Storm Center*, p. 274.

90. Stuart Taylor, "Blackmun Provides Peek at the People Under those Robes," *New York Times*, 25 July 1988, p. B6.

91. " 'Rude' Ruth," *Newsweek*, 11 April 1994, p. 6.

92. See Christopher E. Smith, *Justice Antonin Scalia and the Supreme Court's Conservative Moment* (Westport, CT: Praeger, 1993).

93. Richard Kluger, *Simple Justice* (New York: Random House, 1975), p. 680.

94. David J. Danelski, "The Influence of the Chief Justice in the Decisional Process of the Supreme Court," *American Court Systems*, eds. Sheldon Goldman and Austin Sarat (New York: Longman, 1989), pp. 489–90.

95. Ibid., p. 490.

96. Sue Davis, "Power on the Court: Chief Justice Rehnquist's Opinion Assignments," *Judicature* 74 (1990): 66–72.

97. Beverly Blair Cook, "Justice Brennan and the Institutionalization of Dissent Assignment," *Judicature* 79 (1995): 17–23.

98. Saul Brenner and Harold Spaeth, "Ideological Position as a Variable in the Authoring of Dissenting Opinions on the Warren and Burger Courts," *American Politics Quarterly* 16 (1988): 317–28.

99. See *Plessy v. Ferguson*, 163 U.S. 537 (1896).

100. *Brown v. Board of Education*, 347 U.S. 483 (1954).

101. *Enmund v. Florida*, 458 U.S. 782 (1982).

102. Ibid., p. 801.

103. *Tison v. Arizona*, 481 U.S. 137 (1987).

104. Ibid., p. 137.

105. Lawrence Baum, *The Supreme Court*, 3rd ed. (Washington, D.C.: Congressional Quarterly Press, 1989), pp. 152–53.

106. Stuart Taylor, "Season of Snarling Justices," *Akron Beacon Journal*, 5 April 1990, p. A11.

107. *Wards Cove Packing Co. v. Atonio*, 490 U.S. 642, 662 (1989) (Blackmun, J., dissenting).

108. *Holland v. Illinois*, 493 U.S. 474, 486 (1990).

109. *County of Allegheny v. American Civil Liberties Union*, 492 U.S. 573, 610 (1989).

110. See, e.g., Joel B. Grossman, "Role Playing and the Analysis of Judicial Behavior: The Case of Mr. Justice Frankfurter," *Journal of Public Law* 11 (1962): 285–309; Saul Brenner, "Fluidity on the United States Supreme Court: A Reexamination," *American Journal of Political Science* 24 (1980): 526–35; C. Neal Tate, "Personal Attribute Models of the Voting Behavior of U.S. Supreme Court Justices: Liberalism in Civil Liberties and Economics Decisions, 1946–1978," *American Political Science Review* 75 (1981): 355–67.

111. Jeffrey A. Segal, Lee Epstein, Charles M. Cameron, and Harold J. Spaeth, "Ideological Values and the Votes of U.S. Supreme Court Justices Revisited," *Journal of Politics* 57 (1995): 812–23.

112. *Planned Parenthood v. Casey*, 505 U.S. \_\_\_\_, 112 S. Ct. 2791 (1992).
113. Barker and McCorry, *Black Americans and the Political System*, p. 176.
114. *Dred Scott v. Sandford*, 60 U.S. (19 How.) 393 (1857).
115. *Plessy v. Ferguson*, 163 U.S. 537 (1896).
116. *Korematsu v. United States*, 323 U.S. 214 (1944).
117. See, e.g., Robert Dahl, "Decision-Making in a Democracy: The Supreme Court as a National Policy-Maker," *Journal of Public Law* 6 (1958): 279–95.
118. Thomas Marshall, "Public Opinion, Representation, and the Modern Supreme Court," *American Politics Quarterly* 16 (1988): 296–316.
119. William Lasser, "The Supreme Court in Periods of Critical Realignment," *Journal of Politics* 47 (1985): 1174–87; See also William Lasser, *The Limits of Judicial Power* (Chapel Hill: University of North Carolina Press, 1988).
120. David G. Barnum, "The Supreme Court and Public Opinion: Judicial Decision Making in the Post-New Deal Period," *Journal of Politics* 47 (1985): 652–66.

# Chapter 10

# Courts and Policy Making

The effects of court decisions can extend beyond the individuals, government agencies, or businesses involved in a particular case. Court decisions can affect society in a variety of ways. For example, judicial decisions interpreting the Constitution define the powers of government and the rights of individuals. Many cases concerning constitutional interpretation address difficult and far-reaching questions. Can a state legislature prevent radical political groups from holding rallies on public property? Is the gas chamber a permissible means for state governments to use when imposing the death penalty on convicted murderers? Can public schools sponsor a daily moment of silence permitting students to pray? In considering such issues concerning individuals' rights and government power, court decisions often determine what government can or cannot do. Thus, court decisions have shaped policies concerning such controversial issues as abortion, affirmative action, school desegregation, and the rights of criminal defendants as well as a variety of less controversial issues. In each of these instances, the rules produced by judicial decisions provide guidelines for government and society. Their impact is not limited just to the litigants in the case.

There are two types of court decisions that shape public policy. First, decisions that have a direct effect on public policy are often labeled as "judicial policy making." Cases that confront a policy issue and lead a judge to produce an authoritative rule (or rules) for that issue have a direct effect on public policy. Such decisions formulate rules for policies and practices of government officials. These decisions come most frequently from appellate courts because such actions by trial courts are likely to receive appellate review and subsequent affirmation or reversal. Even if the trial court decision is affirmed by the appellate court, the higher court's decision becomes the most important precedent. For example, when litigants alleged that public schools had intentionally engaged in illegal racial discrimination, judges responded by issuing rulings that limited the authority of school officials. School officials could no longer undertake discriminatory actions, and their school systems were susceptible to judges' remedial orders requiring the implementation of busing plans or other strategies.[1] Similarly, judges have created rules for government practices and policies regarding prison administration, abortion, police investigations, school prayer, and a wide range of other issues.

Second, a different category of court decisions can have an indirect, yet profound, effect on public policy. These decisions emerge from trial courts and often come from juries instead of judges. In civil litigation, individuals may sue businesses, other individuals, or government for injuries or harm to property. Such tort suits can sometimes produce verdicts and judgments that transfer hundreds of thousands or even millions of dollars to injured victims. Although such cases do not necessarily articulate clear mandates for policies and practices, they may profoundly impact policies indirectly when agencies and businesses change their behavior to avoid the risk of future liability decisions.[2] The plaintiff may initiate a case with the intention of gaining compensation, yet the jury's verdict and damage award may shock many agencies into developing new policies. For example, police in Lansing, Michigan, believed that they had taken into custody a drunk man who needed to sleep off his drinking binge. In fact, the man was seriously ill from drinking windshield-wiper fluid in an apparent suicide attempt. When the man died in his jail cell, his family sued the police department, and a jury awarded $1.5 million in damages for the death.[3] As a result, the Lansing police department and other police departments in Michigan developed more careful procedures for evaluating and monitoring people in jail to avoid paying huge sums in subsequent cases. The jury did not purport to articulate a rule for jail policies and practices, but its decision became the catalyst for policy change.

This chapter will discuss both direct and indirect impacts of court decisions on public policy. Particular attention will be given to judicial policy making by judges because such situations raise especially important questions concerning the appropriate role of the judicial branch in the American system of government.

## INTEREST GROUP LITIGATION

Cases that generate direct judicial policy making do not always arise by chance. Although an individual's legal claim may unintentionally produce a judicial decision of broad impact, many political interests intentionally use litigation as a means to advance their policy preferences. Since the early twentieth century, many organized interest groups have used litigation to pursue their public policy agendas. Civil lawsuits have led to the desegregation of school systems, the improvement of living conditions in prisons and jails, the opportunity for women to make choices about abortions, and many other policy outcomes. Typically, reform-seeking litigation involves a lawsuit against a governmental agency by an individual, often backed by an interest group, seeking judicial protection of an asserted constitutional right. Although lawsuits against the government frequently are motivated by a desire for social reform, many other civil actions against the government involve a lone individual merely seeking overdue Social Security benefits and not pursuing social change. Alternatively, private individuals and interest groups may explicitly pursue social change through suits against other private entities. The Southern Poverty Law Center, for example, has filed suits against the Ku Klux Klan and other white supremacists. Although these actions ostensibly seek monetary compensation for racially-motivated murders of innocent African-Americans, the center is quite frank about its underlying goal of eliminating racist organizations by destroying them financially, thereby deterring other such organizations from engaging in violence and intimidation.[4] In the late 1980s, corporations began to use civil litigation against individual community activists who opposed the development of landfills, incinerators, and other pollution-causing business projects. The corporations filed multimillion-dollar defamation suits claiming that their citizen-opponents hurt business by making false statements. Few defamation lawsuits aimed at individual activists succeed in court, but many achieve their intended purpose by scaring citizens away from opposing corporate plans because of the litigation costs required to fight such suits and the fear of losing money after a trial.[5] Thus, civil litigation does not exclusively advance the interests of political underdogs. Litigation is a tool available to any interests that have legal resources and access to the courts.[6] Litigation is simply the form of ''lobbying'' that political interests can employ to influence government and public policy through judicial action.

The characterization of interest groups that employ litigation strategies as political underdogs developed from studies of liberal groups and early litigation activity by conservative groups. These groups sought to advance their policy goals in the judicial branch because they lacked the necessary access and resources to influence public policy developments in the legislative and executive branches. For example, advocates of equality for African-Americans had little ability to influence legislatures during most of the twentieth century. A variety of devices (e.g., poll taxes, complex registration requirements) were employed in many states to prevent African-Americans from voting. Thus, they had little ability to influence the decisions of elected officials. In addition, they lacked the organizational and financial support necessary for effective lobbying campaigns. To eliminate laws and practices that fostered racial discrimination in housing, education, and voting, civil rights groups sought judicial assistance.[7] The courts were virtually the only forum in the government that provided an opportunity for African-Americans to present their claims for full citizenship rights during most of the twentieth century. Civil rights lawyers, especially those from the National Association for the Advancement of Colored People (NAACP), scored significant legal victories that helped enhance equal opportunity and end official racial discrimination by the government.

The success of civil rights groups' attorneys on behalf of African-Americans provided a model for interest group litigation by advocates for women, prisoners, the disabled, environmental issues, and other causes. Although politically liberal groups became associated with the litigation strategy, politically conservative groups increasingly used litigation as a means to achieve their policy goals or to fight against the judicial policy attainments of their liberal opponents. Conservative groups employed litigation strategies early in the twentieth century to oppose unions, government regulation of business, and other societal developments with which they disagreed.[8] After witnessing the success of liberal interest group litigators in the 1950s, 1960s, and 1970s, a variety of conservative groups created their own legal organizations devoted to the pursuit and protection of their favored policy issues. Increased litigation activities by these organizations during the Reagan era, when they had sympathetic allies in other branches of government, indicate that interest groups no longer pursue litigation because they have no other government forums available to hear their claims. Instead, as Lee Epstein's studies indicate ''a wide range of groups regularly resort to the judicial arena because they view the courts as just another political battlefield.''[9]

To successfully employ litigation strategies, interest groups need several attributes and resources.[10] First, interest groups need sufficient longevity to withstand the incremental process of pursuing judicial decisions that shape particular public policy issues. Several decades of continuous litigation were required in dozens of cases before the NAACP finally persuaded the Supreme Court to rule against racial segregation in public schools. Second, organizations need financial resources and adequate legal and clerical staff to maintain litigation, especially when challenging more affluent interests or government—entities that can afford to prolong the litigation process. Third, a group's proficiency at generating well-timed publicity enhances its ability to litigate policy issues. Positive publicity can create financial support, favorable public opinion, and broader circulation of legal arguments and evidence. Law review articles can educate the legal community, including judges, about the soundness of arguments advanced by an interest group. Groups benefit from the respect of judges and the public because a group's reputation may affect its ability to attract other interest groups' support. For example, if an avowedly racist organization wishes to pursue a case concerning government limitations on its members' ability to give public speeches, other organizations concerned with free speech issues may shy away from associating with a group espousing despicable ideas.

## Litigation Strategies

One primary strategy employed by interest groups is the sponsorship of test cases. When organizations sponsor test cases, they represent a claimant whose case raises and carries issues through each level of the court system. Sponsorship of test cases can require significant commitments of time and money because it may take several years for a case to work its way through the state and federal courts. Sometimes organizations will become sponsors after a case has presented a specific policy issue to an appellate court. In such cases, the organizations' attorneys may be more skilled in the preparation and presentation of oral arguments than the litigant's original attorney.

From the interest group's perspective, sponsorship of cases permits the group to control the arguments presented. In other words, the claimant's case serves as the vehicle for the presentation of the political interest's views in the judicial arena. For example, when the officers of the Executive Committee of the Southern Cotton Manufacturers Association sought to fight the implementation of federal laws limiting the working hours of child laborers, they planned the type of case and specific court they would use to challenge federal legislative authority to create labor laws. Within the jurisdiction of the court they selected as the forum for initiating the case, they toured factories to search for desirable plaintiffs. Instead of formally representing the group's members—the factory owners whose labor forces would be affected by child labor laws—they found a family of textile workers who were willing to serve as plaintiffs. Thus, the issue could be presented as the case of a working-class family seeking the freedom to permit their children to keep earning income rather than as a case of business interests challenging unwanted government regulations.[11] Because the carefully planned case fit neatly with the predisposition of that era's Supreme Court justices for preventing government regulation of economic activities, the Southern Cotton Manufacturers Association won a significant (albeit temporary) legal victory on behalf of businesses.[12]

Not all interest groups can successfully "plan" their legislative initiatives. As Stephen Wasby's research on the NAACP's civil rights litigation campaigns indicates, interest groups' litigation activities are shaped by a variety of internal and external factors.[13] For example, interest groups must shape their arguments within the limitations of the particular issues raised by the cases. A "perfect" case may not be available for raising the issues in the most desirable fashion. Organizations' governing boards and central office staff members may disagree with attorneys about the criteria and strategies for selecting and presenting cases. Attorneys must react to their opponents' litigation strategies and to judges' interim decisions (e.g., whether certain evidence is admissible, etc.). Thus, attorneys cannot readily control the pace or direction of litigation in specific cases.

An alternative interest group litigation strategy is the submission of *amicus curiae* briefs to appellate courts. These "friend of the court" briefs are written arguments filed with the court in support of one particular party in a case in which the interest group is not a direct participant. Initially, *amicus* briefs were used to provide judges with useful information from a neutral third party outside of the litigation. Gradually, such briefs came to be used to support one party's position. The use of *amicus* briefs has grown to such an extent that they are now a standard element in cases heard by the U. S. Supreme Court. During the 1940s, only 18 percent of cases heard by the Supreme Court included *amicus* briefs. By 1988, 80 percent of cases included *amicus* briefs.[14]

The *amicus* brief may be an opportunity for the interest group to provide the judges with additional arguments in support of or in opposition to a policy position that was not raised by either party in the case. Interest groups may also build coalitions through the use of *amicus* briefs by demonstrating to the judges how many different organizations agree or disagree with a particular policy position. Thus, groups will invite other interest groups to submit briefs or to "sign on" to a brief filed by an allied interest group.[15] In some instances, the credibility and expertise of a particular interest group may persuade judges about the desirability of a particular outcome. If a case concerns medical issues, for example, medical arguments presented on behalf of physicians' organizations may provide judges with useful and persuasive information that was not effectively presented in the partisan arguments.

As indicated by the discussion of interest group litigation, litigants initiate cases designed to advance specific preferred policies because they view judges as policy makers. Interest groups treat courts as authoritative policy-making institutions which, as the third branch of government, provide an alternative avenue for action. While litigants and lawyers who bring their policy agendas to the courts may treat judges as policy makers, judges are not unified in their views about their own roles in policy making in the American governing system.

## JUDICIAL POLICY MAKING

Judges' characterizations of themselves and their role in the governing system do not reveal a consensus concerning whether they are, in fact, policy makers. Judges have faced this question directly in several legal cases in which laws creating mandatory retirement ages for state judges have been challenged as violations of the federal Age Discrimination in Employment Act. Under the Act, only workers on "the policy-making level" may be forced to retire when they reach a specified age. If judges acknowledge that they are policy makers, then mandatory retirement provisions can be applied to judicial officers. If, however, judges do not regard judicial officers as policy makers, then the application of mandatory retirement provisions to judges would violate the federal law. A federal circuit court in Missouri upheld the regulations, acknowledging that "whatever the philosophy of the particular judge, and whether he views his proper role as broad or narrow, his decisions—some of them, at least—necessarily will resolve issues previously unsettled and thus will create law."[16] By contrast, a federal circuit court in New York ruled that such regulations do not apply to judges, asserting that "[t]he performance of traditional judicial functions is not policy making. . . . The principal business of the courts is the resolution of disputes."[17] Although these decisions reflect traditional divisions in judges' and commentators' assessments and portrayals of the judicial role, it is clear from examining the substance and consequences of judicial decisions that judges can and do have

direct, far-reaching effects on public policy. In fact, although the U.S. Supreme
Court ultimately tiptoed around the question of whether judges are policy makers,
the justices upheld the application of the retirement law to state judges by conced-
ing that judges exercise discretion on issues of public importance and therefore
can be regarded as "on the policy-making level."[18]

Judges do not merely create abstract rules of behavior. Judicial decisions
directly affect people's lives in many ways. An individual court case may decide
no more than whether A owes money to B. Judicial policy making occurs even
in such seemingly small cases because a governmental entity—the judiciary—is
exercising its official authority and power to allocate resources and to influence
the development of rules affecting future allocative decisions. By contrast, other
court cases are more easily recognizable as affecting public policy. Judicial decisions may, for example, determine whether a state government spends millions
of dollars on a new prison or whether women have the right to obtain abortions.
In its most general sense, policy making is "the establishment and application
of authoritative rules."[19] As one of the three branches of government, the judiciary
provides a forum in which people can seek to advance their goals in terms of
directing governmental actions and allocating societal resources. Groups and
individuals who lack the political power to influence policy-making decisions of
legislatures and executive branch officials may present their policy objectives as
legal claims in order to seek judicial assistance.

Because decisions by the Supreme Court affect the entire country, discussions
of judicial policy making frequently focus on the nation's highest court. However,
other courts in the judicial system also influence the development of public policies. State trial courts are the initial forums for cases that will help set the policy
agenda for a state or for the whole country. In state trial court cases, arguments
are developed, political interests are mobilized, and baseline judicial policy decisions are made, and these provide the basis for subsequent reviews, if any, by
appellate courts.[20] Federal district courts similarly provide the initial forums for
many policy issues, and federal district judges have developed and implemented
many of the most controversial judicial policy decisions affecting the administration of school systems, prisons, and other institutions.[21] State appellate courts
influence public policy development on many different issues.[22] For example,
even though the U.S. Supreme Court has declared that the U.S. Constitution
permits Congress and state legislatures to forbid the use of public funds for poor
women's abortions, the Michigan Court of Appeals decided in 1991 that its state
constitution provides broader abortion rights, including access to state funding,
than those contained in the U.S. Constitution.[23] State supreme courts are especially
important policy-making institutions because of their authority over the interpretation of state constitutions and statutes. Because the U.S. courts of appeals are
the final decision makers in many federal cases, their role as policy-making entities
"has continued to grow."[24] Although the processes underlying the development
of decisions differ at each level of the American court system, all courts face

fundamental questions concerning the legitimacy and capacity of judges for developing effective public policies.

## THE LEGITIMACY OF JUDICIAL POLICY MAKING

The United States Constitution vests "the judicial power of the United States" in the Supreme Court and other federal courts.[25] Does this "judicial power" include the authority to formulate and implement public policies? If one examines the intentions of the Constitution's framers, it might be argued that they did not intend to authorize the judiciary to affect the development of policy priorities and the distribution of resources within society. As described by Alexander Hamilton, the judiciary was intended to have limited ability to determine policy:

> The judiciary . . . has no influence over either the sword or the purse; no direction either of the strength or of the wealth of the society; and can take no active resolution whatever. It may truly be said to have neither FORCE nor WILL, but merely judgment; and must ultimately depend upon the aid of the executive arm for the efficacy of its judgment.[26]

Although this quotation from Hamilton implies that the judiciary will not take an active role in policy making, other words in the same essay indicate that judicial decisions will indeed affect public policy. Hamilton could not have anticipated the magnitude of twentieth-century judicial involvement in the development and application of governmental policies, but his description of the courts' fundamental responsibility for protecting the Constitution provides the basis for judicial policy making:

> [T]he courts were designed to be an intermediate body between the people and the legislature, in order, among other things, to keep the latter within the limits assigned to their authority. The interpretation of the laws is the proper and peculiar province of the courts. A constitution is, in fact, and must be regarded by the judges, as a fundamental law. It therefore belongs to them to ascertain its meaning, as well as the meaning of any particular act proceeding from the legislative body.[27]

In the immediate aftermath of the Constitution's drafting, Hamilton's understanding of the intended judicial role included an expectation that judges would define the Constitution and determine whether legislative enactments were appropriate under that fundamental document. Thus, Hamilton presumed that the judiciary would have the power to define the limits of congressional power. The power to tell the legislature what it cannot do enables judges to determine public policy. If Congress wished to limit the extension of slavery into newly acquired territories—as it did in the mid-nineteenth century—and the Supreme Court issued an opinion declaring that Congress lacked the constitutional authority to make such a decision—as it did in the *Dred Scott* case in 1857[28]—then the judiciary decided that the institution of slavery can spread and grow. The judiciary, in effect, determined a policy for the structuring and utilization of labor in the economic system and a policy affecting human beings' liberty. As this example illustrates, courts can influence public policy through their authority to interpret the Constitution.

One argument challenging the *Dred Scott* case and similar examples of judicial policy making is that the judiciary should not oversee and countermand decisions of the legislative and executive branches of government. This power of "judicial review" is not mentioned in the text of the Constitution and, therefore, courts may act improperly when they engage in judicial policy making. According to this argument, judges have no authority to evaluate the actions of elected officials. However, even if courts did not possess the power of judicial review, they would still influence public policy. Every court decision—even those that do not pass judgment on a governmental program but merely determine the outcome of disputes between individuals—arguably involves judicial policy making. A judicial decision in a seemingly small case not only determines a specific allocation of rights and benefits between the two parties, it also contributes to the body of legal precedent, the authoritative rules that will influence, if not determine, the outcomes and allocations of rights and benefits in subsequent cases. Moreover, beyond the pervasive policy consequences of even modest judicial decisions, judicial review remains a political reality despite its lack of explicit endorsement in the Constitution. The concept of judicial review became firmly established when it was exercised by Chief Justice John Marshall in *Marbury v. Madison* in 1803[29] and, as indicated by Hamilton's comments, was recognized and perhaps taken for granted by the generation of leaders who developed the Constitution. It is exceedingly rare in contemporary times for legal commentators to argue that the judiciary lacks authority to review the constitutional basis for acts of other governmental branches. In regard to judicial policy making, the primary debate concerns not whether court decisions can invalidate and shape governmental policies, but whether and when particular judicial decisions "go too far."

Did the judiciary determine public policy in the *Dred Scott* case? Or did the Constitution approve the spread of slavery to the developing western territories? Did the Supreme Court merely effectuate a policy choice dictated by the authors of the Constitution? If so, there must be a single, true, ascertainable meaning to the Constitution, which judges merely enunciate. But, in fact, there is no "true" meaning of all the Constitution's provisions. Many of the phrases in the Constitution are inherently ambiguous, especially those in the Bill of Rights and the Fourteenth Amendment. What is the meaning of the phrase "due process of law"? What about "*unreasonable* search and seizure"? It is difficult for judges to avoid the task of giving meaning to constitutional phrases.

With respect to the Court's actions in *Dred Scott*, it is obvious that the authors of the Constitution were so divided in their opinions about slavery that they simply deferred policy decisions to later generations, declaring in 1787 that the "importation of such persons as any of the States now existing shall think proper to admit shall not be prohibited by the Congress prior to the year [1808]."[30] Moreover, the majority of justices in the *Dred Scott* decision could have resolved that case on procedural grounds without addressing the issue of congressional power. Instead, they went far beyond what they needed to consider to resolve the case because they wished to address the issue of congressional power over slavery.[31] Such actions demonstrate the inevitable influence of judicial officers' values, attitudes, and policy preferences in determining case outcomes. Judges do not merely interpret law; they shape the law and thereby influence and determine public policy.

## Judicial Policy Making and the Concept of Democracy

The legitimacy issue underlying judicial policy making rests on the appropriateness of the judiciary's actions in formulating and implementing public policies. The primary argument against courts' involvement in policy making emphasizes that the principles of democracy require citizen participation and control of government and public policy. According to this argument, public policies should be developed by elected officials because, if the citizenry objects to the policies, they can hold the officials accountable and vote them out of office. Thus, the electoral process permits citizens to control public policy by electing and removing government officials on the basis of the policy agendas those officials pursue. Under this scenario, judges in states that use electoral judicial selection methods might be considered legitimate, accountable policy makers. Federal judges, in contrast, do not fit this conception of democratic control, because they are not elected and are not removable by the electorate. When federal judges make decisions affecting public policy, their decisions are arguably illegitimate because the American people have no way to control the policy imposed on them by the federal judiciary.

If one defines democracy as citizen control of government and public policy, then policy-making decisions by federal judges could be considered undemocratic. However, is this really the appropriate conception of democracy under the American constitutional system? What are the implications of direct and exclusive citizen control of public policy development through electoral pressure on the legislative and executive branches? The elected branches of government are structured to respond to majoritarian and wealthy political interests. Elected officials frequently respond to what they perceive as the wishes of the majority. If public opinion runs strongly for or against a particular policy, it creates pressure on government officials who wish to retain their positions. Elected officials also respond to wealthy interests, which can donate money to political campaigns and thereby advance the politicians' goal of remaining in office. Thus, political action committees, corporations, and other wealthy and well-organized interests exercise significant influence on legislative policy making.[32] The policy-making operations of the legislative and executive branches, with their close links to the electoral process, inevitably favor either the priorities and self-interest of electoral majorities or the goals of special, organized political interests. As a result, there are serious risks that the interests of political minorities and unorganized or disadvantaged groups will be ignored in the policy process. Moreover, the advancement of interests according to public opinion and electoral pressure may create ''tyranny of the majority'' under which political minorities are actually victimized. The maintenance of racial segregation, for example, advanced the interests of the white majority, which gained privileges and advantages through the exclusion of African-Americans from full participation in the economic system and in other aspects of American society. Racial discrimination in the United States was very ''democratic'' in the sense that it was supported by a majority of citizens and by the elected officials they placed in public office.

As the foregoing example starkly illustrates, the American conception of limited democracy is not captured by simplistic definitions equating democracy with majority rule or with complete control of public policy by elected officials. The fact that a Bill of Rights and additional amendments were added to the Constitution to protect the rights of individuals offers clear evidence that the American constitutional system is not based on simple majority rule. The concept of democracy under the U.S. Constitution involves citizen participation in and control of government through the electoral process *plus the protection of rights for individuals*. The specific provisions of the Bill of Rights and subsequent amendments limit policy directives that the majoritarian or special interest-driven elected branches of government may pursue. A majority of citizens may wish, for example, to discriminate against particular racial groups or prevent specific groups from expressing their political views. Indeed, American history is full of episodes in which legislative and executive policies were designed to discriminate against women,[33] African-Americans,[34] Japanese-Americans,[35] Chinese-Americans,[36] Jehovah's Witnesses,[37] Communists,[38] and other groups that lacked sufficient numbers and political power to protect themselves through the electoral process. The protections enunciated in the Bill of Rights require that the majority's policy preferences be limited when those policies impinge on the rights of other individuals. The federal judiciary is explicitly structured to prevent the application of direct electoral pressure on judges, thus permitting judges to make independent decisions. Judges, as interpreters of the Constitution and as decision makers insulated from direct electoral pressure, are the governmental actors who must ensure that the rights of political minorities are protected against violations by the majority and by special interests' influence on the legislative and executive branches. Judicial policy making is not inherently illegitimate in light of the American constitutional system's concept of democracy. Judges must identify and enforce limitations on majority policy preferences that threaten the protected constitutional rights of individuals.

Although the judiciary can play an important role in enforcing individuals' constitutional rights, not all judicial policy making fulfills this function of the courts. As illustrated by the *Dred Scott* case, on many occasions judges invalidated legislative actions that would have protected political minorities. Court decisions that clash with the policy preferences of elected officials may not always serve the judiciary's role as the guardian of individual rights. Depending on the values and ideologies of the judges on the bench, court decisions can represent assertions of judicial power that negate policies generated by the democratic electoral system and do not advance the constitutional interest in individual rights.

## The Legitimacy Issue: Prisoner Litigation

The legitimacy of judicial policy making in the American governmental system can be examined through the example of prisoners' rights litigation. Incarcerated criminal offenders constitute a despised minority without political power to influence the policies of legislative and executive officials, a minority that has earned its despised status by causing harm to society. For most of American history, judges ignored prisoners, declaring that convicted offenders are "slave[s]" of the state[39] or that courts should defer to the expertise of correctional administrators.[40] In the 1960s and 1970s, however, in order to protect the limited rights retained by convicted offenders, judicial decisions began to limit the correctional policies of legislative and state officials.

Is it appropriate for judges to enforce policies that favor the interests of people who have harmed society? The words of the Bill of Rights provide a basis for judicial scrutiny of governmental policies that infringe on individuals' rights—even if the individuals in question have earned their despised status. The Eighth Amendment, for example, forbids the application of "cruel and unusual punishments." If these words have any meaning at all—and presumably they do, because they were placed in the nation's fundamental document—they clearly imply a limitation on what government may do to punish convicted criminals. The government may punish criminals, but that punishment must not violate constitutional standards by being "cruel and unusual." Because these words are general and ambiguous, there is no easy way to determine which punishments violate constitutional standards. Thus, judges face difficult questions when examining whether prisoners' rights have been violated. For example, should someone serving a short sentence for a minor criminal offense be permitted to die of injury or disease by being deprived of medical care? Should corrections officials be permitted to use beatings or electric shocks to kill prisoners who were not sentenced to death? Should a prisoner serving a short sentence be subjected to the lifelong physical effects of malnutrition by being underfed while incarcerated? As these questions imply, government officials may sometimes apply "cruel and unusual punishments'' unless judges can shape correctional policies by limiting the risk of mistreatment of convicted offenders.

Although the responsibility for interpreting and protecting the Bill of Rights inevitably leads judges to influence the development of public policy, there are no precise guidelines to prevent judges from going "too far." For example, judges have sought to prevent overcrowded, unsanitary, and dangerous prison conditions by specifying the number of offenders who may be incarcerated in a particular prison and by reviewing institutional policies and procedures.[41] Although these judicial decisions are designed to protect the Eighth Amendment rights of prisoners, they can have undesirable unintended consequences. Such decisions have led to increasing violence as inmates and staff adjust to new, judicially-imposed rules and procedures[42] and to significant correctional expenditures by state governments that remove resources from other services and programs.[43] People may agree that judges must prevent "cruel and unusual punishments," but there is no consensus about what precisely constitutes improper punishments. Thus, it may be clear that judges have a role in enforcing the constitutional boundaries for public policy initiatives. However, the breadth of judges' proper authority over public policy is subject to dispute.

## LIMITATIONS ON JUDICIAL POLICY MAKING

The recognition that the constitutional system gives judges a role in shaping public policy does not answer all questions surrounding the legitimacy of judicial policy making. Although judicial policy making is a planned component of the American definition of democracy—citizen participation *plus* the protection of individual rights—there are no obvious limits on judges' formal power to determine public policy. If federal judges are removed from direct electoral accountability so that they are free to clash with majoritarian preferences while enforcing the Bill of Rights, what prevents judges from using their protected tenure to go beyond the appropriate boundaries of their power? In other words, without electoral accountability, what keeps federal judges from becoming dictators who make whatever decisions they wish? Obviously, the independence of federal judges in the protection of the Bill of Rights should not become a license for dictatorial behavior. Because federal judges cannot be removed from office, except in extraordinary circumstances producing impeachment, there are no apparent limitations on their pursuit of personal policy preferences, even if those policies are harmful to society or constitutionally improper. The same question may be posed regarding state judges who are appointed to office, and judges selected through merit selection systems who face little likelihood of being ousted through periodic retention elections.

It would be extremely disconcerting if black-robed dictators could direct public policy with complete freedom. Although this behavior might in some way comport with the protection of individual rights, it would clash with the other aspect of the American conception of democracy—citizen involvement in government and public policy. Fortunately, despite the absence of formal constraints on its policy-making authority, the judicial branch is a component of the larger political system, so there are several significant limitations on judges' ability to become dictatorial. These limitations may not be recognized by the public or even by judges themselves, but they keep the judiciary's decisions from becoming too out-of-step with the evolution of values and public policy preferences in American society.

## Judges' Role Conceptions and Self-Restraint

As chapter 7 explained, judges do not merely follow their own policy preferences in deciding cases. Policy preferences are an important underlying factor, but judges constrain their own personal preferences if they believe that the expression of such preferences is inappropriate in a given judicial decision. Research on decision making by appellate judges indicates that judges' conceptions of the proper judicial role limit the breadth of their decisions. If judges view themselves as "Interpreters" or "Realists" as opposed to "Innovators," they will weigh very carefully the propriety and anticipated consequences of any policy-influencing decision.[44] Although a judge may believe that a particular policy would be "best for society," he or she may decline to advance that policy through a judicial decision because of a belief that the issue in question is appropriately reserved for the legislative and/or executive branches of government. A dissenting opinion by four justices illustrated this position in a case in which the majority invalidated a Texas statute designed to prevent illegal alien children from attending public schools. Chief Justice Warren Burger wrote:

> Were it our business to set the Nation's social policy, I would agree without hesitation that it is senseless for an enlightened society to deprive any children—including illegal aliens—of an elementary education. I fully agree that it would be folly—and wrong—to tolerate the creation of a segment of society made up of illiterate persons, many having a limited or no command of our language. However, the Constitution does not constitute us as "Platonic Guardians" nor does it vest in this Court the authority to strike down laws because they do not meet our standards of desirable social policy, "wisdom," or "common sense."[45]

Politically conservative judicial officers frequently employ language of restraint in their opinions about the necessity of restraining the judiciary. However, their use of language should not imply that political conservatism is necessarily associated with judicial self-restraint. When justices appointed by Presidents Reagan and Bush altered the composition of the Supreme Court in the 1980s and early 1990s, they quickly demonstrated their judicial activism by changing case precedents[46] and by altering the meaning of established statutes with which they disagreed.[47] For example, Chief Justice Rehnquist was unsuccessful in persuading Congress to limit prisoners' petitions to the federal courts by altering the governing statutes addressing such petitions.[48] By filing *habeas corpus* petitions, prisoners employ the traditional legal mechanism for asking a court to examine the legality of their incarceration. After the formal appeal process is concluded, *habeas corpus* procedures permit prisoners to raise additional issues of alleged constitutional violations in their arrests and convictions. Although Congress did not follow Rehnquist's suggestions until 1996, the emerging conservative majority on the Supreme Court issued a judicial decision in 1991 to advance the same goal that the legislative branch had rejected.[49] Because procedures for prisoners' petitions are governed by congressional statutes, Justice Thurgood Marshall criticized the Court majority for ''[t]his doctrinal innovation, which repudiates a line of judicial decisions codified by Congress in the governing statute and procedural rules.''[50]

Both liberal and conservative judges may exercise self-restraint because of their beliefs about the proper exercise of authority under the constitutional system and because of their concerns about the judiciary's image in the eyes of the public. The power of the judicial branch is regarded as flowing from its reputation as a ''legal'' rather than a ''political'' institution. Judicial officers concerned about the judiciary's image may restrain their own decision making in order to preserve the courts' legitimacy. The preservation of judicial legitimacy is premised on the practical expectation that people will be less likely to obey legal decisions if they do not regard judges' opinions as proper, legitimate pronouncements based on law rather than on politics. Justice Felix Frankfurter arrived at the Supreme Court with a reputation as a liberal activist but quickly became known as a consistent advocate of judicial self-restraint.[51] He articulated the most well-known warning to the judiciary regarding the maintenance of its image:

> The Court's authority—possessed neither of purse nor sword—ultimately rests on sustained public confidence in its moral sanction. Such feeling must be nourished by the Court's complete detachment, in fact and in appearance, from political entanglements and by abstention from injecting itself into the class of political forces in political settlements.[52]

Justice Antonin Scalia, a conservative Reagan appointee, has issued similar warnings that the judiciary must avoid being viewed as a political branch of government:

> [I]t is not statesmanlike to needlessly prolong the Court's self-awarded sovereignty over a field where it has little proper business since the answers to most cruel questions are political not juridical—a sovereignty which therefore quite properly, but to the great damage of the Court, makes it the object of the sort of organized public pressure that political institutions in a democracy ought to receive.[53]

In Scalia's view, if the judicial branch does not protect its legitimacy through self-restraint, it "will destroy itself."[54] Obviously, judicial officers preoccupied with the courts' image may be inclined *in some cases* to limit the scope of their own decision making. Although Justice Frankfurter and his colleague of the 1950s and 1960s, Justice John Harlan, were fairly consistent in urging restraint by the Supreme Court, the contemporary justices who employ the language of restraint seem to apply the concept more selectively. Justice Scalia, in particular, has provided many examples of activist inclinations when they suited his conservative policy preferences concerning freedom of religion, criminal punishment, and other issues.[55]

Concern for the judiciary's image may also induce judges to follow precedents with which they disagree. Judges may not want the judiciary to appear unpredictable or unstable. They may also feel that certain precedents are so well-established and accepted that it would be disruptive to alter them. Moreover, judges may believe that change should be introduced gradually, so that precedents are modified over a series of cases rather than reversed abruptly in a single decision. This concern for the appearance of stability in law may lead judges to modify and restrain the expression of their policy preferences. In 1992, for example, despite previously joining opinions harshly criticizing the abortion precedent *Roe v. Wade*, Justice Anthony Kennedy declined to cast the decisive vote to overturn *Roe*. Instead, he co-authored a joint opinion with Justices Souter and O'Connor that preserved *Roe* by emphasizing the need to preserve established precedents to protect the Court's image as a legal rather than political institution.[56]

The notion that many judges constrain their own decisions when public policy is involved does not provide firm reassurance that the judiciary will not engage in improper assertions of authority. Self-restraint is, however, only one of several elements that restrict the expression of policy preferences by judges.

## The Structure of Courts

The potential for improper decisions is diminished by the hierarchical structure of state and federal court systems. If lower court judges' decisions go beyond certain boundaries, they will be overruled by appellate courts. One of the functions of the appeals process is to create uniformity in judicial decisions within an appellate jurisdiction and thereby to prevent excessive creativity or unwarranted assertions of judicial power by individual judges.

Although trial courts and intermediate appellate courts are held in check by the highest courts in each jurisdiction, what prevents the U.S. Supreme Court and state supreme courts from behaving dictatorially? State supreme courts are limited, in part, because they come under the authority of the U.S. Supreme Court on issues concerning federal law or the U.S. Constitution. Thus, the U.S. Supreme Court's interpretation of the Constitution limits the potential actions of any state courts.

In addition, the U.S. Supreme Court, state supreme courts, and other appellate courts are constrained by their structures as collegial judicial bodies. No single judge determines outcomes in appellate cases. Judges must compromise, persuade, and otherwise interact with their colleagues to develop a stable majority coalition for each decision. The process of interacting with and pleasing other judges inevitably limits the scope of potential decisions because extreme viewpoints must be moderated and compromised to attract the support of other judges. The likelihood that any particular decision will go "too far" is lessened by the fact that all decisions must satisfy the role orientations and sense of propriety of a majority of the appellate judges.

Individual judges may have their greatest impact on smaller courts. Thus, an extremist judge can influence the outcome of a case by persuading only one colleague on an intermediate appellate panel of three judges. The utilization of three-member panels does not, however, invite excessive assertions of judicial power. In the federal system, other appellate judges in the circuit can rehear controversial cases *en banc* and thereby ensure that policy decisions reflect the views of a majority of the six to fifteen judges who hear *en banc* cases in each circuit. In state courts systems, intermediate appellate decisions are subject to review by the state supreme court. Moreover, the U.S. Supreme Court's nine-member size ensures that the ultimate review and decision in legal cases involves the agreement of at least five justices. Because very few presidents enjoy the opportunity to appoint five justices, Supreme Court decisions usually must satisfy justices appointed by different presidents and whose views were shaped by different historical eras.

The moderating effects of multiple viewpoints on an appellate court may constrain judicial decision making even when a president or a succession of like-minded presidents make multiple appointments that load the Supreme Court and other federal courts with judicial officers from the same political party. The president does not "control" judicial outcomes. Individual judicial officers' decisions may deviate from presidential expectations.[57] Thus, a president who attempts to foster a precise judicial policy agenda is likely to be disappointed with at least some decisions. For example, Reagan appointees Justices Antonin Scalia and Anthony Kennedy disappointed fellow Republicans, including Reagan's former vice-president and successor, George Bush, by joining the most liberal justices to provide the necessary votes for a five-to-four decision protecting flag burning as a form of free political expression.[58]

Judicial selection methods and the composition of courts also limit the risks of excessive judicial influence on public policy. In states with electoral systems, the voters have the opportunity to replace judicial officers whose decisions are regarded as too extreme or as inappropriately influencing public policy. Governors, legislatures, and selection committees seek to appoint new judges with appropriately restrained conceptions of judicial power—especially if previous appointees have seemed to push the limits of judicial authority beyond proper boundaries. Similarly, the president will seek to appoint judges whose views on judicial policy making comport with those of the president's administration and political party. For example, President Reagan and his supporters were not satisfied with the judicial policy making of the appointees of previous presidents. The Reagan administration countered this trend by consciously screening candidates to identify their positions on specific public policies, especially on previously established judicial policies. If the judiciary begins to move too fast or too far in its decision making, the president can pull judicial decisions back to the political center by gradually appointing new kinds of judges when the incumbents die, retire, or resign. Because the president is selected by nationwide election, the process of selecting judges gradually tracks, in a very rough fashion, the general policy preferences of the electorate. When the voters change direction and select a new president from a different political party, judicial appointments gradually reflect the change. The federal judiciary may be rooted in an earlier era and committed to outdated policy preferences when the country undergoes a dramatic political shift,[59] as when Franklin Roosevelt's liberal New Deal coalition gained power in the 1930s. The holdover Supreme Court justices systematically invalidated Roosevelt's economic regulation and social welfare legislation. The infusion of new appointees, however, eventually leads the courts in the direction of evolving societal change as demonstrated by the alteration in Supreme Court decisions as Roosevelt began appointing new justices in 1937. Thus, the judicial selection process helps keep the judiciary's composition and decisions from deviating too far from the general preferences of the voters.

Because judicial appointees are drawn from mainstream American society and have succeeded in mainstream party politics, judges are unlikely to bring to the bench policy preferences that are wholly different from those of large segments of the American public. Very few judges are radical reformers pursuing extremist policy agendas. Judges generally come from the affluent political elite whose values and interests favor the maintenance of the general policy preferences of their historical era. Thus, the policy outcomes produced by judicial decisions are usually very similar to the policy initiatives advocated by other political actors. Judicial policy decisions may be controversial and generate opposition, but the underlying controversies do not generally reflect unique or idiosyncratic policy preferences. Instead, the controversies and attendant condemnations of judicial policy making reflect deep divisions in American society on issues about which there is no public consensus. During the 1970s and 1980s, courts were harshly criticized for decisions affecting such issues as abortion, affirmative action, and school desegregation. In each instance, although substantial segments of the public opposed these judicial decisions, other large segments of society supported the policy preferences advanced by the judiciary. A lack of consensus in American society prevents the Supreme Court from making "final" decisions about controversial policy issues. As long as there are interests pushing to change a specific judicial policy, there is always the possibility that the Supreme Court, especially when composed of new appointees, will revisit and change constitutional doctrines to reflect the views of the high court's current composition.

## External Constraints

Because the judicial branch is a component of the political system rather than a separate entity, judicial policy making is affected by interactions with other branches of government. When courts issue decisions, other political entities react, especially if judicial decisions conflict with the policy goals of other political institutions. Judges are cognizant of the power of other governmental and political actors, and so judicial decisions may be limited by anticipation of external reactions.

Legislatures can take several steps to react to judicial decisions. When judges interpret statutes in a manner with which legislators disagree, the legislators can directly modify the decision by enacting new legislation to clarify the meaning of the statute in question. In 1988, for example, Congress passed the Civil Rights Restoration Act to reverse a Supreme Court decision limiting the application of a gender discrimination statute aimed at colleges and universities.[60] In 1991, Congress passed another civil rights act to reverse several 1989 Supreme Court decisions limiting the scope of antidiscrimination laws.[61] As in other disputes between Congress and the Supreme Court, legislators will continue to initiate new laws when they are unhappy with statutory interpretations produced by the judiciary.

Congress also initiates constitutional amendments when it disagrees with judicial decisions. In the aftermath of judicial decisions on abortion, school prayer, school desegregation, and other controversial matters, members of Congress have proposed constitutional amendments to alter judicial interpretations of the Constitution. Although recent efforts to amend the Constitution have not succeeded, on several occasions in history the amendment process has successfully nullified Supreme Court decisions.[62] The Sixteenth Amendment, which approved federal income taxation in 1913, overruled a Supreme Court decision that struck down congressional efforts to implement an income tax by statute.[63] The ratification of the Twenty-sixth Amendment, which lowered the voting age to eighteen, also followed a Supreme Court decision.[64]

Congress has attempted to enact legislation to limit the judiciary's jurisdiction over issues in which legislators disagree with court decisions. Article III of the Constitution creates the Supreme Court but empowers Congress to create and define other aspects of the federal judicial system. Thus, congressional statutes define the lower federal courts as well as their jurisdiction and procedures. It is possible for Congress to enact statutes that reduce the jurisdiction of federal courts, including the Supreme Court. Congress might attempt, for example, to pass a statute that removes a specific issue from the courts' jurisdictional authority. Except for one notable example that occurred after the Civil War when the

Supreme Court acquiesced in a congressional withdrawal of appellate jurisdiction,[65] this method of constraining judicial policy making has not directly affected the judiciary. Members of Congress are reluctant to tamper with courts' jurisdiction, and questions linger concerning the constitutional propriety of complete withdrawal of jurisdiction over issues—questions that judges themselves will answer if such statutes are ever passed. Because the Constitution declares that ''[t]he judicial power shall be vested in one Supreme Court and in inferior courts [established by] Congress'' and that ''[t]he judicial power shall extend to all cases, in law and equity, arising under the Constitution [and] the laws of the United States,''[66] there is significant doubt about whether the judiciary would acquiesce in a congressional attempt to limit jurisdiction *by statute*. The Constitution declares that the judiciary's power extends over ''all cases,'' so the Constitution itself may have to be amended in order to limit court jurisdiction. The threat of altered jurisdictions, although not frequently exercised and of doubtful validity, may deter judges from forthrightly advancing policy preferences that clash with legislative preferences. During the 1950s, for example, the Supreme Court issued a controversial decision limiting congressional authority to conduct hearings in investigating American Communists[67] as well as other decisions affecting internal security. Two years later, the Court appeared to modify its position in order to grant Congress greater power in such investigations.[68] Many commentators have attributed the change in the Supreme Court's decisions to the threat of jurisdiction-curbing legislation initiated in Congress during the intervening period:

> Bills were introduced aimed at the Court's rulings on internal security matters such as legislative investigations, the executive's loyalty-security programs, state control of teachers and admission of lawyers to the practice of law, and federal preemption of state internal subversion legislation. None of the bills passed, although the Senate vote was very close (a one-vote margin) and the Court appeared to retreat in the face of the attack.[69]

The president may pressure the judiciary by advocating or proposing legislation and constitutional amendments designed to limit judicial policy making. In the most famous presidential threat to the Supreme Court, Franklin Roosevelt, displeased with the Court's obstruction of his legislative program, proposed that the Supreme Court be restructured to permit the president to appoint an additional justice whenever a serving justice reached the age of seventy. The immediate effect of the proposal would have been to permit Roosevelt to make six new appointments and instantly change the balance of power on an enlarged Supreme Court. Although Roosevelt's plan encountered significant political opposition, the confrontation was defused when Justice Owen Roberts changed his position on economic regulation issues—the so-called ''switch in time that saved nine,''— and thereby placed the Court in line with the nation's legislative policy. Soon thereafter, justices began to retire from the Court, and Roosevelt replaced them with his own political supporters.[70] The political threat facing the institution of the Supreme Court may very well have led Justice Roberts and other justices to reconsider their opposition to the policy preferences of the elected branches of government.

## Concerns About Compliance

Because judges have limited ability to implement and enforce their decisions, judicial policy making is constrained by any anticipation of adverse public reactions. During the Supreme Court's deliberations in *Brown v. Board of Education*, for example, the justices' desire to dismantle racial segregation was constrained by their twin desires to maximize the legitimacy of their pronouncement through a unanimous decision and to implement the decision gradually to avoid excessive social upheaval.[71] As a result, the initial *Brown* decision in 1954 was a general policy declaration with great symbolic effect but with few immediate practical consequences.[72] The second *Brown* decision in 1955 concerned implementation and required only that schools be desegregated with ''all deliberate speed'' rather than with dramatic, immediate reforms.[73] The justices' concerns about adverse public reactions limited both the formulation and the impact of their policy decision.

Judges must also be concerned with producing judicial decisions that executive branch officials will obey and enforce. For example, Supreme Court decisions in the 1830s favored the protection of the Cherokee Nation's rights and property against encroachment by whites in Georgia, but President Andrew Jackson refused to enforce the decisions. As a result, those Native Americans were forcibly marched to Oklahoma, with hundreds dying along the way—despite the fact that they had prevailed in court.[74] Jackson is reported to have said ''Well, [Chief Justice] John Marshall has made his decision, now let him enforce it.''[75] Jackson's statement and actions are an extreme example of the practical issues of enforcement that may limit judges' policy-making decisions. If there is noncompliance with court decisions, judges can issue additional orders, but they must rely on governors and presidents to supply law enforcement personnel to ensure that such orders are implemented. The implementation decision in the second *Brown v. Board of Education* decision may have been guided by the justices' concern for the existence and degree of presidential support that would underlie enforcement of the controversial decision. The *amicus* brief submitted by the Solicitor General on behalf of the Eisenhower administration contained the phrase ''all deliberate speed,'' and the justices, in adopting the phrase, may have viewed the brief as a signal that President Eisenhower was willing to enforce the decision, but not on an immediate, massive scale.[76] Indeed, despite his general lack of concern about racial equality,[77] the President eventually deployed military forces to ensure that nine African-American students could attend Central High School in Little Rock, Arkansas, in the face of violent white opposition.

# IMPLEMENTATION OF JUDICIAL DECISIONS

The process of implementing judges' policy declarations inevitably reshapes and limits the application of court decisions. Limitations affecting the interpretation and implementation of judicial policies further constrain policy making by the courts. Because judicial decisions are not self-implementing, they must pass through the hands of various influential actors before they affect people's lives as public policies. The involvement of actors with varying political attitudes, values, and partisan interests can lead to inconsistent and unpredictable outcomes that diminish judicial officers' ability to ensure that policy decisions accomplish their intended goals. In a useful model for illustrating the implementation and impact of judicial policies, Charles Johnson and Bradley Canon identified interpreters, implementers, and consumers who, along with external political actors, determine precisely whether and how judges' decisions will affect society.[78]

## Interpreters

After judges issue a decision, the judicial opinion and its implications must be communicated and explained to the people who will carry it out. Police officers, for example, may not follow closely the developing case law affecting search and seizure, *Miranda* warnings, and the other aspects of their jobs that are shaped by judicial decisions. Police officers do not have easy access to judges' opinions on such issues, nor do they have the time or training to study and interpret the judges' intended meanings. Thus, other actors interpret and explain judicial decisions.

The most far-reaching policy pronouncements come from the Supreme Court and other appellate courts. Frequently, if a trial judge makes a decision affecting public policy, the policy will not be implemented until the issue has been examined by higher courts. When appellate courts issue policy decisions, their decisions are often limited to broad announcements describing the duties of governmental officials or providing directions for officials involved in a particular case. Thus, there remains uncertainty about how the appellate decision applies to other cases with factual circumstances similar, but not identical, to the case decided by the appellate court. The interpretation and explanation of judicial policy is developed gradually by the trial judges who apply the appellate decision to individual circumstances in new cases concerning that particular policy issue. In *Brown v. Board of Education*, the Supreme Court explicitly acknowledged this interpretation and implementation process by instructing the federal district courts to examine alleged racial segregation in school systems and to develop remedies on a case-by-case basis. In other areas, the interpreting role of trial judges is equally inevitable but is based on less explicit instructions. After the Supreme Court declared that criminal suspects must be informed of their rights prior to questioning (the

*Miranda* decision),[79] trial judges had to decide exactly when the warnings must be given, whether the warnings must be precisely phrased, whether any questions could be asked of suspects prior to the warnings, and other questions not specifically answered in *Miranda*. Some of these issues were clarified by the Supreme Court in subsequent appeals, but because not all defendants fully pursue the appeal process or initiate other actions to challenge their convictions, the trial judges' interpretations frequently determine the outcomes of cases.

Other officials may also serve as interpreters. Unlike trial judges who provide authoritative interpretations, other interpreters guide the behavior of officials who enforce judicial policies. Although their interpretations may turn out to be incorrect if a trial court reaches a different conclusion about the same issue, these interpreters still affect judicial policies that affect the lives of citizens. For example, city attorneys advise police departments and school systems on the meaning and implications of judicial policy decisions. State attorneys generally interpret decisions and provide instructions to state and local officials about how to follow judicial policy pronouncements. Thus, teachers, police officers, and other "street-level bureaucrats" use these interpretations, whether accurate or not, to establish policies and practices that affect people in society.

What are the consequences of this interpretation process? Various interpreters may interpret and explain the judicial policies in different ways. Moreover, some interpreters may never even hear of specific judicial decisions, especially if they are in small towns and without immediate access to the latest appellate opinions. Thus, the actual meaning and implementation of the judicial policy may vary from city to city. Varying interpretations of the judges' intentions may stem from ambiguity in the wording of the judicial decision, mistaken perceptions of interpreters, or even willful efforts by interpreters to alter the meaning of the judicial decision. If city officials object to a judicial decision, they may intentionally interpret it as applying to only a limited range of circumstances. This may force a citizen to go back through the lengthy litigation process in order to force the officials to follow a precise directive from the courts. In the meantime, the city officials may succeed in weakening and delaying implementation of a policy that they oppose.

## Implementers

Even if judicial policies are explained, they do not affect society according to the judges' intentions unless the officials responsible for carrying out the policies implement the directives properly. The *Miranda* decision, for example, is primarily a symbolic declaration unless police officers follow their instructions to inform suspects about the right to counsel and the right against self-incrimination. The success or failure of judicial policies can depend on whether implementers have heard about the policies, whether they have understood the explanations of the policy's meaning, and whether they will comply with the policy directives.

A failure to comply with judicial policies may stem from a lack of understanding or from an intentional effort to subvert a policy. When federal courts issued orders to desegregate public schools, many school systems in the South refused to comply. They knew what they were supposed to do, but the judicial policy did not take effect because the implementers disagreed with it and intentionally failed to follow its directives. This willful noncompliance rested on a hope that other political actors—such as Congress—would combat the courts' decisions and prevent desegregation through a constitutional amendment or some other means. Eventually, additional judicial decisions levied fines on school systems, legislative and executive actions withheld funds, and law enforcement or military forces directed compliance in several cities.

Failure to implement judicial policies can take place in more subtle ways as well. For example, an individual police officer who makes an arrest in an alley with no witnesses present can treat, or mistreat, the suspect in violation of judicial policies governing police behavior. If the suspect asserts that the police officer did not inform him of his rights and the police officer says that the suspect is lying, a judge must decide which witness is more credible. Such decisions are likely to go against a criminal suspect—whether or not the suspect is telling the truth. Because the contexts in which suspects are arrested and questioned vary, the Supreme Court cannot protect the rights of criminal suspects. The Court can issue rules, which, if followed, would protect suspects' rights. However, the actual protection of such rights rests primarily in the hands of individual police officers who control the implementation of those rights according to whether they understand and obey the Supreme Court's directives.

Sometimes an individual police officer's failure to follow judicial policies in such areas as search and seizure may stem from a lack of knowledge of the most recent, technical court decisions explaining the nuances of appropriate police behavior. Police cannot be expected to read and understand the most recent judicial decisions, because certain areas of law are refined by new decisions every year. There may be weaknesses in the process of communicating details of judges' decisions to implementers, and these weaknesses reduce the effectiveness of judicial policies. The spate of decisions by conservative judges in the late 1980s and early 1990s exacerbated the difficulties experienced by police officers. These decisions eliminated some restrictions on police behavior affecting questioning suspects, search and seizure, and other areas, and thereby obscured the boundaries of proper law enforcement practices.[80]

## Consumers

The people directly affected by court decisions can also influence their implementation. Although government officials are affected by judicial decisions, their authoritative roles place them in the implementer category. Consumers are the private citizens and corporations affected by judicial decisions. For example, in the case decisions affecting the rights of criminal suspects, the consumers are the individuals investigated, questioned, or arrested by the police. In school desegregation cases, consumers are the parents and schoolchildren directly affected by a court order within a specific school system. Consumers may hear about important judicial policy decisions through the news media, but they rarely learn about the most recent court cases. What if implementers fail to respect the consumers' rights in accordance with judicial directives? If the consumers do not realize that their rights have been violated, the judicial policy will not be effectuated because no one will complain about the lack of implementation. For example, if a public school teacher in a small town leads prayers in the classroom in violation of the Supreme Court's 1962 decision in *Engel v. Vitale*,[81] but no student or parent realizes that this is improper, no one will complain and seek enforcement of the judicial policy. If a consumer recognizes a rights violation but is frustrated by resistance from a school system or other government agency or cannot afford to hire a lawyer, the consumer may not follow through to ensure that the policy is implemented. In small, homogeneous communities, if the entire community disagrees with a judicial policy—such as the prohibition on organized prayer in public schools—the judicial policy may be repeatedly violated, but no consumer will seek implementation of the policy. Alternatively, consumers' resistance may defeat intended policies if they boycott schools to protest desegregation or otherwise refuse to supply the public participation essential to the success of any public policy. Thus, consumers play an important role in the implementation, or lack thereof, of judicial policies.

## Secondary Groups

Many external political actors influence the development and implementation of judicial decisions. The president and state governors are important enforcers. Their commitment, or lack thereof, to the enforcement of judicial decisions can significantly affect implementation of the judges' intentions. Interest groups frequently bear the burden of pressing for implementation of judicial decisions. Because consumers, though directly affected by judicial policies, are frequently unaware of court decisions or lack the resources to require enforcement of such decisions, interest groups utilize their organizational expertise and resources to initiate additional legal action, publicize government officials' failure to obey judges' orders, lobby for enforcement measures, and otherwise seek to effectuate judicial decisions that favor their policy preferences. The public relations activities of interest groups may educate consumers as well as influence interpreters and implementers. The news media play an important role in disseminating information about judicial decisions to interpreters, implementers, and consumers. Moreover, news reports help to keep judges themselves informed about the consequences of their decisions, and thereby influence future judicial decisions, including actions to accelerate implementation. Legislators, scholars, and others are also part of the judicial policy process because their actions influence and inform the actors most directly responsible for interpretation and implementation of judicial decisions. Politicians may, for example, lend legitimacy and encouragement to citizens who resist judicial orders—as often occurred in school desegregation cases—and thereby hinder the effectuation of judicial policies.

### The Consequences of the Implementation Process

Several scholarly studies provide examples of the effects of the implementation process in shaping, changing, or negating judicial policy making. For example, a study of lower court decisions concerning the public's right of access to judicial proceedings indicated that federal district court judges might resist implementation of Supreme Court decisions on their own—even without public opposition or significant controversy surrounding the judicial policy.[82]

Research on judicial policy making indicates that the sources and quality of information available to implementers vary greatly from one city to another.[83] A study of Wisconsin police departments in the aftermath of the *Miranda* decision found varying patterns of compliance with the Supreme Court's directive for police to inform criminal suspects of their rights.[84] The more professionalized departments received information about the decision from several sources, including formal conferences and training sessions.[85] Because the quality and completeness of information varied from department to department, the implementers in different cities had different perceptions of the precise requirements of the judicial policy and its desirability. These mixed perceptions led to differing applications of the judicial policy depending on the arresting officer's knowledge about and commitment to the policy of informing arrestees of their rights.

A study of compliance with Supreme Court decisions forbidding organized religious activities in public schools found that in one city "[w]hile superintendents soberly answered mail questionnaires to the effect that their schools were in full compliance with the Court's interpretation of the Constitution, many teachers led pupils in a wide variety of morning and afternoon prayers, Bible reading, and hymns."[86] In this community and other locales where the Supreme Court's policy directives were ignored, no implementer took responsibility for ensuring compliance. Moreover, school officials had little incentive to clash with the local consensus against the policy, especially when few, if any, consumers were sufficiently interested and able to challenge the lack of compliance.[87]

 As these examples demonstrate, judges are not omnipotent. The practical political world which they attempt to shape through judicial policy making is not readily controllable. Judges' decisions are influenced by internal and external factors. The consequences of judicial decisions are subsequently shaped by the degree of understanding and cooperation exhibited by the political actors who must implement court decrees. Without sufficient cooperation and support from executive branch officials and the public, judicial policies may be rendered ineffective.[88]

Even legendary, courageous judicial policy initiatives, such as *Brown v. Board of Education*, may have more symbolic than substantive policy value because of the difficult implementation process. Gerald Rosenberg's studies of judicial policy making have raised questions concerning the effectiveness of judicial action as a means to generate social change. With respect to school desegregation, Rosenberg argues that the *Brown* decision had little practical impact for most school systems and that measurable national changes developed only after Congress and the president took action in the 1960s.[89] Although courts may be visible actors in many policy issues, analysts need to be wary of either crediting courts with policy successes or condemning courts for policy failures unless they have taken into account the myriad, complex factors that may affect policy development.[90]

# THE CAPACITY OF JUDGES FOR EFFECTIVE POLICY MAKING

In addition to the debates surrounding the legitimacy of and limitations on judicial policy making, there are practical issues concerning the capacity of judges to make good policies. Are courts structured to be viable forums for effective policy decisions? Although judicial decisions are shaped by the personal and political influences that affect decisions in other branches of government, decision-making processes in the judicial branch are structured differently than parallel processes in other governmental institutions. The judicial process involves different actors and different kinds of information. Decision makers in the judiciary possess role conceptions and authority that differ from those of elected officials. The 1950s, 1960s, and 1970s were decades of swiftly accelerating policy-making activities by judges. In the wake of those decades, some commentators believe that courts did not go far enough, and others believe that, in the words of one critic, "The dream of the 1960s and 70s that activist courts can be the agents of social progress has worn very thin."[91] The contradictory assessments of the consequences of judicial policy making frequently stem from divergent analyses of the capacity of the judiciary to develop and implement beneficial public policies.

## Arguments Favoring Judges as Effective Policy Makers

In a well-known article in the *Harvard Law Review*, Abram Chayes presented several arguments advancing the idea that the judiciary has some important institutional advantages for policy-making tasks.[92] Although Chayes was not alone in raising the idea that courts may be suited to the task of policy making, his arguments are a good illustration of justifications for judges' policy-making capacity.

Courts are arguably a good forum for policy making because judges are, compared to other governmental officials, insulated from interest groups, political parties, and other direct partisan influences. Moreover, judges traditionally try to be as neutral as possible when considering competing arguments.

Judges can develop *ad hoc* policies tailored to remedy particular problematic situations. Legislatures' policy decisions tend to sweep with a broad stroke across all relevant situations without regard for subtle but potentially important differences in specific circumstances. By contrast, judges can take particular situational needs and constraints into consideration in carefully designing remedial policies to address specific problems.

The judicial process permits a relatively high degree of participation by interested parties. Unlike the legislative process in which poor and/or unorganized interests are not represented by lobbyists, both sides in a court case are generally represented by professional legal counsel. Additional arguments may be presented through *amicus* briefs and outside experts so that the judge has access to views and evidence from all relevant perspectives.

The adversarial structure of the judicial process creates incentives for both sides to bring forward as much favorable information as possible. In the legislative context, sometimes only specific interest groups have the resources and opportunity to testify at legislative hearings. By contrast, both parties to a court case will bring forward all available favorable information so that the judge can sift through complete presentations of the competing arguments and evidence before rendering a decision.

Unlike legislative and administrative governmental forums, courts must respond to issues brought before them. The policy agendas of judges are determined by the cases initiated in court, and judges do not have the same ability as other governmental officials to avoid difficult questions while consciously pursuing favored policy issues. Legislators ignore intractable problems and address issues of interest that will generate political benefits for them. Judges tackle intractable policy problems because parties bring such issues to court and ask the judiciary to develop solutions. In addition, the judges who hear the complete arguments and evidence are the decision makers in court. Unlike the situation in the legislative and executive branches in which arguments, evidence, and decisions are filtered through layers of different offices and staff personnel, the judicial process provides a relatively nonbureaucratic setting for policy making.

## Arguments Opposing Judges as Effective Policy Makers

Donald Horowitz presented the best known critique of courts' capacity for effective policy making in his book, *The Courts and Social Policy*.[93] Horowitz examined judicial interventions into state and local government institutions to highlight the drawbacks of judges' effectiveness as policy makers.

Judges cannot select their areas of policy emphasis and, because of the constant flow of other judicial responsibilities, they cannot give sustained attention to specific issues. Although legislative committees and executive agencies contain experts on various policy issues, few judges are experts on any public policy issue. They are generalists, trained in law, who have authority over public policy by virtue of becoming judicial officers. Judges are also insulated from the environment affected by their decisions because judicial ethics require judges to withdraw from participation in most social and political organizations. Legislators meet regularly with constituents to keep in touch with public opinion and social concerns. Judges keep to themselves in the protective confines of the courthouse. Because they lack expertise and close contact with affected communities, judges are less able to anticipate the broader consequences of their decisions. Moreover, the *ad hoc* nature of judicial decisions creates policies that lack the comprehensive, coherent perspective that may be developed in legislative and executive settings through the use of policy studies, experts, and long-term planning.

Judges' policy decisions are based on a skewed sample of problems. Judges address the particular case that happens to arrive before them. The case may be highly unrepresentative of the larger problems affecting a policy issue, yet the specific circumstances underlying the case in question could become the basis for policy decisions that may have detrimental effects on a variety of other cases. In addition, the issue addressed by the judge is framed by litigants in accordance with their particular interests, and therefore the judge has little ability to take a comprehensive view of the policy problem, even if he or she desires to do so. In the adversarial process, the parties have an incentive to hide unfavorable information, and the judge has insufficient staff to ferret out complete information. Thus, the judge's decision relies on the potentially biased and incomplete information submitted by the competing parties.

Litigation elicits definitive decisions in favor of one party or the other. Such decisions may be an undesirable means of addressing many policy issues—issues that would be more satisfactorily and beneficially resolved through negotiation and compromise.

## Difficulties in Assessing Judicial Capacity

Which set of arguments concerning judges' capacity for effective policy making is closest to the mark? In fact, it is probably most accurate to say that both viewpoints contain accurate elements but that neither fully captures the complex interactions that underlie judicial policy making. For example, one argument favoring judicial capacity asserts that courts must address tough issues when they are presented. Although judges have tackled many difficult issues, they are able to use such jurisdictional concepts as "standing," "mootness," and ''political question doctrine'' to avoid issues that might generate excessive political controversy. When the first affirmative action case arrived at the Supreme Court in *DeFunis v. Odegaard*,[94] the justices declared it moot because the plaintiff had subsequently been accepted by the law school that he was suing for ''reverse discrimination.'' Although affirmative action was a divisive issue, the Supreme Court managed to delay contact with the controversy. The Supreme Court has the greatest ability to avoid issues because, as explained in chapter 9, justices are permitted to pick and choose the cases that they wish to hear.

By contrast, the opponents of judicial policy making have valid arguments about the risk of skewed information from the adversarial process and judges' lack of expertise. However, judges can bring in expert witnesses to provide more complete information. In addition, judicial decisions do not normally involve a simple, definitive choice between the competing arguments. There are frequently months of behind-the-scenes negotiations involving the parties and the judge before judicial policy is developed and implemented.[95] For example, in Alabama, a federal judge took control of the state's correctional institutions because, among other things, public health inspectors found the prisons unfit for human habitation.[96] A study of prison litigation in Alabama found that the state government and the prisoners' advocates engaged in continuing negotiations during the development and implementation of remedies.[97] Other studies confirm that negotiation can underlie judicial intervention in policy issues.[98]

Some studies indicate that judges rarely foresee the adverse consequences of their decisions. One study, for example, showed that judicial intervention in prison administration could exacerbate prison violence by altering the established procedures and authority structure in the institution.[99] Commentators also note that judicial policy making often fails to accomplish intended objectives. In urban school desegregation cases, for example, some commentators argue that judicial intervention contributed to deterioration of city school systems as middle-class families left the city to avoid court-mandated busing programs.[100] Does the existence of adverse consequences of judicial policy making indicate that judges lack the capacity to formulate and implement effective policies? Or, do the less-than-completely-successful attempts at judicial policy making simply indicate that judges' effectiveness is limited by the same factors that diminish the success of policy initiatives produced by other governmental branches? In fact, court-mandated school desegregation has contributed to increased educational opportunity and reduced polarization in many communities, especially in county-wide school systems and medium-sized cities that contain broad mixtures of racial and socioeconomic groups.[101] The highly-publicized failures of busing programs in the largest cities stem, at least in part, from the Supreme Court's 1974 decision to limit such programs to the rigid confines of relatively arbitrary school system boundaries in metropolitan areas.[102] The slim five-member Supreme Court majority that limited the range of desegregation remedies available to district judges was apparently concerned about the massive political backlash that would be generated if affluent suburbanites were forced to participate in solutions to the problems of predominantly minority urban school systems.[103] There is nothing unique about judges' inability to implement effective remedies for many significant problems of urban education. The legislative and executive branches of government have not dealt effectively with these pressing problems either. Judges, however, often feel a great responsibility to do something to enforce constitutional rights when there is evidence that individuals have been victimized by discriminatory government policies and programs.

In the final analysis, judicial policy making is frequently flawed and ineffective in its attempts to redress societal problems presented in court cases. As Stephen Wasby notes, however, many of the flaws in judicial policy making also limit the effectiveness of policy making by other governmental actors.[104] Legislators are generalists who must struggle to understand experts and to make decisions based on their recommendations. Legislative and executive officials cannot effectively predict the consequences of their policy decisions and rely on skewed information fed to them by interest groups. Thus, the criticisms directed at judicial policy making are not unique and can legitimately be aimed at other governmental policy makers as well.

## THE INEVITABILITY OF POLITICS AND POLICY MAKING

The judiciary's connection to the political system combines with internal and external constraints on judicial decision making to limit courts' potential for dictatorial policy making. Judges' decisions embody policy preferences, but their decisions also reflect a complex mixture of underlying factors and conscious considerations. Critics of judicial policy making may legitimately argue that this complex combination of factors does not always adequately prevent improper assertions of judicial authority. Several scholars have argued that American government and society have suffered from the detrimental consequences of policy making.[105] Their arguments are premised on a narrow conception of "rights" under the Constitution, a reduced concern about the potential harm of simple majoritarianism, and a concomitant presumption that policy making is the exclusive province of the elected branches of government. Although these critics raise serious questions about how the American governing system ought to work, in reality judicial policy making as practiced by both conservative and liberal judges has been and will remain a fact of life in the American system. As authoritative actors drawn from and connected to the political system, judges cannot avoid affecting public policy through the application of their interpretive and remedial powers.

Assessments about the legitimacy of judicial policy making and the limitations on judges' decisions involve evaluative judgments about the nature of the Constitution, the process of judicial decision making, and the judiciary's role in the political system. Simplistic denunciations of judicial policy making as always illegitimate or as entirely dictatorial ignore the constitutional bases and political characteristics that elicit, affect, and limit judges' decisions. Such blanket condemnations of judicial policy making often emanate from critics who disagree with the specific policy advanced by judicial decisions, just as reactive defenders of judicial policy making frequently focus on the policy results that they favor rather than on the constitutional issues underlying the judicial process.

In the 1960s and 1970s, the term "judicial activism" as a label for judges' policy making was associated with liberal judges, and conservative judges, who opposed the policies advanced by the judiciary, argued in favor of judicial restraint. "Judicial activism" is not, however, inherently associated with political liberalism. During the early twentieth century it was political conservatives on the Supreme Court who, in the name of constitutional "liberty" rights under the Due Process Clause, acted to invalidate policies enacted by elected officials. Political liberals applauded judges' decisions that advanced various specific policy preferences from the 1950s through the 1970s—preferences that established legal protections for racial minorities, women, prisoners, criminal defendants, and political dissenters. The ideological shift toward politically conservative judges in the federal courts in the 1980s led to active policy making toward different policy goals—such as limiting access to the federal courts for discrimination cases and for prisoners—despite congressional intentions to the contrary.[106] Political conservatives have criticized liberal interest groups for utilizing judicial policy making as a means to advance policy goals,[107] but conservative interest groups now emulate their ideological competitors by pursuing policy agendas through the courts.[108] As the ideological balance of power shifts in the federal judiciary, political partisans may shift sides as advocates or critics of judicial policy making. Whether or not one agrees with the specific policy decisions of judges during a particular era, there is no escaping the inevitable influence of political factors, internal and external, as limitations on the expression of judges' policy preferences.

## JUDICIAL POLICY MAKING AND THE AMERICAN PUBLIC

One important way to assess the policy making role of the courts is to look beyond controversies surrounding particular issues and to question the judicial branch's larger role in the governing system. Over the course of American history, have judicial actions been consistent with developing political trends? Does the judicial branch lead or follow other branches of government in shaping public policy? A cursory examination of history provides examples of judicial leadership and examples of judicial "foot dragging" on significant societal policy trends. For example, in the 1950s, the Supreme Court moved ahead of other governing institutions in authoritatively combatting the problems of racial discrimination. By contrast in the 1930s, the Supreme Court prevented Congress and the president from implementing legislation designed to redress the widespread economic problems of the Depression. In order to evaluate the judicial branch's overriding role in American society, scholars examine the actions of the Supreme Court in various historical eras. Although the Supreme Court represents only one component of the judicial branch, systematic analyses focus on the Supreme Court and its relationship with other governing institutions and with the American public because of the high court's practical and symbolic importance.

In a classic study of the Supreme Court's role, Robert Dahl examined the instances in which the Supreme Court declared federal legislation unconstitutional and thereby acted against the policy choices of the national governing coalition (i.e., the people's elected representatives in the executive and legislative branches).[109] By 1957—during its first 167 years of existence—the Court invalidated only eighty-six provisions of federal law. Relatively few of these decisions were efforts to protect individual constitutional rights. For example, the Court's efforts to stop government economic regulation and social welfare programs were based on the liberty to contract freely rather than on the rights of political minorities. Political minorities, including women and child laborers, were actually hurt by the judicial decisions because they were the intended beneficiaries of protective regulations (e.g., limitations on working hours, minimum wage laws, etc.). Because the Court's decisions clashed so infrequently with legislative enactments of Congress and the president, Dahl concluded that the Court's actual role in the political system differed from its reputed role as defender of political minorities. According to Dahl, the Supreme Court's primary role in the American governing system is to confer legitimacy on the fundamental policies of the ruling political coalition. The Court's composition changes in accordance with developments in national electoral politics. As officials with particular values and policy goals capture the White House and the Senate, their values are reflected in their nominees for Supreme Court vacancies. Thus, when viewed over the course of many decades, the Supreme Court's decisions tend to agree with, and provide a judicial "stamp of approval" for, the policy decisions emanating from the legislative and executive branches.

Dahl's argument can be illustrated by returning to the example of economic regulation and social welfare legislation. Scholars who subsequently examined Dahl's study found that periods of critical realignment in American politics provided the clearest examples of conflict between the Supreme Court and other branches of government.[110] In the 1930s, the country's dominant political coalition changed, and the Supreme Court eventually became a component of that coalition, but it initially reflected its links to the preceding political era. When the New Deal coalition of Franklin Roosevelt reshaped American politics and public policy during the 1930s, Supreme Court decisions initially clashed with the ruling coalition by invalidating economic regulations and social welfare legislation enacted by Roosevelt and his allies in Congress. As Roosevelt appointed his supporters to the Supreme Court, the Court began to endorse rather than oppose New Deal legislation. Thus, the Supreme Court returned to its usual role as a participating member of the national governing coalition.

Dahl's conclusions were challenged in subsequent studies that examined whether the invalidation of federal legislation by the Supreme Court was an appropriate and accurate indicator of the judiciary's role in policy making. Jonathan Casper, in particular, found that Dahl's failure to consider Supreme Court decisions invalidating state and local legislation enhanced the conclusion that the Supreme Court generally participates in the governing coalition.[111] When the invalidation of state and local statutes and policies are considered, the Supreme Court's influence over public policy is more evident, especially in regard to such issues as prayer in public schools and criminal defendants' rights.

Instead of examining clashes between the branches of government, we can assess how judicial policy making comports with the values and preferences of the American public by examining public opinion about the judicial branch. The most direct method for assessing this aspect of judicial policy making is to look for relationships between public opinion polls and judicial decisions. Public opinion data are always potentially problematic. The value of such data always depends on the size and composition of the survey sample and the phrasing of the survey questions. In addition, the more difficult underlying issue is whether members of the public actually express "opinions" reflecting their knowledge, attitudes, and beliefs or simply respond to questions without knowing or caring about the subject. Because of the inconsistency or unavailability of public opinion data, scholars have had difficulty examining the relationship between judicial policy making and public opinion for many issues and eras. As a result, according to Gregory Caldeira, "A quarter of a century after the launching of the first systematic research on public evaluations of the [Supreme] Court, . . . we have precious few findings and generalizations planted in solid, empirical soil."[112]

Although researchers have produced competing theories about the effects of judicial decisions on public opinion and vice versa, Thomas Marshall finds consistent evidence of the extent to which Supreme Court decisions comport with the dominant views expressed by the public. If Supreme Court decisions conflict with public opinion, judicial policy making may threaten the legitimacy of the judiciary and impinge on the policy making authority of elected officials. Marshall found that "[w]here a clear [public opinion] poll margin existed, over three-fifths of Supreme Court rulings agreed with prevailing public opinion."[113] Because actions by Congress and the president do not always coincide with the public's preferences, Marshall concluded that "the modern Court appears to reflect mass public opinion as often as do popularly elected officeholders."[114] In addition, even when the Supreme Court strikes down a law enacted by elected representatives, the Court, rather than the legislature, often advanced the policy position supported by public opinion:

The modern Court's majoritarian behavior also extends to its judicial activism. About one-half of the modern Court's activist rulings, striking down a disputed law or policy, appeared to reflect nationwide public opinion. These results challenge the commonly cited view that judicial activism is an essentially countermajoritarian practice.[115]

What do these studies tell us about the judiciary's role in policy making? Although the legitimacy of specific judicial actions may be questioned, judicial policy making reflects society's dominant values and policy preferences to a greater degree than many people realize. In influencing public policy developments, the judicial branch is an institution firmly attached to the political system, rather than a force that imposes its will on society from beyond the reach of political influences.

# CIVIL LIABILITY AND PUBLIC POLICY

Most of this chapter has explained direct judicial policy making by judges, the focus of scholarly debates and many studies. Judicial policy making is an especially important topic for students who study courts and politics because it illuminates many enduring questions regarding the proper role of the judicial branch within the governing system. Less studied by scholars and the public is the role of courts as institutional settings for jury verdicts in civil liability cases that indirectly shape governmental practices, the distribution of financial resources—especially insurance costs, product availability, and other consequences of policy making. Civil liability cases involving issues from financial awards to injured plaintiffs are important growing influences on policy in American society.

A private citizen can generate significant consequences by winning a civil lawsuit. Recall the case cited earlier in which a jury awarded a family $1.5 million after a man died in jail from poisoning after, unbeknownst to the police, drinking windshield-wiper fluid prior to being arrested.[116] Or the case in which a jury awarded a state police officer $850,000 to compensate for his claim that the state police department used improper procedures when making promotion decisions.[117] Although neither case involved a judge ordering law enforcement agencies to adopt specific policies and procedures, both decisions undoubtedly produced such changes. The first case will likely lead jail officials to create new and better procedures for evaluating and monitoring the medical condition of arrestees while in custody. The second case is likely to lead police administrators to change their promotion procedures so as to avoid future lawsuits. Moreover, unlike judicial policy making in which interpreters and implementers may find ways to dilute or alter the judges' orders, there are strong incentives in these cases for governmental agencies to implement changes effectively. Otherwise they risk the prospect of losing significant resources.

Both cases illustrate the power of deterrence underlying tort law. If people are threatened with liability, they will change their harmful behavior. New practices will be designed and implemented to avoid the prospect of court-ordered financial losses. When these tort principles are applied to the policies and practices of government agencies, they can have significant policy-making impact.

With respect to criminal justice agencies, the 1980s and 1990s witnessed a reduction of judicial intrusion into policy making for search and seizure, suspect interrogation, and right to counsel—topics that had been shaped by judges' decisions in the 1960s and 1970s. In the 1980s and thereafter, the relatively conservative composition of federal courts placed judges who were disinclined to strengthen rules protecting criminal suspects' rights into policy-making positions. Instead, these judges frequently made decisions that gave law enforcement officials increasing flexibility for making discretionary judgments about handling criminal investigations and other aspects of criminal justice.[118] In sum, direct judicial policy making became less important as an influence over law enforcement policies. By contrast, with respect to other kinds of issues—pursuit driving, use of force, and injuries to suspects in custody—juries increasingly pressured law enforcement agencies to develop new policies by regularly awarding significant financial compensation to people injured in these contexts.[119] As policy-shaping institutions, courts continued to influence law enforcement policies in the 1980s and 1990s, but this influence was produced by juries instead of judges and focused on civil liability instead of constitutional rights.

The impact of civil liability decisions is not limited to lawsuits against government agencies. Successful lawsuits against product makers have potentially massive economic consequences. For example, multiple lawsuits against makers of silicone breast implants and asbestos building products threatened the existence of major corporations faced with the prospect of paying millions of dollars in damage awards. Obviously, such outcomes affect not only the corporation itself but also the employees who may lose their jobs if their employer must go out of business. Such lawsuits also affect product availability. This is beneficial if dangerous products are driven from the market, but it is a difficult issue if there is an adverse impact on beneficial products. For example, vaccines that may be beneficial to millions of people may also cause catastrophic allergic reactions in a small minority of the population. Without financial guarantees from the government or insurance companies, some valuable vaccines might not be produced. The same is true for certain prescription drugs that may be useful for some purposes but harmful (with a liability risk) for others. As described by Peter Huber:

> Chemie Grunenthal, for example, a West German company that once supplied thalidomide to American leprosy victims, announced in 1986 it planned to abandon the U.S. market to avoid the risk of liability that might arise if, for

example, the drug was used in excess or fell into the wrong hands. Until recently, another West German chemical company supplied Americans with botulinum, a paralytic poison that is just right for controlling eye-twitching disease, but the company cut off supplies in 1986 for similar reasons.[120]

Thus, jury verdicts can affect the American economy, including the financial vitality of manufacturing corporations and the availability of certain products.

Civil liability verdicts in product cases can also impact governmental policies. In the asbestos example, not only was a major corporation driven to bankruptcy, but millions of dollars were spent throughout the country to replace asbestos insulation in buildings because of the heightened awareness of the threat of lung diseases suffered by people who breathe asbestos fibers. Because court decisions illuminated health risks posed by a particular product, policy makers throughout the government reacted to minimize the harm caused by the continuing existence of such products.

In addition, civil litigation can have a cumulative effect on public policy. Medical malpractice lawsuits increase the cost of malpractice insurance premiums that doctors must pay. Thus, some doctors have ceased to practice specialties, such as obstetrics, which entail risks of substantial lawsuits. For example, if babies suffer from birth defects resulting from medications prescribed by the doctor during pregnancy or from injuries incurred during labor and delivery, the doctor may be held legally liable. Thus, litigation may reduce the availability of certain medical specialties. In addition, rising insurance premiums add to the cost of medical care for all citizens because doctors pass the costs of insurance premiums on to their patients. The rising cost of medical care in the United States, which is partly attributable to civil liability and insurance impacts, has spurred national debates and policy initiatives concerning reform of medical service delivery and financing systems.

One response to the indirect policy impacts of civil liability decisions has been proposals limiting the power of juries to make damage awards. President Bush, for example, proposed legislation placing caps on potential jury awards in medical malpractice cases.[121] The emphasis of such proposals— the limitation of juries' power—arguably reduces democratic decision making in the judicial branch. Because jury verdicts are produced by citizen-jurors drawn from and intended to represent the community, civil liability decisions are a form of direct democracy in the judicial branch. If juries' policy-shaping decisions are objectionable, it is not because jurors have the potentially dictatorial attributes of federal judges (i.e., life tenure) that make them subject to criticism as undemocratic policy makers. As a "voice of the community," juries apply contemporary societal values to issues of responsibility, accountability, and the allocation of benefits and burdens in society. Civil liability cases' impacts on policy are not necessarily proper, good, or effective simply because juries are the democratic decision-making entity in the judicial branch. However, as contributors to policy development, juries provide institutions with valuable messages about the state of contemporary social values so that such values are considered in governmental responses and corporate reactions to civil liability verdicts and their effects.

# CONCLUSION

Courts are important institutions for the development and implementation of public policy. Their importance stems from both direct judicial policy making undertaken by judges and indirect policy impacts from juries' civil liability verdicts. Civil liability is usually studied as an independent topic seldom connected to courts' influence on public policy. However, because jury trials and verdicts embody an important component of the judicial branch's institutional processes and products, their consequences for policy development must be recognized as part of the courts' overall impact on society.

Interest groups recognize that judges' decisions can shape policies, and therefore they strategically initiate and present cases to advance their preferred policy positions. Although the legislative and executive branches of government are traditionally responsible for policy making, the judicial branch provides an alternative forum for interest groups seeking to advance or hinder particular policy initiatives. Litigation serves as a form of "lobbying" that political interests use to obtain favorable decisions.

The reality of judges' involvement in policy making is inescapable. Decisions affecting school desegregation, abortion, prison reform, and many other issues have contributed to numerous changes in American society. However, debates still rage concerning the propriety and efficacy of judicial policy making. Is it proper for unelected federal judges to influence public policy in a democratic governing system? Are courts' structures and processes effective mechanisms for producing public policy? There are no easy or simple answers. Federal judges' tenure is structurally undemocratic since they cannot be held accountable by the citizens. Yet even federal judges' decisions are kept within the mainstream of society by judges' connections to the political system. While judicial processes provide imperfect means to develop public policies, especially with respect to implementation problems, other branches of government have their own weaknesses that diminish the effectiveness of their policy making, too. In the final analysis, evaluative conclusions about judicial policy making should rest on the analyst's recognition and understanding of the complexity of judicial processes. Because of their political attributes and connections to the political system, courts, as policy-making institutions, are both less powerful than their critics believe and less effective than their supporters claim.

# NOTES

1. See *Swann v. Charlotte-Mecklenberg School District*, 402 U.S. 1 (1971).
2. Christopher E. Smith, *Courts and Public Policy* (Chicago: Nelson-Hall, 1993), pp. 125–42.
3. Mark Andrejevic and David Wahlberg, "Death During Custody Has Happened Before," *Lansing State Journal*, 4 February 1996, p. 5A.
4. See, e.g., Jesse Kornbluth, "The Woman Who Beat the Klan," in *The Ku Klux Klan: A History of Racism and Violence*, 3rd ed. (Montgomery, AL: Southern Poverty Law Center, 1988), pp. 30–31.
5. Ron Hutcheson, "Free Speech Costs Bundles in Court," *Akron Beacon Journal*, 11 November 1990, p. A7.
6. See Lee Epstein, *Conservatives in Court* (Knoxville, TN: University of Tennessee Press, 1985).
7. See, e.g., Clement E. Vose, *Caucasians Only* (Berkeley, CA: University of California Press, 1959); Richard Kluger, *Simple Justice: A History of* Brown v. Board of Education *and Black America's Struggle for Equality* (New York: Random House, 1975).
8. Epstein, *Conservatives in Court*, pp. 16–44.
9. Ibid., p. 148.
10. See Karen O'Connor, *Women's Organizations' Use of the Courts* (Lexington, MA: Lexington Books, 1980), pp. 16–28.
11. Epstein, *Conservatives in Court*, pp. 25–27.
12. *Hammer v. Dagenhart*, 247 U.S. 251 (1918).
13. Stephen L. Wasby, "Civil Rights Litigation By Organizations: Constraints and Choices," *Judicature* 68 (1985): 337–52.
14. Lee Epstein, "Courts and Interest Groups," in *The American Courts: A Critical Assessment*, eds. John B. Gates and Charles A. Johnson (Washington, D.C.: Congressional Quarterly Press, 1991), pp. 351.
15. Ibid., pp. 345–49.
16. Linda Greenhouse, "High Court Justices Face an Issue Close to Home," *New York Times*, 13 December 1990, p. A20.
17. Ibid.
18. *Gregory and Nugent v. Ashcroft*, 501 U.S. 452 (1991).
19. Lawrence Baum, *American Courts: Process & Policy*, 2nd ed. (Boston: Houghton Mifflin, 1990), p. 7.
20. See Lynn Mather, "Policy Making in State Trial Courts," in *The American Courts: A Critical Assessment*, eds. John B. Gates and Charles A. Johnson (Washington, D.C.: Congressional Quarterly Press, 1991), pp. 119–57.
21. See Robert A. Carp and C. K. Rowland, *Policymaking and Politics in the Federal District Courts* (Knoxville, TN: University of Tennessee Press, 1983).

22. See Mary Cornelia Porter and G. Alan Tarr, eds., *State Supreme Courts: Policymakers in the Federal System* (Westport, CT: Greenwood Press, 1982).

23. Judy Daubenmier, "Ban on Abortion Aid Killed," *Akron Beacon Journal*, 21 February 1991, p. A7.

24. Sue Davis and Donald R. Songer, "The Changing Role of the United States Courts of Appeals: The Flow of Litigation Revisited," *The Justice System Journal* 13 (1988–1989): 339.

25. U.S. Constitution, Article III, sec. 1.

26. Alexander Hamilton, "The Federalist, No. 78," in *Courts, Judges, and Politics*, 4th ed., eds. Walter F. Murphy and C. Herman Pritchett (New York: Random House, 1986), p. 15.

27. Ibid., p. 16.

28. *Dred Scott v. Sandford*, 60 U.S. (19 How.) 393 (1857).

29. *Marbury v. Madison*, 5 U.S. 137 (1803).

30. U.S. Constitution, Article I, sec. 9.

31. See Don E. Fehrenbacher, *The Dred Scott Case: Its Significance in American Law and Politics* (New York: Oxford University Press, 1978).

32. See Howard L. Reiter, *Parties and Elections in Corporate America* (New York: St. Martin's Press, 1987), pp. 203–9.

33. See, e.g., *Goesaert v. Clearly*, 335 U.S. 464 (1948) (Michigan statute forbade women from working in taverns unless they were the wives or daughters of male tavern owners).

34. See, e.g., *Nixon v. Herndon*, 273 U.S. 536 (1927) (Texas statute barred African-Americans from voting in primary elections).

35. See, e.g., *Korematsu v. United States*, 323 U.S. 214 (1944) (presidential order requiring Japanese-Americans to leave their homes on the West Coast to be incarcerated in concentration camps during wartime).

36. See, e.g., *Gong Lum v. Rice*, 275 U.S. 78 (1927) (state law prevented Chinese-American children from attending the same public schools as white students).

37. See, e.g., *West Virginia Board of Education v. Barnette*, 319 U.S. 624 (1943) (state law required that children be punished for declining to salute the American flag even if their refusal was premised on principled religious beliefs).

38. See, e.g., *United States v. Brown*, 381 U.S. 437 (1965) (federal law made it a crime for a Communist to serve as an officer in a labor union).

39. *Ruffin v. Commonwealth*, 62 Va. 790, 796 (1871).

40. See, e.g., *Banning v. Looney*, 213 F.2d 771 (10th Cir. 1954).

41. *Holt v. Sarver*, 309 F.Supp. 362 (E.D. Ark. 1970); *Pugh v. Locke*, 406 F.Supp. 318 (M.D. Ala. 1976).

42. Geoffrey P. Alpert, Ben M. Crouch, and C. Ronald Huff, "Prison Reform By Judicial Decree: The Unintended Consequences of *Ruiz v. Estelle*," *The Justice System Journal* 9 (1984): 291–305.

43. See Linda Harriman and Jeffrey D. Straussman, "Do Judges Determine Budget Decisions? Federal Court Decisions in Prison Reform and State Spending for Corrections," *Public Administration Review* 43 (1983): 343–51.

44. See J. Woodford Howard, *Courts of Appeals in the Federal Judicial System* (Princeton: Princeton University Press, 1981).

45. *Plyler v. Doe*, 457 U.S. 202, 242 (1982) (Burger, C. J., dissenting).

46. See *Payne v. Tennessee*, 501 U.S. 808 (1991) in which the addition of President Bush's first nominee, David Souter, created a five-member majority to overturn a two-year-old precedent and a four-year-old precedent concerning admissible evidence in murder cases.

47. See, e.g., *Wards Cove Packing Co. v. Atonio*, 490 U.S. 642 (1989).

48. See Linda Greenhouse, "Judges Challenge Rehnquist Action on Death Penalty: An Extraordinary Move," *New York Times*, 6 October 1989, pp. A1, B7; "Death Row Appeals," *Akron Beacon Journal*, 20 March 1990, p. A6.

49. *McCleskey v. Zant*, 499 U.S. 467 (1991); *Coleman v. Thompson*, 501 U.S. _____, 111 S. Ct. 2546 (1991).

50. *McCleskey v. Zant*, 499 U.S. 467, 529 (1991) (Marshall, J., dissenting).

51. James F. Simon, *The Antagonists: Hugo Black, Felix Frankfurter, and Civil Liberties in Modern America* (New York: Simon & Schuster, 1989), pp. 64, 211–13.

52. *Baker v. Carr*, 369 U.S. 186, 267 (1962) (Frankfurter, J., dissenting).

53. *Webster v. Reproductive Health Services*, 492 U.S. 490, 532 (1989) (Scalia, J., concurring).

54. *Cruzan v. Missouri*, 497 U.S. 261, 301 (1990) (Scalia, J., concurring).

55. See David A. Schultz and Christopher E. Smith, *The Jurisprudential Vision of Justice Antonin Scalia* (Lanham, MD: Rowman & Littlefield, 1996).

56. *Planned Parenthood v. Casey*; see also Christopher E. Smith, "Supreme Court Surprise: Justice Anthony Kennedy's Move Toward Moderation," *Oklahoma Law Review* 45 (1992): 459–76.

57. Christopher E. Smith and Thomas R. Hensley, "Unfulfilled Aspirations: The Court-Packing Efforts of Presidents Reagan and Bush," *Albany Law Review* 57 (1994): 1111–31.

58. *Texas v. Johnson*, 491 U.S. 397 (1989); *United States v. Eichman*, 496 U.S. 310 (1990).

59. See David Adamany, "Legitimacy, Realigning Elections, and the Supreme Court," *Wisconsin Law Review* (1983): 790–846.

60. Louis Fisher, *American Constitutional Law* (New York: McGraw-Hill, 1990), p. 1319.

61. Bob Cohn, "Turnabout on Civil Rights," *Newsweek* 4 November 1991, p. 32.

62. Fisher, *American Constitutional Law*, pp. 1316–17.

63. *Pollock v. Farmers' Loan and Trust Co.*, 157 U.S. 429 (1895).

64. *Oregon v. Mitchell*, 400 U.S. 112 (1970).

65. Ex parte McCardle, 74 U.S. 506 (1869).
66. U.S. Constitution, Article III, section 1.
67. *Watkins v. United States*, 354 U.S. 178 (1956).
68. *Barenblatt v. United States*, 360 U.S. 109 (1959).
69. Stephen Wasby, *The Supreme Court in the Federal Judicial System*, 3rd ed. (Chicago: Nelson-Hall, 1988), p. 309.
70. Fisher, *American Constitutional Law*, pp. 1321–24.
71. Richard Kluger, *Simple Justice* (New York: Random House, 1975), pp. 614, 679, 695–99.
72. *Brown v. Board of Education*, 347 U.S. 483 (1954).
73. *Brown v. Board of Education*, 349 U.S. 294, 301 (1955).
74. See Joseph Burke, "The Cherokee Cases: A Study in Law, Politics, and Morality," *Stanford Law Review* 21 (1971): 500–547.
75. Edwin Miles, "After John Marshall's Decision: *Worcester v. Georgia* and the Nullification Crisis," *Journal of Southern History* 39 (1973): 519.
76. Lincoln Caplan, *The Tenth Justice* (New York: Random House, 1987), pp. 26–32.
77. Kluger, *Simple Justice*, pp. 665, 774.
78. The discussion of interpreters, implementers, consumers, and secondary groups is drawn from Charles A. Johnson and Bradley C. Canon, *Judicial Policies: Implementation and Impact* (Washington, D.C.: Congressional Quarterly Press, 1984), pp. 29–184.
79. *Miranda v. Arizona*, 384 U.S. 436 (1966).
80. See Christopher E. Smith, "Police Professionalism and the Rights of Criminal Defendants," *Criminal Law Bulletin* 26 (1990): 155–66.
81. *Engel v. Vitale*, 370 U.S. 421 (1962).
82. Traciel V. Reid, "Judicial Policy-Making and Implementation: An Empirical Examination," *Western Political Quarterly* 41 (1988): 509–27.
83. Stephen Wasby, "The Communication of Supreme Court's Criminal Procedure Decisions: A Preliminary Mapping," *Villanova Law Review* 18 (1973): 1086–1118.
84. Neal Milner, "Comparative Analysis of Patterns of Compliance with Supreme Court Decisions, " *Law and Society Review* 5 (1970): 119–34.
85. Ibid., p. 123.
86. Kenneth M. Dolbeare and Phillip E. Hammond, "Inertia in Midway: Supreme Court Decisions and Local Responses," *Journal of Legal Education* 23 (1970): 112.
87. Ibid., pp. 115–16.
88. See Charles S. Bullock, III and Charles M. Lamb, "Toward a Theory of Civil Rights Implementation," *Policy Perspectives* 2 (1982): 376–93.
89. Gerald Rosenberg, *The Hollow Hope: Can Courts Bring About Social Change?* (Chicago: University of Chicago Press, 1991), pp. 46–54.
90. Smith, *Courts and Public Policy*, pp. 143–51.

91. Rabkin, *Judicial Compulsion*, p. xiii.

92. See Abram Chayes, "The Role of the Judge in Public Law Litigation," *Harvard Law Review* 89 (1976): 1281–1316.

93. See Donald Horowitz, *The Courts and Social Policy* (Washington, D.C.: Brookings Institution, 1977).

94. *DeFunis v. Odegaard*, 416 U.S. 312 (1974).

95. See Phillip J. Cooper, *Hard Judicial Choices* (New York: Oxford University Press, 1988), pp. 328–50.

96. See *Newman v. Alabama*, 349 F.Supp. 278 (M.D. Ala. 1972); *Pugh v. Locke*, 406 F.Supp. 318 (M.D. Ala. 1976).

97. Tinsley E. Yarbrough, "The Alabama Prison Litigation," *The Justice System Journal* 9 (1984): 276–90.

98. See, e.g., Christopher E. Smith, "United States Magistrates and the Processing of Prisoner Litigation," *Federal Probation* 52 (December 1988): 17.

99. See Geoffrey P. Alpert, Ben M. Crouch, and C. Ronald Huff, "Prison Reform by Judicial Decree: The Unintended Consequences of *Ruiz v. Estelle*," *The Justice System Journal* 9 (1984): 291–305.

100. See, e.g., Lino A. Graglia, *Disaster By Decree* (Ithaca, NY: Cornell University Press, 1976), pp. 203–83.

101. See Gary Orfield, *Must We Bus?: Segregated Schools and National Policy* (Washington, D.C.: Brookings Institution, 1978), pp. 62–67, 119–26; Meyer Weinberg, "The Relationship Between School Desegregation and Academic Achievement: A Review of the Research," in *The Courts, Social Science, and School Desegregation*, eds. Betsy Levin and Willis D. Hawley (New Brunswick, NJ: Transaction Books, 1977), pp. 241–70; Thomas F. Pettigrew, "A Sociological View of the Post-*Bradley* Era," *Wayne Law Review* 21 (1975): 813–32.

102. *Milliken v. Bradley*, 418 U.S. 717 (1974).

103. Kluger, *Simple Justice*, pp. 771–73.

104. Stephen Wasby, "Arrogation of Power or Accountability: Judicial Imperialism Revisited," *Judicature* 65 (1981): 209–16.

105. See, e.g., Richard Morgan, *Disabling America: The "Rights Industry" in Our Time* (New York: Basic Books, 1984); Jeremy Rabkin, *Judicial Compulsions: How Public Law Distorts Public Policy* (New York: Basic Books, 1989).

106. Christopher E. Smith, "Justice Antonin Scalia and the Institutions of American Government," *Wake Forest Law Review* 25 (1990): 801–3.

107. See Morgan, *Disabling America*, pp. 3–11.

108. Karen O'Connor and Lee Epstein, "The Rise of Conservative Interest Group Litigation," *Journal of Politics* 45 (1983): 479–89; Lee Epstein, *Conservatives in Court* (Knoxville, TN: University of Tennessee Press, 1985), pp. 147–56.

109. Robert A. Dahl, "Decision-Making in a Democracy: The Supreme Court as a National Policy-Maker," *Journal of Public Law* 6 (1957): 279–95.

110. David Adamany, "Legitimacy, Realigning Elections, and the Supreme Court," *Wisconsin Law Review* (1973): 790–846; Richard Funston, "The Supreme Court and Critical Elections," *American Political Science Review* 69 (1975): 795–811.

111. Jonathan D. Casper, "The Supreme Court and National Policy Making," *American Political Science Review* 70 (1976): 50–63.

112. Gregory A. Caldeira, "Courts and Public Opinion," in *The American Courts: A Critical Assessment*, eds. John B. Gates and Charles A. Johnson (Washington, D.C.: Congressional Quarterly Press, 1991), p. 326.

113. Thomas R. Marshall, *Public Opinion and the Supreme Court* (Boston: Unwin Hyman, 1989), p. 186.

114. Ibid., p. 192.

115. Ibid.

116. Andrejevic and Wahlberg, p. 5A.

117. "Trooper Wins Bias Lawsuit," *Lansing State Journal*, 24 February 1996, p. B1.

118. See, e.g., Christopher E. Smith, "The Constitution and Criminal Punishment: The Emerging Visions of Justices Scalia and Thomas," *Drake Law Review* 43 (1995): 593–613.

119. See Victor E. Kappeler, *Critical Issues in Police Liability* (Prospect Heights, IL.: Waveland Press, 1993).

120. Peter Huber, *Liability: The Legal Revolution and Its Consequences* (New York: Basic Books, 1988), p. 159.

121. Philip J. Hilts, "Bush Enters Malpractice Debate With Plan to Limit Court Awards," *New York Times*, 13 May 1991, pp. A1, A12.

# Chapter 11

# Judicial Process:
# A Comparative Perspective

The structure and processes of the American judicial system owe much to the British traditions. The adversarial nature of courtroom conflict and the common law system of judge-made legal developments through case decisions are two notable elements of the American judicial process that were inherited from Britain. Despite their common roots, the British and American judicial systems differ in many respects. The United States has developed its own unique judicial character in response to evolving political circumstances. For example, by empowering judges to be the authoritative guardians of a written Constitution through the power of judicial review, the United States has given its judges much greater ability to develop public policies and to block actions by other branches of government. In Britain, the legislative branch (i.e., Parliament) is supreme, and courts may interpret, but not strike down, legislative acts.[1] Why did the American system develop differently in this regard? In part, the differences stem from the American colonists' reaction against flaws that they perceived in the British system. Because of their concern about their mistreatment by the British government, the Americans specified in their written constitution which individual rights were to be protected by the judiciary against governmental intrusion. In addition, the Americans separated the powers of government among three branches (legislative, executive, judicial), which could "check and balance" one another in order to avoid the accumulation of excessive power by one individual or institution. The differing political and historical environments of each country led to differences between the American judicial process and the parent legal system from which it developed.

The American and British examples illustrate differences between closely related legal systems, but there are alternative judicial structures and processes in other countries. To examine the consequences of alternative judicial characteristics, this chapter compares selected aspects of judicial systems and questions whether the United States might usefully borrow certain elements from these systems.

Many of the most frequent complaints about the American judicial system were summarized in a speech by President Jimmy Carter in 1978:

> We have the heaviest concentration of lawyers on earth—. . . three times more than [in] England, four times more than in Germany, twenty-one times more than in Japan. We have more litigation; but I am not sure we have more justice. No resources of talent and training in our society . . . are more wastefully or unfairly distributed than legal skills. Ninety percent of our lawyers serve ten percent of our people. We are over-lawyered, and under-represented.[2]

Carter's criticisms of the American system provide a basis for comparing the United States with selected countries in regard to four important issues: (1) the number of lawyers; (2) the amount of litigation; (3) the system's capacity to produce "justice"; and (4) the distribution of legal services. An examination of these issues can shed light on larger questions about the American judicial process: Does the American system have unique problems? Do other countries' judicial systems more successfully accomplish the functions of courts?

## TOO MANY LAWYERS?

Indeed, the United States does have a remarkable number of lawyers. Each year during the 1980s, more than 20,000 new lawyers joined the legal profession in the United States.[3] With this rate of growth, there were more than 800,000 lawyers in the United States by the 1990s. No other country can match the size of the legal profession in the United States. However, other factors must be analyzed when addressing the question of "too many" lawyers.

For example, the impact of this remarkable growth in the American legal profession since the 1960s is moderated by the fact that many lawyers do not practice law. In addition, during the 1980s, increasing numbers of dissatisfied lawyers left the profession to work in other fields. According to one news report, "[E]xperts estimate that nearly forty thousand lawyers a year are leaving the profession, almost as many people as are entering law school annually."[4] These departures indicate that spiralling growth in the number of licensed attorneys does not mean a corresponding increase in the number of practicing lawyers.

In his quoted remarks, President Carter was not comparing the absolute number of lawyers in each country. In sheer numbers, the United States actually has fifty times as many licensed lawyers as Japan. Instead, Carter was describing the number of lawyers relative to the size of each country's population. This is the most accurate way to compare the respective sizes of different countries' legal professions. While the United States experienced a significant increase in the number of lawyers during the 1970s and 1980s, other countries experienced similar rates of growth. In fact, the growth rates of the legal profession in several other countries exceeded that of the United States. Thus, several nations moved their ratios of lawyers per capita closer to that of the United States. For example, while there was a 52.6 percent increase in the number of American lawyers between 1970 and 1980, the number of lawyers in Germany during that period increased 57.7 percent. In Belgium, the increase was 64.2 percent, and the increases in New Zealand and the Netherlands were 51.9 percent and 74.5 percent respectively.[5] Such increases lowered the population-per-lawyer ratio in several countries:

> [I]n the United States [the lawyer ratio] fell from 572 to 1 in 1970 to 418 to 1 in 1980 [i.e., there was one lawyer for every 418 people]. . . . For all Belgian lawyers, the ratio decreased from 717 to 1 [in 1970] to 466 to 1 [in 1980], [a change which] was appreciably greater than that in the United States. Even more substantial changes may be found elsewhere. In Ontario, Canada, for example, the population to lawyer ratio fell from 1,043 to 1 in 1970 to 599 to 1 in 1980. Similarly, in Scotland the ratio of population (which declined slightly) to practicing solicitors declined from 1,600 to 1 in 1971 to 963 to 1 in 1981.[6]

In sum, although the United States has the heaviest concentration of lawyers, the growth in the American legal profession was not unique and was, in fact, proportionally exceeded by increases in the number of lawyers in several other countries.

Although the United States has the most lawyers per capita, comparisons with other countries are frequently distorted by the fact that legal tasks elsewhere may be undertaken by legal professionals other than lawyers. While the United States lumps certified legal professionals into one category—"lawyers"—other countries have different categories of legal professionals, not all of whom are regarded as "lawyers." Because Japan is often cited as an industrialized economic power that manages to succeed without many lawyers, it is a prime example of the deceptive conclusions drawn from simply comparing the number of "lawyers" in different countries.

As indicated in President Carter's remarks, the United States is frequently criticized for having twenty times more lawyers per capita than Japan. In the mid-1980s, there were more than 650,000 licensed lawyers in the United States, serving a population in excess of 220 million people; but there were only 13,000 *bengoshi* (licensed litigators) in Japan, serving a population of 120 million people.[7] Any comparison of these two figures supports the conclusion that the United States has an overwhelming number of lawyers. There are, however, a variety of other legal professionals in Japan who do the same tasks performed by licensed lawyers in the United States. In Japan, 15,000 *shiho shoshi* (judicial scriveners) draft legal documents concerning real estate and corporate matters and give advice "on a range of matters as broad as any general practitioner in the United States confronts."[8] There are 509 *koshonin* (notaries public), usually retired judges or retired Ministry of Justice officials, who prepare legal documents for loans, deeds, and other matters. In addition, 2,600 *benrishi* (patent practitioners), 49,000 *zeirishi* (tax practitioners), and 30,000 *gyosei shoshi* (administrative scriveners), perform legal tasks that lawyers perform in the United States.[9] There are thousands of people with law degrees in Japan who serve as in-house legal advisors for corporations and government agencies because, unlike in the United States, "[I]t is not a violation of the law under which attorneys are licensed for unlicensed legal experts to give advice to their employers."[10] Because of the diverse law-related careers that attract Japanese law school graduates, Japan has significantly more legal professionals per capita than most people realize. The most revealing evidence of this large number of hidden "lawyers" is the fact that a country only half the size of the United States produces 38,000 law graduates each year, compared to only 36,000 graduates of American law schools.[11]

One cannot make easy judgments about whether the United States has "too many" lawyers simply by comparing American numbers with those of other countries. The growth of the legal profession in the United States reflects the steady growth in the nation's population, expanding career opportunities for women and ethnic minorities previously denied access to the profession, and the increased role of government regulation in American society. When state and federal governments create new laws and administrative rules, businesses and individuals find trained legal professionals to interpret, apply, and challenge complicated or unfamiliar government regulations. Similar developments may occur elsewhere, stimulating the growth of the legal profession in other countries.

Assessments of whether there are "too many" lawyers in the United States require judgments about the lawyers' contributions, both positive and negative, to American society and the national economy. One serious concern is that the legal profession in the United States draws away too many of the best and brightest college graduates. For example, Japan trains many engineers who presumably contribute to the national economy and societal prosperity by developing and improving new products and manufacturing technology. By contrast, there are frequent complaints that many advanced engineering programs in the United States are filled with students from overseas because too many top American students gravitate toward the status and money of a law career rather than toward the study of math and science. While Japanese engineers contribute to their country's economy, lawyers in the United States arguably draw resources away from the economy. Although American lawyers may facilitate beneficial mergers and contracts between American businesses, the lawyers' high fees absorb significant economic resources that might otherwise contribute to economic productivity through reinvestment.

For corporate legal matters, Japan's reliance on salaried (and therefore less expensive) legal professionals in a corporation may produce greater economic benefits than the American use of expensive, independent law firms. Thus, it may be that organization of legal advice, rather than sheer number of lawyers, determines the legal profession's overall impact on a society. Although American corporations increasingly use in-house counsel, the Americans—unlike Japanese corporate counsel—are licensed attorneys accounted for in statistics on the number of lawyers in the country.

Does the United States need hundreds of thousands of licensed professionals to give legal advice, to negotiate business deals, and to process disputes? Certainly, the United States could function well with fewer lawyers. However, because lawyers in American society enjoy status, power, and the potential for affluence, the legal profession continues to attract new entrants. The image of the legal profession continues to draw top students to law school even though many lawyers are not securing high-paying jobs in the increasingly competitive field of law practice.

## TOO MUCH LITIGATION?

Much public criticism has been directed at the purported "litigation explosion" in the United States. As noted by one scholar:

> Yet by now it is a staple of social commentary to cite the myriad laws and abundance of lawyers in the United States. Both have proliferated so rapidly as to suggest (even to lawyers) that American society is choking from "legal pollution"; that Americans as a people are debilitated by the malady of "hyperlexis."[12]

The large number of American lawyers may be the source of excessive litigation, because these legal professionals need to find and serve clients to make money. Lawyers may file lawsuits that have little chance of success because they know that many defendants, especially corporations and insurance companies, are willing to settle the cases by paying a modest settlement rather than spend money on legal fees to fight a case to the end—even if the defendants expect to win the case should it go to trial. In addition to lawyers' self-interest in generating litigation, scholars point to the American "legal culture" as a source of excessive litigation. The term "legal culture" refers to a society's "network of values and attitudes . . . which determines when and why and where people turn to law or government or turn away."[13] Lawrence Friedman argues that Americans expect "total justice," demanding that all wrongs be righted and that compensation be paid for all injuries.[14] These important aspects of American legal culture lead people to make demands upon the judicial system through the litigation process.

Does the United States really suffer from excessive litigation? Although there is a popular belief that the United States has experienced a drastic increase in litigation and that the American courts are burdened by unnecessary lawsuits, many scholars question the accuracy of these perceptions. Long-term studies cast doubt on the proposition that contemporary Americans are uniquely litigious. For example, Wayne McIntosh's study of the St. Louis, Missouri, civil courts from 1820 to 1977 indicated that litigation rates peaked in the mid-nineteenth century and that subsequent rates of litigation were consistent with population growth and changes in economic conditions.[15] Cross-national comparisons also challenge the conclusion that the United States has an excessive litigation rate. A comparison of litigation in the United States with that in courts in other countries found that the American rate of filing civil actions (44 cases per 1,000 population) was similar to that of England (41), Australia (62), Denmark (41), New Zealand (53), and the province of Ontario in Canada (47).[16] The American rate was slightly higher than those of Germany (23) and Sweden (35) and much higher than those of Japan (12), Spain (3), and Italy (10).[17]

What accounts for the differences in civil case filings between countries? The structure of a nation's judicial system may affect how many cases go to court. In Sweden, for example, there is extensive reliance on alternative dispute-resolution mechanisms that Bryant Garth labels "most striking and innovative."[18] Sweden processes disputes through, among other things, a Consumer Ombudsman, a Market Court, a Public Complaint Board, and a simplified small claims process.[19]

Another source of differences may be the distinctive attributes of countries' legal cultures. Japan, for example, is frequently cited as a country whose cultural attributes discourage conflict and litigation.[20] Descriptions of Japan's legal system usually emphasize the country's legal culture as the reason for its low litigation rate:

> The Japanese are a rather remarkably nonlitigious people. They are traditionally suspicious of the courts and of formal legal processes and have a pronounced preference for settling disputes by informal methods of conciliation and mediation. These methods are highly developed, especially in the countryside, and normally recourse is had to the courts only when the issue is very serious and older techniques of mediated settlement have failed. The number of civil suits per capita brought before the courts in Japan is only one-tenth and one-twentieth of that of England or the United States.[21]

In recent years, scholars have criticized the notion that Japan's culture diminishes disputes and litigation. Instead, Japan's low litigation rate apparently stems from conscious decisions about the structure and processes of the legal system. The design of the Japanese judicial process effectively discourages people from utilizing the courts for dispute processing. One reason that there is relatively little litigation in Japan is that the Japanese permit only five hundred aspiring lawyers to pass their national bar examination each year and become the *bengoshi* (licensed litigators) who can conduct litigation.[22] Only 1.6 percent of law school graduates pass the examination and earn admission to the Legal Training and Research Institute in Tokyo. Upon graduation from the Institute and after passing another examination, the new lawyers become licensed litigators. As described by Edward Chen: "Inevitably, the examination process deliberately fails thousands of well-qualified applicants who almost certainly have the capacity to be productive, able members of the legal profession."[23] By limiting the number of available licensed litigators, the Japanese system forces people to find alternatives to formal litigation in order to process their disputes. According to Marc Galanter, "The low rate of litigation in Japan evidences not the preferences of the population, but deliberate policy choices by political elites."[24]

In addition, the cost of civil litigation serves as a serious deterrent to people considering lawsuits. Although there are set court fees for filing in American courts (e.g., $120 for a civil case in federal district court), Japanese courts require litigants to pay a fee equal to a percent of the amount they seek to recover. For example, a lawsuit seeking $1 million would require an initial court fee in excess of $5,000.[25] When considered in light of American lawsuits in which plaintiffs seek many millions of dollars, the initial court fees in Japan can be a considerable expense, well beyond the means of most individuals. Japanese legal fees are also structured according to the recovery sought. Japanese litigants must pay their attorneys an initial fee to initiate the case and a percentage of the recovery if the suit is successful. According to the fee schedule approved by the Japan Federation of Bar Associations, the initial fee would be in excess of $41,000 for a lawsuit seeking recovery of $1 million.[26] As summarized by Richard Miller, "[W]ith such high 'up front' costs, only indigent (and thus eligible for free legal services) and very wealthy litigants can afford to bring a lawsuit and, especially, to seek the level of damages routinely sought in the United States."[27] Thus, the Japanese find it difficult to use the judicial process.

As a result of the structural impediments to litigation, the Japanese are forced to utilize alternative dispute processes. For example, the Japanese Civil Liberties Bureau, despite the civil rights implications of its name, is a general governmental mediation agency that helps to resolve all kinds of disputes between private individuals. The disputes processed by the Bureau range from arguments between neighbors about excessive noise to personal injuries suffered by a corporation's employees.[28] The Bureau's effectiveness in processing more than 375,000 cases each year through mediation is undoubtedly enhanced by the fact that, unlike many Americans, the Japanese have little opportunity to initiate actions in the formal judicial process. When mediation is the only available mechanism for dispute processing, it is likely to be more effective than when other mechanisms, such as litigation, are available as alternatives.

Without access to the courts, the Japanese make use of such dispute-processing mechanisms as formal apologies, which play a much greater role in settling disputes in Japan than in the United States.[29] The Japanese settle many situations by submitting a formal written apology to the aggrieved party. Scholars have argued that ''[a]pology may be given a lower priority in the United States because American society does not place as high a value on group membership, conformity, and harmonious relationships among people as Japanese society does.''[30] Despite this cultural difference, the functional effectiveness of formal apologies in Japan is also related to the lack of access to the judicial process.

Because Japan has little litigation and the United States is perceived to have a ''litigation explosion,'' Americans sometimes express admiration for the cultural attributes of Japan, which purportedly reduce conflicts within society. However, it is clear that many conflicts exist in Japanese society. Japanese society does not fulfill its reputation for absence of conflict between individuals and organizations. Thus, the most important differences between Japan and the United States may not be cultural but may be political—differences that determine the policy choices concerning how disputes will be processed. Japan's efforts to limit access to the judicial process do not fit the American political values favoring procedural and substantive rights: ''The formality and preoccupation with process now so closely identified with the American legal system are not simply a product of lawyers' self-interest and professional training; they are also inextricably tied to the individ-ualistic strain in our cultural traditions.''[31] Americans have greater access to the judicial system and a greater inclination to use it because of the nation's political values concerning protection of individual interests,[32] not because the country is uniquely filled with conflict and litigiousness. Although Japan's use of alternative dispute-processing mechanisms instead of litigation may provide ideas for America's growing alternative dispute resolution movement, Japan is not generally an example that the United States could realistically follow. In fact, critics argue that the Japanese may improve their judicial process by comparing it to its American counterpart. For example, by expressing concerns about Japan's excessive efforts to avoid judicial intervention in disputes, scholars in Japan have actually endorsed some beneficial aspects of the ''litigious'' American judicial system:

> Critics [of the Japanese judicial process] contend not only that the government is insufficiently subjugated to judicial control but that the judiciary itself assumes an administrative outlook toward disputes. That is, the judiciary is accused of actively directing its efforts toward the noncontentious resolution of disputes, implicitly rejecting the aggressive assertion of legal rights. . . . [This] weakens the entire legal system. As the people become less vigilant in defending their rights, the legal order slackens, and an abuse of power may ensue.[33]

In sum, despite widespread perceptions of a ''litigation explosion,'' litigation rates in several other countries are similar to those in the United States. As the Japanese example illustrates, litigation rates do not necessarily reflect a defect in society or an undesirable cultural trait among a nation's people. Instead, utilization of the judicial process is significantly affected by the institutions a society provides for the processing of disputes. Because of American political values concerning the protection of individual rights and interests, the United States, unlike Japan, has made litigation available to many (but not all) individuals and organizational entities.

# ACHIEVING "JUSTICE"?

As illustrated by the preceding chapters, the processes and outcomes of the American judicial process are influenced by a variety of human, political, and historical factors. Individuals and organizational entities possessing wealth and political power have significant advantages in obtaining legal resources, in gaining effective access to the judicial process, and in obtaining favorable outcomes. Obviously, the pervasive political influences that underlie the judicial process prevent the court system from producing neutral, perfect "justice." In other words, adversarial fact-finding tactics (e.g., discovery), negotiated outcomes, unequal legal resources, and other influential characteristics of the judicial process tend to produce outcomes that emphasize efficient case processing and judicial actors' self-interest rather than outcomes that focus solely on idealistic judicial goals of "justice" (i.e., appropriate compensation for victims, liability for those responsible for harms, and fair procedures and principles for neutral decision making). Despite the imperfections that inevitably exist in human institutions, many actors in the judicial system genuinely seek fair outcomes. However, the well-intentioned pursuit of "justice" by judges and lawyers does not create consistent court decisions and balanced negotiated settlements because judicial actors do not always agree about which outcomes are "fair." Moreover, when contending parties possess unequal legal resources, it may be impossible for authoritative figures in the judicial process to give equal and complete consideration to competing arguments and evidence. Some people cannot afford to initiate cases in court. Others cannot sustain litigation through all of the stages of the civil process. Thus, even if they were to agree on the proper outcomes of disputes, well-intentioned judges and lawyers could not ensure that "justice" would be achieved in every case.

In comparing the American judicial system with the systems of other countries, one important question is whether foreign judicial processes include any structures or processes that are especially useful in producing fair outcomes. In other words, are other judicial systems better able to achieve "justice"?

## The Active Trial Judge

One criticism of the American judicial process is that the adversary system is a flawed method of fact finding. Theoretically, when zealous attorneys present arguments and evidence on behalf of their clients, the truth will emerge from the competing presentations. However, there are risks that the adversarial process actually obscures the truth by giving attorneys incentives to hide unfavorable information and to make biased presentations. The risk is increased when one attorney is a more effective advocate than his or her opponent. Dramatic flair and persuasive communication skills may sway a judge or jury if the opposing counsel cannot effectively present the countervailing viewpoint.

Judges in the American adversary system tend to be passive during trials. They prevent attorneys from violating evidentiary or procedural rules, but they do not actively ensure that all relevant evidence is presented. In the adversary system, if evidence favorable to one side is not presented effectively, it is the fault of the attorney. Despite the strength of available arguments or evidence, the client suffers adverse consequences even though competent advocacy should have won the case. Although some American judges take active roles in pretrial conferences that usually lead to negotiated settlements, other judges maintain a passive role at every stage of the judicial process. The judges simply stand aside as opposing attorneys attempt to manipulate, deceive, and overpower each other in the discovery process and settlement negotiations prior to trial.

The alternative approach for fact finding in the judicial process is the *inquisitorial system* used in Germany and other European countries. In an inquisitorial process, the judge takes primary responsibility for discovering the relevant facts by actively questioning witnesses and deciding which evidence is important. In German criminal cases, for example, "[I]t is not the parties but the judge who calls and interrogates the witnesses and who decides upon the order in which evidence is taken. . . . Prosecutor and defense counsel play comparatively minor roles at the trial."[34] After the judge has finished questioning witnesses, the prosecutor and defense attorney may ask further questions. They may also request that the judge consider additional evidence.[35]

The judge also plays the primary role in fact finding in civil cases in German courts.[36] The plaintiff files a complaint asserting key facts, presenting a legal theory, and seeking a remedy. The plaintiff also submits relevant documents. The judge, however, assumes responsibility for determining which evidence is important and for questioning witnesses. Instead of a discovery process and the pretrial maneuvering characteristic of the American system, the German judge holds a series of hearings to examine the evidence. According to John Langbein, "[A] main virtue of German civil procedure . . . is that the principle of judicial control of sequence works to confine the scope of fact-gathering to those avenues of inquiry deemed most likely to resolve the case."[37] Presumably, because the judges control the proceedings, there is no risk of badgering or misleading witnesses, springing "surprise" evidence on the court, or finding one side's attorney overmatched by the opposing lawyer. Thus, the search for truth is undertaken by a neutral party, a legal professional, who will not be swayed by the kinds of attorney tactics frequently aimed at juries in the American system. Although the arguments concerning the superiority of the German system have been challenged,[38] the German example presents an alternative approach to facilitate fair and effective case processing.

It is highly unlikely that the American system would ever emulate the German approach to fact finding. Individual judges may experiment with deeper involvement in pretrial and trial processes, but the adversary system is deeply ingrained and revered by American lawyers. Because the adversary system gives lawyers their greatest influence on outcomes, the American legal profession would resist any effort to impose procedural changes reducing their ability to impress and advocate on behalf of the clients on whom the lawyers depend for their livelihoods. Moreover, the adversary model is well-suited to American political values of zealous advocacy and protection of individuals' and organizations' interests.

## Judicial Selection

In the American adversary system, the responsibility for zealous advocacy entrusted to attorneys helps to prevent detrimental consequences if the judge lacks competence or interest in the case. American lawyers can creatively negotiate favorable settlements or call important arguments and evidence to the attention of the judge. In Germany, by contrast, the judge must be very interested and capable or the fact finding process will be deeply flawed. Because their system limits attorneys' roles in litigation, the Germans need skilled, detached judicial officers to produce fair outcomes. Thus, the Germans employ a judicial selection process intended to emphasize qualifications and competence rather than accountability or representativeness. According to Langbein, "[T]he judicial career [in Germany] must be designed in a fashion that creates incentives for diligence and excellence. The idea is to attract very able people to the bench, and to make their path of career advancement congruent with the legitimate interests of litigants."[39]

While American court systems utilize various methods of judicial selection emphasizing different underlying values (e.g., accountability, qualifications, etc.), many European systems, including those in Germany and France, employ judicial career tracks that emphasize specialized training, qualifications, and subsequent promotions to higher courts. In Germany, aspiring judges take special examinations and enter apprenticeships immediately after graduating from law school.[40] After passing a second examination, candidates may apply for advertised vacancies in lower state courts.[41] In some German states, new judges learn by sitting on three-judge panels with two veteran lower court judges during an initial probationary period, while other states initially give new appointees experience in a prosecutor's office.[42] German judges undergo periodic performance reviews by other judges. After a successful probationary period, judges may be granted life tenure and become eligible for promotion to higher state courts or to the federal courts.

In France, law school graduates who wish to become judges must take competitive examinations for admission to the National Judicial College. After more than two years of specialized training and an apprenticeship, judicial graduates may receive assignments to lower court judgeships.[43] Although judicial offices in the United States are filled by lawyers who develop strong political connections, European courts are served by professional judges who commit themselves to careers as judges on graduating from college. As described by Henry Abraham:

> [I]n France the judge is chosen from the *judicial profession*, for which he or she prepared by special schooling and examination—a profession just as medicine, teaching, and the law are. Although it may not be particularly well-paid, the judiciary enjoys considerable prestige and a high social rating.[44]

Obviously, the German and French systems attempt to produce neutral, detached judges who can assume responsibility for the active judicial role required in the inquisitorial system. This is not to say that these countries have eliminated the influence of politics from their judicial selection processes. Promotions in the French judiciary may be affected by political considerations,[45] and appointment to the highest federal courts in Germany involves decisions by political parties and the national legislature.[46] Although their judicial selection processes are not completely divorced from partisan political influences, Germany and France have apparently succeeded in emphasizing qualifications, training, and specialization when recruiting new judges.

Some commentators have argued that the United States should consider developing similar judicial career tracks involving specialized training and merit promotions for judges.[47] Although there may be a sentimental attraction to the notion that better judges could be produced through specialized training, such thinking shows traces of the lingering notion that law and judicial decision making can somehow be divorced from human, political influences. Research on France and Germany indicates that individuals attracted to and accepted for judicial careers tend to come from particular backgrounds (i.e., middle or upper-middle class) and, in Germany in particular, manifest conservative political attitudes.[48] Because judges under any selection system are imperfect human beings, there is no way to avoid the influence of attitudes, values, and biases. European judicial selection processes do not ensure that their court systems are necessarily able to achieve "justice."

In the United States, there are powerful reasons that a judicial career track is not feasible. As Sheldon Goldman observed, "[A] career, civil-service-type judiciary would be contrary to our political tradition and would be specially inapposite at a point when there is widespread recognition of the policy-making role of our courts."[49] Because American judges generally possess more policy-making authority than their European counterparts, there is a need to emphasize accountability by maintaining connections between the judiciary and the political system. American judges are especially powerful because the common law system explicitly accepts judge-made law in judicial decisions. Moreover, because American judges can overturn the actions of other governmental branches through judicial review, there is a special reason to keep the judiciary connected to other political institutions. If a judiciary focuses on dispute processing, as the European judicial systems seem to do, there may be no impediment to the evolution of a civil service branch of independent judicial "bureaucrats" with limited tasks and authority. When a judiciary possesses broad authority for policy making, however, judgeships are prizes coveted by political interests, and judges are not expected to behave too independently. Thus, for example, political party leaders in American states maintain some control over judicial outcomes by seeking appointments for fellow partisans. Although the political strategies of partisan actors vary according to the selection system employed by each state, there are opportunities for strategic political action in every selection system—including merit selection. Even the federal judiciary, whose judges enjoy the greatest independence through life tenure, is connected to the political system through the appointment power of the president and the political influence of senators. Although many European governing systems have undertaken evolutionary developments toward greater policy-making power for their judiciaries,[50] none matches the authority granted to judges in the American system. The professional judges of Europe may fit their countries' judicial systems, but they would not be appropriate for the political environment in which the American policy-making courts operate.

## DISTRIBUTING LEGAL SERVICES?

Although 13 percent of Americans live below the government's poverty line,[51] fewer than 2 percent of American attorneys work for agencies that provide free legal representation for the poor.[52] The skewed distribution of legal resources is not unique to the United States. Just as the United States initiated the Legal Services Corporation to provide civil representation for the poor, other countries have attempted to distribute legal resources to those without wealth and influence.

Great Britain's Legal Aid Scheme provides legal assistance to individuals with little or no income. In addition, Community Law Centers in large cities provide advice to people with few resources.[53] Like their American counterparts, attorneys in these programs suffer from the problems of low salaries, heavy caseloads, and high personnel turnover.[54] Although seriously injured poor people can be represented by private attorneys on a contingency fee basis in the United States, contingency fees were forbidden in Britain prior to 1996. Moreover, the losing party in British civil litigation must pay for the opponent's attorney, so less affluent people must think long and hard before they risk initiating a lawsuit. Thus, Britain does not provide a model for the United States in regard to making legal resources more widely available.

In Germany, the courts can grant provisional release from paying litigation costs in order to permit less affluent people to initiate litigation.[55] In addition, the inquisitorial process may work to the advantage of poorer litigants by

protecting them from ineffective representation. Despite the existence of mechanisms to increase access to the judicial process, less affluent people may be
reluctant to initiate lawsuits because the losing party in a civil case must pay the
opponent's attorney's fees and court costs.

Italy, Portugal, and a few other countries attempt to equalize distribution
of legal resources by ordering attorneys to represent poor clients without compensation. Because time spent on such cases detracts from lawyers' profitable representation of paying clients, it is not surprising that lawyers put forth little effort
when involuntarily assigned to represent needy clients.[56]

Not surprisingly, the greatest redistribution of legal resources occurs in the
northern European countries, which pursue general policies of redistributing
wealth and resources to elevate the quality of life for low-income citizens. The
Netherlands has such a liberal threshold for free legal assistance that two-thirds
of the working population is eligible for representation in civil cases.[57] Through
its Legal Aid program, Sweden adjusts legal fees according to the income and
assets of people who need representation.[58] In addition, Sweden makes a variety
of alternative dispute resolution forums available to the public.

The United States is unlikely ever to undertake an extensive redistribution of
legal resources. The dominant political values that underlie the American government (e.g., individualism, limited government, etc.) support the continuation of
the current system in which people look out for themselves, and therefore the
wealthy and the politically powerful have better access to legal resources. Economic forces have increased middle-class Americans' access to the judicial process. The increasing competitiveness of the growing legal profession has coincided
with the removal of restrictions on lawyers' freedom to advertise and to offer low
fees. Thus, legal insurance plans and low-cost law office networks (e.g., Hyatt
Legal Services) provide affordable services for routine legal matters. The increased
availability of legal services for the middle class has not led to a corresponding
expansion in services for the poor. America's impoverished citizens lack the political power to gain additional services. They possess neither the votes to push legislative action nor the dollars to attract attention from the competitive economic market
of legal professionals. Just as the redistributive programs of Sweden and the Netherlands reflect those countries' politics and public policies, the skewed distribution
of legal resources and the unequal access to the judicial process in the United States
reflect American political values and interests.

# CONCLUSION

Although there is much to be criticized (and improved) in the American judicial
process, condemnations of the American system are less powerful when viewed
in light of practices in other countries. No nation has developed a system in
which neutral judges apply abstract principles of law to process disputes and
perform other functions of courts. Indeed, no nation can attain the idealized image

of "neutral justice." Courts are staffed by human beings. Laws are produced by the assertion of partisan interests in political institutions, including courts. Judicial structures and processes may take different forms in various countries, but they are always products of a nation's history, governmental structure, and political values.

Comparisons between countries provide a clearer perspective, but not reassurance, for Americans who are concerned about the inadequacies of the judicial process in the United States. Because Americans cling to their high expectations of courts as legal rather than political institutions, the perceived failings of the judiciary cause keen disappointment about the gap between the reality of the judicial process and the ideal of justice. There is cause for disappointment in the unequal distribution of legal resources, inconsistent judicial outcomes, and limited access to the judicial process. Because these attributes of the legal system stem from social conditions in American society and from interactions in the political system, they are best understood through recognition of the influence of politics on the judicial process.

If Americans wish to reform their judicial system by changing structures, processes, and the distribution of resources, changes must be designed in light of the political forces affecting the judicial branch. As indicated by Malcolm Feeley's well-known research on court reform,[59] planned improvements in the judicial system must stem from recognition of how the judicial process really operates—including its political characteristics. The effectiveness of planned reforms will be diminished by any failure to recognize and address political characteristics and influences in the judicial process. By recognizing and anticipating the influence of political factors, reform efforts may be able to refine, limit, or redirect the effects of politics on specific problems in the court system. "Successful" alteration of political influences and consequences in the judicial process is possible, however, only when there is shared consensus about both the goals and methods. Such consensus is difficult to attain when reforms may alter the existing distribution of resources and power in the judicial system. Thus, for example, the noble idea of providing legal services for the poor in civil cases was curtailed when Legal Services attorneys began to win cases against government and business.

The elimination of politics from the judicial process would be undesirable even if it were possible. The political aspects of the American judicial process provide the basis for the accountability of the third branch of government. Judicial selection, for example, binds the judiciary to the political system by drawing authoritative decision makers from the mainstream of society.

# NOTES

1. Henry J. Abraham, *The Judicial Process*, 5th ed. (New York: Oxford University Press, 1986), pp. 308–10.

2. Jimmy Carter, speech before the Los Angeles County Bar Association, 4 May 1978, quoted in Harry P. Stumpf, *American Judicial Politics* (New York: Harcourt Brace Jovanovich, 1988), p. 231.

3. Barbara Curran, "American Lawyers in the 1980s: A Profession in Transition," *Law and Society Review* 20 (1986): 19.

4. Andrea Sachs, "Have Law Degree, Will Travel," *Time*, 11 December 1989, p. 106.

5. P.S.C. Lewis, "A Comparative Perspective on Legal Professions in the 1980s," *Law and Society Review* 20 (1986): 81.

6. Ibid., p. 82.

7. Richard S. Miller, "Apples v. Persimmons: The Legal Profession in Japan and the United States," *Journal of Legal Education* 39 (1989): 27.

8. Ibid., p. 29.

9. Ibid.

10. Ibid., p. 31.

11. Marc Galanter, "Beyond the Litigation Panic," in *New Directions in Liability Law*, ed. Walter Olson (New York: Academy of Political Science, 1988), p. 28.

12. Jerold S. Auerbach, *Justice Without Law?: Resolving Disputes Without Lawyers* (New York: Oxford University Press, 1983), p. 9.

13. Lawrence M. Friedman, *Total Justice: What Americans Want From the Legal System and Why* (Boston: Beacon Press, 1985), pp. 31–32.

14. See ibid., p. 43.

15. See Wayne V. McIntosh, *The Appeal of Civil Law: A Political-Economic Analysis of Litigation* (Champaign, IL: University of Illinois Press, 1990), pp. 181–99.

16. Marc Galanter, "Reading the Landscape of Disputes: What We Know and Don't Know (And Think We Know) About Our Allegedly Contentious and Litigious Society," *U.C.L.A. Law Review* 31 (1983): 51–55.

17. Ibid.

18. Bryant Garth, "The Movement Toward Procedural Informalism in North America and Western Europe: A Critical Survey," in *The Politics of Informal Justice*, vol. 2, ed. Richard L. Abel (New York: Academic Press, 1982), p. 190.

19. Ibid.

20. See Setsuo Miyazawa, "Taking Kawashima Seriously: A Review of Japanese Research on Japanese Legal Consciousness and Disputing Behavior," *Law and Society Review* 21 (1987): 217–41.

21. Robert E. Ward, *Japan's Political System*, 2nd ed. (Englewood Cliffs, NJ: Prentice-Hall, 1978), p. 172.

22. Edward I. Chen, "The National Law Examination of Japan," *Journal of Legal Education* 39 (1989): 7.

23. Ibid., p. 19.

24. Galanter, "Reading the Landscape of Disputes," p. 59.
25. Miller, "Apples v. Persimmons," p. 33.
26. Ibid., p. 34.
27. Ibid.
28. See Joel Rosch, "Institutionalizing Mediation: The Evolution of the Civil Liberties Bureau in Japan," *Law and Society Review* 21 (1987): 243–66.
29. See Hiroshi Wagatsuma and Arthur Rosett, "The Implications of Apology: Law and Culture in Japan and the United States," *Law and Society Review* 20 (1986): 461–98.
30. Ibid., p. 493.
31. Frank K. Upham, *Law and Social Change in Postwar Japan* (Cambridge, MA: Harvard University Press, 1987), p. 223.
32. See Friedman, *Total Justice*, pp. 147–52.
33. Takao Tanese, "The Management of Disputes: Automobile Accident Compensation in Japan," *Law and Society Review* 24 (1990): 686.
34. Joachim Hermann, "Federal Republic of Germany," in *Major Criminal Justice Systems*, eds. George F. Cole, Stanislaw J. Frankowski, and Marc G. Gertz (Beverly Hills, CA: Sage Publications, 1981), p. 100.
35. Ibid.
36. See John H. Langbein, "The German Advantage in Civil Procedure," *University of Chicago Law Review* 52 (1985): 823–66.
37. Ibid., p. 846.
38. See Ronald J. Allen, Stefan Kock, Kurt Riechenberg, and D. Toby Rosen, "The German Advantage in Civil Procedure: A Plea For More Details and Fewer Generalities in Comparative Scholarship," *Northwestern University Law Review* 82 (1988): 705–62.
39. Langbein, "The German Advantage," p. 848.
40. Ibid., pp. 848–49.
41. David S. Clark, "The Selection and Accountability of Judges in West Germany: Implementation of a *Rechtsstaat*," *Southern California Law Review* 61 (1988): 1816.
42. Ibid., p. 1819.
43. See John Bell, "Principles and Methods of Judicial Selection in France," *Southern California Law Review* 61 (1988): 1757–94.
44. Abraham, *The Judicial Process*, p. 95.
45. Alan N. Katz, "France," in *Legal Traditions and Systems*, ed. Alan N. Katz (New York: Greenwood Press, 1986), p. 116.
46. Clark, "The Selection and Accountability," pp. 1826–29.
47. See Robert P. Davidow, "Beyond Merit Selection: Judicial Careers Through Merit Promotion," *Texas Tech Law Review* 12 (1981): 851–907.
48. See Alan N. Katz, "Federal Republic of Germany," in *Legal Traditions and Systems*, ed. Alan N. Katz (New York: Greenwood Press, 1986), p. 95.

49. Sheldon Goldman, "Judicial Selection and the Qualities that Make a 'Good' Judge," *Annals of the American Academy of Political and Social Science* 462 (1982): 123.
50. See Mauro Cappelletti, *The Judicial Process in Comparative Perspective* (Oxford: Clarendon Press, 1989), p. 152.
51. See Christopher E. Smith, *Courts and the Poor* (Chicago: Nelson-Hall, 1991), pp. 3–5.
52. Curran, "American Lawyers in the 1980s," p. 26.
53. See I. H. Jacob, "Access to Justice in England," in *Access to Justice: A World Survey*, vol. 1, eds. Mauro Cappelletti and Bryant Garth (Milan: Giuffre, 1978), pp. 419–78.
54. See Richard Abel, "Law Without Politics: Legal Aid Under Advanced Capitalism," *U.C.L.A. Law Review* 32 (1985): 513–16, 581.
55. Rolf Bender and Christoph Strecker, "Access to Justice in the Federal Republic of Germany," in *Access to Justice*, vol. 1, eds. Mauro Cappelletti and Bryant Garth (Milan: Giuffre, 1978), pp. 527–77.
56. Earl Johnson, Jr., "Thinking About Access: A Preliminary Typology of Possible Strategies," in *Access to Justice*, vol. 3, eds. Mauro Cappelletti and Bryant Garth (Milan: Giuffre, 1978), pp. 150–51.
57. J. C. Houtappel, "Access to Justice in Holland," in *Access to Justice*, vol. 1, eds. Mauro Cappelletti and Bryant Garth (Milan: Giuffre, 1978), pp. 589–90.
58. See Per Olof Boulding, "Access to Justice in Sweden," in *Access to Justice*, vol. 1, eds. Mauro Cappelletti and Bryant Garth (Milan: Giuffre, 1978), pp. 892–93.
59. See Malcolm M. Feeley, *Court Reform on Trial* (New York: Basic Books, 1983).

# Selected Bibliography

Abel, Richard. *American Lawyers*. New York: Oxford University Press, 1989.

———, ed. *The Politics of Informal Justice*. New York: Academic Press, 1989.

———. "The Transformation of the American Legal Profession." *Law and Society Review* 20 (1986): 7–17.

Abraham, Henry J. *Justices and Presidents: A Political History of Appointments to the Supreme Court*, 2nd ed. New York: Oxford University Press, 1985.

Adamany, David. "Legitimacy, Realigning Elections, and the Supreme Court." *Wisconsin Law Review* (1983): 790–846.

Adams, Arlin M. "The Legal Profession: A Critical Evaluation." *Judicature* 74 (1990): 77–83.

Alpert, Geoffrey P., Ben M. Crouch, and C. Ronald Huff. "Prison Reform by Judicial Decree: The Unintended Consequences of *Ruiz v. Estelle*." *The Justice System Journal* 9 (1984): 291–305.

Armstrong, Virginia and Charles A. Johnson. "Certiorari Decision Making by the Warren and Burger Courts: Is Cue Theory Time Bound?" *Polity* 15 (1982): 141–50.

Auerbach, Jerold S. *Unequal Justice: Lawyers and Social Change in Modern America*. New York: Oxford University Press, 1976.

Baker, Thomas E. *Rationing Justice on Appeal: The Problems of the U.S. Court of Appeals*. St. Paul, MN: West Publishing, 1994.

Barnum, David G. "The Supreme Court and Public Opinion: Judicial Decision Making in the Post-New Deal Period." *Journal of Politics* 47 (1985): 652–66.

Baugh, Joyce Ann, Christopher E. Smith, Thomas R. Hensley, Scott Patrick Johnson. "Justice Ruth Bader Ginsburg: A Preliminary Assessment." *University of Toledo Law Review* 26 (1994): 1–34.

Baum, Lawrence. *American Courts: Process and Policy*, 2nd ed. Boston: Houghton Mifflin, 1990.

———. "Specializing the Federal Courts: Neutral Reforms or Efforts to Shape Judicial Policy?" *Judicature* 74 (1991): 217–24.

———. *The Supreme Court*, 3rd ed. Washington, D.C.: Congressional Quarterly Press, 1989.

Berger, Raoul. *Government by Judiciary: The Transformation of the Fourteenth Amendment*. Cambridge, MA: Harvard University Press, 1977.

Best, Arthur and Alan R. Andreasen. "Consumer Response to Unsatisfactory Purchases: A Survey of Perceiving Defects, Voicing Complaints, and Obtaining Redress." *Law and Society Review* 11 (1977): 701–42.

Blasecki, Janet L. "Justice Lewis Powell: Swing Voter or Staunch Conservative?" *Journal of Politics* 52 (1990): 530–47.

Bork, Robert H. *The Tempting of America: The Political Seduction of Law*. New York: Free Press, 1990.

Boucher, Robert L., Jr. and Jeffrey A. Segal. "Supreme Court Justices as Strategic Decision Makers: Aggressive Grants and Defensive Denials on the Vinson Court." *Journal of Politics* 57 (1995): 824–37.

Brace, Paul and Melinda Gann Hall. "Studying Courts Comparatively: The View From the American States." *Political Research Quarterly* 48 (1995): 5–29.

Brenner, Saul and John F. Krol. "Strategies in Certiorari Voting on the United States Supreme Court." *Journal of Politics* 51 (1989): 828–40.

Brenner, Saul and Jan Palmer. "The Law Clerks' Recommendations and Chief Justice Vinson's Vote in Certiorari." *American Politics Quarterly* 18 (1990): 68–86.

Brenner, Saul and Harold J. Spaeth. "Ideological Positions as a Variable in the Authoring of Dissenting Opinions on the Warren and Burger Courts." *American Politics Quarterly* 16 (1988): 317–28.

Bumiller, Kristin. *The Civil Rights Society: The Social Construction of Victims*. Baltimore: Johns Hopkins University Press, 1988.

_____. "Victims in the Shadow of the Law: A Critique of the Model of Legal Protection." *Signs* 12 (1987): 421–39.

Caldeira, Gregory and John Wright. "The Discuss List: Agenda Building in the Supreme Court." *Law and Society Review* 24 (1990): 807–36.

_____. "Organized Interests and Agenda Setting in the U.S. Supreme Court." *American Political Science Review* 82 (1988): 1109–27.

Caplan, Lincoln. *The Tenth Justice*. New York: Random House, 1987.

Carp, Robert A. and C. K. Rowland. *Policymaking and Politics in the Federal District Courts*. Knoxville, TN: University of Tennessee Press, 1983.

Casper, Jonathan D. "The Supreme Court and National Policy Making." *American Political Science Review* 70 (1976): 50–63.

Chapper, Joy A. and Roger A. Hanson. *Intermediate Appellate Courts: Improving Case Processing*. Williamsburg, VA: National Center for State Courts, 1990.

Chayes, Abram. "The Role of the Judge in Public Law Litigation." *Harvard Law Review* 89 (1976): 1281–1316.

Clarke, Stevens H. and Gary G. Koch. "The Influence of Income and Other Factors on Whether Criminal Defendants Go to Prison." *Law and Society Review* 11 (1976): 57–92.

Cofer, Donna P. *Judges, Bureaucrats, and the Question of Independence*. Wesport, CT: Greenwood Press, 1985.

Cook, Beverly Blair. "Justice Brennan and the Institutionalization of Dissent." *Judicature* 79 (1995): 17–23.

Cooper, Philip J. *Hard Judicial Choices*. New York: Oxford University Press, 1988.

Cox, Archibald. *The Court and the Constitution*. Boston: Houghton Mifflin, 1987.

Curran, Barbara. "American Lawyers in the 1980s: A Profession in Transition." *Law and Society Review* 20 (1986): 19–52.

Dahl, Robert A. "Decision-Making in a Democracy: The Supreme Court as a National Policy-Maker." *Journal of Public Law* 6 (1957): 279–95.

Davis, Sue. "Power on the Court: Chief Justice Rehnquist's Opinion Assignments." *Judicature* 7 (1990): 66–72.

DiChiara, Albert and John F. Galliher. "Dissonance and Contradictions in the Origins of Marihuana Decriminalization." *Law and Society Review* 28 (1994): 41–77.

Dolbeare, Kenneth and Phillip E. Hammond. "Inertia in Midway: Supreme Court Decisions and Local Responses." *Journal of Legal Education* 23 (1970): 106–22.

DuBois, Philip L., ed. *From Ballot to Bench: Judicial Elections and the Quest for Accountability*. Austin, TX: University of Texas Press, 1980.

_____. *The Politics of Judicial Reform*. Lexington, MA: Lexington Books, 1982.

Enslen. Richard A. "ADR: Another Acronym, or a Viable Alternative to the High Cost of Litigation and Crowded Court Dockets? The Debate Commences." *New Mexico Law Review* 18 (1988): 1–47.

Epstein, Lee. *Conservatives in Court*. Knoxville, Tenn.: University of Tennessee Press, 1985.

Epstein, Lee and Joseph Kobylka. *The Supreme Court and Legal Change*. Chapel Hill, NC: University of North Carolina Press, 1992.

Feeley, Malcolm M. *Court Reform on Trial*. New York: Basic Books, 1983.

_____. *The Process Is the Punishment*. New York: Russell Sage Foundation, 1979.

Felice, John D. and John C. Kilwein. "Strike One, Strike Two . . .: The History of and Prospect for Judicial Reform in Ohio." *Judicature* 75 (1992): 193–200.

Felstiner, William L. F., Richard L. Abel, and Austin Sarat. "The Emergence and Transformation of Disputes: Naming, Blaming, Claiming. . . ." *Law and Society Review* 15 (1980–81): 631–54.

Fisher, Louis. *Constitutional Dialogues*. Princeton, N.J.: Princeton University Press, 1988.

Fiss, Owen. "The Bureaucratization of the Judiciary." *Yale Law Journal* 92 (1983): 1442–68.

Flemming, Roy B. "Client Games: Defense Attorney Perspectives on Their Relations with Criminal Clients." *American Bar Foundation Research Journal* (1986): 253–77.

Frankel, Marvin. *Partisan Justice*. New York: Hill & Wang, 1978.

Friedman, Lawrence. *A History of American Law*, 2nd ed. New York: Simon & Schuster, 1985.

———. *Total Justice*. Boston, Beacon Press, 1985.

Funston, Richard. "The Supreme Court and Critical Elections." *American Political Science Review* 69 (1975): 795–811.

Galanter, Marc. "Reading the Landscape of Disputes: What We Know and Don't Know (and Think We Know) About Our Allegedly Contentious and Litigious Society." *U.C.L.A. Law Review* 31 (1983): 4–71.

———. "Why the 'Haves' Come Out Ahead: Speculations on the Limits of Legal Change." *Law and Society Review* 9 (1974): 95–160.

Galanter, Marc and Thomas Palay. *Tournament of Lawyers: The Transformation of the Big Law Firm*. Chicago: University of Chicago Press, 1991.

Gates, John B. and Charles A. Johnson, eds. *The American Courts: A Critical Assessment*. Washington, D.C.: Congressional Quarterly Press, 1991.

Gazell, James A. *The Future of State Court Management*. Port Washington, NY: Kennikat Press, 1978.

Gibson, James L. "From Simplicity to Complexity: The Development of Theory in the Study of Judicial Behavior." *Political Behavior* 5 (1983): 7–49.

———. "The Role Concept in Judicial Research." *Law and Policy Quarterly* 3 (1981): 291–311.

———. "Understandings of Justice: Institutional Legitimacy, Procedural Justice, and Political Tolerance." *Law and Society Review* 23 (1989): 469–96.

Glick, Henry R. and Craig F. Emmert. "Selection Systems and Judicial Characteristics: The Recruitment of State Supreme Court Judges." *Judicature* 70 (1987): 228–35.

Goldman, Sheldon. "Reagan's Judicial Legacy: Completing the Puzzle and Summing Up." *Judicature* 72 (1989): 318–30.

Goldman, Sheldon and Thomas Jahnige. *The Federal Courts as a Political System*, 3rd ed. New York: Harper & Row, 1985.

Goldman, Sheldon and Austin Sarat, eds. *American Court Systems*. New York: Longman, 1989.

Graglia, Lino A. *Disaster By Decree*. Ithaca, NY: Cornell University Press, 1976.

Graham, Barbara. "Do Judicial Selection Systems Matter?" *American Politics Quarterly* 18 (1990): 316–36.

Green, Justin J., John R. Schmidhauser, Larry L. Berg, and David Brady. "Lawyers in Congress: A New Look at Some Old Assumptions." *Western Political Quarterly* 26 (1973): 440–52.

Grossman, Joel B. and Austin Sarat. "Access to Justice and the Limits of Law." *Law and Policy Quarterly* 3 (1981): 125–40.

Hall, Melinda Gann. "Justices As Representatives: Elections and Judicial Politics in the American States." *American Politics Quarterly* 23 (1995): 485–503.

———. "Opinion Assignment Procedures and Conference Practices in State Supreme Courts." *Judicature* 73 (1990): 209–14.

Handler, Joel F., Ellen J. Hollingsworth, and Howard Erlanger. *Lawyers and the Pursuit of Legal Rights*. New York: Academic Press, 1978.

Hans, Valerie P. and Neil Vidmar. *Judging the Jury*. New York: Plenum Press, 1986.

Hanson, Roger and Joy Chapper. *Indigent Defense Systems*. Williamsburg, VA: National Center for State Courts, 1991.

Harriman, Linda and Jeffrey D. Straussman. "Do Judges Determine Budget Decisions? Federal Court Decisions in Prison Reform and State Spending for Corrections." *Public Administration Review* 43 (1983): 343–51.

Harrington, Christine B. *Shadow Justice: The Ideology and Institutionalization of Alternatives to Court*. Westport, CT: Greenwood Press, 1985.

Hastie, Reid, Steven D. Penrod. and Nancy Pennington. *Inside the Jury*. Cambridge, MA: Harvard University Press, 1983.

Heinz, John P. and Edward O. Laumann. *Chicago Lawyers: The Social Structure of the Bar*. New York: Russell Sage Foundation, 1982.

Heydebrand, Wolf and Carroll Seron. *Rationalizing Justice: The Political Economy of the Federal District Courts*. Albany, NY: State University of New York Press, 1990.

Horowitz, Donald. *The Courts and Social Policy*. Washington, D.C.: Brookings Institution, 1977.

Howard, J. Woodford. *Courts of Appeals in the Federal Judicial System*. Princeton, NJ: Princeton University Press, 1981.

———. "Judicial Biography and the Behavioral Persuasion." *American Political Science Review* 65 (1971): 704–15.

———. "On Fluidity of Judicial Choice." *American Political Science Review* 62 (1968): 43–56.

Huber, Peter. *Liability: The Legal Revolution and Its Consequences*. New York: Basic Books, 1988.

Irwin, John. *The Jail: Managing the Underclass in American Society*. Berkeley, CA: University of California Press, 1985.

Jaros, Dean and Robert Roper. "The U.S. Supreme Court: Myth, Diffuse Support, and Legitimacy." *American Politics Quarterly* 9 (1980): 85–105.

Johnson, Charles A. and Bradley C. Canon. *Judicial Policies: Implementation and Impact*. Washington, D.C.: Congressional Quarterly Press, 1984.

Kappeler, Victor E. *Critical Issues in Police Liability*. Prospect Heights, IL: Waveland Press, 1993.

Kassin, Saul M. and Lawrence S. Wrightsman. *The American Jury on Trial*. New York: Hemisphere Publishing, 1988.

Kessler, Mark. *Legal Services for the Poor: A Comparative and Contemporary Analysis of Interorganizational Politics*. Westport, CT: Greenwood Press, 1987.

Kluger, Richard. *Simple Justice: The History of* Brown v. Board of Education *and Black America's Struggle for Equality*. New York: Random House, 1975.

Kramer, Ronald C. "Is Corporate Crime Serious Crime? Criminal Justice and Corporate Crime Control." *Journal of Contemporary Criminal Justice* 2 (1984): 2–10.

Landon, Donald D. *Country Lawyers: The Impact of Context on Professional Practice*. New York: Praeger, 1990.

Lasser, William. *The Limits of Judicial Power*. Chapel Hill, NC: University of North Carolina Press, 1988.

Lawrence, Susan. "Legal Services Before the Supreme Court." *Judicature* 72 (1989): 266–73.

Levin, Betsy and Willis D. Hawley, eds. *The Courts, Social Science, and School Desegregation*. New Brunswick, NJ: Transaction Books, 1977.

Lind, E. Allen, Robert J. Maccoun, Patricia A. Ebener, William L. F. Felstiner, Deborah R. Hensler, Judith Resnik, and Tom R. Tyler. "In the Eye of the Beholder: Tort Litigants' Evaluations of Their Experiences in the Civil Justice System." *Law and Society Review* 24 (1990): 953–96.

Lochner, Philip R. "The No Fee and Low Fee Legal Practice of Private Attorneys." *Law and Society Review* 9 (1975): 431–73.

Macaulay, Stewart. "Lawyers and Consumer Protection Laws." *Law and Society Review* 14 (1979): 115–71.

McIntosh, Wayne V. *The Appeal of Civil Law: A Political-Economic Analysis of Litigation*. Champaign, IL.: University of Illinois Press, 1990.

Marshall, Thomas R. *Public Opinion and the Supreme Court*. Boston: Unwin Hyman, 1989.

Melone, Albert P. "Rejection of the Lawyer-Dominance Proposition: The Need for Additional Research." *Western Political Quarterly* 33 (1980): 225–32.

Miller, Mark C. "Lawyers in Congress: What Difference Does It Make?" *Congress and the Presidency* 20 (1993): 1–23.

Miller, Richard E. "Apples v. Persimmons: The Legal Profession in Japan and the United States." *Journal of Legal Education* 39 (1989): 27–38.

Miller, Richard E. and Austin Sarat. "Grievances, Claims, and Disputes: Assessing the Adversary Culture." *Law and Society Review* 15 (1980–81): 525–66.

Milner, Neal. "Comparative Analysis of Patterns of Compliance with Supreme Court Decisions." *Law and Society Review* 5 (1970): 119–34.

Mnookin, Robert H. and Lewis Kornhauser. "Bargaining in the Shadow of the Law: The Case of Divorce." *Yale Law Journal* 88 (1979): 950–97.

Morgan, Richard E. *Disabling America: The "Rights Industry" in Our Time*. New York: Basic Books, 1984.

Murphy, Walter F. *The Elements of Judicial Strategy*. Chicago: University of Chicago Press, 1964.

Oakley, John Bilyeu and Robert S. Thompson. *Law Clerks and the Judicial Process*. Berkeley, CA: University of California Press, 1980.

O'Brien, David. *Storm Center: The Supreme Court in American Politics*. New York: W. W. Norton, 1986.

O'Connor, Karen. *Women's Organizations' Use of the Courts*. Lexington, MA: Lexington Books, 1980.

O'Connor, Karen and Lee Epstein. "The Rise of Conservative Interest Group Litigation." *Journal of Politics* 45 (1983): 479–89.

Orfield, Gary. *Must We Bus?: Segregated Schools and National Policy*. Washington, D.C.: Brookings Institution, 1978.

Peltason, Jack. *Fifty-Eight Lonely Men*. New York: Harcourt Brace, 1961.

Perry, H. W., Jr. *Deciding to Decide: Agenda Setting in the United States Supreme Court*. Cambridge, MA: Harvard University Press, 1991.

Porter, Mary Cornelia and G. Alan Tarr, eds. *State Supreme Courts: Policymakers in the Federal System*. Westport, CT: Greenwood Press, 1982.

Posner, Richard. *The Federal Courts: Crisis and Reform*. Cambridge, MA: Harvard University Press, 1985.

Pritchett, C. Herman. *The Roosevelt Court: A Study in Judicial Politics*. New York: Macmillan, 1948.

Provine, D. Marie. *Case Selection in the United States Supreme Court*. Chicago: University of Chicago Press, 1980.

_____. *Judging Credentials: Nonlawyer Judges and the Politics of Professionalism*. Chicago: University of Chicago Press, 1986.

Rabkin, Jeremy. *Judicial Compulsions: How Public Law Distorts Public Policy*. New York: Basic Books, 1989.

Rehnquist, William H. *The Supreme Court: How It Was, How It Is*. New York: William Morrow, 1987.

Reid, Traciel V. "Judicial Policy-Making and Implementation: An Empirical Examination." *Western Political Quarterly* 41 (1988): 509–27.

Resnik, Judith. "Managerial Judges." *Harvard Law Review* 96 (1982): 374–448.

_____. "The Mythic Meaning of Article III Courts." *University of Colorado Law Review* 56 (1985): 581–617.

Richardson, Richard J. and Kenneth N. Vines. *The Politics of Federal Courts*. Boston: Little, Brown, 1970.

Rosenberg, Gerald. *The Hollow Hope: Can Courts Bring About Social Change?* Chicago: University of Chicago Press, 1991.

Rowland, C. K., Donald Songer, and Robert Carp. "Presidential Effects on Criminal Justice Policy in the Lower Federal Courts: The Reagan Judges." *Law and Society Review* 22 (1988): 191–200.

Ryan, John Paul, Allan Ashman, Bruce D. Sales, and Sandra Shane-DuBow. *American Trial Judges*. New York: Free Press, 1980.

Saari, David J. *American Court Management*. Westport, CT: Quorum Books, 1982.

Scheingold, Stuart A. *The Politics of Law and Order*. New York: Longman, 1984.

Schultz, David A. and Christopher E. Smith. *The Jurisprudential Vision of Justice Antonin Scalia*. Lanham, MD: Rowman & Littlefield, 1996.

Schwartz, Herman. *Packing the Courts: The Conservative Campaign to Rewrite the Constitution*. New York: Charles Scribners' Sons, 1988.

Segal, Jeffrey A. and Albert Cover. "Ideological Values and the Votes of U.S. Supreme Court Justices." *American Political Science Review* 83 (1989): 557–65.

Segal, Jeffrey A., Lee Epstein, Charles M. Cameron, and Harold J. Spaeth. "Ideological Values and the Votes of Supreme Court Justices Revisited." *Journal of Politics* 57 (1995): 812–23.

Segal, Jeffrey A. and Harold J. Spaeth. *The Supreme Court and the Attitudinal Model*. New York: Cambridge University Press, 1993.

Seron, Carroll. *The Roles of Magistrates in the Federal District Courts*. Washington, D.C.: Federal Judicial Center, 1983.

Sheldon, Charles H. "The Role of State Bar Associations in Judicial Selection." *Judicature* 77 (1994): 300–305.

Simon, James F. *The Antagonists: Hugo Black, Felix Frankfurter, and Civil Liberties in Modern America*. New York: Simon & Schuster, 1989.

Slotnick, Elliot E. "The ABA Standing Committee on Federal Judiciary: A Contemporary Assessment—Part 2." *Judicature* 66 (1983): 385–93.

_____. "Federal Appellate Judge Selection: Recruitment Changes and Unanswered Questions." *The Justice System Journal* 6 (1981): 283–304.

_____. "Judicial Career Patterns and Majority Opinion Assignment on the Supreme Court." *Journal of Politics* 41 (1979): 640–48.

Smith, Christopher E. *Courts and the Poor*. Chicago: Nelson-Hall, 1990.

_____. "Federal Judicial Salaries: A Critical Appraisal." *Temple Law Review* 62 (1989): 849–73.

_____. "Justice Antonin Scalia and the Institutions of American Government." *Wake Forest Law Review* 25 (1990): 783–809.

_____. "Polarization and Change in the Federal Courts: *En Banc* Decisions in the U.S. Courts of Appeals." *Judicature* 74 (1990): 133–37.

_____. "Police Professionalism and the Rights of Criminal Defendants." *Criminal Law Bulletin* 26 (1990): 155–66.

_____. "The Supreme Court in Transition: Assessing the Legitimacy of the Leading Legal Institution." *Kentucky Law Journal* 79 (1990–91): 317–46.

_____. *United States Magistrates in the Federal Courts: Subordinate Judges*. New York: Praeger, 1990.

Songer, Donald R. "The Impact of the Supreme Court on Trends in Economic Policy Making in the United States Courts of Appeals." *Journal of Politics* 49 (1987): 830–41.

Stern, Gerald. *The Buffalo Creek Disaster*. New York: Random House, 1976.

Stevens, Robert. *Law School: Legal Education in America from the 1850s to the 1980s*. Chapel Hill, NC: University of North Carolina Press, 1983.

Stow, Mary Lou and Harold Spaeth. "Centralized Research Staff: Is There a Monster in the Judicial Closet?" *Judicature* 76 (1992): 216–21.

Stumpf, Harry P. *American Judicial Politics*. New York: Harcourt Brace Jovanovich, 1988.

_____. *Community Politics and Legal Services*. Beverly Hills, CA: Sage, 1975.

Tate, C. Neal. "Personal Attribute Models of the Voting Behavior of U.S. Supreme Court Justices: Liberalism in Civil Liberties and Economics Decisions, 1946–1978." *American Political Science Reveiw* 75 (1981): 355–67.

Ulmer, S. Sidney. "Are Social Background Models Time-Bound?" *American Political Science Review* 80 (1986): 957–67.

_____. "The Supreme Court's Certiorari Decisions: Conflict as a Predictive Variable." *American Political Science Review* 78 (1984): 901–11.

Vose, Clement, *Caucasians Only*. Berkeley, CA: University of California Press, 1959.

Walker, Samuel. *Popular Justice: A History of American Criminal Justice*. New York: Oxford University Press, 1980.

_____. *Sense and Nonsense About Crime*, 2nd ed. Pacific Grove, CA: Brooks/Cole, 1989.

Walker, Samuel, Cassia Spohn, and Miriam DeLeone. *The Color of Justice: Race, Ethnicity, and Crime in America*. Belmont, CA: Wadsworth, 1996.

Walker, Thomas G. and Deborah J. Barrow. "Funding the Federal Judiciary: The Congressional Connection." *Judicature* 69 (1985): 43–50.

Wasby, Stephen L. "Arrogation of Power of Accountability: Judicial Imperialism Revisited." *Judicature* 65 (1981): 208–19.

_____. "Civil Rights Litigation By Organizations: Constraints and Choices." *Judicature* 68 (1985): 337–52.

_____. "The Communication of the Supreme Court's Criminal Procedure Decisions: A Preliminary Mapping." *Villanova Law Review* 18 (1975): 1086–118.

_____. *The Supreme Court in the Federal Judicial System*, 3rd ed. Chicago: Nelson-Hall, 1988.

Watson, Richard A. and Rondal G. Downing. *The Politics of Bench and Bar*. New York: John Wiley, 1969.

Welch, Susan, Michael Combs, and John Gruhl. "Do Black Judges Make a Difference?" *American Journal of Political Science* 32 (1988): 126–36.

Wheeler, Russell and Cynthia Harrison. *Creating the Federal Judicial System*. Washington, D.C.: Federal Judicial Center, 1989.

Wice, Paul, *Judges and Lawyers*. New York: HarperCollins, 1991.

Wolfe, Christopher, *Judicial Activism*. Pacific Grove, CA: Brooks/Cole, 1991.

Wrightsman, Lawrence, Saul M. Kassin, and Cynthia E. Willis, eds. *In the Jury Box*. Newbury, CA: Sage, 1987.

Yarbrough, Tinsley E. "The Alabama Prison Litigation." *The Justice System Journal* 9 (1984): 276–90.

Yngvesson, Barbara and Patricia Hennessey. "Small Claims, Complex Disputes: A Review of the Small Claims Literature." *Law and Society Review* 9 (1975): 219–74.

Ziegler, Donald H. and Michele G. Herman. "The Invisible Litigant: An Inside View of Pro Se Action in the Federal Courts." *New York University Law Review* 47 (1972): 159–257.

# Index